NO FAULT COMPENSATION
IN MEDICINE

Edited by
Ronald D. Mann
and
John Havard

The proceedings of a joint meeting of
The Royal Society of Medicine
and
The British Medical Association
held at 1 Wimpole Street,
London W1M 8AE
on 12–13 January, 1989

Royal Society of Medicine Services Limited
1 Wimpole Street London W1M 8AE
7 East 60th Street New York NY 10022

©1989 Royal Society of Medicine Services Limited

British Library Cataloguing in Publication Data

No fault compensation in medicine : the proceedings of
  a joint meeting of the Royal Society of Medicine and
  the British Medical Association held at 1 Wimpole
  street, London W1M 8AE on 12–13 January, 1989.
  1. Medicine. Negligence. Law
  I. Mann, Ronald D. (Ronald David, *1928–*) II. Havard,
  John III. Royal Society of Medicine IIII. British
  Medical Association
  342.63'2

  ISBN 1-85315-105-X

Library of Congress Cataloging-in-Publication Data

No fault compensation in medicine.

  Bibliography: p.
  1. Insurance, Health—Law and legislation—Great
Britain—Congresses. 2. Compensation (Law)—Great
Britain—Congresses. 3. Medical personnel—Malpractice
—Great Britain—Congresses. 4. Personal injuries—
Great Britain—Congresses. 5. Insurance, Health—Law
and legislation—Congresses. 6. Compensation (Law)—
Congresses. I. Mann, Ronald D. (Ronald David),
1928–   . II. Havard, John. III. Royal Society of
Medicine (Great Britain). IV. British Medical
Association.

KD3205.A75N6 1989   344.41'022   89-10353
ISBN 1-85315-105-X   344.10422

Phototypeset by Dobbie Typesetting Limited, Plymouth, Devon
Printed in Great Britain at the Alden Press, Oxford

Contents

List of Chairmen and Speakers

MR DAVID BOLT, CBE, FRCS
Chairman, BMA Council's Working Party on No Fault Compensation,
   London

SIR CHRISTOPHER BOOTH, MD, FRCP
President, The Royal Society of Medicine, London

MRS DIANA BRAHAMS, LLB
Barrister at Law; Legal Correspondent, The Lancet, London

DR PETER F. CARPENTER, PhD
Chairman, Strategic Planning Committee, Alza Corporation, Palo Alto,
   California, USA

DR CHRISTOPHER HAM, PhD
Policy Analyst, The King's Fund Institute, London

DR JOHN HAVARD, MA, MD, LLM
Secretary, British Medical Association, London

SIR DAVID INNES WILLIAMS
President, British Medical Association, London

DR RONALD D. MANN, MD, FRCP(Glasg), FRCGP
Medical Services Secretary, The Royal Society of Medicine, London

MR DAVID A. McINTOSH
Senior Partner, Davies Arnold & Cooper, Solicitors, London

MR MARK MILDRED
Partner, Pannone Napier, Solicitors, London

MR ANDREW MORRISON, MB, ChB, FRCS, DLO
Member of Council, The Royal Society of Medicine, London

DR CARL OLDERTZ, Med.dr.h.c.
Senior Vice President, Skandia Insurance Company Ltd., Sweden

DR ROY PALMER, LLB, MB, BS, DObstRCOG
Barrister at Law; Deputy Secretary, Medical Protection Society, London

MR ARNOLD SIMANOWITZ
Director, Action for Victims of Medical Accidents, London

MRS MARGARET A. McGREGOR VENNELL
Barrister of the High Court of New Zealand; Member of the Board of
  Directors, Accident Compensation Corporation, New Zealand; Senior
  Lecturer in Law, University of Auckland, New Zealand

MR BARRY R WEST
Association of British Insurers, London

MR DES WILSON
Chairman, Citizen Action Compensation Campaign, London

List of Invited Discussants

DR ERIC BLACKADDER
Group Medical Director, British United Provident Association, London

MISS CLARE DYER
Legal Correspondent, The British Medical Journal, London

PROFESSOR DAME ROSALINDE HURLEY, DBE
Chairman, Medicines Commission

PROFESSOR IAN KENNEDY
Professor of Medical Law and Ethics, University College, London

PROFESSOR DESMOND LAURENCE
Professor of Pharmacology and Therapeutics, University College, London

RABBI JULIA NEUBERGER
Chairman, The Patients' Association

DR JOHN WALL
Secretary, The Medical Defence Union

SIR JOHN WALTON
President, General Medical Council; Warden, Green College, Oxford

List of Participants

DR F. A. AKBAR
Lane End Road, High Wycombe, Bucks HP12 4HL

MR T. ALBERT
British Medical Journal, BMA House, Tavistock Square, London WC1

MR D. ANTHONY
Lilly Industries Ltd, Kingsclere Road, Basingstoke, Hants

DR A. BAILEY
300 Gray's Inn Road, London WC1X 8DU

MR R. A. BAILEY
Vice-President, Eli Lilly International Corporation, 13 Hanover Square, London W1

DR B. E. C. BANKS
Physiology Department, University College & Middlesex School of Medicine,
    Gower Street, London WC1E 6BT

MISS I. R. BARKER
Fisons plc, Fison House, Princes Street, Ipswich IP1 1QH

DAME JOSEPHINE BARNES DBE.
8 Aubrey Walk, London W8 7SG

DR T. D. BATES
Vice-President (Radiology & Oncology), The Royal College of Radiologists,
    38 Portland Place, London W1N 3DG

MISS S. K. BEAUMONT
General Manager, Usted Park Rehabilitation & Medical Centre, Munstead Heath,
    Godalming GU7 1UW

MS H. E. BEDFORD
Epidemiology Department, Institute of Child Health, 30 Guilford Street, London
    WC1N 1EH

DR L. S. BERNSTEIN
Wellcome Research Laboratories, Langley Court, Beckenham BR3 3BS

DR G. E. BERRIOS
Psychiatry Department, University of Cambridge, Addenbrooke's Hospital,
    Hills Road, Cambridge

DR E. S. BLACKADDER
BUPA, Provident House, Essex Street, London WC2R 3AX

DR C. R. BLAKELEY
43 Mill Stream Court, Wolvercote, Oxford

DR D. BLOWERS
Squibb House, 141–149 Staines Road, Hounslow TW3 3JA

MR M. C. BROMBERG
Ministry of Defence, First Avenue House, High Holborn, London WC1V 6HE

DR D. M. BURLEY
Centre for Pharmaceutical Medicine, Dorna House, West End, Woking GU24 9PW

MRS B. S. BUTTERWORTH
Janssen Pharmaceutical Ltd, Grove, Wantage OX12 0DQ

PROFESSOR K. R. BUTTERWORTH
BIBRA, Woodmansterne Road, Carshalton SM5 4DS

DR P. G. T. BYE
c/o Schering Health Care Ltd, The Brow, Burgess Hill, W. Sussex

DR L. B. CANNELL
Radiology Department, Stoke Mandeville Hospital, Aylesbury, Bucks

MR J. A. CATTON
Fenchurch Insurance Brokers, 89 High Road, South Woodford, London E18 2RH

MR J. F. CHESHIRE
ICI Pharmaceuticals, Alderley House, Alderley Park, Macclesfield SK10 2TF

MR P. CHINQUE
Department of Health, Room A408, Alexander Fleming House, Elephant & Castle,
    London SE1 6BY

DR B. E. M. CLAY
X-Ray Department, Princess Margaret Hospital, Swindon SN1 4JU

MR R. V. CLEMENTS
111 Harley Street, London W1N 1DG

AIR CDRE. E. P. COLLINS
Room 626, First Avenue House, High Holborn, London WC1V 6NE

MR W. F. COLLINS
Eagle Star House, 9 Aldgate High Street, London EC3N 1LD

DR G. COOPER
Cyanamid of GB Ltd, Lederle International, 3 The Potteries, Wickham Road, Fareham
    PO16 7HZ

MME L. CORDIER
Institute Merieux, 58 Avenue Leclerc, 69007 Lyons, France

MR A. B. CRAN
Syntex Research Centre, Research Park, Heriot-Watt University, Riccarton, Edinburgh
    EH14 4AP

MR A. R. DAVIES
The Law Society, The Law Society's Hall, 113 Chancery Lane, London WC2A 1PL

PROFESSOR E. RHYS DAVIES
The Royal College of Radiologists, 38 Portland Place, London W1N 3DG

MR J. DAWSON
Sandoz Products Ltd, Frimley Business Park, Frimley, Camberley GU16 5SG

MRS L. J. DOSWELL
Syntex Pharmaceuticals International Ltd, 23/25 Marlow Road, Maidenhead SL6 7AA

PROFESSOR J. A. DUDGEON
Cherry Orchard Cottage, Bonnington, Nr Ashford TN25 7AZ

MS CLARE DYER
58 Gloucester Crescent, London NW1 7EH

DR J. EDMONDS-SEAL
Association of Anaesthetists, 9 Bedford Square, London WC1B 3RA

DR R. W. ELSDON-DEW
Glaxo Group Research Ltd, 891–995 Greenford Road, Greenford UB6 0HE

MR J. EMERSON
Upjohn Limited, Fleming Way, Crawley RH10 2NJ

DR G. N. ESNOUF
Glaxo Pharmaceuticals Ltd, Greenford Road, Greenford UB6 0HE

DR L. FIELD
Secretary-Elect, BMA, BMA House, Tavistock Square, London WC1

DR B. FREEDMAN
Merck Sharp & Dohme Ltd, Hertford Road, Hoddesdon EN11 9BU

MISS M. FRIDAY
IMS International, York House, 37 Queen Square, London WC1N 3BH

MR C. J. FRIEND
Upjohn Ltd, Fleming Way, Crawley RH10 2NJ

DR F. GABBAY
14 Spring Crescent, Portswood, Southampton SO2 1GA

DR M. D. GAMBLING
Ciba-Geigy Scientific Publications, 100 Wigmore Street, London W1H 9DR

MR D. B. L. GEORGE
ABPI, 12 Whitehall, London SW1A 2DY

MRS S. GORDON-BOYD
Sackville House, 53 New Street, Sandwich, Kent

MR J. GREEN
Health and Safety Information Bulletin, 67 Maygrove Road, London NW6

DR P. GREEN
38 Nightingale Square, London SW12 8QN

MR P. E. GREEN
Department of Health, R108 Eileen House, Newington Causeway, London

MR R. K. GREENWOOD
Glenfield General Hospital, Leicester

MR J. GROOM
BBC Scientific Programmes, BBC Television, Kensington House, Richmond Way,
    London W14

MR T. J. HANDLER
Baker & McKenzie, Aldwych House, Aldwych, London WC2B 4JF

DR J. F. A. HARBISON
Department of Forensic Medicine, 188 Pearse Street, Trinity College, Dublin 2,
    Ireland

MR M. A. HARRIS
Department of Health, Room A406, Alexander Fleming House, Elephant & Castle,
    London SE1 6BY

DR P. A. HARRIS
ICI Pharmaceuticals, Medical Affairs Department, Mereside, Alderley Park,
    Alderley Edge, Macclesfield SK10 4TG

MR P. J. HARRIS
Fisons plc, Fison House, Princes Street, Ipswich IP1 1QH

DR J. R. HILL
4 Grange Road, London N6

PROFESSOR DAME ROSALINDE HURLEY DBE
Queen Charlotte's Maternity Hospital, Goldhawk Road, London W6 OXG

DR V. L. JAMIESON
Roche Products Ltd, PO Box 8, Welwyn Garden City AL7 3AY

MR H. L. JENKINS
Unilever Research, Colworth House, Sharnbrook MK44 1LQ

DR J. L. KEARNS
Medical Director, BUPA Occupational Health, Hogan House, Church Street,
    West Woking GU21 1DJ

MR P. J. KEEN
Glaxo Group Research Ltd, Greenford Road, Greenford UB6 0HE

PROFESSOR IAN KENNEDY
Centre of Medical Law and Ethics, King's College London, Strand,
    London WC2R 2LS

MISS M. A. KING
Beecham Pharmaceuticals International Division, Beecham House, Great West Road,
    Brentford TW8 9BD

MRS L. LAMONT
The Patients' Association, 18 Victoria Park Square, London E2 9PF

PROFESSOR D. LAURENCE
Clinical Pharmacology Department, University College and Middlesex Hospital
    Medical School, The Rayne Institute, 5 University Street, London WC1E 6JJ

DR V. LEACH
59 Mansfield Road, Blidworth, Mansfield NG21 0RB

DR J. LEAHY TAYLOR
18 Thameside, Staines TW18 2HA

MR D. A. LEE
Bayer UK Ltd, Bayer House, Strawberry Hill, Newbury RG13 1JA

MR M. A. LEHMANN
Nuffield Provincial Hospitals Trust, 3 Prince Albert Road, London NW1 7SP

MR J. D. MACDONALD
Department of Health, B.910, Alexander Fleming House, Elephant & Castle,
    London SE1

MS V. McDONALD
Sunday Telegraph, 181 Marsh Wall, Isle of Dogs, London E14 9SR

DR S. McLACHLAN
38 Nightingale Square, London SW12 8QN

IRRIS MAKLER
BBC Scientific Programmes, BBC Television, Kensington House, Richmond Way,
    London W14

DR J. C. MALKIN
Flat 4, Kingswood, 29 Westcliffe Road, Bournemouth BH2 5HG

DR B. A. MANGHAM
BIBRA, Woodmansterne Road, Carshalton SM5 4DS

DR B. T. MARSH
Leo Laboratories Ltd, Longwick Road, Princes Risborough, Aylesbury HP17 9RR

MR T. W. MAWER
TUC, Congress House, Great Russell Street, London WC1B 3LS

MR M. C. T. MORRISON
15 Prospect Hill, Swindon SN1 3JU

RABBI J. NEUBERGER
The Patients' Association, 18 Victoria Park Square, London E2 9PF

DR L. OFFERHAUS
Delta Lloyd Insurance, PO Box 1000, 1000 BA Amsterdam, The Netherlands

MS C. OGILVIE
Pulse, Morgan Grampian, 30 Calderwood Street, London SE18 6QH

MISS J. PARKER
McKenna & Co, Inveresk House, 1 Aldwych, London WC2R 0HF

DR G. D. PARR
Ciba-Geigy Pharmaceuticals, Wimblehurst Road, Horsham RH12 4AB

MISS A. M. PASCOE
ICI Pharmaceuticals, Alderley House, Alderley Park, Macclesfield SK10 2TF

DR I. C. M. PATERSON
Velindre Hospital, Whitchurch, Cardiff CF4 7XL

DR R. M. PEARSON
Consultant Physician (Clinical Pharmacology), Harold Wood Hospital, Gubbins Lane,
    Harold Wood, Romford RM3 0BE

MISS E. PYGOTT
c/o Messrs Barlow Lyde & Gilbert, 1 Finsbury Avenue, London EC2M 2PJ

MR M. D. REDMAN
Glaxo Holdings plc, 6–12 Charles Street, London W1Y 8DH

DR G. A. D. REES
Department of Anaesthetics, University Hospital of Wales, Heath Park,
    Cardiff CF4 4XW

MR P. M. REEVES
BUPA Health Services Limited, Dolphyn Court, Gret Turnstile, Lincoln's Inn Fields,
    London WC1V 7JU

MRS S. ROBERTS
Cyanamid of Great Britain Ltd, Cyanamid House, Fareham Road, Gosport PO13 0AS

MRS V. ROSE
29 Tonbridge Road, East Molesey KT8 0EL

MR W. M. ROSS
62 Archery Rise, Durham City DH1 4LA

DR A. J. ROWE
Haughley Grange, Haughley, Stowmarket IP14 3QT

DR C. N. SCOTT

DR M. J. SEWELL
Clinical Research Department, Pfizer Central Research, Sandwich CT13 9NJ

MR E. R. SHERRING
c/o Davies Arnold & Cooper, 12 Bridewell Place, London EC4V 6AD

MR S. SIMMONS
Royal College of Obstetricians and Gynaecologists, 27 Sussex Place, Regents Park,
    London NW1 4RG

DR I. G. SIMPSON
Medical & Dental Defence Union of Scotland, 144 West George Street,
    Glasgow G2 2HW

MR C. W. SMITH
21 Shipton Road, York YO3 6RE

MR D. R. SMITH
Rehabilitation Studies Unit, Princess Margaret Rose Orthopaedic Hospital.
  Fairmilehead, Edinburgh EH10 7ED

DR M. SMITH
Department of Health, Alexander Fleming House, Elephant & Castle,
  London SE1 6BY

SIR JOHN STALLWORTHY
8A College Green, Gloucester GL1 2LX

MS K. J. STONER
Parke-Davis Research Laboratories, Regional Medical Division, Lambert Court,
  Chestnut Avenue, Eastleigh SO5 3ZQ

MR R. STRIDE
Hospital Doctor, On Call Publishing Ltd, 137–139 High Street, Guildford,
  Surrey GU1 3AD

DR J. S. TEMPLETON
5 Larch End, Horsham RH12 2AZ

MR R. W. THOMSON
North Tees General Hospital, Stockton on Tees

DR J. D. G. TROUP
10 Sandringham Road, Waterloo, Merseyside L22 1RW

MR J. A. VERZIN
8 Derryvolgie Avenue, Belfast BT9 6FL

MR A. D. WALFORD
BUPA, Provident House, 24/27 Essex Street, London WC2

DR J. A. WALL
Secretary, Medical Defence Union, 3 Devonshire Place, London W1N 2EA

SIR JOHN WALTON
Warden, Green College, Radcliffe Observatory, Oxford OX2 6HG

MRS A. E. WARE
Davies Arnold & Cooper, 12 Bridewell Place, London EC4V 6AD

MS S. WHITE
SCRIP, World Pharmaceutical News, 18/20 Hill Rise, Richmond, Surrey TW10 6UA

MS K. WHITEHORN
The Patients' Association, 18 Victoria Park Square, London E2 9PF

MR G. M. WHITFORD
E. Merck Limited, Medical Department, Four Marks, Alton GU34 5HG

MS P. WILKIE
The Patients' Association, 18 Victoria Park Square, London E2 9PF

MR R. A. WILLIAMS
44 Wimpole Street, London W1M 7DG

MR B. WILLS
The Patients' Association, 18 Victoria Park Square, London E2 9PF

DR I. C. F. WISELY
1 Rubislawden North, Aberdeen AB2 4AL

MR S. D. WITHERS
BUPA, Provident House, Essex Street, London WC2R 3AX

MR M. WOODHEAD
MIMS Magazine, 30 Lancaster Gate, London W2 3LP

MR J. WOODMAN
Fisons Pharmaceuticals, Bakewell Road, Loughborough LE11 0RH

MR J. E. WOODYARD
32 Knowle Road, Stafford ST17 0DP

Acknowledgements

The editors wish to acknowledge the approval of the Council of the Royal Society of Medicine and the Council of the British Medical Association for the joint conduct of the meeting of which this volume forms the proceedings. The success of the meeting was entirely due to the speakers and invited discussants and those who spoke so vigorously from the floor and we wish to record our appreciation of these interesting contributions.

We are grateful to The de Lancey and de la Hanty Foundation Ltd, The Royal Society of Medicine, The British Medical Association, The British United Provident Association and the Medical and Dental Defence Union of Scotland for their support of this meeting.

The discussion sections of the symposium were most expertly transcribed from the tape recordings by Dr Mary Firth of 49 Woodstock Avenue, London NW11 9RG. The organisation of the meeting was greatly assisted by Miss Barbara Komoniewska of the RSM and Miss Christine Finlan of the BMA.

Preface

Ronald D. Mann
and John Havard

Ten years ago the Pearson Commission[1] opposed no fault compensation on the basis of high costs and the difficulty of establishing causation. During those ten years successful no fault compensation schemes have been run in Sweden and New Zealand without either scheme running into great trouble over the problem of causation. This experience must challenge the basis of the Pearson Commission's opposition and, with new no fault schemes being set up in Finland and elsewhere, it seems sensible to have another look at this problem.

Interest in iatrogenic harm and compensation, when the latter is appropriate, is part of the changing social environment of medicine. Old, and some would think time-honoured, attitudes have been swept away and indeed, in giving a paper on *Consent, communication and responsibility* to a recent meeting at the Royal Society of Medicine, Lord Scarman[2] said "Medical paternalism is no longer acceptable as a matter of English law; that has gone." The need to make sure that patients are properly informed and give valid consent to medical intervention has become acute. The community has also become more litigious and the massive damages awarded in some actions involving professional negligence have led to a rapid rise in the costs of medical indemnity insurance.

As a profession we have become more willing to acknowledge that rare but unfortunate medical accidents or episodes of iatrogenic harm, some of them due to drugs, do occur. *The report of a confidential enquiry into perioperative deaths* of 1987[3] and the increasing interest of some of the Royal Colleges in medical audit have been landmarks in this respect. Some of these cases of iatrogenic damage are, without doubt, due to negligence and the present law of tort is appropriate to these cases. That tort law needs to be made in several respects more efficient is hardly in dispute and the warm general reception given to some of the initiatives of the Citizen Action Compensation Campaign (CITCOM) is evidence of this.

There are, however, some cases of iatrogenic damage which are no one's fault and this too has to be recognised. Small risks may have to be taken in dealing with the bigger risks of disease and there is a great need for both patient information and patient education—so that patients at large can come to have realistic expectations of what medical science can provide. When the small risks afflict individual patients whilst patients at large enjoy the efficacy of the drug or other medical intervention then, assuming negligence or product defect or the like is absent, no fault compensation seems a humane and reasonable recourse to consider.

Lawyers have often been said to be one of the main forces standing in the way of introducing no fault schemes but this appears to have changed—perhaps with

1

the growing recognition that there are accidents which are no one's fault; perhaps with an increased recognition of the difficulties in the way of the plaintiff in getting a reasonably rapid and effective response from the slow, expensive and unsure process which is involved in the typical action for negligence. At all events it has been reported that support was expressed for no fault compensation by eminent lawyers at the recent annual bar conference and *The British Medical Journal*, in October 1988[4], commented that "The support expressed for introducing such a no fault scheme by the chairman of the Law Commission and the judge who made the first £1m award in a case of medical negligence must thus greatly increase the pressure on the government to act."

Edwina Currie, when in office as junior health minister, has been cited[4] as writing to a member of parliament on 19 September to say: "Whilst there have been some changes in circumstances since 1978, notably an increase in the number of cases coming before the courts, and in the level of damages, these changes are of degree rather than of kind. The basic arguments remain unchanged. The government, therefore, considers that the basis for seeking legal compensation for injuries suffered should continue to be through litigation in the courts." Political parties are, of course, swept into and out of office by changes which are only of degree, rather than of kind. And when rare causes of food poisoning become relatively common the change is one of degree only—but some of its consequences can be unkind. Only those who can secure Legal Aid can hope to obtain redress through "litigation in the courts" and, for example, it would be an unusual doctor who could qualify for Legal Aid and a brave one who would risk his personal assets in a suit at law.

It is, in fact, not obvious that the government, anymore than anyone else in Britain, has any very firm basis for decision making on this subject of compensation for personal injury or, much more narrowly, for medical accident. The recent report on *Medical negligence, compensation and accountability* from the King's Fund Institute[5] provides one of the few systematic attempts to assess the situation. It concludes that an informed debate on the issues and the options is needed—and with this many, including those involved in the elaboration of government policy, seem likely to agree.

The Royal Society of Medicine, with its substantial membership spanning most professional disciplines and its tradition of academic independence and discussion, would seem one suitable forum for such a debate. Since 1983 the British Medical Association has had a Working Party of its Council studying no fault compensation. These two organisations have never before held a joint meeting but the overlap of interests was, on this subject, so extensive that agreement on a joint public review of no fault compensation was easy to achieve even though the plans for the proposed RSM meeting were far advanced.

Thus, the present symposium—and this set of proceedings. One of us (RDM) followed the Opening Remarks with an introductory paper really aimed to establish that there are such things as no fault accidents in medicine. This was followed, as a fact-finding exercise, by three substantial contributions reporting the experience of the existing schemes in Sweden, New Zealand, and Finland. David Bolt, Chairman of the BMA Working Party, then described the BMA proposals and Chris Ham, the lead author of the King's Fund study[5] already mentioned, gave an account of their research and their views on the likely cost of a scheme in the United Kingdom. Two extensive discussion sessions provided vigorous debate.

The second day of the meeting opened with the views of two highly experienced lawyers—one with wide practice as a plaintiff's lawyer and the second looking at the issue from a defendant's perspective. We knew (to our amazement) that Action for Victims of Medical Accidents have a very negative view of no fault compensation. They were, therefore, asked to contribute to the following section of the meeting in which we looked at the objections. The case against no fault compensation was put by Andrew Morrison and the faults in such schemes by Roy Palmer of the Medical Protection Society.

We then sought a North American and International view in the form of a paper by Peter Carpenter of the Alza Corporation. The innovative stand which Alza has taken in elaborating policy to deal with potential iatrogenic harm and the personal views of Peter Carpenter on informed choice (as distinct from informed consent) by patients refreshed, we believe, many of the participants in this strenuous two-day conference. We had Des Wilson to speak on the current CITCOM initiative, as few would doubt that changes in the processes involved in recourse to law must run in tandem, or even precede, attempts to establish no fault compensation. The meeting closed with a very measured discussion of the likely response of the United Kingdom insurance industry to any proposals to establish an insurance-based scheme in this country along the lines of the arrangements in Sweden.

Something more, in introducing this book, should be said about the Discussion sections of the meeting. In many symposia the discussions are bland and many questions are aimed to obtain further detail or clear up obscurities. The debate, as recorded in this volume, was not like that and we believe the discussion, once or twice a little heated, offers a thoughtful and broad range of views on the pros and cons of the basic proposition that we should attempt to establish no fault compensation in this country. The debate shows no easy way. A tightly focused factual study of the data in the possession of the Health Authorities and medical indemnity organisations is needed so that meaningful estimates of the likely costs can be worked out. This would need to be done by, or with the blessing of, the Department of Health.

This meeting caused widespread media interest with major BBC Television and radio and newspaper coverage. It is clear that public discussion, and discussion by the representatives of the public, is appropriate—for patients at large will only be provided with all reasonable care, should they become the victims of medical accidents, if they demand that such care should be provided. And no scheme can succeed without the support and help of the caring professions. The BMA position is, therefore, a caring and considerate position. The principles need to be considered and the details refined in many enquiring minds. If this unique book presents a broad enough view to be of service to those who think about the few incidents of iatrogenic harm that occur in the midst of the massive iatrogenic benefit then those who contributed to the debate in its pages will have been well rewarded.

Note added in press

Not long after this symposium ended the Chief Medical Officer to the Department of Health and Social Security in London wrote to the Chairman of Council of the BMA suggesting "that health authorities should take over financial responsibility for medical negligence".

The Chief Medical Officer made it clear that the Health Departments had been considering a number of options to deal with the problem of the rising cost of medical defence subscriptions. No fault compensation had been one of these options but it raised issues "wider than those of medical defence subscriptions".

As the Department had wanted to maintain its focus on these costs, consideration of the broader subject of no fault compensation had been deferred.

The advantages of an NHS indemnity were seen by the Department as relating to cost savings, quicker settlements and advantages for practitioners. A number of concerns were recognised; these included matters connected with clinical autonomy, the effect on the practice of medicine, the availability of expertise in dealing with claims, the effect upon rising costs and the uneven incidence of damages and, finally, the difficulties of implementation. The scheme, as proposed, was to be limited to doctors working in hospitals and the community health services; general practitioners, as independent practitioners, would continue to be excluded, as at present. The Secretary of the Medical Defence Union[6] was quoted as welcoming the proposals as ''Neat, simple to operate and a scheme with which we could cooperate happily'' and, in mid-May 1989, it was reported that the Council of the BMA[7] accepted, in principle, the proposals for NHS indemnity. It is clear that this acceptance is subject to satisfactory negotiations regarding the details of the scheme and its date of implementation.

A residual minor worry is that hospital physicians, surgeons and obstetricians may find, as the next few years pass, that their managements, who will be involved in the end-costs of Crown indemnity, might challenge them in ways which have not happened in the past—for in the past the doctors' own defence societies have paid when actions have been settled out of court or as a result of the process of tort. The employers of the hospital doctors will now pay—and this may give a new dimension to the concepts of medical audit. Much more important is the fact that all of this makes almost no difference to those few unfortunate patients who become the victims of medical accidents. The patient will still have to prove negligence. The proposed new arrangements determine only who pays when the patient has won and found his or her own way through the unsure and expensive process of tort—a process that schemes for No Fault Compensation would seek to avoid. Thus, it is hard to see how the proposed new arrangements will benefit patients in any substantial way—and the subject of No Fault Compensation, and the need for appropriate schemes in Britain, remains worthy of urgent and informed professional and public debate.

References

1. Pearson Commission (1978). *Royal Commission on civil liability and compensation for personal injury*. Cmnd. 7054, Report Vol. 1. HMSO, London.
2. Scarman, Lord (1986). Consent, communication and responsibility. *J. Roy. Soc. Med.* **79**, 697–700.
3. Buck, N., Devlin, H. B. and Lunn, J. N. (1987). *The report of a confidential enquiry into perioperative deaths*. The Nuffield Provincial Hospitals Trust and the King's Fund, London.
4. Smith, R. (1988). No stopping no fault. *Brit. Med. J.* **297**, 935–936.
5. Ham, C., Dingwall, R., Fenn, P. and Harris, D.(1988). *Medical negligence, compensation and accountability*. Centre for Socio-Legal Studies, Oxford; King's Fund Institute, London.
6. Brahams, D. (1989). Medical defence and crown indemnity. *Lancet*, **i**, 795.
7. Beecham, L. (1989). Council accepts principle of NHS indemnity. *Brit. Med. J.*, **298**, 1320–21.

1

No fault compensation—a discussion paper

Ronald D. Mann

The recent study of *Medical negligence: compensation and accountability* by Chris Ham and others[11] of the King's Fund Institute concluded that "Above all, what is now required is an informed debate of the issues and the options, a debate which recognises the need both to provide compensation and to promote deterrence." This symposium has been organised in order to permit just such a debate between doctors, lawyers, public policy makers, patients, insurance industry experts and others concerned with this important issue.

Most would probably agree that, in this country, only a small proportion of patients who suffer medically-related injuries obtain compensation. Many might also agree that those who are compensated achieve their redress by a slow, expensive, adversarial system in which the results are uncertain—and especially so if accidents which are no one's fault are involved, rather than injuries due to provable negligence.

Those who wish to effect reform or improvements have perhaps four main policy options to consider:

1. The provision of compensation through social security
2. Improvements of the tort law system
3. The prevention of medically-related accidents and strengthening of professional accountability, and
4. The introduction of no fault compensation.

The difficulties in the way of establishing no fault compensation schemes stand, with even greater force, in the way of providing adequate compensation for all, and for all causes, through social security. Some of the contributors to this symposium, including the CITCOM group, refer to improvements in the tort law system and, in a later symposium, the Royal Society of Medicine expects to consider the means of strengthening professional accountability. If we wish now to consider no fault compensation schemes we can begin by noting that their essential characteristic is that they abandon the rule that an injured person has to show that someone was negligent in order to obtain redress.

This is a broad and negative definition. If we narrow the field to personal injuries which are medically-related and seemingly arise from iatrogenic causes—the activities of doctors, dentists, and nurses—and we want a positive definition which describes what such a scheme is (rather than what it is not) then we might define a *no fault compensation scheme* as one which *will relatively rapidly provide for substantial restoration of expected income (or other appropriate financial compensation) for those who have suffered severe, prolonged iatrogenic injury not due to negligence.* The basis for

5

compensation thus becomes patient need, when this need arises from iatrogenic causes, and not the proving of professional negligence or, for that matter, product defect.

The parts of the definition

The definition given above raises many different issues:

1. *"relatively rapidly"*. It does seem clear that the existing no fault compensation schemes, as described in this symposium, provide benefit vastly more rapidly than recourse to the Courts. Patients also recover quicker or adjust better once their complaints are resolved—explanation and reassurance often being helpful even in the absence of financial compensation.

2. *"substantial restoration of expected income"*. In the UK the facilities of the National Health and Insurance Schemes are available to all and do not need to be provided anew. Nevertheless, prolonged loss of income can be profoundly destructive. The income of earning adult taxpayers is already known to the authorities and does not need to be separately and expensively established. It is the difference between this income, annually adjusted according to the cost of living indices, and entitlement to sickness and insurance benefits which, presumably, most needs to be made good, as a minimal criterion. This would make no provision for anxiety, emotional suffering, or loss of enjoyment and the like. However, it seems reasonable to suggest that a first objective in any pilot UK scheme should be the restoration of taxable income which would have accrued to the injured patient or that patient's dependants. Bound up with this is the need to meet the direct costs of home care or domestic expense when a child or non wage-earning adult or care provider is the injured party. Some severe injuries (for example, of the face) produce lasting but not incapacitating injury and might, of course, need to be met by a single lump-sum benefit.

3. *"severe, prolonged iatrogenic injury"*. It is unlikely, despite the ambitions of idealists, that a scheme can be established unless there are limitations on cost. This implies limitations on benefit—at least at a pilot stage. Trivial damage might be excluded and benefit, at least at first, restricted to those in whom the injury was severe enough to interfere with the mainstream activity of the patient's life. Perhaps benefit should not arise unless the injury is of longer than one or even three months' duration.

Agreement on such limits, however difficult, is likely to be easier to achieve than obtaining agreement upon the issue of causation—and this issue invariably arises in deciding that an injury is iatrogenic, and therefore to be compensated if it is not to be dealt with by tort.

Drug-related injuries provide an example. Causation can, in such circumstances, only be established in individual patients and beyond all scientific doubt, if the drug can be withdrawn, the adverse reaction of which it is the suspect cause disappears, and the patient can be rechallenged with the same drug, and the identical reaction (both in clinical and laboratory terms) reappears under conditions in which the changes in the patient's clinical condition cannot be ascribed to the disease for which the drug was being given or to the advent of some new disease. Clearly this process of dechallenge and rechallenge can only be undertaken in a non-lethal suspected drug injury and, even then, it can only very seldom be ethical to attempt it. A demand for absolute proof (or rigid proof on the balance of probabilities) in an individual patient will, therefore, usually lead to a fully predictable result—as we have seen with recent legal actions relating to whooping cough vaccine in this country.

It is necessary, therefore, to accept a standard of proof of causation which falls short of any absolute standard and which equates with the normal clinical judgement of experienced physicians, surgeons, and dentists. The standard to be adopted is that which characterises conventional informed clinical practice; it is not a standard of proof which would satisfy legal inquiry in an adversarial system or attempt some unobtainable scientific absolutism.

This is not to say that drugs cannot be given negligently: when they are, recourse to the law of tort becomes, presumably, appropriate. But it is necessary to recognise that damage due to drugs can arise through no one's fault; and that then no fault compensation becomes relevant.

Damage due, for example, to new drugs can be unpredictable for purely scientific reasons. Even if a drug has been diligently tested before marketing in perhaps 3,000 or so patients, it is unlikely that any cases of a fatal adverse drug reaction with an incidence of perhaps one in 30,000 cases will have been seen. Yet if this drug is subsequently used in three million patients there will be 100 deaths attributed to it.

The action taken in such circumstances will reflect a benefit to risk evaluation which will include consideration of the seriousness of the disease for which the drug is used, its efficacy in that disease, the availability of alternative and safer forms of treatment, and many other factors.

However, neither the size of this kind of risk nor its nature could have been known before the drug was marketed unless a substantially larger number than 30,000 patients were studied at the pre-marketing stage. As this is impossible (unless we grossly retard all innovative new drug development or halt it, preferring to suffer not these drug risks but those of the unconquered diseases) we must accept that the use of new drugs carries with it a very small but entirely unpredictable risk. Those who suffer this risk can be said to have done so as a consequence of all of the other patients who received the drug enjoying its efficacy. It is useless for them to sue for negligence for they have been the victims of malign chance, not human malice or negligence. Does the community that enjoyed the efficacy of the drug not owe those damaged in circumstances which were no one's fault, no fault compensation?

Well-established drugs carry similar but, to some extent quantified, risks. The same issues arise but it has to be kept in mind that, in individual patients, absolute proof of causation is unlikely. This is another reason for not applying the wrong test—that of negligence—to the problem. It is also a reason for accepting that in any reasonable no fault compensation scheme the standard of proof required in respect of causation will have to be that of ordinary informed clinical practice.

The issue does, of course, extend more widely for all human activities are subject to error and it must follow that no medical person can function without there being some very small risk of accident due to human fallibility, fatigue, illness, etc. Thus, however well trained, supervised, and diligent doctors and nurses are, there will always, in any one year, be a small number of iatrogenic accidents through human fallibility. This can express itself as malign chance but there are additional risks for many medical and surgical procedures have their own hazards—which we must take, unless we prefer the risks of disease. But even if the risk of the procedure is one in 10 no one can tell which patient will be the unlucky one: if we could tell, the risk would be one in one and we would not take it.

We must accept then that many, perhaps most, forms of medical, surgical and nursing activity carry some very small but unavoidable risk—and it is reasonable to suggest that means of caring for those unfortunate patients who suffer these risks are essential and, in this country, at present inadequate.

Advantages of no fault compensation

1. The type of scheme described materially assists and cares for those who suffer major personal injuries which can reasonably be ascribed to iatrogenic causes and where provable professional negligence is not involved. No fault compensation can be claimed to be an *essential* component of civilised patient care—and one which is at present totally lacking in Britain.

2. It provides a means whereby the community can fulfil its moral obligation to those who suffer risks which cannot be avoided if patients at large are to benefit from medical intervention in the natural history of disease.

3. It acknowledges that small risks must be taken if big benefits are to be obtained; it provides, therefore, a substantial contribution to the risk-education of the community.

4. It acknowledges that actions at law based upon product defect or on professional negligence are irrational and apply the wrong test if the true cause is no person's fault but arises from the operation of unavoidable malign chance.

5. It can be quicker, kinder, cheaper and more reliable than recourse to the slow adversarial process of tort in which, almost inevitably, substantial legal fees contribute to the total cost. It can represent a realistic response to the real-world balance of probabilities in individual cases.

6. It can provide a proper and wholesome relief to the medical profession and pharmaceutical industry both of whom are, at present, subject to unfavourable public and press comment because these issues are not understood.

7. It can more universally provide an equitable outcome: those whose financial assets at present debar them from Legal Aid but who are not rich enough to risk unaided recourse to the Courts—and this is a large segment of the population— have, at present, no effective means of legal redress and, of course, like everyone else in Britain, no access to no fault compensation.

8. It offers the benefits of a non-adversarial system and this is important as acceptance, when this is true, that an injury was not due to personal fault can be helpful to the patient and preservative of the normal doctor–patient relationships.

9. It may provide better value-for-money and more efficient use of government (i.e. community) funds. The charges for professional indemnity have risen dramatically and general practitioners have their subscriptions to the medical defence societies fully refunded in arrears through their expenses; hospital doctors working full time for the National Health Service have two-thirds of their subscriptions paid by the government under an agreement which runs until December 1989. Thus, the government already bears much of the very considerable cost of the present system. In 1988 it paid about £60 million towards the costs of professional indemnity for doctors; in addition, compensation, legal and administrative costs are said to have amounted to £15 million for health authorities. No fault schemes are surely likely to see a greater proportion of the spend reaching injured patients and less being lost in legal and administrative charges: a more efficient system.

10. A no fault scheme can be run in parallel with improvements in redress at law where product defect or negligence is involved. Thus it need not lessen the incentives for a high standard of non-negligent professional practice. '

The disadvantages

1. The crucial factor is that such a scheme may encounter funding difficulties. It is difficult to predict the number of cases eligible for compensation per year as this would greatly exceed the number who now sue for damages or accept settlements: many who cannot now obtain Legal Aid, and have no effective redress at law, would presumably seek no fault compensation.

However, a reasonable estimate of the number of serious adverse drug reactions per year can be derived from the data of the Committee on Safety of Medicines and from other available post-marketing surveillance data. The number of serious medical accidents can be estimated, possibly with less precision, from the data in the possession of the medical protection societies and NHS Authorities—provided discovery of this information is permitted. Detailed pilot studies in well-chosen areas may be needed. The estimates of the total number of cases of serious, prolonged iatrogenic harm per year could be refined by comparison with general practitioner data, information held by the insurance organisations, and comparison with the experience of those running no fault compensation schemes overseas.

The study of Ham and colleagues[1] estimated that if a Swedish type of system was introduced in the UK then, at the same rates claiming and payment, the estimated cost for England alone would be of the order of £50 million per year. This would be less than present costs but would result in a substantial degree of under-compensation. If claims were compensated at current English rates then the overall cost might rise to £235 million per year. These authors suggest that: "If the average payment per claim were halved, the cost would be around £117 million per year." This, in view of the definition of a no fault scheme (and its limits) as used in this paper represents perhaps the best publicly-available estimate of the costs of the type of scheme under discussion.

Comparison of such estimates with the cost of the present system suggests that funding difficulties should not preclude consideration of a pilot scheme. It is unlikely that these estimates can be meaningfully refined without a study undertaken by, or supported by, the Department of Health and National Health Scheme authorities.

The sources of funding are, of course, critical. In any such scheme the pharmaceutical industry would benefit from the removal of many of the present accusations made against it when the injury is of no person's fault but the company concerned is accused of negligence. The NHS and medical protection societies would benefit as a non-adversarial, non-stigmatising, no fault compensation scheme would enable the settlement of proper claims without providing one example after another of successful actions which progressively elevate the size of the awards made by the Courts—even though the main virtue of some of these claims is that their evidence happens to be unusually complete and identify one responsible individual or organisation and provide unusually complete evidence of causation. The government would benefit from more effective use of public funds and from the fact that unless inappropriate legal actions involving the Committee on Safety of Medicines lessen, the staffing of this Committee and the other Section 4 Committees, is likely to become more and more difficult in a way that threatens the effective continuation of drug regulation in this country.

Avenues to explore include, in respect of funding, the suggestion that the pharmaceutical industry might meet the cost of compensated drug accidents and the NHS the costs of other no fault accidents occurring in its establishments. This might involve two separate schemes, as in Sweden. The medical protection societies might need to meet the costs of compensating accidents arising in private practice and, of course, those due to negligence. As many, perhaps most, of these costs would become ultimate charges on the exchequer the government might well conclude, as suggested by Dyer[2], that it would be cheaper and simpler in the long run to introduce crown indemnity for the staffs operating the National Health Scheme. Other possibilities, perhaps worth considering, are that contributory schemes might be established with insurance-industry or health insurance-industry participation, as occurs overseas.

2. No fault schemes might lessen professional accountability by reducing the fear of being sued for negligence. Most doctors would, I believe, doubt that this fear acts as a positive stimulus to good practice; some would believe that excessive litigation leads to defensive medicine which does not benefit patients (even though actions at law may enrich some lawyers).

However, lessening professional accountability, instead of increasing it, is a real risk and it seems clear that additional measures are needed in addition to no fault compensation. These measures might include:

(i) Improvements in securing legal redress for negligence, product defect, etc. Clearly, steps should be taken to ensure that patients do not receive both compensation and damages for the same injury.

(ii) An improved complaints procedure designed to provide an explanation, apology and corrective action when these steps are adequate, or more appropriate, than compensation or litigation.

(iii) A public education programme on risk in order to teach patients to have realistic expectations and avoid risk whenever possible.

(iv) Improved post-graduate education programmes for doctors so that they are more efficiently helped to reach, maintain, and self-audit high standards of practice.

3. Such a scheme may be unworkable and founder on difficulties related, for example, to definitions of causality, severity, and the like. That these difficulties are real cannot be doubted but prior experience suggests that when the definitions used are consistent with current informed clinical practice then the matter can be handled by medical certification, medical tribunals, and an appropriate appeals machinery involving representatives of a board of acknowledged experts. The real difficulty is, perhaps, not that of medical decision-making so much as the cost implications of relying on humane medical assessments.

4. Defining the non-compensatable would be difficult. A number of exclusion categories may need to be considered. One might be the acceptance of a known hazard about which the patient had been formally warned and had agreed to accept. In these circumstances the patient stands to obtain all of the benefit or all of the hurt for himself and studies in the community at large have established the approximate level of risk involved. The informed acceptance of a well established risk might, therefore, exclude no fault compensation—the patient being expected to cover this risk by way of general insurance.

More difficult is the need to exclude from no fault compensation cases of progression or deterioration of the disease for which the remedy was being given or for which medical or surgical intervention had taken place. Without such exclusions the scheme would become a general sickness indemnity. Again, judgments such as those made in deciding whether a hurt was due to a doctor, a drug, or the disease would need to be made on a clinical practice basis and be weighted in the interests of the patient. In individual patients more than one of these factors may operate so that compensation might need to be apportioned for contributory iatrogenic damage.

Conclusion

The victims of non-negligent medical accidents may be better served by a no fault compensation scheme, provided its benefits are adequate, than by having to have recourse to the slow, cumbersome and expensive processes of the laws of tort, consumer protection or product liability. No fault compensation might also protect those large segments of the population for whom, at present, redress at law is virtually excluded due to the non-availability of Legal Aid.

The doctors, dentists and nurses involved may also, in these cases, be better served by a non-adversarial no fault process which is not only less stigmatising than involvement in claims of negligence but also more rational when real negligence is not involved and the harm arises from, for example, the operation of malign chance.

The community may benefit by accepting its moral obligation to those injured in these circumstances and from the fact that a greater proportion of the funds involved would go to the patients than at present.

The time has come for further review of the no fault compensation schemes running overseas and for continued debate with a view to action by patients, policy makers, doctors, lawyers and those others concerned in this country. Such action should emphasise the need to prevent, whenever possible, iatrogenic harm. It should also aim at a much improved level of communication with patients who have, or believe they have, suffered doctor or drug related damage.

References

1. Ham, C., Dingwall, R., Fenn, P. and Harris, D. (1988). *Medical negligence, compensation and accountability*. King's Fund Institute, London.
2. Dyer, C. (1988) Defence societies' price war. *Brit. Med. J.*, **297**, 1356.

2

Compensation for personal injuries—
the Swedish patient and pharma insurance

Carl Oldertz

Swedish patient insurance and separate pharmaceutical insurance have now been in force since 1 January 1975 and 1 July 1978, respectively. Up to 1 July 1988, approximately 60,000 cases of medical complications have been reported to these insurances. Of these about 35,000 have or will receive compensation.

The insurances are intended to cover a liability in contract based on unilateral, generally applicable commitments by the health care authorities and the pharmaceutical industry. At the same time they will cover any liability that may occur for medical malpractice or drug-related product liability. These insurances include, to a greater degree than conventional liability insurances, a more effective protection for the person who has suffered an injury. In this respect they are similar to Swedish traffic insurance.

Important similarities exist between the two insurances, but there are also fundamental differences. The patient insurance is based on voluntary commitments by the health care authorities and the pharma insurance by the pharmaceutical industries. They provide compensation mainly according to tort law, but as they are voluntary it is still possible, in principle, to sue for damages. The patient insurance—with some significant exceptions—presumes that the injury was caused by some action or omission for which the medical or health care sector is responsible; it assumes the injury could have been avoided if the treatment of the basic disease had been conducted in a different manner. On the other hand, the right to compensation from the pharmaceutical insurance depends only on whether a pharmaceutical product has caused the injury and on whether it is reasonable to provide compensation after considering the nature of the disease being treated and how unexpected and serious the injury was. The element of accident insurance is thus accentuated more in the pharmaceutical insurance system than in the patient insurance system.

The most important similarities between the two insurance systems are:

1. compensation for injuries of any importance is assessed and paid according to the principles of tort law. This means that full compensation for economic losses, for example, loss of income, as well as for non-economic losses such as pain and suffering, is paid,
2. the prerequisite of proving causality has been liberalised,
3. the injured persons will find it more favourable to claim compensation from the insurance than to sue for damages,

4. it is not necessary to prove tort law liability,
5. it has been possible to limit administration costs due to the possibility of basing compensation for pain and suffering and other non-economic losses on standards that are mainly based on existing case law,
6. it has been possible to determine the premiums without paying too much regard to the variation in different injury risks,
7. the more insignificant injuries are excluded from compensation.

Of more general interest, it has been possible to set up the patient and the pharmaceutical insurances on a *voluntary* basis without the need for legislation. This means essentially that all consumption of pharmaceuticals and other medical and health care activities are insured. The systems are therefore applicable to the entire population of Sweden.

Background

The background of the systems is to be found in the trend away from the traditional principles of liability in tort; that is, malicious intent, negligence and strict liability, to systems where greater importance is attached, instead, to the injured person's need of compensation. This goal was first achieved regarding injuries caused during work. In 1972 the first security insurance for work-related injuries (TFA) was introduced. However, this insurance scheme only covered injuries to longshoremen, but as a result of a nationwide collective agreement from February, 1974 the insurance now covers all employees. In this way the possibility of providing additional compensation—in accordance with the general principles governing tort law—was introduced as a complement to the applicable social insurance systems concerning compensation for accidents at work.

This trend was supported by a Government Bill presented to Parliament in 1972 proposing a reform of the Tort Damages Act. It was propounded here that instead of expanding the tort legislation, it would be better to extend the right to compensation through systems of collective insurance which would, within certain defined areas, give more advantageous and effective protection to the injured person than was the case with conventional tort liability. Such systems could simultaneously supersede any tort liability that could arise on traditional grounds. The basic coverage from the national insurance scheme could thus remain intact and would not be affected by more liberal legislation within certain risk areas. In other words, it was recommended that, within those areas where an increased right to compensation was considered justified, preference should be given to insurance solutions where compensation was paid directly to the injured party instead of to solutions where injured persons were treated as third persons whose rights to compensation were dependent on the kind of action that was undertaken by another, for example, the person who caused the injury.

Patient insurance

Patient insurance came into effect on 1 January 1975. Prior to this, the question of compensation for bodily injury in connection with medical and health care had attracted widespread attention. It was generally thought that so-called treatment injuries should be indemnified to a much greater extent than was possible under the applicable tort law where on average only 10 cases per year had resulted in compensation.

An increased right to compensation was considered to be especially justified for those injuries which were unexpected by the patient and unforeseeable, or at least considered improbable by the attending physician. Especially in those cases where a serious injury occurred in connection with medical treatment of a relatively minor disease, it was thought that compensation should be based on more objective grounds than was possible according to tort law, without necessarily describing the act which caused the injury as negligent or wrongful.

A number of private member's bills were introduced in the Riksdag requiring an increased right to compensation for treatment injuries. However, these bills were opposed because of the considerable technical difficulties and issues of principle which would arise if the text of a law had to specify the exact distinction between those cases where liability for the injury lies with the hospital where the treament was undertaken (or with the physician who performed the treatment), and those cases where an injury constituted an unavoidable consequence of the basic disease or a necessary treatment (and should not, therefore, be the liability of the hospital or any of its employees). A system of indemnification based on conventional tort law was also considered to be less advisable as such a system—even if strict liability was introduced—presupposed some kind of malpractice by the medical staff.

A short time after the social security insurance came into effect, negotiations began between the Association of County Councils (which, in Sweden, represent most of the medical care authorities) and a consortium of insurers. These negotiations were concerned with the construction of a comprehensive compensation system whereby a greater number of treatment injuries would be indemnified than was possible under current tort law. The negotiations were monitored by the Ministry of Justice and the Ministry of Health and resulted in the introduction of patient insurance.

Initially the insurance only covered medical care provided by hospitals owned by the state or the county councils. However, insurance contracts were subsequently concluded on a collective basis through which the patient insurance also provided coverage for all privately employed doctors, dentists, physical therapists, etc.

It is of interest to mention some of the reasons which motivated the choice of a comprehensive compensation system through a voluntary insurance programme instead of a system based on legislation and compulsory insurance coverage. The latter system could possibly have been more natural because most of the cost for health care is financed by taxes, which is also the case as regards social insurance.

Initially, these were "new areas" and it was impossible to assess with any certainty the extent to which the system of compensation which had been chosen would be viable in the future. However, it was thought that it would be easier to rectify possible errors with a flexible voluntary insurance system than with a more rigid system where the conditions were established by law. It was also thought that those who had accepted the system would feel a greater responsibility and commitment to it than if the right to compensation had been regulated by legislation. In the latter case they would not be able to influence the system once the law had become effective and they would probably not feel any responsibility to try to change it even if the public found it too restrictive.

It was also assumed that the introduction of the insurance would make lawsuits unnecessary, which would lead to reduced investigative costs as well as reduced legal costs. It also seemed possible to reduce the work load of the law courts as well as the investigative medical authorities. Legal protection for the injured person was assured through claims committees and through the possibility of having a dispute decided by arbitration which was free of cost for the injured person. Comprehensive rules which permitted flexibility of application and interpretation could also be improved or changed faster through the decisions of a claims committee than would be the case if it was necessary to wait for decisions in cases brought before the courts by dissatisfied injured parties.

In a voluntary system it was also thought easier to introduce standardised rules for assessing compensation, thus avoiding the rigidity of the law of damages which does not permit such simplification. The resultant streamlining of the administrative procedure would, it was hoped, lead to considerable savings in claims handling costs. These costs would also be lessened if minor injuries, which normally should be of little or no importance, were excluded from the system. Thus it was stipulated that the injured party must have:

1. been reported sick for a minimum of 30 days, or
2. been hospitalised for at least 10 days, or
3. suffered permanent disability, or
4. died.

Treatment costs and loss of income in excess of SEK 700 are, however, always idemnified.

Pharmaceutical insurance

The pharmaceutical insurance has to some extent the same background as the patient insurance. Serious and complicated injuries could be unexpectedly and unforseeably caused by drugs. If a patient was treated with a medicine for a relatively minor disease or if he, for example, used a drug as a prophylactic, it was considered unacceptable from a consumer's point of view that there was no right to indemnity if the treatment subsequently led to serious injury. This applied even if the risk of injury was already statistically established and adequate information was available; for example, in the labelling. Even if a patient or his doctor knew that it was possible that an injury could occur, they might not think that using a drug in this individual case would result in an injury.

The debate regarding injuries from thalidomide and oral contraceptives caused considerable discussion and brought pressure on the legislative authorities to establish a new system of compensation for the victims of drug injuries. There was also considerable interest on the part of the manufacturers of pharmaceuticals in constructing a system that was less complicated and more easily administered than the existing system based on conventional tort law. It was particularly inconvenient to be involved in time-consuming lawsuits where it was necessary to engage qualified scientific staff to assist in the unproductive task of providing evidence for more or less unjustified legal cases.

Scientific experts in the drug industry were considered to be better employed in the development of new or better products. The industry also thought that a system where the right to compensation was based on causation was better than a system which was based on proving a defect in the product.

In 1972 a Products Liability Committee was appointed by the Government and assigned the task of conducting an enquiry regarding extended liability for injuries caused by especially dangerous products. The findings of the enquiry quickly established that drugs were the foremost among those products which could cause the most serious injuries and medical complications. In 1976 the Committee presented a report together with a proposal for legislation regarding compensation for drug injuries. According to this proposal the introduction of strict liability for injuries caused by unknown side effects of drugs was recommended. Furthermore—a point that must be regarded as rather surprising in the context of conventional tort legislation—the introduction of strict liability was recommended for certain injuries caused by statistically known adverse reactions, which the patient had to accept if he wished to receive treatment for his disease. However, the Committee's recommendations with regard to the latter issue were somewhat restrictive in that compensation was recommended only for those cases where the injury led to death or to at least a 50% impairment of working capacity during a comparatively long period.

While this proposal was being considered, strong requests were put forward that the administration of drug injuries and the administration of the patient insurance should be handled together. There was no reason why an injury caused by a drug should be compensated in a different manner from an injury caused by an operation or vice versa. When a patient is being treated for a disease at a hospital, such a treatment could be effected either through drugs or through surgery and in both cases complications might occur. The degree of the risk of complications was probably decisive in the choice of treatment. It was also considered inappropriate, contrary to what had been declared in the Bill of 1972, to introduce strict liability if it was possible instead to implement a comparable compensation scheme through a voluntary insurance solution.

After lengthy negotiations agreement was finally reached regarding a voluntary insurance solution, and this came into effect on 1 July 1978. It had approximately the same scope as was originally recommended in the Committee proposal—with the important difference that the requirement of an impairment of working capacity by a minimum of 50% no longer applied. The most insignificant injuries were, however, excluded.

Fundamental principles behind the patient and pharmaceutical insurance schemes

One of the basic aims of both systems is to establish rules that meet the patient's actual need of compensation, bearing in mind the type of injury and its consequences, in a more satisfactory manner than is possible according to tort law. Another is to provide a system where claims can be handled in a more rational way than tort law permits and without unnecessary delay. Law suits should also, as much as possible, be avoided. However, the systems should be able to cover situations in which it is questionable whether the injury was caused by an incorrect or inappropriate treatment, or was due to, for example, insufficient testing of the drug (or the instructions for its use were not absolutely clear). If these prerequisites were not met, it would still be a reality, within a system which is not regulated by law, that a number of compensation questions must be decided according to conventional tort law, with all the disadvantages that this would imply.

For reasons of cost, as well as the desirability of having a simple claims procedure, such systems had to be constructed in such a manner that a relatively clear border line could be drawn between those injuries which should, and those which should not, reasonably be indemnified. Consequently, they should not ascribe importance exclusively to the need for compensation of the injured party. Therefore, neither the relative seriousness nor the rarity of a complication were considered to be the decisive factors. A compensatable injury could not, in other words, be defined as being an injury which has arisen as a consequence of an unexpected, undesired or unfortunate complication which occurred during, or as the result of, a medical treatment; nor could it be defined as the result of an unsuccessful treatment for which the desired result had not been achieved.

With respect to the patient insurance the basis for extended liability was considered to depend on a decision or an act for which a doctor, a nurse or a hospital was responsible, whether the decision or the act in itself was negligent or not. With that fundamental approach the indemnification system could, to a considerable extent, be related to the general principles governing tort law—and a relatively clear border line could be drawn between injuries, complications or undesired results of treatment and unavoidable consequences of the basic illness or its necessary treatment, which, as such, should not be compensatable.

The injuries (complications) which should thereby be indemnified without the necessity of proving negligence are, therefore, mainly those in which the injury could have been avoided, if:

1. in objective terms, another equally effective but less risky treatment method was available and therefore should have been chosen, or
2. the injury was caused by a treatment that, although undertaken for medical reasons at the time, is shown, after the treatment, to have been completely unnecessary or meaningless and therefore can be classified as inappropriate, or
3. hypothetically—with the knowledge that a complication actually occurred—it would have been possible to avoid the complication by carrying out the treatment in a somewhat different manner that was at least as effective, or
4. it was probable that the right diagnosis would have been made if the patient had been treated by a doctor who was a medical specialist in the disease that was to be treated.

Among others, the following injuries or complications fall outside this liability:

1. those which arise in connection with accepted and medically appropriate treatment methods and which could not have been avoided if the treatment-method had been applied in a different manner,
2. those which resulted from unavoidable delays in diagnosis or treatment,
3. those that resulted from insufficient resources being provided to the health care system, because of policy decisions.

These basic principles do not, however, categorically exclude accepting a broader liability within certain limited and clearly defined areas, for example, when there are considerable difficulties in investigating whether the injury is an unavoidable complication, or if it could have been avoided if the treatment had been performed in a different manner. An example of this is injuries caused by infection. In many situations it is difficult to determine whether it is probable that the infection was transmitted to the patient through a treatment, or if the infection is the result of bacteria carried by the patient himself. In such borderline cases it is considered rational to accept a definition for compensation that is so broad that in some cases compensation will be given for injuries which, in fact, are unavoidable.

However, a different method was chosen for determining which kinds of injuries should be indemnified under the pharmaceutical insurance. As stated earlier it must be accepted that drugs may cause adverse reactions. A drug can consequently—in spite of the fact that it can cause serious side effects—be registered and released for public use by the authorities. This is because the positive effects of the drug are much greater than the negative. For this reason it must be accepted that a few people will suffer injury so that many more people will be cured. One cannot, therefore, justifiably maintain that a drug is defective or faulty because it causes injuries in some cases. In fact, in order for a drug to have any effect on a disease, it must be biologically active and have an influence on the course of the disease. Normally the curing, alleviating or prophylactic effect is obtained. However, as humans are biologically complicated, it cannot be expected that all will react in the same way. There can be other factors in an individual which, just like the disease, are affected by the drug. Biological variations exist among human beings, and it seems that such variations can also be temporal.

Consequently, it is possible that in certain cases or situations, precisely that property of the drug which should have given a desired effect on the disease can also affect a biological factor which is not normally found in most patients and thereby cause an unavoidable injury. Somewhat simplified, it could be said that there is not actually any defect in the drug in such a case, but rather that it is an abnormality in the patient which is the reason for the injury. Such a biological abnormality cannot in many situations be foreseen and it is, therefore, impossible to foresee that a drug can cause injury to a specific individual. Nevertheless, the complication is unexpected and unforeseen in regard to a treatment which is normally considered effective and safe. Even the prescribing physician, in many cases, has no reason to anticipate that an injury might occur and has therefore not warned the patient about the risk, or, if information about the risk has been given, neither the patient nor the physician had reason to expect the actual occurrence of an injury.

Special problems can arise when a new drug is introduced. Even if it has been sufficiently tested from a scientific point of view before it was brought onto the market, it is possible that the drug sooner or later will cause injuries. If that occurs it is not always appropriate to conclude that the drug is defective. Especially in cases when a new drug is unquestionably much better than other drugs on the market, this argument regarding a defect seems to be very dubious. It seems to be unreasonable to delay too long in introducing important drugs if this will delay treatment of patients suffering from a disability or prolonged sickness. An example of what can be achieved by a new medicine is the introduction of polio vaccine. As a result of a national, mass immunisation programme in the USA a devastating figure in 1952 of about 58,000 cases of polio, of which about 21,000 resulted in serious paralysis, was reduced to about 20 cases. However, it is impossible to avoid some individuals suffering injury because of adverse reactions. From this point of view it seems reasonable that with a system from which many will gain but a few will lose, those who gain should contribute to those who lose.

If such rare and unexpected injuries are to be indemnified, it is not possible to create an effective system for indemnification along the same philosophical lines as those for the patient insurance. The injuries cannot be related to any specific conduct by the manufacturer of the drug, or the prescribing physician. Obviously, the injury could not have been avoided if the drug treatment had been carried out in a different way. This means that indemnification must be based on an assessment of whether or not reasonable grounds exist for compensating the complication which has occurred. Is it reasonable or unreasonable that the patient himself should bear the risk of injury? Such questions must obviously be answered in the light of all known data about the risk of side effects, the seriousness of the basic illness, the patient's general state of health and the severity of the injury. This also means that in principle the so-called "development risks" are included.

According to the pharmaceutical as well as the patient insurance systems, the assessment of whether an injury is indemnifiable or not is based, in general, on such objective and easily ascertainable facts as are evident after the injury has occurred. In comparison with other systems based on traditional tort law, where it is necessary to prove that someone has been negligent, this facilitates the decision on whether or not an injury should be compensated. It also makes it easier to explain to the injured person why compensation could, or could not, be paid. In tort law systems it is important to investigate the manner in which the injury occurred: was the drug defective, how did the tortfeasor act and what were the reasons for conducting the treatment in a certain manner.

If the right to compensation is dependent on all the facts which are present after the occurrence of the injury, it is possible—in a system whose primary goal is to decide whether or not compensation should be paid—to evade the prerequisite, in itself illogical, that the right to compensation implies that some fault, has been committed by somebody who has contributed to the chain of events and decisions which led to the injury.

Once the injury has occurred, one has access to all relevant information which will indicate whether the injury will be indemnifiable or not. Thus it is not necessary to investigate whether any of the medical personnel—at the time of the treatment—ought to have been aware of the risk of injury, or why the injury occurred. Also, there is no reason to investigate or enquire whether a possible side effect in a medicine was known or whether a warning of such a side effect should have been more clearly given.

As the right to indemnification has been defined in this way, it has been possible to reach a relatively effective demarcation regarding those complications which should reasonably be indemnified and those which (because they are unavoidable consequences of a disease or its necessary treatment) should not be indemnified. The latter can, even if they were very unexpected, be compared with conventional diseases and accidents, which can suddenly affect a human being. Those should instead preferably be covered by other forms of generally applicable insurance and should not be included in the general costs for medical and health care and, of course, should not be paid for by consumers through their purchases of pharmaceuticals.

Conditions

Patient insurance

A condition of benefit is that a compensatable injury must have occurred during medical or health care activities. Such a "treatment injury" must be of a physical nature. The expression "health care" refers only to health care with a medical connection that is directed to individual persons in the form of treatment. Measures like the addition of fluoride to drinking water in order to further general dental health are not included in this definition. Health and medical care, of course, also means dental care, prophylactic care, vaccinations, blood donation, physical or other kinds of therapy, etc.

There must be a direct connection between the injury and such health and medical care as is provided through the health care system. As a rule a care measure has to be carried out by a person—a doctor, a nurse, etc—who is employed in the health care system.

As mentioned earlier, a treatment injury is an injury or disease of a physical nature. Thus the main principle is that purely mental injuries, psychological symptoms without any direct anatomical connection, are not covered by the insurance. However, if a mental injury has resulted from a physical injury, it will be covered. The reason for this limitation is, or course, that mental complications relating to treatments are in most cases either unavoidable, and as such are not compensatable according to the basic philosophy of the insurance, or are the result of a treatment which was not successful.

The treatment injuries which are included in the insurance can be classified systematically into five groups:

1. Real treatment injuries
2. Injuries caused by diagnostic intervention
3. Injuries caused by incorrect diagnosis
4. Accidental injuries
5. Infection injuries

REAL TREATMENT INJURIES

These are defined as those injuries arising in connection with interventions—surgical, diagnostic, etc. The principal philosophy behind the right to indemnification for this kind of injury can be expressed by a relatively simple, frequently applied rule: "A treatment injury should be indemnified if the injury could have been avoided if the treatment method, just as effectively, could have been applied in another way."

To decide whether or not any injury can be compensated, the investigation of the case should answer the following questions.

1) Has the injury been caused as a direct consequence of a treatment for which the health care system is responsible? If the answer is no, there is no right to compensation. If the answer is yes, the right to compensation depends on the answer to the following questions.
2) Was the treatment which caused the injury appropriate from a medical point of view? If the answer is no, compensation will be paid. If the answer is yes, the third question must be answered.
3) Could the injury have been avoided if the patient had been treated as effectively in another way? If the answer is yes, compensation will be paid, and if the answer is no there will be no right to compensation.

The first question is in general, comparatively easy to answer. The second question must be answered from a purely medical point of view. When the doctor has to decide which method of treatment he should choose, he must consider how the disease can be treated as effectively as possible, as well as the risk of more or less serious complications of the alternative forms of therapy. If this decision is made according to accepted scientific knowledge, no compensation will be paid for a complication that occurred, even if it was very serious or, in the individual case, totally unforseeable. The decision must, of course, be based on all the facts available at the time of treatment. If it is, for example, possible to identify a certain risk factor but this is not done, compensation will be paid if the injury could have been avoided if a better method had been chosen.

The following example illustrates the problems involved in the interpretation of this condition. If it is properly decided that a baby should be delivered normally and not by caesarean section, this decision has been made after considering the risks for the mother as well as the baby. Should a complication then occur in regard to either the mother or the baby which could not be avoided, any injury arising as a result of the treatment is not compensatable, even if it could have been avoided if a caesarean section had been performed. The injury in this case is an unavoidable complication of a medically appropriate treatment. The method was chosen because it involved the least risk for the mother and baby. The possibilities for obtaining compensation in such a case, would relate to any possible mistake in the diagnosis or the performance of the delivery.

The third question should also be answered with reference to the knowledge and experience of a senior physician. Compensation can be paid if—with knowledge of the fact that the treatment resulted in a complication—it would have been possible to avoid the injury if the treatment could have been performed as effectively in another way. This means that if an injury is unavoidable, compensation will not be paid even if the risk of the complication was known or if the risk was very remote.

Injuries which occur after the treatment has been performed are not normally indemnifiable, for example, injuries caused by a haematoma or by a thrombosis.

Even if a certain kind of complication is extremely rare, compensation will not be paid if the complication was unavoidable and the chosen treatment was proper and appropriate from a medical point of view. Such a situation cannot, as indicated earlier, justify indemnification. On the other hand, if a complication was due to a lack of knowledge of a special deviant condition in a patient, compensation would be paid if the injury could have been avoided if the surgeon had known about it. For example, if an intravenous injection unexpectedly extravasated and thereby caused a necrosis, compensation would be paid. The result will be the same if a dislocated nerve is damaged during an operation, and the operation could normally have been performed without causing such damage—but not if the nerve was infiltrated by cancer. The outcome will be the same if a patient is caused pain because some of the small and unidentifiable nerves in the skin are injured as a result of an operation. However, if a nerve which should be identified is injured, indemnity will be provided. That is the case, for example, when the sciatic nerve is damaged as the result of an injection. Sometimes a paresis of a patient's arm or leg is discovered after an operation. In many cases it is not possible to find out exactly how this kind of injury was caused, but it is generally known that such injuries result from a compression of the relevant nerve due to the positioning of the limb during operation. Such injuries are normally indemnified because they could most probably have been avoided if the arm or leg had been placed in a different position. Injuries to nerves caused by plastering are also indemnifiable, in most cases, for the same reason. The principles for the application of this condition can also be shown by the following cases: during a kidney biopsy the needle injured a major blood vessel which resulted in serious bleeding. The bleeding could probably have been avoided if the artery had not been injured; compensation would therefore be awarded. But in a case where the bleeding was caused when a sample was taken from a suspected cancer area in the stomach, no compensation would be paid.

DIAGNOSTIC INTERVENTION

The right to compensation for injuries resulting from diagnostic intervention, is based on a liberalisation of the conditions which was introduced in 1979. The reason for the change was that certain diagnostic interventions can cause serious complications without any possibility of avoiding them even if the intervention had been performed in a different manner. Examples of this are injuries which occur with angiographic examinations. Where a serious condition is suspected, for example a tumour in the brain, cerebral angiography has to be undertaken and it would constitute a serious omission to refrain from such an examination. In this kind of intervention it is not entirely uncommon that, due to arteriosclerosis in the catheterised blood vessels, a plaque can be loosened which can cause considerable cerebral damage.

In these cases, when the examination proves that the patient did not suffer from any serious disease, it is now thought reasonable that compensation should be paid to the patient, even if, from a medical point of view, the risk was perfectly proper, and the subsequent complication was an unavoidable result. The insurance has therefore been extended to include complications caused by diagnostic interventions, if this is found reasonable with regard to the nature and severity of the disease which was diagnosed, the seriousness of the injury and the general health of the patient.

INCORRECT DIAGNOSIS

With respect to diagnostic injuries, it has not been possible to abandon totally the conventional principle of negligence which serves as a prerequisite for compensation. If an incorrect diagnosis was made, compensation will be paid for any additional injury which could have been avoided if the right diagnosis had been made. The prerequisites for the right to compensation have, however, been made more objective, so that if examination results obtained with technical aids have been incorrect, and this fact has led to the injury, then compensation will be paid. Furthermore, if symptoms of illness have actually been interpreted in a way that does not agree with generally accepted practice, compensation will also be paid. In the latter example, the assessment is based on the level of knowledge and experience of a senior physician specialising in diagnosing the particular type of disease. There is consequently, in relation to tort law, a somewhat broader liability, as the circumstances which led to the mistake in the individual case are not relevant.

ACCIDENTAL INJURIES

The fourth special group concerns accidental injuries. In many instances, these can be directly related to the care a patient has received, or should have received. Because of his illness a patient is more easily exposed to risks of accidental injury than a healthy person. The patient often requires a higher degree of care and attention.

The extent of such care cannot always be foreseen in the individual case; perhaps a bed has not been provided with protective bars, the floor has been too slippery, appliances and help devices are worn out and therefore unable to give full service, the resources are insufficient to monitor and supervise a patient effectively and continuously, etc. The scope or type of care that should have been provided in the individual case cannot, perhaps, be assessed before the accident has actually occurred. However, even in this case, a prerequisite for indemnification is that the accident is at least in some way related to the care. This means that compensation can be paid for an injury sustained as the result of any activity for which the personnel of the hospital are responsible, or as a result of any fault in the health care equipment. Thus accidents which could as well have happened in the home of the patient are not compensated.

Furthermore, indemnity cannot be paid for injuries which have either been caused directly by the basic illness—and whose occurrence evidently could not have been prevented through a measure connected with the care of the patient—or which are direct symptoms of the basic disease. In the former case special attention must be directed to injuries sustained by those who are mentally disturbed, epileptics or patients with pronounced aging symptoms. In the latter case such diseases as cancer of the bone or pronounced osteoporosis could be of importance.

INFECTION INJURIES

The final special group consists of so-called infection injuries. In this respect the patient insurance has, in some cases, acquired the characteristics of an insurance covering unavoidable complications because the real reason for the infection is often difficult to establish. The underlying principle is that compensation will not be paid for infections that have, in all likelihood, been caused by the patient's own disease or bacteria, rather than by other bacteria transmitted through treatment. However, if it is probable that the infection was caused by organisms which were transmitted through surgery, compensation will be paid to the patient. For example, if an abscess requires surgery, no compensation will be paid if the infection persists or spreads. Nor is compensation paid if surgery is performed in an area of the body where it is known that a concentration of pathogens exist, for example, in the colon or the respiratory system. Furthermore, generally no compensation is paid when an infection is considered probable because of the patient's reduced resistance or because there is a particular risk of infection as, for example, during an extensive operation for cancer.

EXCLUSIONS

There are relatively few exclusions to the insurance cover provided. Compensation will not be paid if the injury is a consequence of a risk assumed in order to avoid a threat to life or seriously disabling conditions of illness. This can be the case especially during treatment of serious accident injuries, but the exclusion can also apply to complications caused during operations which are necessary because the treated disease is very severe. In these cases, where a deliberate risk is taken, it has not been considered reasonable to compensate injuries which have not been caused by negligence. This principle also appears to be natural as health care can neither furnish an absolute guarantee of a given result nor can it guarantee that there are no risks involved in, for example, surgery.

Hepatitis non A non B caused by blood transfusion is not compensatable if it was necessary to give the patient large quantities of blood, which is usually the case in heart operations. In such cases an intentional risk must be assumed, as it is not possible to identify blood infected with the virus that will cause this kind of jaundice. However, if only a lesser quantity of blood is needed, compensation would be paid if the transfusion was not absolutely necessary.

In a patient with suspected recurrence of cancer of the uterus, a biopsy with a thin needle was made through the rectum. This intervention caused damage to the sciatic nerve as well as sepsis. The infection was not compensated, because an intervention of this kind was necessary and the risk of infection was well-known. The damage to the nerve, on the other hand, was compensatable because such damage is not a calculated risk connected with this kind of intervention and should have been avoided.

If an injury has been caused by a drug, compensation would only be paid if the directions for use have not been followed by the medical personnel.

A claim must be made within three years from when the injured party became aware of his injury and that it was caused by a treatment. There is also a maximum limitation of 10 years from the time when the injury was caused.

Pharmaceutical insurance

According to Swedish legislation a drug is defined as a preparation intended to be administered internally or externally for the purpose of preventing, revealing, alleviating or curing illness or the symptoms of illness. The insurance covers injuries that are caused by such drugs. Injuries caused by so-called natural drugs are not included. As in the patient insurance, and mainly for the same reason, only diseases or injuries of a somatic nature are covered. Mental complications are, consequently, excluded. An additional argument for this decision is that sometimes mental effects are unavoidable or even intended during the period of drug treatment. The insurance also does not cover the consequences of a drug not giving the desired effect. For example, if a patient takes medication for an infection, and the infection is not cured, he cannot receive compensation.

This inevitably follows from the fact that medical care cannot guarantee that a disease always will be cured. Nor can compensation be granted if the injury was sustained during activities that are inconsistent with the known or desired effects of the medication, such as when a person takes a sleeping pill and falls asleep while driving a car. The same will be the case if the injury is due to a fainting-fit because the patient's blood pressure was intentionally lowered by a medicine.

Owing to the considerable difficulties which sometimes can arise in proving a clear and unquestionable connection between the injury and the use of a drug, a rule of evidence regarding causal relations has been introduced. To receive compensation the injured person has only to prove with preponderant probability that the injury was caused by the drug. In practice this more lenient evidentiary requirement has resulted in an acceptance in the individual case of a generally known statistical causal relationship. Causality is accepted if it is not otherwise evident from the investigation that a certain factor or predisposition in the individual case could, in itself, have caused a similar injury. In the same manner, a chronological connection can be given substantial weight. If the injury occurs within a relatively short period of time after the drug has begun to be used, this is taken to be a relatively strong indication of causality. If, on the other hand, the drug consumption has been going on for a long period of time without the appearance of any side effects, this will be taken as evidence against causality.

This rule of evidence has been of particular importance for women who have used oral contraceptives and been affected by thrombosis. If the woman is under 40 years of age and is neither a heavy smoker nor overweight, compensation is normally paid. However, in a case where a 41 year old woman, who had used oral contraceptives for more than 10 years, was affected by thrombosis a few days after she had had a knee operation, compensation was not awarded primarily because this kind of complication risk was known to be increased by the operation.

As indicated earlier, when it has been established that there are no other obstacles to compensation it must be decided whether or not it is reasonable that the injury should be indemnified. In this respect importance is given to:

1. the nature and severity of the disease for which the treatment was given
2. the general health status of the injured party
3. the seriousness of the injury
4. the opportunities and reasons for the medical profession to foresee the effects of the drug.

A central provision of the pharmaceutical legislation is that drugs shall be of a high quality and be manufactured in such a way that normal use of a drug shall not produce side effects which are disproportionate to the intended effects of the drug. As this condition must be interpreted from a general point of view it is obvious that the risk of side effects must intentionally be taken and accepted. Consequently it is reasonable that some risks can and must be taken without any right to indemnification. In the treatment of a serious disease a greater risk must be taken than in the treatment of a less serious disease.

The reasonability test assumes that the injury shall not be compensated if it must reasonably be accepted as a known adverse reaction to the drug. In the application of this principle, consideration is given to all of the circumstances and the specific reasons for the medical profession to anticipate the consequences of the side effects of the drug, and to the type and seriousness of the disease that is being treated, as well as to the general state of the health of the patient, the extent of the injury and other relevant factors.

In general the degree of risk—even the risk of death—that must be accepted by the patient without the right to compensation stands in direct proportion to the severity of the disease. One must also consider the fact that an injurious effect could cause a more serious injury to a patient with a reduced state of health than if a person in a good general state of health had been exposed to the same risk. In such a case the person with the poorer state of health must inevitably accept a more serious injury without the right to compensation.

In addition to these factors, which are directly related to the injured patient, the probability of the particular injury in question occurring must also be taken into account. Accordingly, uncommon or totally unknown side effects should entitle the victim to indemnity to a greater extent than more frequent ones. Even if it is known statistically that minor side effects could occur, it might happen in actual clinical practice that an injury became so serious that it must be regarded as unexpected. Such a circumstance also weighs in favour of indemnity.

The most typical situation where compensation is paid is when comparatively serious injuries are caused with low frequency during treatment of less serious diseases, for example, sulphonamides and skin diseases (such as Lyell's syndrome); acetylsalicylic acid and stomach bleeding. If a medicine is used as a prophylactic compensation is paid even for comparatively trivial injuries, e.g., oral contraceptives and livery injury, vaccines and infections. Examples of injuries with high frequency are those where dangerous drugs have to be used, for example, to save lives; for example, anticancer drugs and blood disease or damage to the bone marrow. One further example of a case where a serious risk has to be assumed without any right to compensation is the treatment of a fatal infection with antibiotics which can cause permanent impairment of hearing.

As stated above, even if the borderline between accepted side effects and unacceptable side effects seem theoretically difficult to draw, most cases can be solved comparatively easily if they are carefully analysed. As an example: compensation was paid in a case where a sulphonamide was prescribed in normal doses for a mild urinary tract infection and the patient sustained serious skin damage. Compensation was not, however, paid in a case where the patient was suffering from fatal cerebral meningitis and unusual doses of sulphonamides had to be administered. If, for example, the victim suffers damage to the organ of balance after the use of gentamicin to cure a potentially fatal septic condition, compensation is not payable. In another case, because the wrong disease was diagnosed the wrong medicine was used to treat the patient. Notwithstanding the fact that this medicine has well-known side effects, compensation was paid for an injury which was caused by the medicine.

In principle, compensation could be paid if an injury is caused by the intended effect of a drug but in practise compensation is seldom paid for this reason. This is the case when, because heparin is used to dissolve a thromboses, a concealed wound starts bleeding.

Another application of the basic rule of reasonableness is that a drug injury should be at least as great as the injury that would probably have resulted, had the drug not been used. This principle could of course also follow from the definition of the concept of ''loss''. In other words, a loss (economic or otherwise) can hardly be considered to have occurred if the use of the drug cures the basic disease but gives rise to an injury that is less than would have resulted if the basic disease had not been treated with the drug in question.

The general health status of the patient should also be taken into consideration. In one case a patient with a serious heart disease underwent surgery for a fractured leg. Because of a serious fall in blood pressure during the operation, macrodex was injected. The patient suffered an anaphylactic shock which caused severe brain damage. Due to the necessity of treating the fall in blood pressure, compensation was not paid. However, another similar case was indemnified because, in that case, the patient's state of health was normal.

Thus far, with two exceptions, most reported injuries have been caused by side effects which are well-known. The most important factors determining whether compensation is to be paid is that sick leave must normally be in excess of three months if the injury is due to a known side effect. However, if the suffering was especially severe or if the drug was used as a prophylactic agent in otherwise healthy persons, then compensation may be paid in spite of shorter sick leave.

As is apparent, there are important differences between the Swedish pharmaceutical insurance and the German 'Arzneimittelgesetz' as well as the EC product liability directives. Under those compensation systems injuries caused by known side effects are compensatable only if, for example, warnings or instructions are insufficient or misleading. On the other hand, the Swedish compensation system will not pay so much attention to possible faults or omissions in the contents of warnings or labelling but will instead consider the reasonableness of whether or not an injury should be compensated.

It is of interest that it has been possible to provide compensation to about 100 haemophiliacs who, through injections of blood fractions, have contracted the HIV virus which can cause AIDS. The infections were most probably contracted during the period of 1978 to 1981 when the disease and its causes were completely unknown. This is obviously a development risk which is to be excluded according to the basic conditions of the EC directives.

Liability Sums

Liability, according to the drug compensation scheme, is limited as follows:

— SEK 3 million for each injured person
— SEK 150 million for injuries that have occurred during one and the same calendar year
— SEK 100 million for so-called serial injuries which are caused by the same type of substance or property in one or more drugs, regardless of which insurance year the injuries occurred

The reason for these limitations is that certain serial injuries can give rise to extensive cumulative economic consequences. It is possible, for example, that a drug might cause injuries that become manifest or proven only after many years of use. A great number of injuries must, in such situations, be indemnified at the same time, and it is therefore necessary to limit the total liability.

The maximum limit for compensation of so-called 'serial injuries' is set at SEK 100 million which is considered to be more than sufficient if another catastrophe similar to that caused by thalidomide should occur in Sweden. Injuries which are part of a series injury would be attributed to the calendar year during which it first became apparent that a series injury had occurred. The reporting of serious, previously unknown side effects will always lead to a review of the registration and use of the product. In such cases it is necessary to consider whether the drug should be withdrawn from the market. If, however, the product is found to have such great therapeutic value that it should still be used despite the risk of injury, injuries that occur after publication of the possible harmful effects would not be included in the serial injury. In such cases, when frequent and possibly serious side effects must be accepted due to the other properties of the drug, compensation may still be paid according to the reasonableness assessment.

Waiver of the right to claim damages

An important provision—especially for foreign drug manufacturers—is that the injured person cannot accept compensation from the insurance without first waiving his right to claim compensation from other potentially liable persons. This is made by assigning to the insurers his right to tort damages.

Limitation periods

A claim must be made within three years from the time when the injured party became aware of his injury and that it was caused by a drug. No other time limitation exists, which means that it is of no importance when the injury was caused or when the injured person finished using the drug which caused the injury.

Claims Committees and arbitration

If a person does not wish to accept the decision of the insurer regarding his right to compensation, he can have the case referred to an advisory claims committee. The opinion is not binding on the patient or the insurer.

The Patient Injuries Committee consists of six members and the Pharmaceutical Committee of eight members. In both cases, the chairman and one medical expert are appointed by the government. There are two government-appointed members on the Pharmaceutical Injuries Committee who represent the interests of the patients, and one such appointee on the Patient Injuries Committee. On the Pharmaceutical Injuries Committee, one member represents the hospitals and two members represent the pharmaceutical industry, one of whom represents the importers and the other the manufacturers. The committee which deals with the patient insurance also includes two representatives for the hospitals. The consortium of insurers appoints one member on each committee.

If the injured person does not accept the recommendation of the committee, he can invoke arbitration proceedings. In such a case the consortium of insurers disburse the costs for the arbitrators if the injured person's claims were not obviously unfounded.

One of the arbitrators appointed by the parties to the dispute may request that a third arbitrator be appointed by the government.

Prevention of injuries

Because the right to compensation is not bound to the question of whether or not the injury was caused by malpractice—but rather to questions concerning the unforeseeable nature of the complication—it ought to be possible to obtain a fairly accurate idea of those risks which can be connected with different types of treatment methods. It is also possible to assume that medical personnel are more inclined to give information regarding complications that have occurred, as this will influence eligibility for compensation in favour of the patient. It is also the experience of the insurance scheme that medical personnel—because the insurance does not look for scapegoats and normally does not make more detailed enquiries regarding the reasons for the treatment decisions of the doctors—have become much more open to providing information concerning what, in reality, caused the injury, than when malpractice alone justified compensation. The information passed to the insurance is obviously confidential and is, in principle, not released to the authorities or to private persons.

As claims statistics, which are computerised, include details about basic illnesses, treatment methods, injuries, places where treatment was performed, ages of injured persons and the total cost of the injuries, it is obvious that the claims statistics constitute a basis for analysis regarding injury prevention. In total about 50,000 cases have been reported to the insurance. It is probable that this material provides a unique medical database of complications which could have been avoided (normally compensatable) and injuries which are considered impossible to avoid (not compensatable).

The accumulated experience and information about injuries which has been collected by the consortium could be used with the aim of investigating whether certain risks can either be avoided or, if this is not possible, if they can be reduced.

Compensation

In both insurance systems indemnities are mainly paid in accordance with the general principles of tort law for assessing damages for personal injury. This means that compensation is paid, regarding acute illness, for loss of income, costs for medical treatment, pain and suffering, and in cases of permanent disability in the form of annuities for loss of income and lump sums for loss of amenities and for general inconvenience. In cases of death compensation for burial costs is paid as well as for loss of support. Compensation for pain and suffering and for other kinds of non-economic losses is standardised. Tables based on Supreme Court decisions are used. This facilitates the handling of claims and is also an advantage from an informational point of view. Indemnities are not reduced because of contributory negligence. Recourse against the insurances is not permitted which also means that compensation from collateral sources will be deducted.

Premiums and claims experience

Pharmaceutical insurance

In 1988 the premium for Swedish pharmaceutical insurance amounted to approximately SEK 17.7 million which corresponds to about 0.31% of the industry's total business volume in Sweden. Part of the premium is used for paying compensation for injuries caused by known side effects which occurred during the insurance year. The size of this part is SEK 3,170 million which corresponds to the actual costs for paid out indemnities. The other part provides coverage for serial injuries caused by unknown side effects and for the costs of administering the compensation scheme. This part amounts to SEK 14.5 million and is paid by the Swedish Pharmaceutical Insurance Association which has all Swedish manufacturers and importers of pharmaceuticals as members. They contribute to the premium in proportion to the business volume of each company.

The number of pharmaceutical injuries registered during the period of 1 July 1979 to the end of July 1988, was approximately 2,308. Of these, 778 cases (34%) were indemnifiable, 1,242 cases (55%) were not compensatable and 288 cases or 12% are still under investigation. Approximately 50% of the latter cases are expected to be indemnified. Of those injuries which were denied compensation, about 623 did not qualify for compensation according to the basic rule of reasonableness. About 214 of these were relatively insignificant injuries with periods of sick leave of less than three months. In the remaining 407 cases the basic disease was very severe. In 333 cases the investigation did not show that it was probable that the injury had been caused by a drug. In 69 cases the instructions for use of the drug were not followed and these injuries were, therefore, transferred to the patient insurance which paid the compensation. The total cost for injuries reported up to 31 July 1988 is estimated to be about SEK 70 million and the average cost per case is estimated to be about SEK 50,000.

Until 1983 all the reported claims were caused by well-known side effects of drugs. However, during 1982 a new antidepressant drug was introduced on the Swedish market. It soon became very popular. However, many adverse reactions—some of them comparatively serious—were reported to the National Social Welfare Board during the spring of 1984 and the drug was withdrawn in September 1984 after about 70,000 persons had used it. In all about 400 adverse reactions were registered by the Board. Of these, 79 were reported to the consortium, mostly during 1983 and 1984, 36 were not compensable, 40 received indemnities and three are still under investigation. All of the reports to the National Board were examined and the conclusion was drawn that at least 300 would not have been indemnified even if they had been reported to the consortium. The injuries were mostly too insignificant or, in some cases, the basic disease was too severe. The total cost for this serial injury is estimated to be about SEK 5.2 million.

Since the insurance went into effect on 1 July 1978, only one court case has been filed regarding an injury that occurred after that date. This case is still in its pre-trial stages in the district court. The Pharmaceutical Committee has heard 83 cases. Of these 19 were considered to be matters of principle while 64 cases involved factual disputes. Regarding the latter cases the Committee recommended compensation in nine of them. In 17 cases the issue has been whether or not the injury was compensable in accordance with the basic assessment of reasonableness. In 15 of these it was concluded that the injury was not compensable; in 13 cases it was because the injury was minor. In two cases concerning questions about causal connections, the injured persons have requested an arbitration hearing. However, their claims were denied by the arbitration panel.

Patient insurance

For the insurance year 1988 the total premium for patient insurance for hospitals is estimated at SEK 98.5 million, or about SEK 12 per inhabitant. The premium is payable on a continuous basis which corresponds to the actual compensation paid out. For 1988 this part of the premium will be estimated to SEK 52.7 million (for 1987 SEK 43.2). The premium for the administration will be about SEK 17.6. The total payable premium will be SEK 70.4 million which corresponds to about SEK 8.40 per inhabitant. The cost for the administration of the insurance will be the annual premium for private physicians, physical therapists and dentists amounts to SEK 400, SEK 250 and SEK 750, respectively. The administrative cost for the insurance can be estimated to be about 16% of the premiums.

Up to 31 July 1988, 60,203 reported injuries had been registered. Of these, 24,408 did not receive indemnification or were under investigation. Of the remaining 35,795 cases, 23,876 were injuries which had occurred within the health care system administered by the County Councils. Of these 19,307 have been accepted as compensatable and 4,569 are under investigation. 10,413 cases came from dentists in private practice, 228 cases were reported by physicians in private practice, 76 cases related to company medical care and 45 cases to private hospitals or nursing homes. Of the total of 35,795 injuries, 29,282 had already received compensation. A decision regarding the right to compensation had not been reached in 6,511 cases because of incomplete investigation. The number of reported injuries has continuously increased each year and today it is estimated that the total number of indemnifiable injuries which occurred during 1988 will be approximately 4,000.

The total cost for injuries reported up to 1 July 1988 amounts to approximately SEK 605 million. For injuries which occurred during 1975 and 1976, the total compensation can relatively well be estimated as SEK 40 million.

About 65% of the compensation paid out relates to pain and suffering or other kinds of non-economic losses. Loss of income corresponds to about 14%. Costs for hospitalisation or fees to doctors amounts to about 13%. The cost in connection with cases of death is estimated at about 2%. The figures are about the same regarding the pharmaceutical insurance.

The average cost per accepted claim for 1987 is estimated to be about SEK 36,000.

Of the 19,307 indemnifiable injuries which occurred within the hospitals, 13,313 were caused in connection with surgery or similar interventions, 1,344 were caused in connection with diagnostic faults and 3,420 were caused by accidents. Quite naturally most cases involve individuals over the age of 50 and the frequency is greater among women patients than men.

The Patient Injuries Committee has passed judgment in 1,364 cases, of which about 2% involved questions of principle. Of the latter, the Committee concurred with the decision of the consortium in about 90% of the cases and reversed it in about 10%. Thirteen cases have been tried by arbitration. Of these, four were decided in favour of the injured person. In about 10 cases legal proceedings have been brought against hospitals or doctors. In one case the plaintiff received more compensation for care in his home than the insurance was prepared to pay him. The other cases are still under consideration or have been lost by the plaintiffs. No judgment has yet been issued in these cases which also means that, thus far, no decisions at all have been rendered concerning any injuries sustained after 1 January 1975.

3

Medical misfortune in a no fault society

Margaret A. McGregor Vennell

Background to no fault in New Zealand

Prior to 1974, it was only in limited circumstances that there was a legal remedy for those who suffered personal injury in New Zealand. New Zealand, along with other English-speaking former colonial territories, had inherited the English common law. This meant that the victims of personal injury were restricted in their right to bring a claim for damages for those injuries, and the claim was predicated on there being a "tortfeasor". The right was enforced principally through the tort of negligence but where the action of the defendant was "intentional" a claim could be brought in the ancient tort known as trespass to the person, which includes assault, battery and false imprisonment. An injured person had to be able to prove liability on the part of the perpetrator of the injury to be successful in a tort action. The establishment of liability, particularly in negligence, is not simple. It requires proof of fault and the protection it provides is limited. The essentials of negligence are that it is necessary to establish: (1) A duty of care; (2) A breach of the appropriate standard of care (the reasonable person test); (3) Damage to the plaintiff of a kind which is recognised by the law (that is injury or loss); (4) The damage suffered must be causally connected with the breach of duty. (This is sometimes described as "remoteness of damage" or "proximate cause"); (5) The defendant's conduct must have been the actual and legal cause of the plaintiff's injury; and, finally, (6) if the plaintiff has contributed to his or her own injury the damages may be reduced according to the extent that the final damage is caused by the plaintiff's own "fault". Liability for Trespass to the Person is easier to prove since for the wrong to be actionable it is not necessary to prove damage, but it is necessary to prove "intention".

Workers' compensation

For injured workers compensation was available without proof of fault under the *Workers Compensation Act 1956*. This entitled a worker, or the dependants of a deceased worker, to compensation which was payable during periods of total or partial incapacity for work, provided that the injury arose out of and in the course of his employment or the incapacity resulted from certain industrial diseases. It was not available for the self-employed.

For the majority of people who suffered "personal injury by accident", the legal system did not provide either a remedy or compensation. For the fortunate few who had personal accident insurance cover, benefits were available under the policy. A compulsory system of third-party insurance against liability arising out of motor-vehicle accidents had existed since 1928[1]. Those who could not bring a tort claim or who were not covered by the workers' compensation scheme were entitled to benefits under the social security scheme.

By 1966 there was dissatisfaction with the workers' compensation legislation, and the Government of the day wished to consider New Zealand becoming a party to the International Labour Convention (No. 121) and to the International Labour Recommendation (No. 121)[2]. Accordingly a Royal Commission of Inquiry was appointed to examine the existing workers' compensation scheme and to make recommendations for legislative change. It was given the additional power to examine any associated matters which it deemed relevant to the objects of the inquiry[3]. When the Royal Commission reported in December 1967[4] its proposals were radical in that it recommended that the tort action for personal injury should be abolished. In place of the common law claim it recommended its replacement by a comprehensive scheme of compensation for every person in New Zealand (whether or not they were a permanent resident and irrespective of whether or not they were earning).

The Royal Commission reached the conclusion that it could not examine the question of compensation for work-related accidents in isolation from motor vehicle and other accidents. In its view the existing systems of compensation and the common law claim for damages were capricious since the right to compensation depended not on need but on whether an injured person was covered by an existing scheme or could succeed in a common law claim for damages[5]. In 1972 the *Accident Compensation Act* was passed by a National Government. Under this act cover was restricted to all earners, wherever the accident occurred, and the victims of motor vehicle accidents, whether earners or non-earners. This meant that the scheme would exist side by side with the common law claim for damages based on proof of "fault" which would have still been available for non-earners such as housewives, the retired, students and overseas tourists injured elsewhere than in motor- vehicle accidents. At the end of 1972, after the Act implementing the scheme had been passed there was a change of Government, and the new Labour Government enacted amending legislation so that non-earners were covered from the scheme's inception in respect of all types of accidents.

When the scheme first came into force (on 1st April 1974), there was no definition of "personal injury by accident" and there was a degree of uncertainty as to what was covered by the term. The scheme was essentially a workers' compensation scheme but one which covered all accidents so the uncertainty is not surprising. There was undeniably a lack of awareness of the many different types of "accident" which are compensatable under a scheme wherein "fault" on the part of another person is irrelevant[6]. To remedy this defect amending legislation was passed in late 1974 providing a definition of "personal injury by accident" which has remained unchanged ever since and which, with some minor changes, was re-enacted in the 1982 Act[7]. It seems that inadvertently little thought was given to the scope of the scheme and to what was encompassed by the term "personal injury by accident". In relation to medical accidents there had been no particular dissatisfaction with the common law system, and it is quite clear that medical accidents were covered by the scheme as part of the package which provided a comprehensive system of compensation for "personal injury by accident". The scheme has been re-examined recently by the Law Commission and the principles of the scheme endorsed.

Medical claims in New Zealand before 1974

Prior to 1974 when the *Accident Compensation Act* 1972 came into force, common law claims against medical practitioners or hospitals were uncommon[8]. There was little "claim consciousness". Nevertheless, hospitals, both public and private[9], carried insurance against liability. The medical profession belonged to one of two of the British medical defence societies, and thus received the same benefits and protection as their colleagues in Great Britain[10]. It is not possible to obtain exact figures on the number of claims which were brought; most were settled out of court, and those that were not settled were heard by a judge sitting with a jury in the Supreme Court and were thus not reported. The law in New Zealand did not differ markedly from other Commonwealth jurisdictions. Claims were available in both contract and tort. In tort, the principal action available was in negligence, where the standard of care applied was that laid down in **Bolam v. Friern Hospital Management Committee**[11]. In addition, the New Zealand Court of Appeal had recognised, in **Smith v. Auckland Hospital Board**[12], that a claim in negligence was available when a patient had asked a specific question about the risks inherent in a particular procedure and there was a failure to inform the patient about those risks.

This action, brought in negligence (not trespass to the person) had arisen out of an incident at Green Lane Hospital. The patient had been examined by a process which outlined his aortic artery by using a radio-opaque dye. Its condition could then be determined by X-ray photographs. During the examination an unexpected complication interrupted the flow of blood to his right leg and finally demanded a decision that his leg be amputated.

When the plaintiff filed his first statement of claim in 1961 he had alleged negligence in regard to the aortogram and negligence in failing to save the leg. Later the pleadings were amended to include two further acts of negligence. The jury absolved the doctors and the Board in relation to the original allegations. The amended pleadings made further and quite different complaints namely— that he had not been adequately informed of risks inherent in the procedure and that failure amounted to negligence. The jury found in the plaintiff's favour and awarded damages of $3,000. The defendant moved that the verdict of the jury be set aside and for judgment upon the grounds that there was no evidence on which the jury could properly find that there was negligence in *failing to warn* the plaintiff. (Alternative grounds for the award being upset were also pleaded). The plaintiff had asked a specific question about the risk. In reply he was told that there were none and that he would be home in a couple of days. Woodhouse J. expressed the issue thus: "It is solely concerned with the extent to which a doctor must describe the contingencies in beneficial treatment. How far can he be made liable in negligence for the chance occurrence of medically acceptable risks in a necessary procedure which he has competently performed, merely because the patient was not forewarned?" This, he said, is a question which is easier to define than resolve. Woodhouse J. also mentioned that the claim was not that an absence of informed consent had given rise to a cause of action in trespass to the person (assault). Indeed the plaintiff had signed forms of consent which included an acknowledgement that the nature and effect of the procedure had been fully explained to him[13]. Had he not done so a claim in battery might have been available. After analysing all the evidence Woodhouse J. concluded that even if some detailed warning was necessary, there need not be an elaboration of the risks which might occur.

When **Smith**[12] went to the Court of Appeal it can be assumed that the question was regarded as important since a bench of five judges (in contrast to the usual three judges) heard the case. Woodhouse J.'s judgement was reversed. The Court unanimously applied the principles of **Hedley Byrne v. Heller**[14] and held, in particular Turner J., that ''the particular relationship of doctors and patients is sufficient to impose upon the doctor a duty to use due care in answering a question put to him by the patient where the patient, to the knowledge of the doctor, intends to place reliance on that answer in making a decision as to a treatment or procedure to which he is asked to consent''. The Court of Appeal recognised that although there is a duty, breach had to be established; that is what a reasonable doctor would have said when asked about the risks, and the causal chain also had to be established. This meant that if a proper answer had been given, the patient would have refused to undergo the treatment or procedure either immediately or after further questions and answers. There had been two earlier reported cases about medical negligence. In **Furniss v. Fitchett**[15] there had been a negligent disclosure of confidential information about a patient's mental health during judicial proceedings. Damages, including a punitive sum, were recovered in a subsequent action in negligence.

In 1953, in **MacDonald v. Pottinger**[16], North J. held that although proof that a pair of forceps was found in a patient's body after an operation of itself raises an inference of negligence against someone, this is not free from doubt. In his view the doctrine of *res ipsa loquitur* (an aid to proof for the plaintiff) did not apply in the circumstances of a complicated surgical operation performed by a team of workers. The problem there was that although there was a clear inference of negligence, the maxim did not operate to single out any one member of the team. The operation had been performed in a private hospital by the patient's own surgeon. The situation might well differ if the operation was performed in a public hospital situation with a clear chain of command.

It seems that if the accident compensation scheme had not been implemented the law of torts in respect of claims for medical negligence would have followed the same process of development as has occurred in other common law jurisdictions. Indeed in other areas of professional negligence the law has continued to develop[17].

Statutory provisions

On 1st April 1974 the *Accident Compensation Act 1972* (which has now been largely replaced by the *Accident Compensation Act 1982*) came into force. The key provision of the 1982 Act is Section 27[18] which abolishes the right to bring a claim for damages at common law (whether it be based on contract, tort, breach of statutory duty, or administrative action or inaction), provided it arises directly or indirectly out of ''personal injury by accident''[19]. ''Personal injury by accident'' is not as such defined in the Act, however, there is an inclusive and exclusive definition, which is the meaning unless the act otherwise requires[20]. Although there has been some litigation involving the extent of the definition, its precise meaning is still far from clear. Nor is it clear what claims for negligence are precluded[21]. The New Zealand Court of Appeal decided in **Donselaar v. Donselaar**[22] that section 5 of the *Accident Compensation Act 1972*[23] did not preclude a claim for exemplary damages where the conduct amounted to a trespass to the person.

Benefits available under the scheme

The aim of common law damages is to place the injured person in exactly the same position, so far as money can do, as he or she would have been in had the accident not occurred[24]. Common law damages are awarded once and for all, for all past, present and future losses[25]. The purpose of the accident compensation scheme is quite different. It is to shift a fair share of the burden which suddenly falls upon individuals as a result of personal injury. The Woodhouse Commission intended it to be a form of social insurance not a form of social assistance[26]. The benefits are available wherever and however the accident occurred. The scheme cushions losses due to injury largely by a system of periodic payments. For "earners" (employees and the self-employed), whose injury causes them to lose earnings either totally or partially, and either permanently or temporarily, the Act provides for earnings related compensation[27]. The scheme is based on loss of earning capacity not on where or how injury occurred. An employer is required to compensate his or her employees for the first week[28] after a work-related accident, but if an injured person is self-employed or injured away from work there is no compensation for the first week[29]. The rate of payment of earnings related compensation is 80% of the amount of the loss of earning capacity due to the injury. This rate was set in the belief that it would provide a balance between the needs of an injured person for compensation and the prevention of undue financial hardship. There was a need to provide a financial incentive for the injured to return to work. The maximum earnings on which compensation can be paid is at present NZ$70,326 p.a. (UK £25,169.68)[30]. This sum is increased from time to time by Order-in-Council to take account of wage increases. The average weekly wage at May 1988 was NZ$572.09 (UK £204.75) or approximately NZ$29,749 per annum (UK £10,647). About 1.7% of the labour force are estimated to have earnings above $70,326. In certain limited circumstances there is provision for compensation to be paid in respect of loss of potential earning capacity[31].

Where an earner dies as a result of "personal injury by accident" earnings related compensation is payable to the dependent spouse, children and other dependants[32]. The total payable cannot exceed the total earnings related compensation which would have been payable had the deceased lived[33]. In general, there are no earnings related payments for non-earners, apart from those who may be compensated for the loss of potential earnings[34]. The scheme provides for medical treatment for both earners and non-earners. This includes all the necessary ancillary treatment such as physiotherapy, provision of drugs and artificial prosthetic aids[35]. The Law Commission has recommended that non-earners should receive a periodic benefit reflecting the degree of the impairment or disability[36].

Both earners and non-earners can receive two kinds of lump sums. The first of these is for permanent loss or impairment of bodily functions[37]. Payment is based on an assessment of permanent partial incapacity based on a percentage system and cannot exceed $17,000 (UK £6,084.30). The other lump sum is payable in respect of loss of amenities or capacity for enjoying life, including loss from disfigurement, and pain and mental suffering, including nervous shock and neurosis. The maximum payable under this head cannot exceed $10,000 (UK £3,579.00)[38]. This latter provision has raised enormous difficulties in its application. This was mainly because the Commission applied it by calculating a scale of pain and suffering which was related to the injuries suffered and which was really an *ad hoc* percentage system. In **Jones *v*. A.C.C.**[39], in considering the equivalent provision in the 1972 Act (section 120), Casey J. rejected the Commission's approach and said that the sum awarded should be such as to afford proper compensation for the injury, and that the award should not be fixed in relation to a scale in which $10,000 represented an appropriate payment for the worst possible injury[40]. In his view the Commission's approach was contrary to the spirit of the provisions. Although the sums payable under these two sections are small, section 79, in particular, has created more difficulties in relation to its application than almost any other section in the Act[41]. These difficulties will disappear if the Law Commission's recommendations to abolish these lump sums are implemented.

Under section 80 provision is made for certain other losses to be compensated as the Corporation "sees fit"[42]. These are proved losses necessarily and directly resulting from the injury or death (section 80(1))[43]. There is also provision under section 80(2)(a) for weekly compensation, for any proved "quantifiable" loss of household or domestic service, to be paid to "any member of the house-hold of which the injured or deceased person was a member," as the Corporation sees fit[44]. Section 80(2)(b) provides for the Corporation "as it sees fit" to pay "for any identifiable and reasonable expenses or losses incurred . . . in giving help to the injured person"[45]. If it is thought necessary the Corporation may pay for the constant personal care of an injured accident victim[46].

Where a person has died as a result of "personal injury by accident" the Act contains provision for two additional compensation payments. First funeral expenses are payable to the extent that they are "reasonable by New Zealand standards"[47]. Secondly, a lump sum may be paid to a dependent surviving spouse, children and certain other dependants[48].

Funding of the scheme

The scheme is financed from three different sources. First, from compulsory levies on employers and self-employed persons; secondly from compulsory levies on owners of motor vehicles; and thirdly, from money obtained by general taxation. There is only one scheme, although the Accident Compensation Corporation maintains three separate accounts: earners, motor vehicle and supplementary.

Earners' account

All employers and self-employed levies are paid into this account, which is used for expenditure on claims by earners for all work and non-work accidents, except those which involve the use of a motor vehicle. At present the maximum leviable earnings (which is the same as the maximum earnings for the assessment of earnings related compensation) is NZ$70,326 (UK £25,169.68). Every year the Corporation makes a recommendation to Cabinet so that levies may be set for the following financial year. Levies are based on an industrial classification system and the rates are laid down by Order-in-Council. The maximum levy rate for the 1988–89 financial year is NZ$22.80 (UK £8.16). (See Table 1). The minimum levy rate is NZ$1.30 (UK 0.47p)[49]. The average levy is NZ$2.53 (UK 0.91p). A proportion of the levy is set aside to pay claims arising out of earners' non-work related accidents. At the present time this proportion is NZ$1.05 (UK 0.38p).

Motor vehicle account

The motor vehicle scheme is funded by a levy on all owners of motor vehicles. The funds can be used only for expenditure on claims by persons (earners and non-earners alike) who are injured by accident, through, or in connection with the use of a motor vehicle. The levy on most types of motor vehicles is

Table 1   *Comparison of New Zealand earners' levies with Canadian provincial workers' compensation levies*

	New Zealand	Quebec	Ontario	British Columbia
Maximum levy	NZ$22.80 =UK £8.16	C$15.00 =NZ$18.87	C$14.27 =NZ$17.95	C$8.71 =NZ$10.96
Minimum levy	NZ$1.30 =UK 0.47p	C$1.09 =NZ$1.37	C$0.75 =NZ$0.94	C$0.67 =NZ$2.53
Average levy	NZ$2.53 =UK 0.91p	C$3.17 =NZ$3.99	C$3.09 =NZ$3.88	C$2.01 =NZ$2.53

Currency exchange rates at 15 November 1988
NZ$1.00=UK 35.79 pence
NZ$1.00=Canadian 79.05 cents

NZ$100.00 (UK £35.79), and on motorcycles under 50cc, vintage and veteran cars is NZ$35.30 (UK £12.60).

Supplementary account

All expenditure on claims by non-earners (other than claims for accidents involving a motor vehicle) is paid from this account. Recovery is not based on a levy system, but instead each year the Corporation recovers from Government the sum paid out in each year. The account is funded by general taxation and is set aside by Government for the purpose.

Investment income

The scheme receives some funding from investment income. For the six months 1 April–30 September 1988 the Corporation achieved an 8.1% (16.2% per annum) return on funds. The total funds invested stood at about NZ$850 million (UK £280 million).

Tensions in the scheme in relation to funding and benefits

Levy rates

In 1986 the Corporation recommended to Government that there be a large increase in earners' levies. This was due in part to increase in costs such as medical and related fees but it was principally due to changes in the scheme's funding base. Originally the scheme had been fully-funded. In such a scheme, levies are set at the rate which is necessary to meet the estimated future costs of accidents occurring in that year. The *Accident Compensation Act 1982*, apparently partly because of recommendations made by a Caucus committee in 1980, was drafted with the intention that the scheme should not be fully funded. It was not clear whether it was to be partially funded or pay-as-you-go. The Corporation, in recommending the levy rate for the 1984/85 year, based its recommendations on a partially-funded approach. Accordingly the average levy rate was decreased by 30% and in practice part of the reserves were refunded. At the time when the levy rate was decreased there was a wage-price freeze in operation. Because of the time lag between levy rate recommendations and the expenditure financed from the levy, the Corporation's funds suffered from the effects of a "costs and expenditure blow-out'' when the wage price freeze was lifted in late 1985. This meant that in 1986 the levies had to be raised.

This was criticised widely by employers and the self-employed. It was largely because of the criticism that Government referred the operation of the scheme to the Law Commission in 1987. Much of the criticism by employers and the self-employed related to the narrow funding base of the scheme and to the fact that the earners' scheme was funding nearly all non-work related accidents apart from road accidents and accidents to non-earners. Sporting injuries were singled out as being a financial drain on the scheme despite the fact that they represented only 7% of payments from the Earners Account. The scheme received criticism because motor vehicle users were not funding the scheme unless they were owners.

Apart from those two areas there was no suggestion that the scheme's funding base should be widened. For example, this might be done by levying, inter alia, manufacturers, importers, occupiers and health care providers on an enterprise basis. The Law Commission issued an Interim Report on Funding on 30 October 1987[51]. Widening the funding base did not commend itself except in so far as it recommended that there be an additional tax on petrol (which would be in effect a levy on road users). Indeed the Law Commission apparently rejected the notion of enterprise liability and recommended that the scheme should be financed on a flat-rate basis.

Health care providers

The Report of the Committee of Inquiry into the Treatment of Cervical Cancer (Cartwright Report) was released on 31 July 1988[52]. This Committee had been set up to examine the treatment of women with cervical carcinoma *in situ* (CIS) at the National Women's Hospital in Auckland. Amongst its many conclusions, the Committee of Inquiry said that in the absence of a Bill of Rights, and in a jurisdiction where the financial accountability of the medical profession has been distorted by no fault Accident Compensation legislation, there needs to be a procedure which patients or their relations can follow if they want more information about their health problems; if they need someone to negotiate or mediate on their behalf; or if they want some form of sanction to be considered[53].

Judge Cartwright concluded that the vast majority of patients do not want financial redress. Rather they want information so that they have a chance to take part in a treatment decision, with the attendant opportunity to decline inclusion in a trial. Patients may also want the right to ensure that a negligent, rude, or incompetent doctor's reputation is known so that other patients can choose alternative health care[54]. Judge Cartwright recommended that these difficulties would be resolved if patient advocates were appointed. She did not give consideration to medical responsibility as such, through the disciplinary process. Nor did she suggest widening the funding base to provide for financial accountability. Although it was outside her terms of reference consideration does need to be given to both these issues. There are signs of a reaction against the accident compensation scheme as a result of the inquiry[55].

Benefit tensions

Under the existing scheme, both earners and non-earners are entitled to the two lump sum payments mentioned earlier, together with medical treatment and rehabilitation. There is, however, no pension scheme for non-earners. Ullrich[56] has pointed out that this creates anomalies. The Law Commission has recommended that the lump sums be abolished and that they be replaced by pension-based periodic payments[57]. It has also recommended that non-earners receive weekly pension-based payments in respect of temporary incapacity[58]. In New Zealand at present nearly 10% of the work-force are unemployed[59] (See Table 2). This has created tension in the scheme. There are indications that the injured are not being certified as being fit either for a complete return to work or for a partial return (or for light duties). One reason for this may be because medical practitioners know that if a person is certified as fit for work but no work is available then the person will join the ranks of the unemployed. Unemployment benefits are less than earning related accident compensation benefits. Tension has also arisen because the costs of medical treatment for minor injuries are high. This is due in some degree to problems in the organisation of health services in general.

The role of the medical profession in the scheme

The medical profession plays an important role in the scheme because the profession is the gate-keeper. The profession makes the initial decision as to whether a person has suffered "personal injury by accident". This may place the profession in a difficult position when the question of deciding whether a patient has suffered "medical misadventure" has to be considered. There may be a reluctance to infer that a fellow practitioner's actions may have resulted in harm to a patient. If that is so then a patient may have difficulty in obtaining the necessary certificate to establish "personal injury by accident as a result of medical misadventure".

Boundaries of the scheme as it relates to medical misfortune

"Accident" requirement

When the accident compensation scheme was originally enacted, Parliament did not define "personal injury by accident", but this was rectified to an extent soon after by the insertion of the limited definition already set out[60]. Nevertheless, the partial definition is not a complete aid to interpretation. The phrase derives from earlier workers' compensation legislation, where it was also necessary to establish that the events occurred "during the course of employment". It is the word "accident" which has most frequently been the subject of judicial interpretation.

Table 2 *Unemployment statistics–30 October 1988*

	Number of registered unemployed subsidised workers and trainees[a]				
	Oct 87	Sept 88	Oct 88	% of Labour force Oct 87 (%)	Oct 88 (%)
North Island	75,078	104,472	107,077	7.5	10.7
South Island	31,007	42,080	41,709	9.2	12.4
New Zealand	106,085	106,552	148,786	7.0	11.1

[a]Figures exclude Maori access and trainees in employment-rich and Link courses, for which no regional breakdown is available.

One of the earliest definitions of accident was that given by Lord Macnaughton in **Fenton** *v.* **Thorley**[61] where he said "the expression 'accident' is used in the popular and ordinary sense of the word as including an unlooked for mishap or an untoward event which is not expected or designed". The words of Earl Loreburn in **Trim Joint District School** *v.* **Kelly**[62] are frequently cited. He said: "We are to construe it in the popular sense as plain people would understand it, but we are also to construe it in its setting, in the context, and in the light of the purpose which appears from the Act itself . . . When people use this word they are usually thinking of some definite event which is unexpected, but it is not always so . . . ." Both limbs of the phrase were considered by the House of Lords in **Jones** *v.* **Secretary of State for Social Services**[63]. Lord Diplock[64] said that "personal injury" (in the context of the statute being considered by the Court) was a "term embracing all adverse physical or mental consequences of an 'accident' . . . But accurate diagnosis of the personal injury is not necessary in determining entitlement to injury benefit or death benefit if it is obvious that there has been personal injury of some kind and that its consequence has been incapacity for work or death." Those decisions were decisions where the statutes under consideration were narrower in their scope than the Accident Compensation Act.

Since the Act first came into force the phrase has been considered in a number of cases by the High Court and the Accident Compensation Appeal Authority. An exhaustive consideration of the meaning of the phrase was given by the Chief Justice, Sir Ronald Davison in **Wallbutton** *v.* **ACC**[65], who concluded that the expression "accident" in the definition "personal injury by accident" embraces two situations–"(a) An event which was not intended by the person who suffers the misfortune; and (b) An event which, although intended by the person who caused it to occur, resulted in a misfortune to him which he did not intend"[66].

It seems that if "an external causative incident", which assumes the character of an accident because of its result, can be proved, then a claim for personal injury will fall within the scheme[67]. Thus, many situations of "medical maloccurrence" will come squarely within the scheme[68].

Medical misadventure

The definition of "personal injury by accident" includes "medical, surgical, dental or first aid misadventure"[69]. This raises the question as to what situations arising out of medical treatment fall within "medical misadventure"[70]. The cases which have so far arisen for consideration appear to fall into three groups: (1) a positive action by a member of the medical profession, which results in injury to the patient; (2) a failure to treat the patient for either injury or sickness; (3) a failure to obtain informed consent to treatment. (This latter arises when there is a failure to fully explain the risks.) The issue is then to what extent a situation falling into any of these groups is a "personal injury by accident". For it may still be open to a patient provided he has not suffered a "personal injury by accident", and thus does not have cover under the Act, to bring an action in negligence against a doctor, surgeon or hospital or other paramedical service[71].

Mr K. L. Sandford, the former and first Chairman of the (former) Accident Compensation Commission who wrote a Commentary on the meaning of "Personal Injury by Accident"[72] said that "what is misadventure for accident compensation purposes turns on the principle that a person receiving treatment for his own benefit consents (either expressly or impliedly) to the treatment given, provided it is reasonably chosen, and administered to a standard which is to be reasonably expected in the circumstances". Blair takes a somewhat different view[73] explaining that the Act is remedial and that its fundamental purpose is to cushion the losses suffered by accident victims regardless of fault. In 1981 the Accident Compensation Corporation developed guidelines explaining the applicable principles to be used in deciding whether or not medical misadventure had occurred[74]. These are based on the decisions at the time when the guidelines were issued. Before the guidelines, the only High Court decision which had considered the question was that of Speight J. in **Accident Compensation Commission v. Auckland Hospital Board and M**[75]. Since then there have been two others; **MacDonald v. Accident Compensation Corporation**[76] and **Viggars v. Accident Compensation Corporation**[77].

In the first case, Mrs M. had become pregnant after a sterilisation operation. Evidence was available that the forceps which were used for the laparoscopic technique of sterilisation by tubal ligation were defective.

The Court held that in these circumstances Mrs M. had suffered personal injury by accident in the form of medical misadventure. It would be beyond the intention of wording of the Act that cover should be granted on the basis of personal injury by accident merely because medical treatment had not been 100% effective. Where there was an unsatisfactory outcome of treatment which could be classified as merely within the normal range of medical or surgical failure attendant on even the most felicitous treatment, it could not be held to be a misadventure. The failure of Mrs M's operation was caused by a mechanical and remediable fault and was not therefore due to its falling within an accepted failure rate. Thus, she had suffered "personal injury by accident" due to "medical misadventure".

In **MacDonald's**[78] case, the claimant had had a complex surgical operation which had resulted in an adverse consequence, the development of a faecal fistula which, in the view of the surgeons who had performed the operation was a surprising and extraordinary event. The Accident Compensation Corporation, and the Accident Compensation Appeal Authority, held that such an event was not "surgical misadventure". When it was appealed, Bisson J., after considering the meaning of "misadventure" in the dictionary sense, and the legislative history of the accident compensation scheme, held that the claimant had suffered surgical misadventure. His Honour appeared to shift away from the previous objective approach namely that if the risk was known to the medical profession then it was not medical misadventure, to a subjective approach which involved looking at things from *the point of view of the victim* (and her medical advisors). If as a result of treatment things "turned out badly" for the individual patient then the Act afforded cover. The patient's misadventure was within the terms of the phrase. Bisson J. thought that the Act, by using the word "misadventure", intended to look at bad fortune from the viewpoint of the accident victim. In each case, a person starts with a certain physical state, whether good, bad or indifferent, which is adversely affected either by accident, which is bad fortune of one kind, or by the treatment turning out badly despite all proper care and attention, which is bad fortune of another kind.

It is apparent therefore, that the happening of an injurious event must be examined, in relation to each victim, to see whether either the event itself is unlikely, or that the consequences are unlikely. Bisson J. provided further guidance by examining earlier cases and listing a number of different situations which, he thought, would qualify as medical misadventure.

These may be summarised in the following four propositions.

1. Where the risk of an adverse consequence is slight, but nevertheless the patient suffers that adverse consequence, then such an unlikely occurrence will be injury by misadventure, because the factor of mischance or bad fortune is present.
2. Risk of some minor adverse consequence is likely but in the event the consequence proves to be grave; such a grave consequence will be injury by misadventure
3. An unforseen adverse consequence will clearly be injury by misadventure.
4. An adverse consequence from a known risk which might well have been avoided had certain damage been detected (without negligence or medical error) could also be injury by misadventure, as the patient is either the worse from the mishap or has been the victim of a "piece of bad fortune".

Bisson J. concluded that an injury will not be covered by the Act as "personal injury by accident" unless the essential element of mischance or bad fortune or mishap brings it within the ambit of misadventure. In the third case **Viggars**[79], Tompkins J. followed the two previous High Court decisions, and concluded that knowledge that certain problems could arise cannot be the test, because the chances of the problem arising may be so remote that the problem could not be considered to be within the normal range of medical and surgical failure. The appellant had suffered a stroke during the performance of a carotid arteriogram. The essential question which the Court had to answer was whether the event that occurred was so unusual and unlikely that it could properly be described as mischance or bad fortune for the particular patient. The unsatisfactory outcome, though known to medical science, was so unusual or unlikely, and statistically so rare, that it was clearly not within the normal range of medical or surgical failure attendant upon an arteriogram. The event was therefore a medical or surgical misadventure.

From these decisions it it difficult to deduce all the situations which will qualify as "misadventure". The scope of the term is much wider than Sandford thought in 1979. The question of whether it is a mischance must be looked at subjectively from the point of view of the individual patient. A rare occurrence for that particular patient will amount to medical misadventure.

Inherent risks of treatment

Difficulties have arisen in interpreting the term "medical misadventure" when a patient suffers an adverse reaction to either a drug or an artificial device. The difficulty is compounded by questions of causation. For example, the reaction may be caused by an inappropriate prescription or insertion which could amount to error on the part of the medical practitioner, or the reaction may be a known side-effect. In the first case, the reaction must surely be medical misadventure, in the second case it is more questionable.

PHARMACEUTICAL DRUGS

The Accident Compensation Corporation has issued a medical bulletin which lays down guidelines for medical practitioners and claims officers to use in deciding whether an adverse drug reaction is "medical misadventure"[81]. It is based on the premise that most drugs have known side effects, and that some of these side effects will be adverse either to patients generally or only to particular patients.

Where the nature and/or extent of an adverse side effect may be reasonably expected by the physician as likely to arise from the course of treatment prescribed that adverse side effect will not be personal injury by accident. The patient is assumed to have accepted that side effect as a consequence of the treatment when consenting to the course of treatment prescribed. If, however, the nature and/or extent of an adverse side effect goes beyond that which could be reasonably expected by the physician as likely to arise from the course of treatment prescribed, the patient is not assumed to have accepted and consented to that adverse side effect. It will be accepted as personal injury by accident and an entitlement to compensation will be recognised. The extent to which a patient's consent ought to be obtained if drugs are being administered as part of a medical trial programme is another difficult question and since the *Report of the Cervical Cancer Inquiry* needs serious consideration[82].

ARTIFICIAL DEVICES

Claims in respect of intra-uterine devices (IUDs) and other artificial devices have been considered under the heading of medical misadventure and have generally been declined. This is because embedding or wandering IUD's are regarded as an inherent risk of the use of such devices even when the insertion has been carried out by a skilled operator using an appropriate technique and with proper care. Medical advice has generally been that the complications would normally be taken into account in deciding whether their use is appropriate[83].

Disclosure and consent

There is a difficult question which has not as yet been finally answered and that is whether any doctrine of "informed disclosure" or "informed consent" applies[84], either to create the right to compensation under the Accident Compensation scheme or at common law.

The Accident Compensation Corporation guidelines in relation to "medical misadventure" including drug injuries and injuries from medical devices suggest that if there is even a minimal risk of injury then the event is outside the accident compensation scheme[85]. Two possibilities seem to follow from this, first that if there has been no explanation of the risks, however slight, so that the patient can make an informed decision, then the likelihood (and magnitude) of the risk of harm eventuating is increased because the patient has lost the opportunity to refuse treatment[86]. Thus it may bring the situation within the umbrella of "personal injury by accident" due to "medical misadventure". The other possibility that might be argued is that if there is a failure to make an "informed disclosure" of the risks, then such failure is also "medical misadventure". Indeed a similar argument appears to have been accepted by the Appeal Tribunal in **Re K**[87]. In that case incorrect information about the need for contraception was given to a patient by the hospital staff after a sterilisation operation had been performed. This was held to be medical misadventure, although it was suggested that a complete failure to inform at all would not have been medical misadventure. Undoubtedly there are difficulties of a causal nature in such an approach, but they may not be insurmountable. There are inferences in the judgement of Willis D. C. J. (sitting as the Accident Compensation Appeal Authority) in **Re Priestley**[88], which seem to support such a view.

The argument advanced by the claimant in **Priestley**[88] was, in effect, that if she had known of the operation's risks she would not have undertaken the medical treatment at all. The claimant, (who appeared on her own behalf) did not advance the argument that the risk of injury was therefore increased so as to bring it within "medical misadventure". In such a case, if it is not "medical misadventure" provided proof of causation is available, it should be sustainable as an action in negligence[89].

Negligent mis-statement

Closely related to disclosure and consent are those situations where incorrect information is given to a patient. Sometimes this will result in consent being given when it otherwise might not have been. Since the Appeal Authority decision in **Re K**[90] the scope of "medical misadventure" may have been widened so that provided the causal claim can be proved some if not all cases of negligent misstatement may be covered.

Smith v. Auckland Hospital Board[91] illustrates some of the issues. In **Smith**[91] a risky medical examination of the heart was undertaken. The risk eventuated and resulted in the amputation of the leg. After the coming into force of the *Accident Compensation Act*, because of the risk the plaintiff might not have succeeded in establishing that he had suffered a medical misadventure. He might, however, have succeeded in a claim in tort based on the negligent statement made by the medical practitioner employed by the Hospital Board. The plaintiff had placed reliance on the doctor's statement that nothing untoward was involved in the medical procedure. In other words, a claim for damages for a negligent misstatement would lie (even although the damage suffered was physical), whereas a claim for compensation would not be available since no "personal injury by accident" had been suffered. This, however, may be straining the words "indirectly" used in section 27 of the Act.

Smith[91] is a difficult case. In the Court in the first instance[92] Woodhouse J. treated the situation as one about the appropriate standard of care to be applied to the duty to warn. In Woodhouse J.'s view, "the paramount consideration is the welfare of the patient, and given good faith on the part of the doctor . . . the exercise of his discretion in the area of advice must depend on the plaintiff's overall needs"[93]. Account should be taken of the gravity of the condition to be treated, the importance of the benefits expected to flow from the treatment or procedure, the need to encourage him to accept it, the relative significance of its inherent risks, the intellectual and emotional capacity of the patient to accept the information without such distortion as to prevent any rational decision at all and whether the patient has appeared to surrender the decision-making power to the doctor. In the Court of Appeal liability was held to exist on the ground that a specific request for information had been made[94]. If there is a lack of "informed consent" an action in battery or assault may lie. The question then remains whether a claim for exemplary damages would be recognised.

Omissions to treat

Omissions to treat patients have given rise to difficulty. The original view was that these were not "personal injury by accident". Thus there was no cover under the Act, and accordingly a claim in tort for medical negligence would lie. One of the first cases where this question was considered was **Collier's**[95] claim. Blair J. sitting as the appeal authority, held that a causative link must be shown between the act or omission complained of and the injury or, as in that case, death. The injured person had been admitted to hospital after being in pain for several days. The pain increased and an operation for the removal of his appendix was carried out. On the following morning he died from heart failure and shock. A post-mortem examination disclosed that there had been an infarction of the bowel, which had been undiagnosed. His death was due to that condition. Blair J. stressed that the Act deliberately excluded cover in respect of disease and that therefore there must be an inquiry into whether death was indeed by accident or merely by disease and thus outside the Act. Here the patient had entered hospital with a complaint which went undiagnosed and untreated, and he had died from that complaint. Although it was not expressed, the Judge apparently thought that "medical misadventure" arises when there has been a positive action on the part of a doctor. This positive action must be causally linked with the injury. When there is a disease condition which is not treated there will be no causal connection between the disease and the failure to treat. Thus failing to diagnose and treat a disease will not be "medical misadventure" but may be medical negligence.

In other jurisdictions, without an accident compensation scheme, there have been decisions which have found that the failure to treat, or to treat in an incorrect way so that the illness goes untreated, may amount to medical negligence[97]. It is argued that if the failure to give medical treatment arises in circumstances which amount to medical negligence, or as in **Collier's**[95] case if the wrong treatment is given so that the illness goes untreated in circumstances which would also be medical negligence, and there is no entitlement under the *Accident Compensation Act*, then a claim in medical negligence may still lie. It may not be so if the condition would not normally be expected to be detected. In such case it would probably qualify as a medical misadventure.

There have been two claims which illustrate the difficulties which can arise. These are **E's claim**[98] and the **Appeal by B**[99]. In **E's** case the applicant's husband died of pneumonia after an illness lasting for about a week. Two days before his death, he attended a surgery, where he complained of stomach pains and vomiting, and received tablets as treatment for the symptoms. His condition worsened. The following day his wife attended the surgery, but failed to obtain assistance. Treatment was given the next day, but the husband died before admission to a hospital. The applicant's claim that her husband had died as a result of medical misadventure was declined by the Commission. She sought a review. When proceedings were brought by his widow in the Supreme Court the question of whether or not there was cover was referred to the Commission for a determination. In giving his decision the Commission delegate made the following statements:

1. "Medical misadventure occurs when: (a) a person suffers bodily or mental injury or damage in the course of, and as part of, the administering to that person of medical aid, care or attention, and (b) such injury or damage is caused by mischance or accident, unexpected and undesigned, in the nature of medical error or medical mishap".
2. "The non-availability of medical assistance is not related to medical treatment of a patient, and to the actual delivery of such treatment".
3. "It must be established that the harm suffered was causally connected with a 'personal injury by accident'". In addition the Commission delegate discussed the difference between "medical error", that is a failure to observe a reasonable standard of care and skill, and "medical mishap" which "describes the situation when there is the intervention or intrusion into the administering of medical aid, care or attention of some unexpected and undesigned incident, event or circumstances of a medical nature that has harmful consequences to the patient".

E's claim[98] was referred to in the **Appeal by B**[99]. The appellant's husband, who suffered from severe coronary disease, was admitted to hospital for an artery vein graft. Following surgery, his post-operative progress was monitored daily by hospital staff, and his symptoms noted. He was examined by his own surgeon and the chief cardiac surgeon before a decision was made on whether he should be discharged. The diagnosis was that his condition was satisfactory, with no evidence of risk. He was therefore discharged 14 days after surgery. Three days later, he died from a massive pulmonary embolism. His widow contended that there had been a medical error on the part of the surgeon in not detecting the possibility of an embolus in her husband's condition and that but for this error he would not have died. She alleged that the failure to diagnose correctly and to take appropriate post-operative measures, such as the administration of anti-coagulants, amounted to medical misadventure in the nature of medical error. The appellant and others who had visited the deceased in hospital gave evidence that the deceased's condition indicated the symptoms of impending fatality. The opinion of a cardiologist was that, "on the assumption that the descriptions given by [the appellant] relating to her husband's condition were as described", this should have signalled the pulmonary embolism. He concluded however that he did not think it could be claimed that the error resulted in the death of the deceased.

In deciding that there had not been medical misadventure Blair J. (the appeal authority) held that:

1. Medical misadventure in the sense of medical error arises only if the service to the patient, including the performance of medical attention or the diagnosis which leads to it, was of a lower standard than was reasonably to be expected in the circumstances.
2. The correct test of medical error to apply in the circumstances of the case was whether in the pre-discharge period, in the light of the evidence available, the post-operative hazard should reasonably have been foreseen and steps taken to avoid it.
3. The evidence of the deceased's symptoms in the pre-discharge period, as recorded in hospital post-operation notes and the observations of the surgeons, was not sufficient for the surgeon to have diagnosed the hazard of a pulmonary embolism as a reasonable possibility.
4. The evidence was not sufficiently persuasive to establish that death was the result of medical misadventure. The appeal was therefore dismissed.

Blair J.'s decision appears to narrow the distinction between medical error and medical negligence. The applicant failed to establish that her claim was in respect of personal injury by accident and thus covered by the Act, therefore on the face of it, a claim in medical negligence might have been available. The discussion of what medical errors will amount to medical misadventure seems however to suggest that, in most circumstances, medical misadventure will coincide with medical negligence. It must be remembered, however, that **E's Application**[98] involved a failure to treat a disease whereas in **B's Claim**[99] the allegation of "medical error" arose where there was continuous treatment but the worsening of the deceased's condition was not recognised. It is interesting to note that the claim made in **Re E**[98] subsequently proceeded as a negligence claim based on standard medical negligence principles, and was successful before a jury[100]. The claim of **Mrs B** went through a convoluted legal process before being referred by the High Court to the Corporation for a decision as to whether the deceased had "cover" under the Act. The Corporation delegate[101] concluded on the available evidence that "personal injury by accident" had been suffered. This decision and that in **Re K** may open the way to some "omissions" falling within the scope of "personal injury by accident". The Corporation issued a determination reversing the earlier decision in **B** after further evidence was adduced at a Commission of Inquiry. The additional evidence showed that the death was not due to "personal injury by accident". **E's** case is distinguishable because it was an omission to treat a pre-existing disease. These are outside the scheme as the definition of "personal injury by accident" excludes damage to the body or mind caused by disease, infection, or the ageing process.

The wrong diagnosis cases undoubtedly cause difficulties. If one applies a strict causal test then some of the cases will clearly fall within "personal injury by accident". For example, in **Barnett v. Chelsea and Kensington Hospital Management Committee**[102], where the defendant's negligence in failing to diagnose arsenic poisoning was not a cause of death and therefore there was not liability, the arsenic poisoning would surely fall within "personal injury by accident". This *cannot* be said with any certainty about situations such as pregnancy after a sterilisation operation[103]; a negligent abortion followed by the subsequent birth of a healthy baby[104]; a pregnancy after a vasectomy, where there was a failure to warn of the risk of conception[105]; or where a pregnancy resulted after a sterilisation operation, and there was a refusal to have an abortion, which events concluded with the birth of a congenitally abnormal child[106]. The situation in **McKay v. Essex A. H. A.**[107] where there was a failure to diagnose rubella in the mother and the child was born with deformities would not be "personal injury by accident". The deformities were caused exclusively by infection and thus excluded from the scheme.

Tensions in the scheme in relation to "personal injury by accident" and medical misfortune

Coverage

One of the principal difficulties in the scheme has undoubtedly been the unsatisfactory nature of the definition of "personal injury by accident"[108]. Quite apart from claims for "medical misadventure", claimants have had difficulty in establishing that the effects from which they are suffering are the "physical and mental consequences of an accident"[109]. There are causal difficulties inherent in establishing that the incapacity results from disease or in establishing that cardio-vascular or cerebro-vascular episodes are compensatable.

The Australian Committee of Inquiry (also chaired by Sir Owen Woodhouse) suggested that the difficulties could be avoided by not using the word "accident" at all, but instead linking injury to Chapter XVII of the *International Classification of Diseases*[110]. This is a publication which is well-known to the medical profession (usually the first arbiters of the question of whether a person has suffered "personal injury by accident"). It is used principally for statistical purposes in hospitals and elsewhere. It prescribes exhaustive categories of both injury conditions and the external causes of injury[111]. The Law Commission has also adopted this proposal[112]. Nevertheless, the World Health Organisation list uses words such as "accidental" and "excessive"[113]. A doubt remains as to whether it would resolve all the difficulties which arise from the term "medical misadventure". The Law Commission believes that most of the problems would disappear since the classification specifies particular consequences which are likely to occur. It suggests that one of the main consequences of this will be that the concepts of recognised risk and informed consent will no longer be relevant. In the area of medical misadventure, such a schedule would adjust and state more precisely the line between illness and injury[114]. How the International Classification can help in the absence of disclosure or lack of informed consent if the result of the treatment is not unexpected by the medical profession is open to question. It does nothing to ensure that patients receive full and clear information about their treatment and the available options; nor does it do anything to ensure the accountability of the profession to their patients[115].

Tension between "disease" and "medical misadventure"

There is another difficult area due to the scheme excluding recovery for "damage to the body or mind caused exclusively by disease, infection, or the ageing process", but recognising cover for "medical misadventure"[116]. The tension arises because in most cases where "medical misadventure" is alleged to have occurred, the patient will have presented for treatment suffering from the disease. Before the claimant can succeed in recovering under the scheme there has to be proof that the predominant cause of the ultimate harm is the treatment rather than the underlying disease. In many cases the patient cannot establish that the treatment is the predominant cause and therefore fails in the claim for compensation[117]. Whether the Law Commission's proposal to tie "personal injury" to the World Health Organisation's classification will resolve this difficulty is a moot point.

Insurance arrangements

All members of the medical profession in New Zealand belong to one or other of the British medical defence unions. The Medical Defence Union has 3295 full members (both doctors and dentists). The Medical Protection Society has 3700 full medical members. The subscription rates for both are set out in Table 3.

There are two different hospital providers in New Zealand[118]. Hospital services are provided free for all New Zealand residents under a system of publicly funded hospitals. These are administered by regional elected hospital boards. Some hospital boards have insurance cover against their residual liabilities. Most of these are carried by the state-owned State Insurance Office; details of the arrangements and cover provided are set out in Table 4. The Auckland Area Health Board, for a population of about 900,000, administers four large surgical and general hospitals and one large gynaecological hospital. Parallel to the free hospital system there is a system of privately operated hospitals, for both medical and surgical procedures. In Auckland there are six private hospitals carrying out surgical procedures and a similar number of medical and convalescent hospitals. These are mostly administered by trust boards. Some are affiliated to religious organisations. (In Auckland the Mercy Hospital, one of the largest private

Table 3 *Subscription rates of medical defence societies—1988 New Zealand*

	Medical practitioners	Dental practitioners
Trainee Interns	Free	—
Newly qualified 1st year	NZ$28 (UK £10.02)	$28 (UK £10.02)
Standard (full)	$168 (UK £55.08)	$56 (UK £20.04)

Table 4 *Hospital Board—insurance arrangements*

Number of Hospital Boards or Area Health Boards:	25
Number *replying* to my inquiry:	12
Number *with insurance cover* for negligent treatment	9
Number with *no insurance* cover	3

Premiums: in a range from NZ$144.85 (Marlborough AHB) to NZ$15,387.94 (Auckland AHB) Average appears to be around $900.

Cover: $20,000 (3 boards, including Auckland AHB did not advise the amount of cover).

Insurer: In most cases, State Insurance Office.

Claims: Two boards said there had been claims since 1 April, 1974:—
   Taranaki AHB— No claims proven within the terms of the policy.
           Two claims.
           One claim proceeded to either settlement or litigation.
   *Auckland AHB—*Many claims (Number not specified)
           "It would take a great deal of research to ascertain how many of these claims were settled or proceeded to litigation".

hospitals, is administered by a Roman Catholic religious order, the Sisters of Mercy). Other private hospitals are administered by the companies which operate health insurance schemes. It is presumed that private hospitals hold insurance cover against any residual liability, but no information is available.

Responsibility and quality control

It has been said earlier in this chapter that the fact that some medical misfortunes are covered by New Zealand's no fault compensation scheme was almost by chance. There was no clear perspective of the role either of claims or of tort liability as systems of quality control. There was no inquiry about the role the tort of negligence can play in providing an incentive structure which would induce the medical profession "to invest optimally in injury prevention"[119]. Danzon argues that in principle negligence liability can provide an efficient system of quality control. The medical malpractice (tort system), Danzon says, makes no sense if its sole function is compensation[120]. In some common law jurisdictions concern has been expressed about the tort system. This may not be because there are deficiencies in the tort system but because the cost of claims and the costs of premiums is high. It may be that the tort system in a perfect society would be quite adequate. In the United States, and to a lesser extent in the United Kingdom, the catalyst for change has not been medical malpractice litigation so much as the fear of litigation, defensive medicine and high insurance premiums. In New Zealand criticism of the effect of the Accident Compensation scheme on medical practice and medical defence subscriptions has stemmed in part from feelings of annoyance emanating from other professional groups which pay high professional indemnity premiums. Courts, too, have been active in developing the doctrine of professional responsibility. In the last two decades the New Zealand Court of Appeal has been particularly active in all areas of professional responsibility other than medicine from which it has been barred by the Accident Compensation Act[121]. So, too in other jurisdictions, where the same trend is evident, the medical profession has largely escaped. This is in part because courts have been unwilling to find a breach of duty by that profession. Some of the New Zealand criticism stems from the belief that persons who suffer "personal injury" at the hands of others ought to be compensated whereas there is less justification for compensating those who are economically injured.

In a no fault society quality control has to be achieved outside the compensation system. Thus the approach to dealing with complaints becomes all important. In New Zealand discipline within the medical profession is divided between two bodies both of which derive their status from the *Medical Practitioners Act 1968*. This Act is at present under review. It is hoped that substantial proposals for change will shortly be introduced. The proposals include more or less equal lay participation in the disciplinary process. It is also proposed that some or all of the penalty by way of fine be paid to the complainant. (This proposal is comparable with recent changes in the Criminal Justice system where the courts can issue orders for reparation or that part of the fine be paid to an injured person.) One level of complaint is to the Medical Practitioners Disciplinary Committee which deals with allegations of professional misconduct. The disciplinary committee consists of four registered medical practitioners (appointed by the Council of the New Zealand Medical Association), one registered medical practitioner appointed by the Minister of Health, and one lay person appointed by the Minister. There are also Divisional Disciplinary Committees consisting of six medical practitioners and one lay member. The Divisional Committees inquire into charges of conduct unbecoming to a practitioner. The Disciplinary Committee has the power to impose a fine not exceeding NZ$1000 (UK £357.90). Under the legislative proposals the fine will be increased to NZ$10,000 (UK £3,579). It has powers of censure and may limit practice rights. The Divisional Committees have the power of censure. There is a right of appeal from the Disciplinary Committee to the Medical Council (this body is the equivalent of the General Medical Council). This body acts in two different capacities: first, as an appellate tribunal for appeals from the Disciplinary Committee; and second, it has original jurisdiction to hear complaints alleging "disgraceful conduct". This jurisdiction is exercised by the Preliminary Proceedings Committee deciding what further action should be taken. The Medical Council is made up of 11 members of the medical profession, appointed on the recommendation of different bodies. There is one lay member appointed by the Minister of Health. As mentioned already, lay membership of both the Disciplinary Committee and the Medical Council is limited to one. This needs to be compared with the GMC, which has nine lay members[122]. In New Zealand, as in the United Kingdom, there has been a growth in consumer groups. This is a result in part, because of rising public dissatisfaction with the medical profession, heightened public awareness of the patient's right to complain, and public dissatisfaction with a disciplinary system which focuses on internal professional issues rather than on responsibility to patients.

The Cartwright inquiry into the Treatment of Cervical Cancer[123] brought into sharp focus defects in the system of ethical and peer review. Since the Report was issued the process of ethical review is being reorganised. The final form that it will take is not yet decided but it seems apparent that there will be much greater lay input than there has been hitherto. There have been suggestions that the Accident Compensation Corporation should police medical practice by reporting doctors whose patients suffer injury. In my view this would be counter-protective. It is difficult enough for the injured to obtain the medical evidence necessary to establish "medical misadventure". If the profession came to regard the Corporation as a public watchdog the task of the patient in proving causation would be made harder. Surely the profession itself should be able to exercise a degree of control. Another model worth studying is the Swedish Medical Responsibility Board, which operates in the setting of a no fault patient injury compensation scheme[124]. In any system the successful operation of a system of medical responsibility depends on heightened awareness of both the complaints procedure and of the right to compensation. In New Zealand I believe that those injured who manage to enter the system either as complainants or as the victims of "medical misadventure" are only the fine point at the tip of the iceberg. Even in Sweden, I suggest that the group recovering compensation may only be the tip of the iceberg. There is, as I have said earlier, no statistical information about the number of claims to the Corporation for "medical misadventure", since such claims are not separated from other forms of "personal injury by accident". There have been at least seventy-seven appeals to the Appeal Tribunal in the scheme's fifteen years of operation[125]. (The population of New Zealand is about 3.3 million.) *I believe that quality control is of the utmost importance, and that it should run parallel with a right to fair and reasonable compensation for medical misfortune.* I do not believe that either can be looked at in a vacuum. The two must also run parallel with the right of patients to full information about their condition and the treatment options. In part this needs greater consumer awareness. Madam Justice Picard, a commentator on Canadian Health Care liability, has said that groups "formed primarily from the professions of law and medicine may tend to be too introspective; the public and patients must be a part of the search for information and solution"[126]. She stresses that "the patient is the raison d'être of the health care system. This fact seems to be forgotten. Associations of citizens as patients should not be feared but fostered. Lawyers, doctors and other health care professionals should be prepared to work with them and to join them"[127].

An overall assessment of the scheme

The scheme itself

The accident compensation scheme protects the whole population against the consequences of all kinds of personal injury. National surveys show that the scheme has universal acceptance[128]. For the average injured person who suffers minor injuries only, and requires medical and para-medical treatment, there is little or no financial cost to be met. For the person whose injuries keep them away from work for more than a week, then compensation payments are paid promptly and regularly. In spite of the prolix nature of the legislation, the scheme is a model of administrative efficiency[129] and is not costly[130].

The scheme has, neverthless, attracted public criticism for a number of reasons:

i) The financing of the scheme, given the major and sudden increase in employer and self-employed levies in 1987. This was the principal reason for the government referring the scheme to the Law Commission for examination in 1987[131].

ii) There has also been concern about the escalating costs of compensation and the level of compensation, especially for minor injuries.

iii) There is tension in the relationship between the scheme and the provision of health care generally. This is perhaps exacerbated by the "gatekeeper" role of general practitioners. Accident victims are clearly in an advantageous position as compared with the "sick".

iv) The Corporation has expressed concern about its small role in accident prevention, given the parameters of the present legislation. An important question which needs to be addressed is the use of incentives, penalties and other methods of deterrence in influencing individuals and organisations to engage in safer practices.

The Law Commission has recommended a flat rate levy for all employers[132], and considers that variable or other levying processes have no effect on safety[133]. Others would disagree most vehemently, and argue that the lack of deterrent and safety incentives in the scheme is one of its greatest weaknesses[134].

The Corporation itself has also expressed concern about the difficulties inherent in the lump sum for non-economic loss[135]. As the Law Commission rightly says, these awards are a recognition of the common law principle of awards and such lump sum awards have no place in a compensation system[136]. Nevertheless, the Law Commission accepts that in theory they can be valuable but suggests they be converted to a system of periodic payments[137].

Medical misfortune

In my own view the scheme has not worked satisfactorily in relation to "medical misadventure". Claimants have had a disproportionately difficult task in establishing a right to compensation in comparison with other claimants, although some easing of their difficulties seems to have been evident since the **MacDonald** and **Viggars** claims were successful in the High Court[138]. There is another problem because some of those who suffer from "medical misadventure" may not be aware of their right to claim[139]. There are also difficulties about medical responsibility and accountability[140].

In theory, a successful common law claim results in an award of damages to compensate for all the injured person's proved losses, both economic and non-economic. The award will include damages for loss of past wages, future wages, medical and other out-of-pocket expenses, as well as all future losses (which can be ascertained in advance) and non-economic losses such as pain and suffering. It is difficult, accurately to predict and prove future losses. The court may underestimate them for fear of being over-generous. In some cases, it may be impossible to prove accurately what future losses and other losses not easily quantifiable such as non-economic loss will be. In practice, few claims actually reach the courts. Instead the legal principles form the basis for negotiation and settlement. Many settle for much less than they might recover in successful litigation, largely through fear of failure in the courts.

The tort system is based on the plaintiff balancing the advantages of allowing the claim to proceed to court successfully as against the risks of not being able to prove the losses and therefore failing completely. Many claimants with meritorious claims settle for less than their losses rather than bear the risk of litigation. In contrast under an accident compensation scheme one does not have to establish "fault" or pin the blame on a defendant. The claimant has only to prove compensatable losses. Therefore many more people recover proved losses under an accident compensation scheme, especially when one remembers that such a scheme can compensate on a pension-basis, than would ever recover adequate compensation at common law.

Other

In making an overall assessment of the New Zealand accident compensation scheme, it is necessary to ask whether an all-embracing scheme which selects accident victims regardless of cause and treats them differently from sickness victims is truly equitable. If accident victims are to be treated differently from sickness victims, then it might be argued that not all accident victims should be treated in the same way. Some accident victims cannot establish their right to compensation as easily as others. Is an all-embracing scheme equitable or might there be advantages in having different schemes for different accident situations, or schemes within a scheme? These are all questions which need to be considered even if they cannot be answered. In this country, in any event, an all-embracing scheme has been rejected[141].

Apparent weaknesses in the New Zealand scheme

The scheme is based on the philosophy that accident victims are a special class of people, deserving of special treatment, and that it is the responsibility of the community as a whole to cushion people from the effects of accidents. It replaced the Workers Compensation scheme, the Criminal Injuries Compensation scheme and the Third-party Motor Vehicle Insurance scheme. It also of course replaced the tort system, and purported to harness and divert the money expended on the tort system and the other schemes, to cover all accidents. This in itself has created problems.

First the scheme is frequently inaccurately described as a no fault scheme. It is in truth a welfare scheme which provides benefits for a selected group of people who are the victims of accidental misfortune. Those who come within the parameters of the scheme are advantaged in respect of the benefits they receive as against those who are outside the scheme. One of the principal purposes of the scheme was to replace the old Workers Compensation scheme which was a no fault scheme under which employers could cover themselves against their liability by insurance, albeit compulsory insurance. Employers who formerly paid premiums to insure against their no fault liability for work-related accidents now find themselves required to pay levies (not premiums) which fund a scheme of welfare payments to their employees if they happen to suffer accidents in or outside the work-place. It is hardly surprising that the employers feel that they have somehow lost control, that the sums they pay are no longer based on perceived risks in the work-place, and that what they are required to pay is no longer, and cannot be, influenced by any steps they take to prevent harm. Nor is it surprising that many employers regard the levies as a kind of additional form of taxation.

Secondly, because the benefits under the scheme largely replaced benefits available under the workers' compensation scheme, and in addition, some common-law damages concepts[142], many would see this as being too generous for some accidents, in particular, those accidents for which no-one can be said to be responsible. The question many ask is: Why should the victim of such an accident be advantaged over the sick?

Thirdly, and this follows from the previous two considerations, in the work-place, on the road, in public buildings, in the doctor/patient relationship and in other circumstances, there ought to be an element of individual responsibility or "control"[143]. But in a comprehensive scheme, based on community responsibility, real individual responsibility becomes irrelevant. Under the former insurance-based schemes, individual responsibility acted as a device to limit the numbers of claims, but once such responsibility becomes irrelevant other devices have to be found.

In New Zealand the device used to limit the parameters of the scheme has been by the selection of the threshold "personal injury by accident". This term was devised by the courts, as a control test operating alongside "in the course of employment", which was itself a test of particular individual responsibility and relationship. When the test of particular responsibility is divorced from "personal injury by accident" the rules of the game are changed dramatically. On the other hand, there is a widening of the boundaries of cover, for example, minor accidents outside the work-place are now included. On the other hand there is a narrowing of the boundaries, because, without the link between responsibility (control) and accident, it is harder for the claimant to establish "personal injury by accident". This effect is illustrated by some industrial diseases[144], and by "medical misadventure[145]. The latter is exacerbated, in particular, by the tension between "medical misadventure" and sickness (disease).

A framework for a medical injury scheme

An equitable scheme first and foremost must be comprehensive. It must be administratively efficient and simple to operate. Above all an equitable scheme must provide real compensation. I believe that many of the problems of the New Zealand scheme have arisen because of its framework. It was believed that if all accidents were treated in the same way and by the same organisation that administrative efficiency would be achieved. Undoubtedly the scheme is administratively efficient. I believe that in part this has been to the advantage of those suffering from the more common accidents who have received their benefits quickly. This has been at the expense of those injured through medical misfortune, including those harmed by the use of pharmaceuticals, medical appliances and vaccines[146]. It is important to draw the parameters for a scheme in such a way that patients do not have to expend time, money and energy in establishing their entitlement to compensation. This is easier said than done. There is no magic answer. If the stigma of fault is removed, and if the burden of proof is heavily weighted in favour of the patient so that entitlement is presumed, then one may be part way to achieving comprehensive entitlement. On the other hand those whose treatment does not turn out as well as they would like should not be compensated. How can the two groups be differentiated? Patients need to be educated about their right to compensation. Patients' associations are important in education and in disseminating information. Panels, made up of equal numbers of lay and medical members, may help in deciding what events are medical misfortune.

Any scheme, if it is to be efficient and comprehensive, cannot be instituted without some consideration of issues of responsibility. As I have said earlier, responsibility has been divorced from the New Zealand no fault scheme. Sir Owen Woodhouse believes that there is no interrelationship between compensation schemes and responsibility. Therefore our scheme has a narrow funding base. There is no enterprise funding. We are told that it is in no sense an insurance scheme. "The scheme replaced compulsory insurance schemes which had been underwriting the risk of claims in the Courts or under workers' compensation legislation. That fact, together with its use of funds collected from those who earlier had paid premiums to insurers for their indemnity, has left behind for some people the misconception that it is simply a new means of obtaining cover against new risks".

"It is wrong and a cause of confusion to think of it in this way. This scheme is not in any sense an insurance system. Its benefits are provided as of right without reference to cause and regardless of risk. It is simply one component of the general social welfare provisions of the country"[147].

In my view by regarding the scheme as an aspect of social welfare, and abandoning the insurance basis, the scheme has a fundamental flaw. This is one of the essential differences between the New Zealand and Swedish schemes. The Swedish schemes are unashamedly insurance schemes, covering workers' compensation, motor vehicle accidents, drug injuries and patient injuries. In an insurance scheme there is a built-in prevention incentive since the reduction of risks and the reduction of accidents may reduce the premiums. In a social welfare scheme funded by a "form of taxation", levy payers, rightly or wrongly, believe that there is nothing that they can do either to influence the levy rates or to prevent accidents from occurring[148]. It is true that risky behaviour can be controlled by imposing penal sanctions. These are not always desirable. It is questionable, too, whether penal sanctions are as effective as economic incentives. An insurance scheme on the Swedish model does not solve all the problems. Difficult questions of causation remain. Proof is still required that the injury would not have occurred but for the treatment. Nevertheless, since the premiums are related to claims there must be some incentive for the prevention of injury.

Whatever type of scheme is adopted, there needs to be a close relationship with the bodies responsible for maintaining ethical standards, quality control and standards of responsibility. A close watch must be kept on the criteria both for drug trial programmes and for treatment protocols.

A satisfactory scheme must provide real compensation. The New Zealand scheme provides real income-related compensation for earners but for the non-earner the benefits are far from generous. Medical misfortune, when it happens, does not distinguish between earners and non-earners. The benefits system does distinguish one group from the other. The Law Commission's recommendation for periodic pension-based benefits for non-earners would remove this anomaly. Pension-based benefits are, I believe, preferable to a system where, as in Sweden, the benefits are related to tort damages awards.

The views expressed are the personal views of the writer and not those of the Board of Directors or of the Management of the Accident Compensation Corporation.

Notes and References

1. *Motor Vehicle Insurance (Third party Risks) Act* 1928.
2. In 1942 Lord Beveridge in his report had been highly critical of the U.K. Workers' Compensation legislation on which the New Zealand Act had been modelled. He had recommended a unified plan for social security (Cmnd. 6404).
3. Report of the Royal Commission, Section 8.
4. *Report of the Royal Commission of Inquiry into Personal Injury by Accident*. N.Z. Government Printer, Wellington, 1967. (The Report is referred to usually as the Woodhouse Report after its Chairman, the then Mr Justice Woodhouse, later Rt. Hon Sir Owen Woodhouse, President of the Court of Appeal. Sir Owen Woodhouse is now the President of the Law Commission.)
5. Report at para. 171, p. 77, where the disadvantages and inadequacies of the tort claim are discussed.
6. The submissions made to the Royal Commission related to its principal term of reference (defects in the workers' compensation scheme). Defects in the tort claim in respect of non-work accidents were peripheral to the inquiry. If the terms of reference had been wider then it can be assumed that the accident insurance industry would have been able to provide statistical information about the causes of "accident".

7. "'Personal injury by accident'—
   (a) Includes—
       (i)   The physical and mental consequences of any such injury or of the accident;
       (ii) Medical, surgical, dental, or first aid misadventure;
       (iii) Incapacity resulting from an occupational disease or industrial deafness under sections 28 and 29 of this Act;
       (iv) Actual bodily harm (including pregnancy and mental or nervous shock) arising by an act or omission of any other person which is within the description of any of the offences specified in sections 128, 132 and 201 of the *Crimes Act 1961*, irrespective of whether or not any person is charged with the offence and notwithstanding that the offender was legally incapable of forming a criminal intent;
   (b) Except as provided in the last preceding paragraph, does not include:
       (i)   Damage to the body or mind caused by a cardio-vascular or cerebro-vascular episode unless the episode is the result of effort, strain, or stress that is abnormal, excessive, or unusual for the person suffering it, and the effort, strain, or stress arises out of and in the course of the employment of that person;
       (ii) Damage to the body or mind caused exclusively by disease, infection, or the ageing process."
   Some might argue that these changes were cosmetic rather than substantive. Prior to the passing of the original Act, New Zealand had had a criminal injuries compensation scheme, *Criminal Injuries Compensation Act* 1963, which merged in the comprehensive accident compensation scheme.
8. Geoffrey Palmer, *Compensation for Incapacity*; Oxford, 1979 says at p. 43 that in 1970 there were "no more than 60 arguably serious medical malpractice claims in New Zealand and that the total payout from insurance companies was $150,000." Palmer's statement is based on information obtained by Professor Marc Franklin (Franklin, (1975) 27 Stan. L.R.653 at 670). Common law claims for personal injury arising elsewhere than in work-related accidents or motor-vehicle accidents have increased to a marked extent in other Commonwealth jurisdictions since 1974. Such developments could not take place in New Zealand after the scheme's inception.
9. In New Zealand public hospitals are state financed but there are also private hospitals which are subsidised by the State.
10. The Medical Protection Society has a larger membership in New Zealand than the Medical Defence Union.
11. [1957] 1 W.L.R. 582 (Q.B.).
12. [1965] N.Z.L.R. 161 (C.A.) reversing the decision of Woodhouse J. in the Supreme Court, [1964] N.Z.L.R. 241.
13. The interview as described in the evidence is set out in Woodhouse J.'s judgment at 244, lines 24–44.
14. [1964] A.C. 465 (H.L.).
15. [1958] N.Z.L.R. 306. Fleming, *Law of Torts*; 6th Edition Law Book Company Ltd, Sydney, 1983, at p. 161, footnote 38, remarks that this decision is perplexing in that it countenances liability for nervous shock from foreseeable misuse of an *accurate* certificate. He does not refer to the issue in his 7th Edition, 1987.
16. [1953] N.Z.L.R. 196.
17. **Gartside *v*. Sheffield, Young & Ellis** [1983] N.Z.L.R. 37: **Rowe *v*. Turner, Hopkins and Partners** [1982] 1 N.Z.L.R. 178 (C.A.).
18. S.5 of the Accident Compensation Act 1972 is not materially different from s.27, but it is not identical.
19. *27. Act to be a code.* (1) Subject to this section, where any person suffers personal injury by accident in New Zealand or dies as a result of personal injury so suffered, or where any person suffers outside New Zealand personal injury by accident in respect of which he has cover under this Act or dies as a result of personal injury so suffered, no proceedings for damages arising directly or indirectly out of the injury or death shall be brought in any Court in New Zealand independently of this Act, whether by that person or any other person, and whether under any rules of law or any enactment.

(2) Nothing in this section shall affect

    (a) Any action which lies in accordance with section 86 of this Act; or

    (b) Any action for damages by the injured person or his administrator or any other person for breach of a contract of insurance; or

    (c) Any proceedings for damages arising out of personal injury by accident or death resulting therefrom, if the accident occurred before the 1st day of April 1983.

(3) Subject to this Act, the Corporation should have *exclusive* jurisdiction to determine whether or not any person has suffered personal injury by accident in the circumstances specified in section 26(2) of this Act or has died as a result of personal injury so suffered, and its decisions shall be *conclusive*.

(4) Where, in any proceedings before a Court, a question arises as to whether or not any person has suffered personal injury by accident in the circumstances specified in section 26(2) of this Act, or has died as a result of personal injury so suffered, the Court shall refer the question to the Corporation for determination.

(5) The Corporation may, on the application of any person who is a party to any proceedings or contemplated proceedings before a Court, determine any such question.

20. S.2, the interpretation provision. The definition is set out in n.7.

21. It is noteworthy that not all cases of medical negligence come within the scope of "medical misadventure". While acts of operational negligence will obviously be included, an act of omission, for example in failing to respond to a call for treatment, would not be included (cf **Application for review by E** (77/R1352) ACC Report, July 1978, p. 44 considered by Speight J in **Accident Compensation Commission v. Auckland Hospital Board and M** [1980] 2 N.Z.L.R. 748. The case of "E" did in fact proceed to trial; a civil jury found the doctors liable for damages (A225/75 Rotorua Registry. Hearing date: 28 November–5 December 1979). For a discussion of the meaning of "mental consequences" see Vennell, "The Mental Consequences of Accident—Problems of Interpretation of the Accident Compensation Act" [1988] 14 Recent Law 28.

22. [1984] 1 N.Z.L.R. 97.

23. S.27 of the Accident Compensation Act 1982 is not identical to s.5 of the 1972 Act, but this is not material to the results of **Donselaar v. Donselaar**.

24. **Liesbosch Dredger v. S.S. Edison** [1933] A.C. 449, per Lord Wright at 459.

25. **Fitter v. Veal** (1701) 12 Mod. Rep. 542.

26. See Report of the Royal Commission, 1967, para. 279 at pp. 107–108.

27. S.59 provides for earnings related compensation after the first week for temporary loss of earning capacity; s.60 provides for the assessment of permanent incapacity.

28. S.57.

29. It is, or course, possible for the self-employed to insure against loss of earnings in the first week, or thereafter. The Law Commission also presided over by Sir Owen Woodhouse has recommended that the waiting period be extended to two weeks: Law Commission, Report No. 4, "Personal Injury Prevention and Recovery", Wellington, 1988.

30. The conversion date for all figures in this paper is 15 November 1988 when the New Zealand dollar was the equivalent of 35.79p Sterling.

31. S.63.

32. S.65. A totally dependent spouse receives earning related compensation at the rate of three-fifths of deceased's earnings related compensation based on permanent total loss of earning capacity. Children receive one-fifth of the earnings related compensation calculated on the same basis.

33. S.65(7). Under s.65(8) the Corporation is given a discretion to reduce the earnings related compensation when it considers that, having regard to certain specified factors, it would be just so to do. Cf. cl. 62 of the Draft Bill appended to the Law Commission Report, which provides for a different approach to determining dependency.

34. S.63.

35. Ss. 72–75.

36. Report, above n.29, paras. 213–214.

37. S.78. The Law Commission has recommended the replacement of lump sums by a periodic payment for loss of earning capacity, see Report, above n.29., paras. 188–205.
38. S.79.
39. [1980] 2 N.Z.L.R. 379.
40. *Ibid*, at 382; **Re Nikorima** 4 A.C.C. Report (1980 September) p. 82.
41. For a discussion of some anomalies in the scheme, see Ullrich, "Unemployed? Do not pass go . . . Accident Compensation and Unemployment" (1982) 12 V.U.W.L.R. 47.
42. S.80 is a re-enactment of s.121 of the 1972 Act. The effect of s.121 was discussed by Willy, "The Accident Compensation Act and Recovery for Losses Arising from Personal Injury and Death by Accident" (1975) 6 N.Z.L.R. 250 at 258–260; Blair, at pp. 19–23. Cf. Draft Bill cl. 59.
43. In **Accident Compensation Commission** *v.* **Nelson** [1979] 2 N.Z.L.R. 464 (C.A.), Richmond P. and Cooke J. (Woodhouse J. dissenting), this was described as a "more stringent test than ever prevailed as to remoteness of damage in either tort or contract. *Directness* of causation is not enough". The loss must necessarily result from the injury.
44. In **A.C.C.** *v.* **Kivi** [1980] 2 N.Z.L.R. 38, the Court of Appeal considered what s.121(2)(a), the corresponding provision in the 1972 Act, meant. The scope of s.80(2)(a) has been narrowed by the additional requirement that the loss of service must be "of a domestic or house-hold nature which was previously provided on a regular basis . . .".
45. In **Re Hales** [1982] N.Z.A.C.R. 446; [1983] 3 N.Z.A.R. 324, where the claimant was virtually unconscious and was unlikely ever to become fully sentient again, Blair J. held that in the circumstances hospital visits had no therapeutic value to the claimant, and therefore since the visits were solely for the visitor's benefit or solace the expenses incurred in travelling were not recoverable.
46. S.80(3).
47. S.81. In **Wall** (1976) 1 N.Z.A.R. 89 a fairly large sum was claimed for the expenses relating to a Maori tangi (funeral). It was held that s.122 (the predecessor of s.81) covered the expenses directly related to the burial (without unreasonable extravagances), but that all the indirect expenses were not recoverable; cf Draft Bill, clause 69.
48. S.82; spouse, up to $4,000 (UK £1,431.60) depending on the extent of dependency; children and other dependants, $2,000 (UK £715.80) each calculated on the basis of the extent of dependency, but no more than $6,000 (UK £2,147.40), abated according to a formula set out in the provision which ensures that if there is more than one spouse, or more than three dependants then no more than $4,000 or $6,000, as the case may be, will be paid out. The draft bill has no provision for lump sums to be paid to dependants of a "deceased person".
49. See Table 1 for a comparison with levies set in some Canadian provinces under Workers' Compensation schemes.
50. This was more than double the average return of 3.6 percent achieved by the superannuation funds managed by life insurance companies for the same period.
51. Law Commission, Report No.3.
52. *Committee of Inquiry into Allegations Concerning the Treatment of Cervical Cancer at the National Women's Hospital and Into Other Related Matters*, Government Printing Office, Auckland, July 1988.
53. *Ibid*, at p. 172.
54. *Ibid*.
55. Geiringer, "Trial in Error", N.Z. Listener, November 26, 1988, 18 at pp. 47 and 50.
56. Above, n.41.
57. Law Commission Report No. 4, paras 194–203.
58. *Ibid*, paras. 212–213.
59. See Table 2, for the unemployment figures at October 30, 1988.
60. Above, n.7.
61. [1903] A.C. 443. In this and other cases, including **Trim Joint District School Board of Management** *v.* **Kelly** [1914] A.C. 667, the Court was considering the phrase 'personal injury by accident' but was in reality merely interpreting the word 'accident'.
62. *Ibid*, at 680–681 (this was a case in which a school-teacher was killed by the deliberate act of violence of a pupil).

63. [1972] A.C. 944.
64. *Ibid*, at 1005.
65. (1980) 5 ACC Report 56, in which **Fenton v. Thorley** (n.61 above); **Jones v. Secretary of State for Social Services** (n.11 above) and **Mills v. Smith** [1963] 2 All E.R. 1078 were considered.
66. *Ibid*, at 58. See also the Accident Compensation Corporation guidelines on 'Personal Injury by Accident' [1981] N.Z.A.C.R. 242.
67. Accident Compensation Corporation guidelines, *ibid*.
68. **Re Firmstone** (tituled Re **Attorney-General** [1983] N.Z.A.C.R. 553). This case was not a medical case. Examples of a medical case which would clearly fall within the scheme as being the result of another accident would be **Robinson v. Post Office** [1974] 1 W.L.R. 1176, but the chain of causation from the original accident to the final injury must be complete. If the wrong operation is performed, the occurrence will clearly fall within the phrase 'personal injury by accident': see **Re Penn** [1982] N.Z.A.C.R. 250.
69. S.2 'Personal injury by accident', (a) (ii), above n.7.
70. Blair, *Accident Compensation in New Zealand*. (Second Edition) Butterworths, 1983 at p. 77, lists a number of situations which could be regarded as 'medical misadventure', although as he says, the list of possible medical misadventures is infinite:
    "(a) A patient fails to recover from treatment as expected, or reacts abnormally to appropriate treatment.
    (b) A doctor's failure to diagnose the patient results in a worsening of his condition. The failure might be justifiable—the condition may have been extremely rare or it might have been swamped by symptoms of other unrelated problems.
    (c) A wrong diagnosis is given and, for similar reasons, this might be justifiable.
    (d) A patient develops psychological problems following proper treatment.
    (e) A patient is left with unexpected ugly scars following an operation properly carried out."
    As Blair points out whether or not all of his examples amount to medical misadventure will depend on the particular facts and the interpretation of para (a)(ii) in its context.
71. Accordingly to **L v. M** [1979] N.Z.L.R. 519, the claimant must first ascertain from the Corporation (formerly the Commission) whether s/he has cover under the Act, otherwise the defendant may ask the Court to stay its proceedings pending this issue being decided by the Corporation.
72. Sandford, Personal Injury by Accident under the Accident Compensation Act—A Commentary, ACC Wellington (1979) at 61.
73. Blair, op cit, at 81.
74. Notes on "Personal Injury by Accident" [1981] N.Z.A.C.R. 242 at 243; Medical misadventure". "As stated, the Accident Compensation Act specifically provides that the partial definition 'personal injury by accident' includes . . . medical, surgical, dental or first aid misadventure. The meaning of this phrase has been considered in various cases, both by the Corporation and by the Courts. The Accident Compensation Appeal Authority has said, in a definition approved by the High Court, that medical misadventure includes: A mischance or accident, unexpected and undersigned, relating to medical treatment and arising out of a lawful act. [Dictum of Blair J in Appeal by **S. M. Collier** (1976) 1 N.Z.A.R. 130; approved by Speight J, in **Accident Compensation Commission v. Auckland Hospital Board and M** [1980] N.Z.L.R. 748]. "The effect of the definition is that it is not necessary to show that there has been negligence on the part of a medical practitioner before a claim will lie for medical misadventure. The definition embraces the case where the correct procedures were carried out but where a mischance or accident, unexpected and undesigned occurred.
    "All treatment, whether medical or surgical has a chance of being unsuccessful. There is a natural and expected failure rate. The Act does not provide a guarantee of complete success in medical treatment. Where there is an unsatisfactory outcome of treatment which can be classified as merely within the normal range of medical or surgical failure, this would not be held to be a medical misadventure.
    "It is noteworthy that not all cases of medical negligence come within the scope of medical misadventure. While acts of operational negligence will obviously be included,

an act of omission, for example in failing to respond to a class for treatment, would not be included (cf Application for **Review by E** (77/R1352) ACC report July, 1978 p. 44, considered by Speight J, in **Accident Compensation Commission** *v.* **Auckland Hospital Board and M** cited below). Public liability insurance would be required to cover this type of situation."

"The above comments apply equally to all other forms of medical misadventure, including surgical, dental or first aid".

75. **Accident Compensation Commission** *v.* **Auckland Hospital Board and M** [1980] 2 N.Z.L.R. 748.
76. (1985) 5 N.Z.A.R. 276. It is interesting to note that, at an Auckland District Law Society Continuing Legal Education Seminar in 1984, Hon Dr. Martyn Finlay Q.C. said that: "If we assume the true criterion for interpreting and applying the Act to be to include disability resulting from accident but to exclude that caused by disease, is not any disability that may be attributable to the failure of medical intervention to secure its intended result more akin to accident than sickness?"
77. (1986) 6 N.Z.A.R. 235. Evidence was available to the effect that there was a 1% chance of the event happening (since 1972 550 arteriograms had been performed at Greenlane Hospital, of these none had resulted in the consequences suffered by the appellant).
78. Above, n.76.
79. Above, n.77.
80. Examples of successful claims are:—
    Re Muir [1981] N.Z.A.C.R. 828, in which serum hepatitis was contracted from an unsterile instrument. (An unsterile instrument was not a normal risk of an operation); **Re Bulter** [1982] N.Z.A.C.R. 300, in which a baby was damaged prior to birth, as a result of a nurse giving an incorrect injection.
    Examples of unsuccessful claims are:—
    Re Lloyd [1982] N.Z.A.C.R. 259 in which the patient developed dermatitis as a result of medical treatment. This was held to be within the normal risks of treatment; **Re G** [1982] N.Z.A.C.R. 329 (possible mis-diagnosis held not to be 'medical misadventure', but, *quaere*, some incorrect diagnoses may amount to medical misadventure). cf **McKay** *v.* **Essex A.H.A.** [1982] 2 W.L.R. 890 (C.A.) in which a failure to diagnose was held not to be medical negligence; **Re Kishor Bava** [1983] N.Z.A.C.R. 669 (aggressive treatment of cancer held not to be medical misadventure); **Re Stopford** [1984] N.Z.A.C.R. 783 (known complication of high dosage of drug): **Re Priestley** [1983] N.Z.A.C.R. 787 (no evidence that a failed sterilisation was due to medical misadventure); **Re Murtagh** [1984] N.Z.A.C.R. 801 (events and pain under anaesthesia was held not to be a rare and unusual occurrence).
81. Medical Information Bulletin No. 23 (July 1982).
82. Above, n.52. See Brahams, *"The Need for Consent in Medical Trials"* (1982) N. L.J. 687.
83. The decision in **Re Wilson** (1985) 5 N.Z.A.L. 33 (A.C.A.A.) seems to follow the narrow approach. The claimant had received an intramuscular steroid injection to alleviate hay fever. A blood vessel was damaged, resulting in a painful abscess which required surgical treatment. Middleton D.C.J. held that the crucial issue was whether the complication which arose could have been anticipated at the time when the treatment was undertaken. As there is always the risk, in any injection, of the needle penetrating the wrong area, any ensuing complication which, though it may be rare, is not completely unknown does not amount to medical misadventure. (This decision was given whilst the appeal in **MacDonald's** case was awaiting hearing in the High Court). Since **MacDonald** the question would perhaps have to be: Was there any risk, and if so, was the risk one capable of being guarded against? If the answer to either or both is in the negative, then the circumstances may well have amounted to 'medical misadventure'.
84. "Informed consent" is the term of art used in Canada and in the United States, but the same principle has been considered in New Zealand without giving it the formal title (see **Smith**, above n.12). In England, first in **Chatterton** *v.* **Gerson** [1980] 3 W.L.R. 1003, and more recently by the House of Lords in **Sidaway** the Canadian "full disclosure" standard was rejected in favour of the "professional standard", i.e. for

information to be disclosed relating to the risks of medical treatment (this may be quite close to the standard discussed by Woodhouse J. in **Smith**, above n.43). See also **F** *v.* **R** (1983) 33 S.A.S.R. 189 (adoption of the Canadian standard). A full discussion of the Canadian position is found in Picard, **Legal Liability of Doctors and Hospitals in Canada** (1984), (Carswell) Chapter 3, pp. 41–147. For a discussion of the New Zealand position since the introduction of the accident compensation scheme, see Mahoney, "Informed Consent and Breach of the Medical Contract to Achieve a particular Result" (1985) 6 Otago L.R. 103; Vennell, "Medical Negligence and the Effect of the New Zealand Accident Compensation Scheme". ZVg1R Wiss 80 (1981) 228. Vennell, "Informed Consent or Reasonable Disclosure of Risks", (1987) 13 Recent Law 160.

85. Notes on "Personal Inquiry by Accident—Medical Misadventure" [1981] N.Z.A.C.R. 242 at 24.
86. Particularly if the patient cannot exercise his or her choice of whether or not to proceed with the medical treatment.
87. (1987) 6 N.Z.A.R. 231.
88. [1984] N.Z.A.C.R. 787.
89. The judgement in **Re Priestley**, n.88, is surprising for the interpretation, at 790, placed on the Court of Appeal's decision in **Smith** *v.* **Auckland Hospital Board**, that "the doctor's duty is fully to inform the patient *if* the question is asked, but that otherwise, there would be no duty. Such a view, it is suggested, is based on too loose an interpretation of **Smith** which still requires conduct in conformance with the appropriate standard of care, and that an application of such standard may or may not require a disclosure of risks in the absence of a request. This would seem to accord with the **Sidaway** doctrine. (**Sidaway** *v.* **Bethlem Royal Hospital** [1985] A.C. 871.)
90. Above, n.87. This area of tort liability has developed throughout the Commonwealth since the House of Lords decision in **Hedley Bryne & Co Ltd** *v.* **Heller & Partners** [1964] A.C. 465.
91. [1965] N.Z.L.R. 191 (C.A.). The test laid down by the Court of Appeal was adopted in Ontario in **Neale** *v.* **Hopmans** (1966) 54 D.L.R. (2d) 165 (C.A.).
92. [1964] N.Z.L.R. 241.
93. Above, at 250–251.
94. Above, n.91.
95. (1977) 1 N.Z.A.R. 130.
96. See Blair, **Accident Compensation in New Zealand** (Butterworths, Wellington 1978), at 44. "This case may be regarded as a somewhat unsatisfactory one, in the sense that the evidence furnished at both the Review Hearing and the Appeal was meagre as regards the central question namely whether the omission to diagnose the trouble was, in the circumstances, 'medical misadventure'. The only medical evidence available consisted of copies of the inquest reports, which included a statement by the surgeon concerned and the statement of the pathologist. In the absence of proper medical opinion the decision cannot be regarded as really definitive, but rather as deciding that medical misadventure was 'unproven'". (This case is not discussed by Blair in his Second Edition 1983.)
97. **Barnett** *v.* **Chelsea and Kensington Hospital M.C.** [1969] 1 Q.B. 428 is an example.
98. **Application for Review for E.** (Review N77/R1352), 1981, July A.C.C. Rep. 44.
99. 1980, September A.C.C. Rep.
100. Information supplied to the writer by J.P. Gittos, Barrister, counsel for the widow of "E".
101. Unreported (dated 14 June, 1984).
102. Above, n.97.
103. **Udale** *v.* **Bloomsbury A.H.A.** [1983] 1 W.L.R. 1098 (Q.B.D.).
104. **Sciuriaga** *v.* **Powell** [1980] C.A. Transcript 597.
105. **Thake** *v.* **Maurice** [1986] Q.B. 644 (Q.B.D.), 670 (C.A.).
106. **Emeh** *v.* **Kensington, Chelsea and Westminster A.H.A.** [1985] Q.B. 1012 (C.A.).
107. [1982] Q.B. 1166 (C.A.).
108. S.2. The definition is set out in n.7. at the beginning of these footnotes.

109. See Vennell, "The Mental Consequences of Accident—Problems of Interpretation of the Accident Compensation Act" (1988) 14 Recent Law 28.
110. World Health Organisation, Geneva, 1967.
111. *Compensation and Rehabilitation in Australia* (Report of the National Committee of Inquiry, July 1974) Vol 1 paras. 350–351, 147–148.
112. The Law Commission is presided over by Sir Owen Woodhouse. Law Commission, Report No. 4, *Personal Injury: Prevention and Recovery*, 1988. Recommendation 8. Paras. 165–166 (pp. 47–48).
113. *Ibid*, E850–E858 at p. 172; E870 at p. 174; E878–E879 at pp. 178–179.
114. *Ibid*, para. 165.
115. Both these issues were considered in the *Report of the Cervical Cancer Inquiry*, at pp. 132–142.
116. Above, n.10, where the definition is set out.
117. In **Re Lloyd** [1982] N.Z.A.C.R. 259, dermatitis, which developed as a side-effect of treatment, was held to be within the normal risks of treatment; in **Re Kishor Bava** [1983] N.Z.A.C.R. 690 it was held that side effects from the aggressive treatment of cancer were not 'medical misadventure'.
118. The Report of the Hospital and Related Services Task Force, "*Unshackling The Hospitals*", 1988 discusses and contrasts the public and private hospital systems.
119. Danzon, *Medical Malpractice—Theory, Evidence and Public Policy* (Harvard U.P. 1985) p. 9 referring to Posner, *Economic Analysis of Law* (1977).
120. *Ibid*, at p. 221.
121. For example, **Gartside v. Sheffield Young & Ellis** [1983] N.Z.L.R. 37 (solicitor); **Allied Finance and Investments Ltd v. Haddow & Co** [1983] N.Z.L.R. 22 (solicitor); **Scott Group Ltd v. McFarlane** [1978] 1 N.Z.L.R. 553 (solicitor); **Rowe v. Turner Hopkins and Partners** [1982] 1 N.Z.L.R. 178 (solicitor); **Day v. Mead** [1987] 2 N.Z.L.R. 443 (solicitor).
122. The work of the General Medical Council is described from an outsiders viewpoint in Rosenthal, *Dealing with Medical Malpractice—The British and Swedish Experience* (Tavistock, 1987).
123. Above, n.52.
124. Rosenthal, above n.24, Chapters 9–12.
125. This should be compared with the number of 5000 p.a. patient injury claims which was the figure given to me when I visited Sweden in June 1988.
126. Picard, *Legal Liability of Doctors and Hospitals in Canada* (Second Ed., 1984, Carswell) at p. 345.
127. *Ibid*, at p. 352.
128. Law Commission, Report 4, paras. 1 and 2.
129. Ison, *Accident Compensation* (1980, Croom Helm, London).
130. The levy rates compare more than favourably with the levies paid in respect of Workers' Compensation schemes in Canadian Provinces. Table 1. When one remembers that the whole population is protected against nearly all types of injury wherever they occur the level of costs can be described as "reasonable".
131. The Law Commission, Reports Nos. 3 and 4.
132. Report No. 4, para. 73; Report No. 3 Recommendation 1.
133. Report No. 4, paras. 105–149.
134. Brown, "Deterrence and Accident Compensation Schemes" (1978–79) U.W.O.L.R., 111; Brown, "Deterrence in Tort and No Fault: The New Zealand Experience (1985) 73 Cal. L.R. 976; Professor Richard Miller of the University of Hawaii, Submission to Law Commission on Accident Compensation, 1987.
135. S.79.
136. Report No. 4, paras. 188–194.
137. *Ibid*, Recommendation 11. Miller, "Should Social Insurance Pay Compensation for Pain and Suffering?" (1982) 31 I. C.L.Q. 550. In this article Dr. Miller canvasses the arguments both for and against the payment of lump sums in compensation schemes and concludes that they do not fit. Nevertheless, he believes that it is too late to remove them, and that compensation schemes should accommodate them. Another solution would be to allow tort claims for pain and suffering.

138. It is very difficult, if not impossible, to reach any conclusions, because of the lack of statistical information separating 'medical misadventure' claims from claims arising out of other accidents.
139. In a scheme where the medical profession acts as the gate-keeper of the scheme, (and plays a leading role) there may be a psychological incentive not to inform patients of their rights (if only to protect the medical profession's relationship with the patient).
140. Vennell, "Informed Consent or Reasonable Disclosure of Risks; The Relevance of an Informed Patient in the Light of the New Zealand Accident Compensation Scheme" (1987) 13 Recent Law 160 at pp. 169–170.
141. *Royal Commission on Civil Liability and Compensation for Personal Injury.* (Pearson Commission) Report, 1978. Cmnd. 7054.
142. E.g., Lump sums for non-economic loss, see s.79.
143. This term is used to mean more or less the same thing in respect of the doctrine of "vicarious liability" as it does in workers' compensation cases.
144. If work-place conditions are irrelevant then it may be difficult to establish either the causal link or that the disease is work-related.
145. If responsibility is established then it may be easier to establish that the ill-effects are part of the chain of cause and effect and thus depends on the assumption of responsibiltiy.
146. There is no separate compensation scheme for vaccine related injuries. The problems in establishing 'medical misadventure' from their use are similar to those arising out of the use of pharmaceuticals.
147. Law Commission Report No. 4, op. cit, pp. IX–X.
148. Levies are seen by many employers as a form of taxation.

4

Discussion

Chairman: Sir Christopher Booth

Mr R. K. Greenwood *(Leicester):* The figures quoted both for the compensation to patients and defence society subscriptions in New Zealand are frankly very small by UK standards. I cannot see the population of this country accepting that kind of level of compensation. If such a scheme were brought in here in a similar fashion I suspect the corporation would quickly go bankrupt.

Mrs Vennell: In saying that the figures quoted are very small in respect of compensation, it should be remembered that someone can be on earnings-related compensation for 20 or 30 years, getting 80% of their earnings for that period. When I was involved in advising people on settlements in an air crash I did some calculations. As a result I am sure that the sums people receive from the New Zealand scheme are far greater than anything they would get from the common law. The common law is guesswork, damages are guesswork, and it is not possible to guess what people will need. Our scheme can identify a need such as alteration to people's houses, which the common law cannot do adequately.

I love the common law and I teach torts—but I do not think it is satisfactory for personal injury claims.

Dr J. Leahy Taylor *(Staines):* Dr Mann told us that the standard of proof of causation would need to equate with the normal clinical judgement of experienced clinicians. One of the problems of the present system is that experienced clinicians give totally opposite evidence in the witness box. Their normal clinical judgement varies widely.

A second problem of the present system is its all-or-none nature—the 51% rule. The judge thinks it is 51% likely that there was negligence, so 100% compensation is paid. If he thinks it is 49% likely, nothing is paid. Surely, in any new system there must be some arrangement whereby, if the clinicians together could come to a figure, perhaps it might be 40% or 35%, there should be a coefficient of causality and not an all-or-none method of compensation.

Dr Mann: It is, of course, true that there are difficulties with causation and attribution, and that they are inescapable. They are at their worst in an adversarial system such as we have at the moment. When one group of clinicians is pitched against another group of clinicians, working in an adversarial environment, the situation itself maximises the differences of view and does not seek to resolve them to the patient's advantage. In a non-adversarial system, as Dr Oldertz has told us, causality has not been found to be the problem it might be expected to be.

In the kind of no fault compensation that we might be discussing, when people are trying to come to a reasonable view in the patient's interest, we might hope, therefore, to have less of a problem than some would anticipate.

I would accept the idea that there cannot be an all-or-none type settlement in some cases. Things are more complicated than that and in some patients an adverse outcome might be due in part to progression of the disease and in part to doctor or drug related damage. I suggested, therefore, that compensation might need to be apportioned for contributory iatrogenic damage.

Sir Christopher Booth: On the point of professional differences of view, for example, industrial injuries boards dealing with compensation for coal-miners suffering from pneumoconiosis, the system works reasonably well and, as I recall, is entirely based on clinical judgement. It may be, therefore, that the non-adversarial situation brings us into a different position.

Mrs Jean Robinson: I am very glad that Dr Leahy Taylor raised the question of clinical judgement which was referred to earlier as if it were some kind of gold standard. Those of us who have been involved in helping patients are aware that this is not so. For example, the Ombudsman will only take cases where there is no question of litigation. Nevertheless, case notes disappear. On the rare occasions when he takes evidence under oath some very odd medical opinions are given.

I, too, was going to raise the question of industrial injuries and industrial diseases. Those of us who work with victims of those diseases, as I do as a trustee for the Society for the Prevention of Asbestosis and Industrial Disease, know that doctors can behave very differently towards someone who they know is applying for compensation, even if it is nothing to do with the medical profession, or any question of accident or injury by the medical profession, than towards someone who is not. They can behave differently towards a private patient, for example, with regard to the need for induction of labour, than towards a National Health Service (NHS) patient.

With regard to clinical judgement, users of health care services are not as naive as they used to be. We are not dealing with the kind of population for whom clinical judgement is infallible, and we are aware of the differences that may occur.

One of the constructive things which I would like the medical profession to consider is the question raised in Dr Mann's paper, that no fault compensation preserves doctor–patient relationships because it is non-adversarial. I am most concerned about the preservation and restoration of relationships between injured patients, their relatives, and doctors when, for whatever reason, some kind of medical mishap has occurred.

Although a no fault compensation scheme *may* preserve or be less damaging to doctor–patient relationships, this is not necessarily so. I think it cannot be assumed that this will happen unless some serious study is made of what happens to the relationships, and where they go wrong, and how.

Many of us deal with people who have not only been medically injured, originally perhaps through nobody's fault—or think they have been, when they have not—but are emotionally damaged because of what happens in their subsequent encounters with health care personnel. That is what needs to be avoided. Please do not assume that no fault compensation alone will answer this problem. It is something that all of us will have to work at through medical and public education, and through study of what happens in those encounters, and why.

Sir Christopher Booth: Speaking about differences of view between doctors, I think the whole situation has to be put in perspective. Basically there is a large proportion of situations in the clinic in which doctors will agree. Differences in everyday clinical work are not a big problem. When we are talking about no fault compensation, litigation, and resulting differences of view, we are talking about the exceptions within medicine, and not the general rule. I would like to make the point clear. That is certainly the professional view; I suspect it is also the lay view.

Dr Oldertz: The Swedish experience is that there is always sensitivity about the relationship between the doctor and the patient when an accident occurs. In our experience the doctor is often the lawyer of the injured patient. He argues his case, and always tries—at least, in most cases—to give an objective view of what happened. We think that the doctor gives the true facts, which is very important, because then we have the information on which to base a decision.

Mrs Vennell: It is true that an accident compensation scheme is not a panacea for the problems that arise in doctor–patient relationships, particularly when something has gone wrong. The New Zealand experience—perhaps because we have the common law, and the medical profession in New Zealand still thinks in terms of the common law—indicates that when something goes wrong there is a fear of the litigation process. Even though the litigation process no longer exists, there is fear in the backs of the doctors' minds that they may still be sued.

One of the answers, although not the complete answer, is education. If there is to be a compensation scheme, a massive education process has to be mounted. There must also be quality control.

The point was raised about the different treatment of patients depending upon whether they are in or outside the national health system. This was highlighted in New Zealand by the cancer inquiry that I mentioned. The women who were treated in the National Women's Hospital were ''free'' patients and the treatment they received was absolutely appalling. They were not treated as individuals—or people—at all. I do not think that the accident compensation scheme made the situation any worse because the experimental programme had begun before the accident compensation scheme was introduced.

A health system creates problems, the resolution of which is largely educative. It is a fault in the legal profession in New Zealand that lawyers do not always think of their clients as individuals or as people. It is a fault of the medical profession as well. The answer is education and resources.

Sir Christopher Booth: The problems of the Auckland women's study might well have been avoided had there been a medical audit system of a reasonable quality. Such systems are now more frequently used.

Sir Michael McNair-Wilson MP: Could both Dr Oldertz and Mrs Vennell say what percentage of those seeking compensation under their schemes actually receive compensation? Secondly, would Mrs Vennell confirm categorically that the financing of the New Zealand scheme is now on a proper basis? Thirdly, can Dr Oldertz say anything about the young man who sued for many millions of kroner, in a way which seemed likely to upset the Swedish system?

Dr Oldertz: In Sweden we do not talk about ''seeking compensation''. We try to have the injuries reported so that it can be decided whether or not they can be compensated. About 50% of the reports received will receive compensation. The other 50% will not be compensated for various reasons.

There is a limit to the liability per person of 3 million Swedish kroner (about £300,000). Compensation from social insurance is comparatively high, and we pay only the excess over what it and other kinds of compensation schemes provide. The actual cost for an injury in most cases will be less than the maximum. For instance, there are about 20 or 25 cases of newborn children who have been injured during delivery. As far as I know, none of these children has yet received the maximum compensation. It depends upon such factors as how much care needs to be provided. Should private care be provided, or is it sufficient to provide care by the social authorities? This is a problem for us. If private care has to be provided for a brain-damaged child for the whole of his life, 3 million kroner will probably not be sufficient.

[*See also comment by Dr John Wall later in this discussion—Ed.*]

Mrs Vennell: I believe that our scheme is on a sound financial footing; 94% of every income dollar is returned in compensation, which is a far better record than any of the North American workers' compensation schemes.

The question about how many people who claim compensation for medical accidents are actually paid is very difficult to answer. Unfortunately, we do not separate accidents into categories. This is because the cause of accidents is irrelevant to us—we have merely to decide whether or not an accident has been suffered—and since accidents are not categorised by cause there are no separate statistics of what could be regarded as medical accidents.

Since 1974 three cases have gone to appeal in the High Court—the three cases I mentioned (M's case, MacDonald's and Viggars')—and 77 cases have gone to the appeal authority, which is the lower level. Although only 80 people, unhappy at being declined compensation in the first place, have gone to appeal we do not know what percentage that 80 represents.

Dr J. D. G. Troup (*Waterloo, Merseyside*): My main interest in no fault compensation concerns injuries and accidents at work, I am involved in accident research, and thus in prevention. What is the effect of these schemes on the safety profession in general, and on active prevention in particular?

Dr Oldertz: One of the criteria for paying compensation for injuries is if it can be established that the injury could have been avoided. Compensation is not paid if the injuries are unavoidable. With enough claims experience if should be possible to ask why do injuries still occur in spite of their being avoidable and there being no negligence? The other question that could be asked is why are injuries unavoidable—and is that really true?

Claims experience should be used as a basis for scientific investigation. For example, the use of angiography is now very much reduced in Sweden. Instead, we have computerised tomography and the nuclear magnetic resonance (NMR) scanner. The introduction of such machines and procedures has been furthered by our increased knowledge of the hazards of angiography. Another issue now being studied intensively is why children are damaged by lack of oxygen. It is now possible to take blood samples continuously during delivery but babies are still being born with brain damage. This is a problem for the medical profession but our claims experience is available to the medical profession, who have the opportunity to use it for investigations, and we would hope that the data would indicate research areas of interest from the point of view of medical accident prevention.

Mrs Vennell: Our Corporation is in many ways misnamed as the Accident Compensation Corporation. We are actually charged with *preventing* accidents. Compensation is in a way, "locking the stable door after the horse has bolted". We do not move into the prevention area directly in relation to medical accidents, but we do have a considerable budget with which research is funded into many avenues of accident prevention. One must remember that we cover everything from work-related accidents, through to unsafe products and road accidents. Medical accidents are only one category. People apply for funds from our research budget. If an application was for medical research into the prevention of medical accidents, it may well get research funding.

Mr David Bolt (*Chairman, BMA No Fault Compensation Committee*): Would Dr Oldertz tell me whether there is any provision in the Swedish system for lump sum payments or whether payment is made at regular intervals?

Secondly, I am not clear from Mrs Vennell's presentation whether there is any definition of what does and does not constitute a medical accident. Do I understand that in New Zealand the routine complications of a surgical operation, because they are not part of the proper course of the operation, would be accepted without demur? My impression was that there was a very generous approach to this problem in New Zealand which I confess I found slightly surprising.

Dr Oldertz: Pain and suffering, and loss of amenity are normally paid in the form of lump sums, but there are occasions when they will be paid as an annuity. With regard to loss of income, if the loss is considerable it is paid in the form of annuities. If it is a small loss, it is paid in a lump sum—because that is practical.

Mrs Vennell: There is no definition of a medical accident—of what amounts to personal injury by medical misadventure. We use the interpretation that has been placed on personal injury by accident. If it is an untoward event arising out of medical treatment, it will be regarded as an accident which means in effect that only those untoward events which are unusual are covered. What can happen is illustrated by the three cases I described. Each case is argued on its merits, and if the outcome is unexpected for that patient, it will be compensated—but if it is likely to happen, then it is part of the treatment.

Prof. D. Laurence (*University College Hospital, London*): Mrs Vennell said that her Corporation is concerned with accident prevention. She also said that the Corporation does not classify the applications and categorise them. If that is not done, it seems to me that valuable data are being lost with which to detect trends in accidents which would be useful for promoting research.

Mrs Vennell also used a memorable phrase, saying that the medical profession are the ''gatekeepers'' of the scheme. I am sure that this must be true—and will become true in the United Kingdom, because eventually such a scheme will be introduced here. Dr Mann referred to clinical judgement beings its basis, and that is surely what it will have to be—clinical judgement on causation, severity and prognosis—and, indeed, we all know it is very various.

We are naturally interested in all the aspects of any scheme, but what can the medical profession do *now* to help facilitate the introduction of a good scheme? I suggest that we look at the clinical issues which will be the gatekeeping issues of the scheme which the medical profession will have to assess, judge and recommend, on causation, severity and prognosis. These will be very difficult issues, and they need to be viewed in relation to a no fault scheme. I hope that the profession—and possibly this Society—will start work on this now and not wait until a scheme is imminent.

Sir Christopher Booth: These are all matters to be discussed in relation to Mr Bolt's presentation of the British Medical Association's proposals.

Dr J. A. Wall (*Secretary, Medical Defence Union*): I do not want to pre-empt what Mr Bolt will say, but just to respond to a point made by Sir Michael McNair-Wilson about the Swedish scheme. As Mrs Brahams described it in the *Lancet* in January 1988, one of the points the BMA likes about the Swedish scheme is that it does not bar the citizen from suing the doctor, if that is what he wishes. In fact, it is assumed in Sweden that the damages awarded in the courts are roughly of the same order as that paid by the compensation scheme—which is one reason why there is so little litigation.

In the case of Mpanda, for instance, the plaintiff chose to sue on the basis that he preferred to have private care. He did not go to the compensation scheme. There was an award of a capital sum which amounted to the equivalent of some millions of pounds which caused some consternation, although it only arose in a district court.

Secondly, a comment on the New Zealand scheme. My colleague in Sydney has worked with the Secretary of the New Zealand Medical Association on research (shortly to be published) into the frequency with which complaints have been made during the 15 years in which the scheme has been in operation. The number of complaints dealt with by the equivalent of the General Medical Council in New Zealand between 1974 and 1987 has gone up by 1800%, a 19-fold increase in complaints dealt with by the disciplinary body. It must surely have some association with the fact that people cannot go to court.

Dr D. M. Burley *(Centre for Pharmaceutical Medicine):* What has been the impact of the schemes, particularly the Swedish scheme, on legal practice? One of the arguments in favour of a no fault scheme is that the costs of litigation are high, and that perhaps for every £1 of compensation there is £1-worth of legal costs. Have actions for negligence virtually disappeared now from the Swedish courts in relation to both medical and pharmaceutical injuries?

Dr Oldertz: When the Swedish scheme was introduced this problem was not so acute. There were only a few relevant law suits at that time, perhaps no more than 10 every year. Law suits concerning negligence have almost disappeared. During the past 13 years there has been a total of between 10 and 15 such cases, most of which have concerned the amount of compensation. In Sweden it is not accepted that we should pay for private care and this creates problems because there is legislation which states that every Swedish citizen is entitled to receive reasonable care. So we cannot accept that the Courts can maintain that the patient treated within the social security system has not received good care.

Mrs D. Brahams *(Legal Correspondent, the* Lancet*):* Sir Michael McNair-Wilson asked what proportion of claims are accepted in Sweden. I understand about 60% are accepted and 40% rejected.

Dr Oldertz: I normally say about 50%, but it varies slightly and could be nearly 60%—it is not easy to give an exact figure.

Dr E. S. Blackadder *(BUPA):* I would welcome a no fault compensation scheme in the United Kingdom but I am slightly uneasy about schemes which concentrate so much on damage caused by doctors, drugs and accidents. In a civilised society I wonder whether patients should not be compensated for the need, for the outcome, so that we should not worry about the causation.

We have heard about New Zealand and Sweden, and Finland also has a scheme, but these are small countries with populations of four or five million. Would these schemes work in a country of 55 million or, say, in the USA with 300 million?

Dr A. J. Rowe *(British Medical Association):* Dr Oldertz raised the question of the implications of compensation in the private sector, which has now been raised on three occasions. Would I be correct in saying that the "cradle to the grave" social security system which he has just outlined, and indeed underlined, as the general philosophy of life in Sweden, allows his scheme to be successful? In a country without such an extensive social security system, and where a no fault compensation scheme would have to do more than "top-up" existing extensive benefits, would he have doubts about the viability of his scheme?

Dr Oldertz: That is difficult to answer. The cost of a scheme depends very much on what has to be paid for loss of income. It has to be remembered that many of the patients who are injured are old and are pensioners. In my opinion, the importance of paying compensation for loss of income should not be over-estimated. Furthermore, in a modern society, at least the smaller degrees of permanent disability will not cause any permanent loss of income. Of those who are 100% disabled it is probably only those who are brain-damaged who have real difficulty about going back to work. Our experience is that when the compensation matter has been cleared up most people can return to work.

Sir Christopher Booth: The political dimension is important, in the sense that both Dr Oldertz and Mrs Vennell are from high taxation, high social security, high government spending countries. In the United Kingdom we have a political situation in which in three successive elections a party has been to the country on the basis of reduced taxation, reduced government spending and increased private sector activity. That situation has to be accepted politically—we may not agree with it, but it happens to be the policy of the country—and the party has been elected with huge parliamentary majorities. This point has been repeatedly made to me by Permanent Secretaries of the Departments of Health and Education—and that is the policy to which we work.

The situation in the USA is exactly the same, as witnessed by Mr Bush's famous comment, ''Read my lips''.

Nevertheless, the need to care properly for those injured through no fault of their own probably unites countries and political parties—it is the most appropriate means to accomplish this that may seem to vary.

5

No fault compensation in Finland with an overview of the Scandinavian approach to compensation of medical and drug injuries

Diana Brahams

Introduction

In October 1987 I visited Stockholm together with my husband, Malcolm Brahams, a solicitor, and Dr John Wall from the Medical Defence Union, which organisation, together with the *Lancet*, helped to support the trip to investigate the workings of the Swedish no fault compensation scheme. My findings were published in the *Lancet* (1988)[1] and my husband's in the New Law Journal of January 8 and 15th. Almost a year later, following an offer of support for the trip from the Medical Protection Society, my husband and I visited Helsinki to study the workings of the newly introduced Finnish schemes. My report was published in the *Lancet* (1988)[2] and Malcolm Brahams' report in the New Law Journal of 23 September 1988.

In 1984, Finland (population 4.9 million) introduced comprehensive insurance for patients suffering from injuries induced by pharmaceutical products and a limited voluntary insurance for treatment injuries to patients in the private sector. In 1987 a statutory comprehensive scheme was implemented for treatment injuries in both the state and private sectors. Though inspired by the Swedish schemes and fashioned broadly on Swedish lines, there are some fundamental differences of approach.

The social background to the medical and pharmaceutical insurance schemes

There is a strong social security base providing for pensions, disability benefits and welfare benefits, etc. Accordingly, taxation is heavy with the rates for large income earners very high indeed. (The Government has stated its intention to lower the maximum rates payable in the near future.)

Ninety-three percent of medical care (including almost all hospital care) is provided by the state. There are 22 health districts each with a central hospital, five of which are attached to a University. Patients are normally cared for within their own district. Primary health care is provided at health centres rather than by individual general practitioners and home visits by doctors are unusual. In the large southern cities, private sector primary care has been expanding, though

---

For the purposes of calculating awards and costs of benefits, there are 7 Finnmarks (FIM) to £1 sterling.

hospital care is still almost entirely carried out in the state sector. Waiting lists for routine operations vary from a few months to under a year, but the health care system has been put under increasing pressure over recent years as demands grow, particularly from the elderly, who form an increasingly large proportion of the population.

The Finns (like the Swedes) traditionally prefer insurance to litigation as a means of obtaining compensation for personal injuries. Originally a national traffic insurance scheme was set up and this was followed by employment compensation insurance schemes, so that litigation in these fields is now almost extinct.

The case for improved means of compensation for injuries following medical and pharmaceutical treatment

Why insure?

As more and more people were subjected to medical care, the risk of injury (as well as recovery) from such treatments increased. Malpractice (or negligence) was difficult to prove and many felt that such proof should not be a basic requirement in cases of medical or drug injury. The Finns took the view that an injury occurring during health care should be insured on a national scale in the same way as traffic and employment injuries. Nation-wide insurance would dispense with the need to prove negligence in the courts which in turn would improve patient and medical staff relationships and also relationships between doctors and health employees themselves.

A stage by stage introduction of nationwide medical and pharmaceutical insurance

The medical insurance scheme in neighbouring Sweden (population 8 millions) was set up in 1975 and appeared to be working well. By contrast, in Finland, the (inquisitorial) tort system for running negligence claims through the courts was generally accepted to be extremely unsatisfactory. Few patients received compensation via this route—and most did not even bother to try to claim any as the process was very slow, expensive and likely to fail. Indeed, a Finnish lawyer specialising in insurance work, Henrik Gahmberg, said that since those badly off would receive legal aid and that many home insurance policies covered litigation costs sufficient to fund such an action, before the new schemes were introduced, plaintiffs were deterred by the poor chances of success and the slowness of the procedure as much as by the costs. Doctors practising in a relatively small community were usually very reluctant to testify against a colleague and both hospitals and doctors tended to defend such claims fiercely, since reputations and cash from the health budget could be at stake.

Accordingly, in 1978, the Finnish Medical Association proposed that a no fault patient injury insurance scheme should be introduced in Finland. In 1980 it presented a petitionary Act of Parliament. Subsequently, the Finnish Bar Association and various Law Societies altruistically supported a change to insurance as being in the patients' best long term interests.

Phased introduction of no fault compensation in Finland—some lessons learned

In 1980 the Ministry of Social Affairs and Health set up a Committee whose task was to:

(1) Investigate whether there was a need for a system which would compensate patients injured while undergoing medical care, whether this occurred by accident, negligence or non-negligent error. If so (and the Committee was to take into account any experience gained abroad by other countries), whether this should be achieved by legislation and to estimate the cost of such a scheme.

(2) Investigate the extent to which existing provisions needed amendment (taking into account any developments abroad) and to recommend any changes which it felt should be made.

(3) Investigate the need for, and the possibility of, founding a national body of experts who would provide statements on injuries sustained in medical treatment which could be handed to the authorities, the courts, the insurance companies and the claimant.

The Committee's report recommended that a Patient Injuries Review Board be set up and that two Acts of Parliament be passed, one setting out patients' rights *per se* and the other relating to compensation for treatment injuries and obviating the need to prove negligence. The Act on patients' rights is not yet law, but the *Patient Injury Act 1986* came into force on 1 May 1987. This Act has dispensed with the need to prove negligence for medical treatment injuries. However, not everybody favoured a statutory solution and before that end could be achieved, a number of interim measures, which are of interest in themselves, were instituted to pave the way bit by bit.

The interim stages in patient treatment injury compensation

Although there was general agreement that comprehensive insurance cover for medical treatment injuries should be created there were ideological disagreements on how such a scheme should be administered. These disputes caused considerable delay in providing "no fault" insurance compensation for treatment injuries in the public health sector. The "Left" favoured a nationalised civil service management of claims while the "Right" supported claims handling by the experienced Insurers' Association. There were some 450 different (and independently minded) local government organisations and other interested parties who had to be involved and agree to the scheme. Ultimately, hopes of a voluntary agreement had to be abandoned and legislation was enacted in the form of the *Patient Injury Act 1986*. The Act makes insurance compulsory on health carers and lays down the conditions for compensation.

In the interim period, patients claiming compensation for medical negligence could invite an opinion from the National Board of Health and, after 1984, from the Patient Injuries Review Board newly set up within the Ministry of Social Affairs and Health. In theory, therefore, the position of patients was improved. The Review Board's task was to advise whether or not compensation should be paid in connection with medical, health or hospital care and then, if requested, make recommendations as to the amount of compensation payable. The Board had power to investigate the claims and call for documentary (not oral) evidence when required; take medical advice and then make recommendations.

Though these findings were not legally binding decisions, the idea was that if they were favourable, patients could show them to hospital administrators or the doctors' insurers to encourage them to settle the claim, or they could use it in court proceedings. Even after a claim had gone before the courts, the courts were entitled to seek an opinion from the National Board of Health and, after 1984, from the Patient Injuries Review Board, to enable the court to decide whether there had been negligence.

In practice the procedure proved slow and bureaucratic and proof of negligence was still required. Few statements were requested and few patients received compensation through this route.

There are proposals from some groups in Britain for a similar sort of board (though perhaps more multidisciplinary in its composition) to be set up to advise on compensation levels in personal injury claims. It is, therefore, worth pointing out that in Finland this half-way house for easing the route to compensation foundered, at least in part, on the rocks of bureaucracy and the requirement to prove negligence.

A further, but more positive lesson, for Britain and any other country looking to replace its tort system with a no fault based insurance can be found in Finland's experience with its cooperative private sector. On 1 June 1983 this sector pioneered a voluntary pilot agreement for no fault compensation for medical treatment injuries. The scheme worked well, paving the way for the statutory nationwide insurance provisions which came into force on 1 May 1987 and which superseded it.

The pharmaceutical insurance scheme

In 1984 a comprehensive voluntary scheme designed to compensate for injuries caused by pharmaceutical treatment was introduced. This was modelled on Swedish lines with all importers (48% market share) and manufacturers (52%) of pharmaceutical products participating and funding the scheme. (The scheme is considered in more detail later.)

The ambit of the patient treatment injury insurance scheme

As in Sweden, the Finnish treatment injury scheme is designed to provide payments for pain and suffering, loss of amenities and top-up financial cover for loss of earnings over and above any benefits (state or private) which may be received. Unlike the Swedish Scheme, the Finnish patient treatment injury compensation scheme is statutory and there is no maximum limit either for an individual claim or as a cap on the year as a whole. All the schemes pay out on a monthly or annual basis; lump sums are not the norm in Finland or Sweden.

The Finnish Patient Injury Act 1986

Table 1 and Figure 1 provide helpful summaries. The Act is given in translation in Appendix 7. It provides that compensation is payable for personal injury caused to a patient in connection with health and medical care and that volunteers for medical research are to be classed as patients. The scheme encompasses all aspects of medical care including that given in mental institutions, prisons and military hospitals, etc.

Table 1 *Patient Injury Act*

Essential benefits:
Full coverage by insurance
Culpability not a prerequisite for compensation
All compensations paid by the same bureau
Appeals without difficulty and free of charge (Patient Injury Board)
Courts of justice

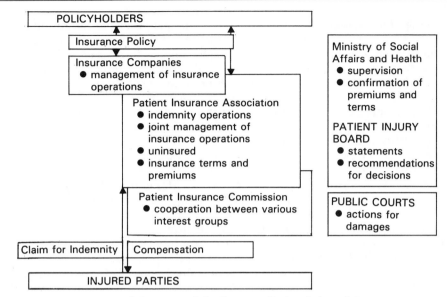

Figure 1 *The Operational Structure of the Statutory Patient Injury Act.*

According to Section 2 compensation is payable for any injury which:

(1) probably arose as a consequence of examination, treatment or any similar action, or neglect of the same;
(2) has been caused by an infection or inflammation which probably has originated in the circumstances connected with examination, treatment or any similar action or;
(3) has been caused by an accident: (a) connected with examination, treatment, or any similar action, or (b) occurring during ambulance transportation or in connection with fire or other damage to treatment premises or treatment equipment, or (c) resulting from a defect in medical care equipment or in a medical care device;

The consequences of medically justifiable treatment that could not have been avoided by any other procedure equally effective in the care of the patient shall not be regarded as being patient injury in the sense of (1) and (2) above. An injury resulting from a diagnostic . . . (procedure) shall, nevertheless, be compensated as a patient injury if the consequence is unreasonable considering the quality and severity of the illness or injury to be diagnosed and the state of health of the patient as a whole.

Section 3 states that compensation will be assessed in accordance with the provisions (applicable in court) laid down by the Tort Damages Acts and that compensation will not be payable for minor injuries. (A minor injury is one which does not require the claimant to be off work for two weeks and/or causes no persistent injury, and/or loss or damage of less than 500 FIM.) (In Sweden a claimant must be off work for thirty days, and fourteen days for a drug injury claim.) If the patient has contributed intentionally or through gross negligence to his injury, then any award will be discounted in proportion.

The Act imposes a positive duty on those practising in health or medical care to insure; failure to do so renders the uninsured party liable to pay ten times the normal premium due from him.

Section 5 enables the Association to issue policies and attend to claims settlement on behalf of the member companies. Where a party is uninsured the Association has to pay out any damages due and collect the increased premium under S4. In practice, the Association grants much of the state cover and re-insures it, whereas the private sector tends to be covered by an individual policy.

By S6 the Ministry of Health and Social Affairs has to confirm the insurance terms and premiums, and S7 imposes a duty on the Association to issue and/or maintain a policy if individual companies refuse to do so.

A claimant may choose to apply to the Association for compensation in full and leave it to the Association to reclaim (under S9) all benefits available to the patient. Further, the Association has the right to reclaim damages paid out to compensate for an injury caused intentionally through ''gross negligence''. Both Dr Huittinen (the President of the Finnish Medical Association and a senior medical adviser to the Insurance Association) and Mr Pentti Ajo, the Association's managing director, thought such recourse unlikely save in a really extreme case. By contrast, the traffic scheme imposes a duty on the Association to attempt to reclaim damages caused by grossly negligent driving.

There is a three year limitation period with a longstop of 20 years.

The Act provides for a Patient Injury Board to be appointed by the government. It is the duty of the Board to issue recommendations for decisions on compensation for patient injury and to anyone who carries insurance against liability under the Act and also to issue statements to courts dealing with patient injury claims. The Board must strive for uniformity in its decisions. It has the right to inspect and seek any necessary information from the parties and it may take further specialist medical advice as required.

The Act imposes an obligation on all those concerned with claims handling to preserve secrecy; violation may render a person liable to a fine or a maximum of six months' imprisonment.

The Act specifically preserves the claimant's right to pursue an action for damages through the courts based on the provisions of the Act. So far nobody has done so. (By contrast, in Sweden anybody opting out of the scheme and going to court has still to prove negligence and causation under the original tort laws; there have been five cases in 13 years.)

A cautious start in the first year

The Patient Insurers' Association (the Articles of which are given in Appendix 2) and Appeals Board both admitted that they were concerned to keep the scheme within manageable and affordable limits. Finland is not a rich country and resources are limited and the Finnish scheme rejected some 62% of all claims made in the first year. (In Sweden on average some 60% of claims are accepted each year.) By 1 May 1988 there had been 1381 claims decisions out of 1902 reported injuries with 529 accepted (see below).

Many of the claims which were rejected were made by relatives of elderly demented patients who had, for example, fallen while going to the lavatory. Dr Huittinen, the scheme's senior medical adviser considered this a growing social problem. He estimated that by 1990, a thousand old people would suffer femoral neck fractures while resident in institutions. Since the Finnish welfare state took care of all their needs such patients would not qualify for compensation in any event. The scheme is designed to compensate only the patient not his relatives unless they too have suffered actual loss as a consequence of the injury.

In the first year, 296 women and 165 men had been compensated, with 452 and 239 claims rejected respectively. The Association had compensated seven deaths under the Act, but had not so far met any claims for babies allegedly brain damaged by the birth process and was prepared to compensate in a case where the patient's unusual anatomy (for example, a displaced nerve) had caused a treatment injury.

Injuries which do not qualify for compensation

The scheme has built in limitations and is not all-embracing of medical failures. "Trivial" treatment injuries (see above and Appendix) and injuries caused by shortages of resources, are not compensated. However, the Association is prepared to compensate for mental or psychological disturbance. (Compare the position under the Finnish pharmaceutical scheme and in Sweden where mental injury is not compensated under either scheme unless it emanates directly from a physical ailment.)

Medical treatment which has been correctly carried out but which fails to achieve the desired result is not classed as an "injury". Cosmetic surgery or treatment which was not medically indicated (for example, a facelift) could fall outside the scheme, but cosmetic surgery which was justified for other reasons (as affecting the mental or physical welfare of the patient) would qualify. Injuries resulting from the patient's basic underlying condition and/or by necessary risk-taking in treating them are not compensated. For example, a patient who underwent endoscopical examination for suspected gall bladder complications who subsequently developed pancreatitis (a recognised complication) did not qualify.

In her description of the workings of the scheme, Paula Kokkonen (Director of Administration) points out that the scheme will not pay out for injuries which were sustained following sound medical treatment and which were not avoidable with that procedure even if another method was available which would have been as effective as the chosen method, and this method might have avoided the injury occurring (for example, vaginal birth/caesarian section).

Two other examples of uncompensatable injury due to necessary risk taking suggested by Dr Huittenin were (a) where a patient suffered an aneurysm of the cerebral arteries and during the operation a subarachnoid haemorrhage developed leaving the patient with impaired brain function. Failure to treat would result in death; thus, similarly (b) if the patient had a malignant tumorous growth in the parotid gland. If the removal of the growth necessitated severing the enveloped facial nerve, the ensuing facial paralysis would not be compensated. However, a patient who underwent an operation on the cervical spine for relief of pain and became paralysed would usually be compensated even if there had been no error in her treatment because the injury was so catastrophic, not inevitable, and the aim of the scheme was to alleviate and compensate suffering where this was possible.

Infection injuries:

These fall into four categories depending on the site and state of the wound: (1) clean (for example, uninfected ankle), (2) clean but contaminated by patient's own bacteria; for example, operation on the bowel, (3) infected; for example, perforated appendix, (4) dirty wound with long standing sepsis. Class 1 infections would normally be compensated and occasionally those occurring in class 2. Classes 3 and 4 are not compensated.

The scheme as applied to individual cases

Case 1. A 40-year-old married country woman fractured her ankle. During treatment, a metal plate which had been inserted was later removed, following which the patient suffered severe prolonged infection which required her to spend several weeks in hospital and prevented her from returning to work. She received compensation for pain and suffering, the cost of medicines and hospital treatment and any loss of earnings which could be validly shown. (She was self-employed).

Case 2: A woman of 75 had treatment for a broken hip joint. Unfortunately while being transported home in an ambulance her scar was opened and had to be re-sutured. No persisting disability in consequence; losses less than 500 FIM. Rejected as too minor.

Case 3: A 48-year-old labourer was admitted for treatment of a damaged medial collateral ligament of his left knee joint. The patient claimed for compensation as he was disappointed to find that he still had considerable restriction of movement in his knee and after walking the knee was prone to swell and become painful. The patient had suffered with rheumatoid arthritis for some 20 years. The examination, treatment and follow up of his condition had been reasonable and without error. Accordingly, the claim would be rejected since the disappointing result was due to the patient's own underlying condition. (Where a treatment (or drug) fails to achieve the desired effect no patient injury is caused.)

Case 4: A 43-year-old woman with fibroid growths of the uterus was admitted to hospital for a hysterectomy. After the operation she was found to have a vesicovaginal fistula. She had to undergo a further operation necessitating an extra month's stay in hospital and extra time off for sick leave. She received 4,000 FIM for pain and suffering, reimbursement for hospital and medicine charges and also for loss of earnings. (She had registered for work which would have necessiated her accepting a job offer or losing her unemployment benefits.)

Case 5: A woman of 65 suffered from stomach pains. An exploratory laparotomy was performed. The scar became infected and healed badly causing her to stay extra days in hospital and leaving an unsightly appearance. She received 4,000 FIM for pain and suffering, 2,000 FIM for unsightly scarring, and was reimbursed for hospital expenses etc.

Case 6: A 61-year-old (retired) man was treated for dental caries. The dentist broke the root of a tooth while putting in a screw in the upper jaw. The tooth had to be removed and a three tooth bridge made. Though technically a "minor" injury, the expenses of the reparative dental work were refunded after the estimated cost of 6,530 FIM were checked and found to be fair.

Case 7: A young woman who suffered from serious bronchial pulmonary asthma was allergic to aspirin. She injured her ankle and presented for treatment, first alerting the doctor to her condition and her allergy. Unfortunately, the doctor while acknowledging her warning, wrongly prescribed indomethacin which he should have known would aggravate her allergy. On returning home and taking the medicine she had a serious attack of asthma from which she died. The injury was compensatable. (The scheme will pay for funeral expenses as well as loss of support to dependants etc.)

Case 8: A young soldier suffered serious injuries during a training session. He was admitted to hospital (over the weekend) but owing to the fact that his symptoms were incorrectly interpreted and treated he was not admitted to intensive care until the third day, whereafter he died.

Other deaths compensated had been caused by haemorrhage at home following a tonsillectomy, an endotracheal tube becoming twisted and another which had been misplaced.

Appeals

Professor Henry Troupp (a senior neurologist) chaired a discussion on the appeals process. The appeal board meets privately every Friday afternoon when it discusses some 10–15 cases having first read the papers. (Patients and insurers are not represented.) He said that in Finland there was not the range of expert opinion available in larger countries and that in specialty subjects there was likely to be a dominating figure whose views would command the most respect. Opinions imported from outside Finland would not normally be welcomed for claims assessment purposes. Professor Troupp said that about 10% of rejected claimants appealed.

Appeals allowed

1) A 44-year-old labourer was admitted to hospital following a fall from his bicycle while drunk. He had developed a subdural haematoma which later displayed classic symptoms which were not recognised, (very severe headaches, dizziness etc). The hospital did not have a computer tomograph but did have an isotope scanner which they did not use. The patient suffered brain damage, and a claim was made on his behalf by his wife. FIM £110,000 (£16,000) for pain and suffering and loss of amenities. The Board members we met admitted this was a relatively small sum for serious loss of amenity etc.

2) A patient was treated for a Colles fracture of the wrist. She suffered severe pain as the bandage and plaster of paris cast were too tight and pressed on the median nerve. A diagnostic operation was performed. Although the fracture healed without permanent disability she was awarded compensation (2,000 FIM) by the Board since it disapproved of the doctor's failure to release the bandage and cast after the patient had returned complaining that her wrist was aching.

Under appeal

A patient who had undergone a laparotomy suffered subsequent failure of bowel movement owing to 10 cm of gut having become anchored into the wall of the stomach during the procedure. A further serious operation had to be performed to correct the situation which could be regarded as a known rare complication.

Causation

The Finns, like the Swedes, adopt a practical approach to the problems posed by causation. As Paula Kokkonen explained, 'In practice, proving an unambiguous cause-effect relationship may be impossible. For this reason, from the point of view of getting compensation for damages it is now sufficient if the injury was in all probability caused by the activity or procedure on which the claim is based, or by negligence.' The schemes' assessors weigh into the balance the overall circumstances, the statistical probabilities, the timing of events and general experience with regard to an injury occurring in such circumstances.

Funding the scheme

Private doctors and practitioners pay their own premiums individually to cover any treatment they may offer, while health districts pay their premiums based on a *per capita* basis as in Sweden (about 8 FIM). Pharmacists carry individual professional indemnity cover but are not part of the scheme. Where, for example, a patient was injured due to taking medicines prescribed incorrectly the Association would pay out the whole award and reclaim any proportion due from the dispensing chemist's insurers.

How the claims are processed

All (15) insurance companies offering cover under one of the four schemes belong to the Association (Potilasvakuutusyhdistys) which has its headquarters in Helsinki. It is the Association's employees (and not those of a particular company which may have granted the policy) who will handle and settle all the individual claims which are processed centrally in Helsinki. All four types of insurance claims are handled by the same settlement clerks who, therefore, do not specialise in any single type of claim. Everything is highly computerised, with treatments classified by a code letter under the WHO definitions. These have, however, proved insufficiently detailed to cover the wide variety of complications which have occurred following treatment.

Claims are processed promptly. After the patient fills in a simple claims form the Association takes over the investigation. The patient's details are entered into the computer system and the hospital and doctors' notes are requested. These are now almost always neatly and routinely typed (originals) as doctors are encouraged to dictate their notes and the hospital or care centre's typists will transcribe them. Once the notes are received and the handler has satisfied himself that the claim is not excluded, for instance, as too minor or unconnected with treatment or outside the limitation period, then the claim and all the necessary medical records are sent to one of the Association's medical advisers who may seek specialist opinions if required. (Dr Huittinen considered that many claims were sparked off by a doctor's rudeness and/or poor patient handling).

Finnish law requires the Association to explain the reasons for rejection in clear simple terms. Patients would be advised of their right to appeal and were entitled to see the medical notes and reports.

There are differently constituted appeals boards for the different schemes (all based in Helsinki) so that dissatisfied claimants can seek an alternative recommendation. The assessors' and appeal boards' recommendations are not legally binding but in practice will be adopted and would carry considerable weight if produced in court.

Levels of damages

Finnish tariffs for damages, which are index linked and set out in a book compiled by the Traffic Insurers, are relatively low by British standards, perhaps two-thirds or three-quarters of awards payable in Sweden and a third of those payable in the UK. For example, the maximum award for pain, suffering and loss of amenity would be approximately £30,000, in Sweden £40,000, in Britain £85,000. Everybody, whether on benefits or not, is expected to pay 60 FIM (about £8.25) per day towards the cost of hospital treatment and dental care is not comprehensively subsidised. The cost of treatment and medicine would be refunded if the injury was considered to be compensatable, as would the costs payable in a private hospital, though the patient would have to move out of private care as soon as possible after the accident and prospective future care would be within the state sector. (If the patient had private care insurance the costs of his treatment would not be refunded as he would have suffered no loss.)

Loss of earnings (subject to benefits available) are compensated.

The drug scheme

The number of *reported drug injuries between 1984–1988* was as follows:

    1984   30 cases
    1985   86
    1986   67
    1987   119 (after patient insurance injury publicity was increased)
    1988   51 cases by April 28

In 1987, 119 claims were made of which 97 were settled, 22 not determined finally and in two cases decisions not yet made: 51 injuries were indemnified; 66 rejected. (There were no AIDS deaths due to contaminated blood products.)

As in Sweden, if a patient elects to claim under the pharmaceutical scheme he forfeits his right to sue for damages in court and his rights are subrogated to the Insurers' Association. Similarly, the limitation periods are shorter than for the patient treatment injury scheme and claims must be made within 1 year of discovery of injury with a 15 year long-stop. To qualify for compensation, the claimant must have suffered permanent injury or been prevented from working for at least 14 consecutive days or have died. There are maximum payments allowable: FIM 2 million per person; FIM 50 millions for serial injuries; FIM 100 million total payable for all injuries occurring within one calendar year. The Finnish Pharmaceutical Insurance Pool appoints the Drug Injury Appeals Board which has a legal chairman and vice chairman, a pharmacologist, a specialist in internal medicine, a member proposed by the manufacturers and another by the importers.

The Rules of the pharmaceutical schemes are set out in full in Appendix 3.

Conclusions

The patient injury scheme

The interim measure of setting up a government appointed board to investigate medical negligence claims and advise on compensation was not considered a successful option since few people received compensation. The two new schemes, particularly the patient treatment injury scheme, has greatly increased the number of patients now compensated but who would, formerly, have received nothing. The scheme seems to work efficiently and compensates at full rate with no discount for early receipt (see the Opren settlement where awards on Britain were substantially reduced for this reason). Finnish law has never allowed for massive lump sum awards and payments for pain and suffering are low by British standards in a country where the cost of living and levels of taxation are high (over 80% top rate) and salaries not especially so.

The Finns propose to introduce legislation giving the patient rights to receive more information. At present the system works relatively paternalistically and no written consent forms are used in hospitals. Peer monitoring in Finland is less well organised than in Sweden, although, once a patient puts in a claim for patient compensation, the hospital's medical chiefs learn of it as they have to sign a junior doctor's report and add any additional comments of their own. Patients can complain to the licensing board if they consider a doctor's practice should be reviewed or he should be disciplined. The Patient Insurance Association (when asked) said it would consider the idea of publishing a report but there are no definite plans to do so. (None have been published by the Swedish insurers either.) So far (but it is early days), the Finnish scheme has not availed itself of the opportunity to tackle practising black spots which are beginning to surface in some areas and becoming apparent to the medical advisers.

Some claims statistics

Statistics on premium rates, claims reported, kind of claims compensated, proportion of claims compensated and reasons for rejection are given in Appendix 5.

The pharmaceutical scheme

The drug insurance was established by an agreement which came into force on 1 July 1984. The policyholder is a cooperative society and the Finnish Pharmaceutical Insurance Pool takes care of indemnity operations (there is a corresponding system in Sweden). The insurance is covered by a pool of insurance companies who maintain a Pool office and operate in the same building and in connection with the Finnish Motor Insurers' bureau and the Patient Insurance Association which avoids extra costs and ensures professional claims handling and uniformity of approach.

A drugs related injury is defined as an illness or bodily injury apparently caused by a drug; the injury has been caused by a side effect which, in view of the circumstances, was unexpected either at all or in its gravity.

The conditions for indemnity are that the drug was issued for use in Finland and that the injury caused temporary or permanent disability for work for a minimum of 14 days, permanent bodily injury or death. But where costs or losses exceed 500 FIM claims are always entertained.

Compensation will not be awarded if the drug failed to achieve the desired effect; the use of the drug was connected with unsuitable activity or activities; the injury was a reasonable side effect following the use of the drug; the drug was illegally obtained; the injury was caused wilfully or through misuse of the drug; or for psychic reactions without physical injury.

Compensation

Compensation is made up to the full level provided by the Finnish Tort Damages Act (412/74). The scheme is run on the basis that full compensation will be made (after first deducting any benefits or income available to the claimant) and the scheme provides secondary (and complementary) financial security to the claimant in the event of injury flowing from drug treatment. It will compensate for the cost (if any) of medical treatment, permanent disability and/or injury and/or handicap, pain and suffering, loss of income, funeral costs and survivor's pension.

The claims handling process is almost identical to the patient treatment injury process, but the patient has only one year to claim from the date when he learned of his drug-related injury and there is a fifteen year long-stop which runs from the date that the patient ceased using the drug.

Where a patient is dissatisfied with a decision either on the merits or as to quantum, he must lodge a notice of appeal within six months to the Drug Injury Board. There is also the possibility of arbitration and the patient has the option of a court hearing rather than a claim through the scheme.

The Drug Injury Board is appointed by the Finnish Pharmaceutical Insurance Pool and consists of a chairman and vice chairman who must be lawyers and four members, one of whom must be a pharmacologist, one a specialist in internal medicine, one a member proposed by the manufacturers and one a member proposed by the importers.

Unfortunately, in Finland the claims handlers considered that requirements of strict confidentiality prevented them from giving us any examples of claims made or rejected even if the patients' names were withheld. This was very disappointing.

Total secrecy of this sort is not, in my view, in the public interest; where a drug has caused a compensatable injury this information should surely be a matter of public record even if the patient's name and identifying details are excluded. We were told that this information was, however, made available to the Ministry of Health.

An overview of the Scandinavian schemes

The Finnish and Swedish "no fault" insurance systems seem to work well and the removal of the need to prove negligence has greatly increased the number of claimants. Norway is the next Scandinavian country on course to introduce a no fault insurance for drug induced injuries. The Norwegian parliament has approved legislation and a statutory scheme (as compared with the voluntary ones in force in Finland and Sweden) is expected to be in force from the middle of next year.

Unlike the British adversarial litigation, the schemes are cheap to run, cost-efficient, prompt, and patient and doctor friendly. They provide a rapid trouble-free investigation of the incident at no charge to the patient (which is what many patients most want initially), and whether or not compensation is payable, the patient and/or his relatives will receive a full and clear explanation of what occurred.

About 60% of claimants will have received a decision within six months of making a claim and the patient is compensated in full according to local tariffs.

However, when putting these Scandinavian schemes into a British perspective, it is important to remember that they operate side by side with established national traffic and employment insurance schemes. Further, social security benefits are considerably higher in Finland and Sweden than they are in Britain; while awards for non-economic losses are lower. This puts less strain on the Scandinavian insurance systems which act as a topping up of benefits; all other benefits received are first deducted from the compensation finally payable. Lump sum payments were never the norm and are not normally made. Payments are made monthly and are calculated and reviewed on an annual basis. There is considerable stress on rehabilitation.

The schemes compensate for a failure to treat as well as for failed treatment (unlike the New Zealand scheme where a failure to diagnose or treat is not an 'accident'). But the schemes are not a kind of disguised, all-embracing sickness benefit and their financial viability probably depends, in part, on their selectivity.

They offer compensation without aggravation, delay and cost to many patients who would formerly have either not have bothered to apply or would have been denied compensation through a negligence claim in the courts. The insurance schemes have improved doctor/patient relationships and inter/professional relationships between health carers, they have also taken the pressure off hospital budgets which were formerly at risk from negligence claims.

There are considerable opportunities for improving medical standards and practices by using the insurance statistics for research purposes and publishing the results. Thus far, the Swedish and Finnish insurers have not put pressure on doctors to limit their practice, though there is some stress on education in quarters seen to need it. There is concern in Sweden that avoidable errors continue to be made, for example, over the thirteen years of the patient insurance some 26 babies have been born with serious brain damage caused by hypoxia during birth—about two a year, and these claims continue to trickle in at the same rate notwithstanding that the dangers are well recognised. Finland has not yet compensated a brain damaged infant.

Rates of claims—before and after—Finland, Sweden and Britain

In Finland (population 4.9 million) only a tiny number of claims were mounted each year through the courts and of these very few were successful. The litigation process was regarded as excessively slow and cumbersome and experience proved that it deterred even those who had litigation insurance. Thus, although the Finnish patient treatment injury insurance scheme has only been running a short while, the rise in the numbers of people making claims and being paid compensation is nothing short of dramatic. Indeed, the figures for the first full calendar year, May 1st 1987 to April 30 1987, show that there were 1,902 claims in this period. Of these 1,902, 521 had not yet been decided and 529 had been accepted with 852 rejected. Claim rate=40 per 1,000.

In Sweden, (population 8 million) the position before the introduction of the patient treatment injury insurance scheme was not unlike that in Finland with no more than a very few cases proceeding through the court process. The first eleven years show that in this period some 48,167 claims were submitted with 19,959 rejected. Claim rate 60 per 1,000.

In Britain, (population approx 52 million), where litigation has increased threefold over the last ten years, and is certainly greater than it was in Finland and Sweden before the schemes, the claims rate is now 10 per 1,000.

"No fault" compensation—reform long overdue in Britain

In Britain, the traditional adversarial system of litigation is the only avenue for claiming compensation in the field of drug or medical treatment injuries.

Many lawyers and managers of drug companies are apparently still unconvinced by the arguments in favour of introducing some sort of no fault compensation scheme.

It is obvious that many of the lawyers who argue against change are those who have a vested interest in the status quo and whose practices would suffer if such claims were removed from the legal system. But there are also many lawyers who seem to be genuinely convinced that the best or only way to pursue compensation for medical or drug injuries is through adversarial litigation.

I suggest that this attitude stems largely from a combination of ignorance and prejudice. Let me define my terms and take prejudice first. From the start of our training, we as British lawyers, (and indeed also American, Canadian, Australian and other Commonwealth country lawyers) are educated in the public, adversarial, oral tradition. It is tried and tested, its faults are well known to the public and the profession, as are its strengths. In many ways it has served us extremely well, and our judges are second to none for their impartiality and fairness. But, in my opinion, an adversarial combat between two unequal sides funded largely by the taxpayer is a quite inappropriate route to compensation for patients injured while undergoing medical treatment or drug therapy. Times have changed and the law must change to accommodate the needs of society.

As to ignorance: by ignorance, I mean a lack of knowledge and real understanding of what the alternatives could be. I would like to see a nationwide no fault insurance for injuries arising from medical treatment and a nationwide no fault insurance for drug injuries funded by the drug industry, manufacturers, importers, suppliers and so forth.

In my view, litigation in medical disputes is not the way for the future. It is by its nature an expensive, protracted obstacle course where the injured party must try to pursue the stronger, fitter one and convince a judge that his injury was caused by negligence. The parties are usually locked into a struggle for many years at enormous cost. Those who do not qualify for legal aid will be deterred from bringing an action at all. In the result, few injured patients receive compensation and many of those who do have to wait for many years becoming more and more embittered with the system which produces such unfairnesses.

By contrast, in a growing number of countries, such as Sweden, Finland and New Zealand, this slow, cumbersome lottery has been replaced by a form of nationwide insurance from which minor injuries and losses are excluded. In Japan, following the clioquinol disaster, a "no fault" compensation insurance was set up by the drug industry. Later this year, Norway also is to institute a statutory drug scheme to compensate patients for adverse drug injuries which are not due to erroneous prescribing.

Product liability in Britain

We have moved a few steps forward—under pressure from the EEC—with regard to product liability. In March 1988, we introduced in Britain a form of "strict product liability", but reserved the "state of the art" defence and have imposed a ten year long-stop. Most of the drug insurance schemes have long-stops of fifteen years. Some drugs have very long latent periods for major adverse effects. An example was diethylstilboestrol which, when given in pregnancy produced neoplastic lesions in the teenage children of the treated mothers. A ten-year long-stop seems, therefore, too short a period to me.

Our so-called "strict" product liability does remove some of the difficulties faced by the injured consumer, but it still leaves most of the obstacle course in place. I do not believe the way forward for Britain lies in the kind of litigious consumerism, presently so active in the USA.

There, a few individuals, lawyers and claimants, will profit from hefty jury awards and punitive damages, but the average patient will not benefit. Rather the contrary. Indeed, Derrick Owles (1988)[3] says that in 1985, the USA spent between $29 billion and $36 billion on tort litigation. Most of this vast sum went to lawyers and court administrators; plaintiffs received only between $14 and $16 billion.

Further, the author asks if strict product liability has prevented the marketing of defective products? Over the years the number of product liability actions has steadily increased: from 1976 to 1985, the number trebled to produce 13,500 product liability actions in the federal courts in 1985. The experience of the federal courts is reflected in the state courts, and product liability is largely a matter of state law. Some 866,000 tort actions were concluded in the state courts in 1985. As a deterrent to marketing defective products, strict liability does not seem to provide an answer. On the contrary, the current trend looks to harm the consumer both by working against innovation, withdrawing products for fear of litigation, despite the fact they are useful and safe for the majority, and for adding additional costs on to the purchase price payable for the product.

Indeed, at the 1988 annual meeting of the American Bar Association, George Frazza, general counsel of Johnson and Johnson, said that if his company developed an AIDS vaccine he would advise withholding it from the market until Congress had passed protective legislation. However, other speakers thought differently.

Another source (personal communication) advises that in the USA lawyers refuse to handle some nine out of ten claims on a contingency basis as they consider the outcome too uncertain or likely to produce too small a sum of damages to be worth the trouble.

Thus, I believe that if there is more and more litigation, more and more Legal Aid (funded by the tax payer), and perhaps the introduction of contingency fees, then the average patient and the taxpayers in this country will lose in both cost and in the variety of treatments and appliances which could be of real benefit. If litigation raises the price of drugs and appliances then the National Health Scheme, as the largest buyer of such goods, will become more expensive to run. Either more taxpayers' money will be required or the health service will suffer.

As the Civil Justice Review (1988)[4] has pointed out, it may take up to a pound or more in costs to recover a pound or less in damages and the complexity of a claim may bear little relation to the level of damages claimed or awarded. If one takes into account the low level of Legal Aid fees, this pound for pound outlay represents quite extraordinarily poor value for effort and time.

Reform is, therefore, long overdue

The needs of the patient should be put first. Clearly, the patient needs a quick, cheap process which will not involve him in anxiety, expense, difficulty or stress.

Sweden and Finland have drug injury insurance schemes. So does Japan. Ironically, in Japan so few people have claimed that the fund grows and grows. The drug companies are now asking for their premiums to be reduced!

In Sweden, which has been running patient insurance for thirteen years and drug injury insurance for ten, relationships between doctors and patients have improved. Side by side with compensation insurance we must introduce good peer monitoring and complaints procedures and perhaps the insurers should be entitled to recommend for and against certain practices on the basis of their claims experience.

Cost of administration must inevitably be a crucial factor

The King's Fund report (Ham *et al.*, 1988)[5] states that the Swedish patient insurance administration costs amount to about 15% in relation to the awards made. Taking into account the fact that the average award is relatively low, £3,500, this indicates that the scheme is cheap to run. This makes far better economic sense than adversarial litigation, which, in this complex field, can amount to 100% and more and where small claims are simply not worth pursuing at all.

Who should be compensated?

Our present negligence-based system does recognise a distinction between naturally occurring or self-inflicted misfortune and injuries suffered as a result of outside forces. Those of us who believe that there should be increased benefits for the disabled and sick so that they have a better basic standard of living and comfort have to recognise that we could not, as a society, afford to provide all those in need with top level compensation. I therefore propose that we can move only at one step at a time, and that we should adopt the Scandinavian logic of classifying medical and drug treatments as endangering activities which should carry insurance. The need to prove negligence is then dispensed with, and claims can be made simply by filling in a form.

How should they be compensated?

Though structured settlements are now possible they have to be sought and pleaded by the parties and may not be imposed by a judge. Many judges are unhappy with our current situation of required lump sums which are inevitably a matter of guesswork and which can produce unexpected windfalls for the family of a patient who dies early and shortfalls if the patient lives longer than estimated.

Provided annual payments emanate from a guaranteed source, judges should be entitled to impose awards based on annual needs which are subject to re-assessment in changed circumstances and discontinuance after the patient's death. Lump sums (over perhaps £25,000) should be discontinued in Britain. Further, care should be taken to avoid a double benefit situation. If a patient suffers an injury while being treated under the National Health Scheme it should not be permissible to award damages for the cost of reparative treatment performed in the private sector if such treatment was available in the health service. Similarly, with regard to nursing and residential care.

In Scandinavia payments are made monthly and benefits received (including the availability of national health service treatment) are fully discounted from awards payable. We would need to adopt a similar approach and for any scheme to be affordable, there would have to be capping of damages which would be payable both through the courts and through the scheme. It is notable that in Florida the malpractice crisis has become so severe that the state has passed legislation limiting the sums which may be claimed in this field.

Where then should we begin?

Reforms take time even where there is a commitment to change, and in Britain the government has so far been resistent to suggestions made by the British Medical Association and others that a pilot no fault compensation scheme should be pioneered. However, it is worthwhile remembering that Finland pioneered her patient injury compensation insurance within the private sector. Perhaps the British United Provident Association and Private Patients Plan, and the private hospital organisations, should be prepared to take the initiative in this direction in Britain? Some four million people carry private health care insurance. This would seem a good starting point.

One must conclude that Finland has a population approximately one-tenth the size of ours, but we have proportionately greater resources. If they can introduce such a scheme, then we should be able to do so in Britain, given the will and the necessary commitment.

Experience has shown that there are relatively few claims made for drug injuries, but these injuries can cause considerable distress to the patients and be unduly expensive to litigate. This cannot be in the interest of either the consumer or manufacturer. The time has come, therefore, for an initiative from the leading companies to get together with the Government and agree a comprehensive compensation scheme with a tariff of payments available.

In conclusion, it is important to bear in mind two final points:

Firstly, that adversarial litigation is of its nature destructive and protracted for both doctor and patient. It keeps the patient's grievances festering and may delay the recovery processes for him and his family. Equally, it may affect the doctor's confidence and ability to practise and care for future patients. Confronted with even the possibility, let alone the reality, of negligence litigation, the doctor may become nervous, defensive and over-anxious and it may adversely affect his ability to treat other patients and to cope with the stresses of practice.

Secondly, that compensation given without a parallel system providing medical audit and for the consideration of complaints and doctors' accountability will not and should not be acceptable either to patients or to medical profession itself.

Acknowledgements

I am indebted to the *Lancet* for permission to reproduce some of the material which has appeared in their columns. I am also indebted to my husband for a collaborative review of the schemes, to Dr Carl Oldertz, of Skandia Insurance, Stockholm, and to Dr Matti Huittinen, Dr Pentti Ajo, Mrs Barbro Walther and to the Medical Defence Union and the Medical Protection Society for their help and support in compiling the information in this publication.

References

1. Brahams, D. (1988). The Swedish medical insurance schemes. The way ahead for the United Kingdom. *Lancet*, **i**, 43–47.
2. Brahams, D. (1988).
3. Owles, D. (1988). Product liability: lessons from America. *New Law Journal*, Sept 9, 648.
4. Civil Justice Review 1988. Command paper 394. HMSO, London.
5. Ham, C., Dingwall, R., Fenn, P., and Harris, D. (1988) *Medical negligence, compensation and accountability*. King's Fund Institute, London.

6

No fault compensation—the BMA proposals

David Bolt

It is widely assumed that the interest which the medical profession is showing in the topic of no fault compensation is inspired principally by the recent sharp increase in the cost of medical indemnity. This assumption is less than fair to the profession because, in fact, its interest in the matter antedates the rise in Defence Society subscriptions by several years. Since 1983 the Association has had a Working Party of its Council studying the matter and it is my duty, as the current Chairman of that Working Party, to inform you about the Association's present attitude to the subject. In doing so, I would emphasise that the views I express, while representing current thinking in the Association, should not be seen as immutable. The Working Party is still meeting regularly and it, and the Council to which it reports, are fully open to new ideas and willing to modify their position in response to persuasive arguments.

The profession is very unhappy about the present position regarding the compensation of patients who have been inadvertently damaged during the course of medical investigation or treatment. It is inevitable that, as compensation depends upon the proof of negligence on the part of those responsible for patient care, any attempt by the victim to secure recompense will be strenuously resisted, as no professional person is happy to be found guilty of negligence in relation to the care given to the person for whom he is responsible. Consequently, at the first suggestion that litigation is being considered, the normal relationship between doctor and patient is destroyed and replaced by an adversarial situation, totally foreign to everything for which the profession stands. Moreover, even when the basis for possible litigation exists, further progress towards compensation is desperately long drawn out and highly uncertain, so that no matter how deserving the patient may be of financial help, there is no certainty that he will receive it. At the same time, many other patients who have suffered from medical mishaps but have no grounds for litigation will receive no compensation, regardless of the fact that their need may be no less real than that of the individual obtaining large sums of money through the Courts. It seems to the profession that the time has come when compensation for medical mishap should be related to the patient's need and not to the possibility of proving negligence against the doctor or other professional staff concerned.

The title "no fault compensation" is, perhaps, an unfortunate one. It may well be understood to imply that, in the cases judged to deserve compensation, no one has been, in any way, at fault in relation to the mishap they have suffered. Of course, if decisions taken about patients were invariably correct, if drugs always functioned in a predictable way, if the technical difficulties encountered during investigations or operations or during obstetrical deliveries were always capable of immediate and satisfactory resolution and equipment always functioned satisfactorily, no medical mishaps would arise. Unfortunately, as patients are well aware, the real world is not like that and it can be argued that, when failure occurs under any of those headings, someone is at fault. However, the basis of the no fault concept is not that there has been no fault but that it is not necessary to establish that there has been a fault, much less that the fault arose as a result of negligence on the part of those concerned, in order to obtain compensation. The fact of the injury is sufficient and the scale of compensation will be strictly related to the needs of the unfortunate victim. This is the principle which we are all concerned to establish.

Sadly, there are a number of difficulties about creating a system to implement this principle and it is with these that we are mainly concerned. They could best be considered in four groups, covering the relationship between the no fault scheme and the Courts; the criteria for eligibility for compensation, under the scheme; the basis for actual compensation; and the cost of the scheme and who will meet it. I will now comment on each of these in turn.

The relationship between the no fault scheme and the Courts

Without pre-empting what I have to say about the cost of the scheme and who will pay for it, it is clear that an important element in financing it must come from consequent savings in legal costs. It is, therefore, tempting to suggest that some barriers should be created to restrict the right of patients to seek compensation by litigation and then, if unsuccessful, turn to the no fault scheme. Equally, it might appear desirable to stipulate that those using the no fault scheme should give an undertaking not to seek redress from the Courts if, for example, they are dissatisfied with the compensation offered by the no fault scheme. Clearly, as the law stands, such an undertaking could not be enforced but it might, at least, have some moral authority. This issue has been frequently discussed within the Association and our present conclusion is that no such efforts should be made. We feel that, if a patient wishes to seek redress through both channels, it should be open to them to do so, hoping that the existence of the no fault scheme might tend to influence the view of the Judges in making awards in Court. We are conscious that this decision will cause problems if a no fault scheme comes into operation, as it will limit the resources available for the scheme, particularly during the early years when it is, hopefully, establishing its reputation for fairness and promptness in meeting claims. Nevertheless, it is the view of the medical profession that it would be wrong to seek to interfere with the right of patients to have recourse to the Courts, if such is their wish.

The criteria for eligibility for compensation

Sadly, it is evident that all medical mishaps cannot be compensated. The cost would be prohibitive, even if Government finance was freely available. The compensation must clearly be restricted to unforseen mishaps and those resulting from recognised risks of medical diagnosis and treatment excluded. We have been impressed by the system in use in Sweden, both for its clarity and because it has been shown to work in practice, and we feel that it would form a satisfactory basis for no fault compensation in the UK. Clearly, much work would need to be done by lawyers to formalise such a document for use but, in the BMA, we have used a very condensed form, which allows some discussion of principles. I will comment briefly on the seven headings we have employed.

1. Only physical injury will be compensated. The implication that psychological damage consequent upon medical mishap will not be considered for compensation caused us some anxiety. On balance, it is accepted that to open the door to psychological problems would almost certainly cripple any scheme and simply prove too expensive to operate. It has been argued that, on this basis, compensation for pain and suffering would be excluded but, possibly illogically, we feel that such considerations should be included, as having more than a psychological basis.

2. Injury resulting from the natural progression of the disease under treatment should certainly be excluded.

3. Injury resulting from diagnostic error which could be regarded as reasonable in accepted medical practice should be excluded. This particular criterion creates some problems, because by its nature it is subjective. It would be ideal if the majority of claims could be dealt with by staff, without reference to the experts, but clearly, in this instance, expertise would be necessary for decision and appropriate panels would be needed.

4. Injuries resulting from unavoidable complications of any procedure competently performed for valid clinical reasons would be excluded. This criterion suffers from some of the objections to the previous one, often requiring expertise for assessment. It may also be regarded as too exclusive. It might be felt that the exclusion from compensation of some very remote complications, recorded in the small print of textbooks but hardly entertained by those regularly performing the procedure, was unreasonable.

5. Injury resulting from infection implanted during a procedure would be accepted for compensation but exclusions would apply to operations involving naturally infected organs or tissues, tissues of diminished vitality, prolonged catheterisation or drainage, prostheses *in situ* for a year or more and patients with defective immune resistance.

6. Injury resulting from the use of drugs in accordance with the manufacturer's instructions would be excluded but we are conscious that this view is not universally held and that extension of no fault compensation to intrinsic defects of drugs is advocated. It might be best if, as in Sweden, a separate but related scheme to cover such problems was instituted.

7. Injury resulting from extraneous factors, such as equipment failure, errors in patient handling and the like would be accepted, although, if not covered by insurance, they would tend to be the responsibility of the Health Authority. I will refer later to the relationship between the no fault scheme and the Health Authorities.

Compensation under a no fault scheme

It is the view of the BMA that the emphasis, in this context, should be upon the reimbursement of identifiable financial loss or of expense consequent upon injury. We share the view of our Swedish colleagues that there should be a mechanism to exclude the trivial and a minimum disability of 30 days (or of 10 days' excess hospitalisation) seems reasonable. In this context anxiety has been expressed by some of our General Practitioners about the likely pressure they would experience if certification was imposed upon them. This is clearly an issue requiring further consideration.

It is thought that reimbursements should take account of other sources of income, such as National Insurance or entitlement to salary under contracts of employment and that some ceiling, such as twice the national average wage, should be imposed. Evidently, if payment needed to be extended over long periods, protection against inflation should be provided. Where a medical mishap caused the death of an individual with dependants, provision would be made for support for the family, on similar lines, modified to take account of any insurance or state pension to which the family was entitled. Expenses consequent upon injury to a non-wage earner, such as a housewife, where help in the home or professional care for the individual was required, would be a charge upon the no fault funds. Similarly, the cost of services required by a damaged child, beyond whatever was available from the National Health Service or the Social Services, would be met by the no fault scheme and, effectively, where the consequences of the injury proved life-long, the responsibility of the scheme for him or her would continue indefinitely.

Clearly, there are some injuries which could only be compensated by a capital sum. For example, facial scarring affecting marital prospects and social life, damage to an organ not affecting capacity to work or expectation of life, or the accidental creation of sterility could not reasonably be compensated in any other way. Equally, the balance of opinion in the Association favours the acceptance of claims relating to pain and suffering and their recognition by payment of a capital sum, which in appropriate cases might be additional to the provision of finance for income or to meet expenses. It should be said that BMA Council was particularly concerned that the response of the no fault scheme to claims should be quick. I was reminded, when talking to them, that many patients would not be in a position to meet expenses resulting from medical mishap and await reimbursement. In such cases, speed in accepting claims and paying appropriate allowances would be of the very essence of an acceptable system.

The cost of the scheme and who will meet it

It is fair to assume that, whatever estimates we may make about the cost of a no fault compensation scheme, they will be exceeded if it comes into operation. The only estimates I have seen are those in the King's Fund paper "Medical negligence: compensation and accountability"[1] and I have no doubt that the authors would be the first to agree that they are extremely tentative. It might be possible, with the collaboration of the Health Authorities and the Defence Societies, to reach a more accurate estimate based on retrospective assessments but I have little doubt that, because many incidents which might be eligible under this scheme go unreported, the figure would seriously underestimate the eventual bill. Nevertheless, since a prospective study, on the same basis, would occupy two or three years and would not necessarily be more reliable, a retrospective paper exercise may be the best available. Eventually, a pilot scheme may be necessary. If based upon particular patient groupings, the result might well not be capable of being translated to cover all patients while a geographically based study, if it did not lead on to a full scheme, would leave someone with a continuing responsibility for numerous individuals receiving regular compensation for medical accidents. However, it would evidently be quite irresponsible to leap into such a scheme without the most detailed assessment of likely cost, so that, if it is to be contemplated, the help of Health Authorities and Defence Societies, with actuarial advice, seems the only practical way forward.

It is clear that a substantial contribution to the eventual cost must be made by the medical profession. Already, the profession puts of the order of ninety million pounds a year into indemnity insurance, of which less than 50% actually reaches damaged patients. Evidently, there is a substantial margin for improvement in the application of the profession's money, if the element of litigation could be reduced in favour of providing help in a non-adversarial manner for those with real need. Clearly, the Health Authorities also have a responsibility in this field, which they meet out of current budgets. If the concept of an insurance-based system to deal with their obligations was acceptable to Government, the possibility of a no fault compensation scheme, based upon the same financial principles as that in Sweden, might well become a reality. There is clearly a lot of work to be done before any firm decisions can be taken but, it seems to me, there are real grounds for hope that a serious deficiency in our provision for patients can be made good.

Conclusion

It is unfortunate that Ministers seem to have taken so firm a position against no fault compensation. Progress in the matter will hardly be possible without their help. Serious exploration of the possible cost would be, to say the least, greatly facilitated if the Department of Health were willing to offer help with a retrospective study which seems the only way to make progress, at the moment. It is certainly the view of the medical profession that, if a no fault compensation scheme were to come into existence, its financial arrangements must not, under any circumstances, erode the resources available for patient care in the National Health Service. Perhaps this assurance may relieve Ministerial anxieties enough to allow them to consider the proposals which emerge from this Conference.

Reference

1. Ham, C., Dingwall, R., Fenn, P. and Harris, D. (1988). *Medical negligence, compensation and accountability*. King's Fund Institute, London.

7

Should a no fault compensation scheme be introduced and what would it cost?

Christopher Ham

Doctors and their defence societies have been thrown into turmoil by the decision of the Medical Protection Society to introduce risk-related subscriptions in 1989. With obstetricians facing a bill of over £4000, compared with £1080 in 1988, there is concern that it will be difficult to recruit doctors to high-risk areas of medical practice in future. In fact, although recruitment problems may arise, the impact on doctors will be limited by the arrangement under which the Government reimburses the subscriptions of general practitioners as expenses and meets two-thirds of the cost of subscriptions paid by hospital doctors working whole-time for the National Health Service (NHS). The bulk of the increased cost of medical liability insurance will thus be met by the Treasury, and this may help to precipitate a much-needed review of arrangements for dealing with medical negligence claims.

Such a review will be welcomed by patients and their relatives. Despite a doubling in the number of claims paid and in the average value of damages awarded between 1984 and 1987, claimants face great difficulties in suing doctors and health authorities. These difficulties are illustrated by the case of Melinka Head, recently awarded £800,000 damages in the High Court. Melinka underwent surgery for appendicitis in 1981. The operation was a success but subsequently she was given the wrong fluid intravenously. This caused brain damage and Melinka was left with the mental capacity of a baby. She requires constant care and attention and suffers frequent fits and seizures.

Melinka's case highlights three major shortcomings in the way in which negligence claims are handled. First, the procedures involved are lengthy and expensive for patients, doctors and health authorities. In Melinka's case, it took seven years to settle the claim and only persistence on the part of her parents ensured that compensation was awarded. Second, claimants often find it difficult to obtain the services of a solicitor with relevant expertise. Melinka's parents sacked the solicitor who first handled their case before finding one who was competent to deal with medical negligence. Third, the legal process is adversarial

The analysis in this paper draws heavily on my work with Robert Dingwall, Paul Fenn and Donald Harris. I would like to emphasise my debt to them. Many of the ideas presented here are drawn from our King's Fund Institute Briefing Paper, Medical Negligence: Compensation and Accountability *(King's Fund Institute, London, 1988), although I am responsible for this paper.*

and causes those involved to close ranks. Consequently, patients and their relatives are not given adequate explanations or apologies when things do go wrong, and doctors may be distressed by the apparent hostility and ingratitude of their patients.

Melinka's case is not unique. Although doctors and health authorities warn that the UK is about to experience a malpractice crisis similar to that which has occurred in the USA, the real problem is that too few cases are compensated because of the hurdles that claimants have to overcome. Only about three out of ten people who seek compensation receive a payment, and many fail along the way because of the obstacles involved. In particular, it may be difficult to establish that a doctor failed to use reasonable care and, as a consequence, caused injury to a patient. This means that in practice the tort system becomes something of a lottery with injuries being compensated quite differently depending on the cause and on the availability of evidence. It is for this reason that various proposals for reform have been put forward, including the introduction of a no fault compensation scheme.

It is important to recognise that a no fault scheme is only one of several options available to policy-makers contemplating reform. As Ham, Dingwall, Fenn and Harris[1] have argued, a range of policy instruments exists. Some of these instruments are concerned primarily to deter doctors from acting negligently, while others aim to provide compensation. The critical test of any proposals of any reform is whether they are likely to be more effective than existing arrangements in meeting these two objectives[1].

Options for reform

Of the options available, those that require serious analysis can be grouped into three categories:

1. modifications to the existing tort system
2. the abandonment of the tort system in favour of providing compensation through social security
3. the introduction of a no fault scheme

As the main purpose of this chapter is to consider the case for a no fault scheme, the other two options will be discussed only briefly. Other contributions to these proceedings will review ways in which tort can be improved and the suggestions discussed on this issue are simply illustrative. One point to emphasise is that these three options are not mutually exclusive and it may be possible to modify the tort system, provide more generous income support through social security, and move towards a no fault scheme.

1. Modifying the existing system

Much could be done to change existing arrangements for dealing with negligence. For example, access to the legal system could be made easier and claimants could be helped to identify solicitors skilled in medical negligence work. There is evidence that public awareness of the possibility of claiming for damages has increased in recent years and this could be taken further by encouraging solicitors to market their services and by developing the Law Society's Accident Legal Advice Service. These initiatives might be accompanied by the establishment of a panel of solicitors who specialise in medical negligence cases.

Some attention could also be given to the barriers to access created by means testing on civil Legal Aid. Eligibility levels are at present so restricted that they prevent a large part of the population from obtaining redress. At the same time, structured settlements could be introduced to overcome the difficulty of determining appropriate levels of compensation when the expectation of life of plaintiffs is uncertain.

A further change would be to transfer negligence liability from individual doctors to health authorities. This would put doctors on the same basis as other NHS staff, with their employer assuming vicarious liability for negligence. The medical profession has in the past resisted this suggestion, fearing that health authorities would take a more active role in promoting high standards of medical practice if they were liable for negligence. However, the turmoil created by increases in defence society subscriptions has led to this idea receiving a more sympathetic hearing.

If health authorities were to assume liability for medical negligence, then it would certainly create a stronger incentive than at present for authorities to reduce mistakes by doctors. In particular, it would encourage authorities to take a lead in ensuring that doctors review the quality of their work and participate in medical audit. There is increasing evidence that doctors themselves recognise the importance of audit and it should be possible to build on this interest in future to establish audit as a routine part of clinical practice.

Health authorities could also introduce revised procedures for handling complaints to enable patients and their relatives to find out what went wrong with their treatment without recourse to the law. The existing complaints machinery is complex, fragmented and slow, and lacks the impartiality needed if patients are to be confident that their grievances are to be properly investigated. In the longer term, it should be possible to simplify complaints procedures to establish one point of contact whatever the nature of the complaint and to guarantee that those hearing complaints are genuinely independent.

A final change worth considering concerns the procedures for disciplining doctors. At present, the General Medical Council (GMC) investigates cases of serious professional misconduct, and health authorities follow the guidance set out in circular HM (61) 112 in assessing the professional competence of hospital doctors. Neither procedure is wholly satisfactory and proposals are currently under discussion to allow the GMC to consider less serious examples of misconduct and to simplify and accelerate local disciplinary arrangements. Relatively minor administrative reforms could help these procedures to operate more effectively and fairly *if* the government is prepared to override the objections that will undoubtedly be raised.

While this does not exhaust the list of options available to policy makers, it does illustrate some of the possibilities for overcoming the weaknesses of the existing system. By strengthening medical audit and reforming complaints and disciplinary procedures, the accountability of doctors could be strengthened and doctors might be deterred from acting negligently. Furthermore, by increasing access to the legal system it would be easier for claimants to obtain compensation. However, there would still be a basic inequality between defendants, represented by a small group of experienced and specialised lawyers, and plaintiffs, represented by a dispersed, heterogeneous group of lawyers, often with infrequent involvement with medical negligence cases. It would also continue to be difficult to prove fault. The inadequacies of the tort system may, therefore, encourage its replacement by a more equitable alternative. Providing compensation through social security is one such alternative.

2. Social Security

The issue of income support for disabled people is a major area of analysis in its own right, and in this section of the paper it is possible only to illustrate its potential role in the case of medical negligence. The replacement of tort by social security is both radical and potentially expensive. As such, it is probably best viewed as a long-term possibility. The advantage of a general disability income is that individuals would receive support on the basis of the fact of their injury or their disability and its consequences, and would have to establish neither fault nor cause. This would overcome the inequities between accident victims and the sick and disabled which arise when special schemes are created for accident compensation (see below). Also, the payment of benefits periodically rather than as a lump sum would remove one of the unsatisfactory aspects of tort awards.

The principal advantages of social security as a means of providing compensation lie in its relative accessibility and simplicity. As a result a large number of people can be compensated and administrative costs can be kept to a minimum. These advantages are the result of a uniform system of determining compensation. Consequently, benefits are not tailored to the individual's circumstances, as happens under tort law.

It should be emphasised that social security could meet one of the objectives of tort law, to provide compensation, but it would not, of itself, deter doctors from acting negligently. The latter objective would need to be pursued by other means such as the extension of medical audit, and more effective procedures for disciplining doctors. This might include giving a regulatory body the power to monitor medical practices, receive reports of accidents, and determine appropriate action to be taken. A body of this kind might develop out of the GMC.

Replacing tort with social security at a level where the disability income adequately substituted for the damages provided by tort is likely to be expensive. As a recent review of benefits for disabled people by the Social Security Advisory Committee has shown, the present patchwork of benefits provides neither an adequate basic income for the disabled nor sufficient help toward the extra costs which people incur because of their disabilities (Social Security Advisory Committee, 1988)[2]. Estimates of the costs of meeting these objectives vary, but, as an example, the proposals of the Disability Alliance for a comprehensive disability income scheme, cited by the Social Security Advisory Committee, would cost an additional £3 billion at 1987–88 prices. In view of the concern of the present Government to be more selective in the provision of social security and to target benefits on those most in need, the introduction of a *general* disability income is probably not a feasible option in the near future. In view of this, a special scheme to compensate the victims of medical accidents assumes greater importance, and we now consider the case for such a scheme.

3. No fault compensation

Other papers in this volume discuss the operation of no fault compensation schemes in New Zealand and Sweden. The principal features of these schemes have also been described in detail in Ham, Dingwall, Fenn and Harris (1988)[1]. I now wish to draw out the general lessons which emerge from experience in New Zealand and Sweden and highlight the principal points which need to be addressed if serious consideration is to be given to the introduction of no fault compensation in the United Kingdom.

It is clear that the operation of no fault compensation is, in general, viewed positively in Sweden and New Zealand. However, it is also apparent that various difficulties have arisen in the operation of these schemes. On the positive side, the schemes enable accident victims to be compensated quickly and at little administrative cost. Legal fees are eliminated, and the adversarial features of the tort system are avoided. Claimants do not have to find a skilled solicitor to act on their behalf, and in some cases they may be supported in making a claim by their doctors. As a consequence, it is possible to provide compensation to a larger number of people than under tort law, and the bulk of the expenditure involved goes directly to the claimants[5].

Against these advantages, a number of difficulties and lessons emerge from experience. First, while victims of accidents do not have to prove negligence, they are required to show that their injury was caused by an accident as defined by the scheme concerned. In practice, there are various exclusions, including minor injuries, injuries resulting from the natural progression of an illness, and injuries which could not have been avoided. *The key consideration in both schemes is that an injury should be caused by medical intervention and should be avoidable.* Although the range of accidents included in the schemes is broadening as new cases arise, difficulties still occur in demonstrating eligibility. *It is clearly not the case that a no fault scheme will result in all claims for compensation being paid.*

Second, as we noted in the discussion of a general disability income, the existence of special schemes for accident compensation creates inequities in the treatment of accident victims and the sick and disabled. This issue has received particular attention in New Zealand. Recent reviews of the accident compensation scheme by both the Law Commission (1988)[3] and the Royal Commission on Social Policy (1988)[4] have argued that there should be equal treatment of accident victims and the sick and disabled. It has yet to be determined whether this will be achieved by reducing the level of benefits available through the no fault scheme, by increasing social security benefits to the sick and disabled, or by a combination of these approaches.

Third, and leading on from this, the nature of the support available through social security to people with illness or disability is a key consideration. In Sweden, 90% of earnings lost because of illness or injury are paid up to £17,000 a year, after which benefits taper off[5]. The existence of a comprehensive social security system and a health service largely free at the point of use casts the Patient Insurance Scheme in the role of a supplementary source of finance. About 70% of Swedish payments are for non-economic losses such as pain and suffering, with 14% allocated to loss of earnings and 13% for medical costs. In contrast, in New Zealand, where the social security system is less generous, 48% of payments are for loss of income, 21% are allocated to non economic losses such as pain and suffering, and 14% are for medical costs. In comparing these figures, it should be emphasised that the New Zealand scheme covers injuries for all accidents whereas the Swedish scheme is concerned only with medical accidents.

Fourth, both schemes appear to be more effective in providing compensation than in preventing accidents. The New Zealand Accident Compensation Corporation is intended to have a role in accident prevention but this role has not been carried out effectively. As the Law Commission's review of the Accident Compensation scheme noted[3], there is an urgent need for accident prevention to be given higher priority.

In Sweden, the Patient Insurance Scheme plays some part in accident prevention by analysing the causes of accidents and feeding back the results to doctors. However, responsibility for setting and maintaining standards rests principally with doctors and professional self-regulation is strongly emphasised. The disciplining of doctors in Sweden is handled by the Medical Responsibility Board.

This is a government agency which receives and investigates complaints. As Rosenthal[6] has argued, the Board is an important instrument for holding doctors to account for their actions. While the Board may refer patients to the Patient Insurance Scheme for compensation, the reverse never happens. This is to ensure that doctors are not deterred from helping patients obtain compensation by the fear that they may later be disciplined.

Fifth, it is clear that taking cases out of the context of tort does not necessarily enable patients and their relatives to obtain an explanation of why an accident happened. Certainly in New Zealand, this appears to be just as much of a problem as in the United Kingdom. Indeed there has been concern recently about the lack of accountability of doctors in New Zealand, in the wake of the inquiry into the treatment of cervical cancer patients at The National Womens' Hospital in Auckland[7].

As these comments suggest, careful thought needs to be given to the arrangements for preventing accidents, investigating complaints and disciplining doctors *before* a no fault compensation scheme is introduced. While no fault compensation may enable a larger number of people to be compensated than tort law, it does not of itself help to deter doctors from acting negligently. Indeed in some cases removing the threat of legal action may encourage doctors to be less careful. If the deterrent effect of the law is to be removed (and the extent to which it is a deterrent is questionable), an alternative way must be found of promoting high standards of medical practice. Here again, medical audit has a crucial part to play.

Costs

The potential cost of a no fault scheme varies greatly according to the assumptions that are made about the rates of claiming and the size of awards. Furthermore, any attempt to compare costs has to overcome the absence of reliable data on the costs of existing arrangements. The figures presented below should, therefore, be regarded as tentative until better data become available.

At present, there are roughly ten claims relating to hospital treatment per 100,000 population in England each year. Approximately three of these claims are compensated and the average award is around £15,000. The total cost of the system, including both damages payments and legal expenses, is estimated to be £75 million, of which £65 million can be attributed to the NHS, either directly or through the cost of subsidising doctors' subscriptions to the defence societies.

The Swedish scheme generates about 60 claims per 100,000 population from all health care contacts, although the majority of these relate to hospital treatment. Fifty per cent of these claims receive compensation, averaging £3,200 at current exchange rates. If we assume that a Swedish style system were introduced in the UK, at the same rate of claiming and payment, the estimated cost for England alone would be of the order of £50 million per year. This would appear to represent a saving.

In fact, the actual cost of a no fault scheme in England is likely to be considerably higher than £50 million. The reason for this, as we noted above, is that Swedish compensation payments are made in the context of generous income support provided through social security. Given the more limited nature of our own social security system, average settlements would almost certainly be higher. If claims were compensated at current English rates, the overall cost would be around £235 million per year.

In practice, the average payment per claim is likely to fall since the introduction of a more accessible scheme would probably be associated with a reduction in the severity of claims. In Sweden, for example, a large number of claims are received concerning dental injuries and payments made in these cases are often low because the injuries are minor. If the average payment per claim were halved to reflect a reduction in claim severity, the cost would be about £117 million per year.

As a final comment on costs, two other points are worth highlighting. First, in the Swedish scheme, there is an upper limit on individual payments of £272,000 at current exchange rates. Second, the payments made for non-economic loss are lower than in England. Maximum awards under this heading are £40,000 compared with £80–100,000 in England[5].

One of the reasons for these limits is the concern to keep the overall costs of the scheme within manageable proportions. *This suggests that there may be a trade-off to be made between compensating a small number of cases at current levels and compensating a large number of cases with somewhat smaller awards.*

Conclusion

Should a no fault compensation scheme be introduced? The answer suggested by our analysis is a qualified "yes". The shortcomings of tort law present a good case for reform. However, it is difficult to argue strongly for any one of the several options on offer because each has drawbacks. While the possibilities of modifying the existing system have not been exhausted, some of the weaknesses of the system would remain however extensive the package of reforms. Equally, while a general disability income has many attractions, and would certainly lead to greater equity in the treatment of sickness and disability, it seems unlikely to win the support of politicians in the near future. *Nevertheless, incremental changes both to the tort system and to social security provision for disabled people may offer the best prospect for reform and these changes could be introduced in stages while the case for more radical options is considered.*

A no fault scheme would overcome many of the shortcomings of existing arrangements and would be a more effective mechanism of providing compensation than tort law. Against this, as our analysis has illustrated, such a scheme would not prevent accidents occurring and deter doctors from acting negligently. Nor would no fault compensation necessarily enable patients and their relatives to obtain an easier explanation than at present of what went wrong with their treatment. To meet these objectives, parallel arrangements would have to be introduced to promote high standards of medical practice, reduce mistakes, strengthen disciplinary procedures against doctors, and improve complaints procedures. Indeed, regardless of whether a system of no fault compensation is introduced, a strong case can be made for reform in these areas. These reforms would not help those who require financial support to meet the cost of errors in their treatment but they would go a considerable way toward strengthening professional accountability. Also, greater openness between doctors, health authorities and patients, and more effective methods of accident prevention, may help to reduce the number of legal claims. *The failure of the BMA's proposals for no fault compensation to consider the issue of professional accountability is a serious weakness which needs to be addressed as these proposals are developed further.*

As our discussion of costs has shown, it is likely that a no fault scheme would be more expensive than existing arrangements. Against this, a larger number of people would be compensated, and claims could be settled quickly and at little administrative cost. Ultimately, it is a matter of political judgement whether the additional price is worth paying. Also, a judgement would need to be made about the level of compensation to be made and the probable trade-off between providing large damages to a few or more modest damages to many.

Finally, it is important to ask who would run a no fault scheme? The experience of New Zealand and Sweden indicates two possibilities. First, a statutory scheme could be established, as in New Zealand, with a public agency taking responsibility for handling claims and making payments. Second, a voluntary scheme could be established, as in Sweden, involving a consortium of those agencies currently involved in medical negligence claims. The choice between these options depends to a great extent on the attitude of government to no fault compensation. If ministers continue to resist pressure for reform, then a voluntary scheme is the only realistic way forward. Even in this case, however, the Government would need to give its blessing to the participation of health authorities in such a scheme.

One other lesson which emerges from our analysis is that special schemes of accident compensation give rise to inequities between those who fall inside the scheme and those who remain outside. At a time when the possibility of a no fault scheme for children injured during birth is being canvassed, this conclusion should give pause for thought. On what basis can the special treatment of one category of medical injuries be justified? Indeed, to return to the case cited at the beginning of this paper, why should the parents of children like Melinka Head have to continue to fight their way through the legal process while the parents of children who suffer injuries at birth with similar tragic consequences be eligible for compensation through a no fault scheme?

In summary, it seems likely that the pressure to reform the medical negligence system will grow. In view of this, the sooner the options for reform are clearly identified and analysed, the better the prospect that the resulting changes will represent an improvement on the present position. As the debate develops, it will be important not to lose sight of the fact that any alternative to existing arrangements must seek to promote deterrence (or prevention) as well as to provide compensation.

References

1. Ham, C., Dingwall, R., Fenn, P., and Harris, D. (1988). *Medical negligence: compensation and accountability*, King's Fund Institute Briefing Paper 6, London.
2. Social Security Advisory Committee (1988). *Benefits for disabled people: A strategy for change*, HMSO, London.
3. Law Commission (1988). *Personal injury: prevention and recovery*, Report no. 4, Wellington.
4. Royal Commission on Social Policy (1988). *Working papers on income maintenance and taxation*, Wellington, NZ.
5. Brahams, D. (1988). The Swedish medical insurance schemes. The way ahead for the United Kingdom, *Lancet*, **i**, 43–47.
6. Rosenthal, M. (1987). *Dealing with medical malpractice*. Tavistock, London.
7. Paul, C. (1988). The New Zealand Cervical Cancer Study: Could it happen again? *Brit. Med. J.*, **297**, 533–539.

8

Discussion

Chairman: Dr Ronald D. Mann

Dr D. M. Burley (*Centre for Pharmaceutical Medicine*): Mrs Brahams mentioned that in the Finnish scheme the sum of money in any one year is limited. Does that mean that if a claim is brought in December, and the money has all gone, the individual does not get anything? How is it possible to operate a scheme where the money may run out in any given year?

Mrs Brahams: Naturally the scheme is monitored and as I understand it the awards would be retrospectively reduced, but I do not think that has yet happened. There is a "fail-safe" mechanism. If there were claims amounting to say, £110,000, and only £100,000 available for 11 claims, each one would be discounted by a percentage. The last person to claim is not told that there is no cash left for him. Each claim is reduced proportionately.

Ms H. Wilkinson (*National Consumer Council*): Towards the end of her presentation Mrs Brahams mentioned the question of accountability and improving clinical standards. Do the Finns have a system similar to the Medical Responsibility Board in Sweden, and are all the cases that are brought through the patient insurance scheme also brought to the attention of the Board? My understanding of the Swedish scheme is that some, but not all, of the cases are referred to the Medical Responsibility Board.

As the King's Fund paper recently pointed out, if we are to have a no fault compensation scheme we also need a very good, solid system of accountability. I wonder whether it will be necessary to tighten our arrangements in this respect.

Mrs Brahams: I have the impression that the peer monitoring in Finland is not as strict as it is in Sweden. It is a smaller country, and they tend to know where the black spots are. I think that unofficially pressure can be put on people and in a small community, clearly, it sometimes is brought to bear. Dr Huittenin, for example, told me that in the year the scheme has been running he came to the conclusion that there were certain parts of the country where he would not wish to have a car accident and be taken into intensive care!

There is a problem concerned with the handling of confidential material; the doctors are encouraged to be truthful and forthright and to help the patient make a claim. If a doctor knows he could be attacked with that same information, he will be discouraged from being honest and forthcoming. This is a fact of human nature, and is the reason why the Swedes are very concerned to keep their peer monitoring separate from their insurance.

The subject of patient–doctor relationships was raised earlier. The chief medical adviser to the Swedish scheme commented that the scheme had greatly improved patient–doctor relationships—"now the doctors can defend their patients and not themselves". I think that is a very telling comment. The Swedish doctors were originally opposed to the scheme, feeling that it would take away from their autonomy and, in a sense, that it was challenging what they were doing. But now they are pleased and the Finnish doctors are also very pleased with their scheme.

In Sweden there is the Board of Medical Responsibility which is a self-regulating board, run by doctors for doctors. It is not like the General Medical Council. The power to remove licences lies with a separate licensing board. Anybody who has a complaint can write to that licensing board and does not need to have a sworn deposition. In addition, if a complainant is a foreigner and cannot speak Swedish, he can write in another language and the letter will be translated. This is very encouraging—the system is made easy.

Dr J. Havard *(British Medical Association):* I have the impression that the options put forward by Dr Ham are mutually exclusive, except for the need to take the medical profession to task. In this connection, I would point out that more than seven million surgical and medical procedures are carried out each year in the United Kingdom. We have record low infant mortality figures. There are only a relatively few cases in which damage occurs as a result of incompetent or careless medical treatment.

With regard to Dr Ham's remarks about the National Health Service (NHS) Review suggesting medical audit, I suggest that this is highly unlikely because the first thing it would show would be the appalling state of the supporting services for the medical staff—which would be a very expensive matter to put right.

Dr Ham suggested we should learn from overseas experience. It would not be possible to introduce a no fault compensation scheme in this country without reforming the law of tort. The calculations which have been carried out have been based very properly on the Swedish system. However, there is a spectrum with Sweden, Finland and New Zealand at one end, where relatively small amounts are awarded and hardly any negligence actions take place; at the other end of the spectrum is the USA where, as we all know, things are very different. The introduction of no fault compensation in the USA would, it is estimated, increase the number of negligence actions about six times. The US Congressional Report probably ruled out no fault compensation because it was not at all convinced that any money would be saved.

Dr Ham: I am sure that the options are not mutually exclusive, and that we could proceed on a number of fronts at the same time.

I will wait until after 31 January to see whose assessment regarding the forthcoming White Paper is correct.

I agree with Dr Havard's rough estimate of the additional number of claims. It is broadly in line with what we calculated in our report, comparing current English rates of claims with those in Sweden. There would be something like a six-fold increase in the number of claims coming forward and probably being compensated which would account for some of the estimated increase in cost. I would not argue—and hope I did not imply—that no fault compensation is a way of saving money, in the way Dr Havard suggested. Almost certainly, we will have to spend more if there is any kind of no fault compensation scheme, but there are judgements to be made about maximum payments, average payments and the kinds of exclusions which would pertain.

Mrs Brahams: According to statistics from Finland, they had an extremely low rate of claim, of the order of six per 1,000. In the first year of the scheme, however, there were 1902 claims, which is a rate of about 40 per 1,000. In Sweden the rate is now about 60 per 1,000, and in Britain perhaps 10 per 1,000. From almost nothing the rate rose instantly to 40 per 1,000 in Finland, and it will probably increase.

With regard to the rate of satisfaction of claims, compensation was awarded in 529 claims, denied in 852, with 521 still pending. About three-quarters of the claims were decided by the end of the first year.

Prof. J. A. Dudgeon (*Great Ormond Street Hospital, retired):* I was interested to learn that Dr Ham gives the idea of a no fault scheme a qualified approval. He also referred to Lord Justice Pearson's Commission to which I gave evidence over a decade ago. In paragraph 1.5.31 in the chapter on medical injury, the Commission said:

"We do not at present recommend a no fault scheme in the United Kingdom but do recommend that the schemes in New Zealand and in Sweden should be looked at with great care."

That was in 1978—and it is now 1989.

Mrs Jean Robinson: A factor that has been left out of the debate is the massive social injustice in the United Kingdom caused by people's lack of access to the courts. This applies not only to medical actions but also to many other forms of legal action. A society in which people do not have access to the courts has an in-built injustice and that is something which has to be considered. I do not see medical actions as apart from that.

I think Mrs Brahams greatly underestimated the evidence for improvements in the safety of medical care which have taken place in the USA directly as a result of litigation. It has not been in the interests of the medical profession to seek and to provide such evidence. Nevertheless, it can be detected in medical journals. For example, many doctors said that they had improved note taking and history taking as a result of threats of litigation. Would that more doctors in this country would make such improvements, and without the threat of litigation.

However, one of the major causes of people wishing to sue in this country is the wish to get access to case notes and to know the truth. If such information were available, many actions which are being fought at the present time would never have been brought.

Mr Bolt referred to the fact that standard complications known to occur with certain procedures would be excluded. It would be of great interest to me to know the actual components of the overall complication rate, for example, the complications which develop with laparoscopic sterilisation. Some of them must be due to negligence; some to the learning curve of new doctors; some to lack of supervision—and so on.

Confidential inquiries into maternal, neonatal and surgical deaths show that a great many avoidable injuries take place because inadequately supervised junior doctors are doing work which senior doctors should do. Yet all of that is included in the "standard complication rate" of many procedures.

My final point is my extreme concern at the exclusion of non-physical injury. Some of the most serious, distressing and worrying cases with which I deal are psychological injury following some kind of medical mishap. One component of that is the iatrogenic injury following the way patients who complain are treated by health care personnel. For many years I have seen psychological injury result from high-technology childbirth. Women say they have suffered the equivalent of technological rape. The effects are very long term, very serious, and the effect on the family is profound.

Unfortunately, the medical profession has not looked sufficiently in its basic research at the psychological effects of many new treatments. It is bad for medical care, for the profession, and for the patients, that medical research often leaves out something which is profoundly important and causes an enormous amount of suffering.

Mr R. K. Greenwood *(Leicester):* Unfortunately, I think that no fault compensation will not come about. Sir Christopher Booth summed it up adequately by saying that the political and economic background of this country is against it.

Mrs Brahams made an important point when she said that we should think of the effect of what we propose both on the economy and on the next patient. The doctor becomes nervous, defensive and over-anxious (her words) when threatened with litigation. Most people present today and almost every newly qualified doctor will be sued some time during his career.

With regard to the time taken to resolve complaints: six months, which Mr Bolt thinks is too long, and which Mrs Brahams thinks is good for the Finns, is certainly very much quicker than what happens in this country at the moment.

Prof. D. Laurence *(University College Hospital, London):* I agree with Dr Ham that there is a deep irrationality in compensating according to cause and not according to simple need, regardless of cause. I also agree that the road of selective compensation is the one that society is determined to go down. It is probably right to do so and, should economic conditions improve, it may expand into something more comprehensive.

I support Prof. Dudgeon's remark about the Pearson Commission. My recollection is that it said quite clearly that it liked the idea of compensating medical accidents, but that *at the moment* (and this was in 1978) it saw overriding reasons why this was not practicable. It even added that it might become practicable, and should be borne in mind.

I am, however, worried about the British Medical Association's exclusion criterion number 6 regarding "injury resulting from the use of drugs in accordance with manufacturers' instructions". Many medicines do not have manufacturers' instructions; they are generic medicines. It may be that the law will demand prescribing instructions in the future, but there is no requirement at present. That criterion would exclude compensation for the practolol incident when a number of people went blind, and some people lost their lives with polyserositis. There was no suggestion of negligence and of course ICI compensated. The attitude "leave it to the patient and the pharmaceutical company" is acceptable when dealing with a firm like ICI, but not if a small generic company is involved.

The Pearson Commission said that drugs were the area in which most demand for compensation had been seen, and this was an international phenomenon. Any scheme that excludes rare but horrifying effects from drugs used in accordance with the manufacturers' instructions will not be accepted by the public. Practolol was a new medicine, but it took four years to find out what was happening. People still get aplastic anaemia from antirheumatic drugs and some still drop dead from penicillin. I wonder whether it is acceptable that such incidents should be excluded from a no fault system. I doubt if it is proper to exclude the rare, very severe adverse effects of drugs, whether or not they are known, and whether or not they are warned about.

I would urge the BMA to look more deeply into the area of the adverse effects of drugs. I agree that anti-cancer drugs can be put to the patient as a matter of life and death, and that patients should accept the risk. But I think the BMA's exclusion number 6, as presently written, would probably exclude more than the BMA wishes to exclude.

Mr Bolt: The main difficulty is that mishaps in the drug area are infrequent and unpredictable, and they may affect thousands of people and cost a great deal of money. Therefore, our suggestion is that it is not appropriate for them to be included in this no fault scheme. It would be sensible and reasonable if the drug manufacturers created a no fault scheme of their own, to cover the problem of the adverse effects of drugs. It would be a burden round the neck of the general scheme which we are discussing, and would make it much more difficult to get under way.

Mrs Brahams: I agree that drug injuries should be compensated under a separate scheme. A number of countries have started drug injury schemes even when they do not have no fault treatment schemes.

A new scheme is beginning in Norway, and I believe that Parliament has passed legislation to set it up this year. There is also a compensation scheme for drug injury in Japan.

Prof. Laurence: I can see the merits of a separate scheme for drug injuries.

Dr Mann: Most clinical pharmacologists will agree with Prof. Laurence. The problem is with, for example, a one in 30,000 risk of aplastic anaemia for an effective drug in a serious disease. That is the one sort of situation which could rationally be dealt with on a no fault basis without reforming the law of tort. It is perhaps the clearest case of all.

Dame Rosalinde Hurley (*Queen Charlotte's Maternity Hospital, London*): I was a little disappointed in Dr Ham's modification of the tort system because I had expected to hear of a modification of the legal system rather than peripheral matters.

There is much wrong with our system in tort, not just in actions for negligence. It seems to me that no fault—or no blame—compensation would remedy two of the grosser defects. One is the delay. The statute of limitations may be helpful to the plaintiff but it is not helpful to the luckless doctor who is being sued. Very often the action is not lodged for many years after the initial letter from the solicitor. It is to be hoped that no fault compensation would remedy that situation.

The second aspect that might be remedied by such a system would be the method of payment of damages, already alluded to. It is sometimes very distressing for the impoverished and the poor to receive a huge lump sum from the court. They have no idea how to deal with it or how to invest it and ironically enough, they often find that their only friend and adviser is the surgeon or physician whom they have just successfully sued.

Dr Ham: I agree. In talking about modifying the tort system, I hope I made it clear that I was giving some examples rather than an exhaustive list of the possibilities.

Dr C. Oldertz (*Skandia Insurance Co. Ltd., Sweden*): Dr Ham mentioned the Swedish system as a basis for estimating the cost of a no fault insurance system in the UK. In my opinion, the figure he mentioned is probably too high. I hold this opinion, firstly, because smaller injuries are probably being compensated as highly in Sweden as they are in the UK, in terms of non-economic losses, and secondly, because most of the cohort of patients who are injured are old. They are pensioners, they are sick from other causes, and they are not wage earners.

Dr Ham is probably right about the frequency of occurrence of injuries. However, I do not think that any decision on the total cost should be taken without making a more thorough investigation. I am sure that the injuries in themselves will be the same in the UK as in Sweden, so the basis for compensation should be the same—but, of course, the amount of compensation could be different. Exact figures could be obtained to show how many of the injured are wage earners, how old they are, how sick, and what compensation they presently receive.

With regard to the very high awards that are given in the UK, they are higher than in Sweden.

I investigated the question of how many newborn children are injured and receive compensation in Sweden. On average, it is about two children each year, so probably the number receiving serious injuries is not very great.

Mrs Brahams: It is my declared aim to try to get the law on damages changed in the United Kingdom and I would have the support of most of the judiciary who have pleaded for Parliament to change the way in which compensation is awarded for personal injury. Judges would like to be able to offer structured settlements—that is, payments per year—which could be amended according to need. This cannot be done at the moment. Judges cannot impose such a settlement; they have to make a lump sum calculation.

There has been a small change for the better, in that "structured settlements" have been introduced, but they have to be pleaded, that is, asked for by the plaintiff. This arrangement has been made possible because of a concession by the Inland Revenue. Previously, no tax was payable on a large lump sum that an individual received, but the income produced by it was taxed. The feeling against annual awards was because people would be taxed on the money in their hands each year, so that they would be at a disadvantage; they would not have the lump sum and would be taxed on the income. About a year ago the Inland Revenue conceded that people will not be taxed on the income if it is paid annually. That is quite an attraction, and it is a move forward. However, judges still cannot *impose* such a settlement on the parties and a change is required in this area.

If we are going to move realistically towards any kind of no fault scheme there must be some sort of limit on the damages, and the limitation would have to be across-the-board. Clearly, if someone could get £1 million in court and £250,000 through the scheme, the latter would be wrecked by people all the time going outside it.

The case of Mpanda which was referred to was a situation in Sweden. The boy had foreign parents, and the case was not appealed, which was surprising. It capitalized up to £4 million—a staggering award for private care. We could not create a system with such an enormous built-in defect.

Mr S. Simmons (*Royal College of Obstetricians & Gynaecologists*): Dr Ham wondered why there is a special case arising for babies damaged in labour. I was intrigued by the Swedish figure of two in a year. Perhaps Dr Ham does not know that in the UK at the moment about 300 or 400 such cases are awaiting litigation. There are only 800 consultants in the country, so a simple sum shows that by the end of next year we will all have been sued.

Therefore, not only would it be good for obstetricians to change the system, but in the end it will probably also be good for the patients. At the top end of the scale, the senior doctors are leaving the discipline. Many of my older colleagues have already said that they are not prepared to go on doing obstetrics unless something happens to change the present position. Those at the bottom end of the salary scale are not coming into the discipline. We have conducted careful survey in our discipline, and it is clear that in the last year there has been about a 20% drop in recruitment—thus, there may be inadequate numbers to fill the posts already available.

There is very hard evidence that the present situation is having a profound effect on professional recruitment and, if you like, there is the soft evidence of talking to junior doctors who say "No, thank-you". A junior doctor who works for me at the moment told me that in her year at Queen Charlotte's (which is the cream of our training group) the whole year had come out of the obstetric discipline because of what is happening in litigation.

To talk about litigation being a benefit to the obstetrician or to obstetrics does, I think, miss the mark entirely.

Moreover, in a sense we are victims of our own success. Litigation is inversely proportional to perinatal morbidity and mortality. There have been very profound improvements in our discipline in the last 10 years, and they are almost equalled by the rise in litigation. If somebody tells me that litigation is improving the quality of practice, then I must reply that he simply does not understand the subject. In fact, it has done completely the reverse. Defensive medicine in obstetrics is presently taking place. There is no question that this is something that *might* happen. It is happening *now*. We have looked very carefully at the figures of caesarean section in relation to this, and there is no doubt that the sharp increase is directly related to litigation. Unless something is done—and it is no good talking about "maybe", and "when", and "5 years' time"—the service in obstetrics may founder totally.

Let us not be under any illusion that this is something we can talk about in an academic sense in the Royal Society of Medicine. Unless we come to grips with this issue of litigation in obstetrics, we will find that there is no service to talk about.

Dr Ham: Of course, there is a problem, and it is not only obstetricians who are suffering. I take the point entirely about patients also being at risk because of the developments that are now occurring.

However, Mr Simmons has not answered my problem about equity in the treatment of different kinds of medical accidents and medical injuries. I would like to hear from Mrs Vennell of the experience in New Zealand, because equity is already a problem there, even with a no fault compensation scheme which covers *all* accident victims and not just medical accident victims. How can we get around the problem of different treatment for different cases?

Mr Simmons: My reply, quite simply, is that it is a matter of priorities. If we want to debate the finer issues, we must keep the service going. If the whole service is lost, the finer issues that have been raised will not be relevant.

Mr A. J. P. Ross (General Surgeon, Member of the BMA No Fault Compensation Committee): There is growing evidence that much of the brain damage that occurs in neonates actually occurs *in utero* long before labour takes place. This is one reason why that area should be taken out from the rest. I am in no doubt that there is no negligence. I do not know how the cases are won, but certainly there is very little proof that the action of the obstetrician produced the brain damage in the child.

I want to address a point relating to one of Dr Ham's concepts on deterring negligent action. Personally, I believe it shows a lack of understanding of why people go into medicine. We do try to do our best for every patient. A doctor does not think that because he might be sued, maybe he will do a little better. To speak like this shows a lack of understanding of why we practise medicine and what motivates us—it certainly is not the threat of litigation.

I talked to a group of young doctors when I was in the USA, and I asked them whether they thought that the threat of litigation improved their standard of medicine. They said, "No, on the contrary". They said what Mr Simmons has just been saying: that they practise defensive medicine, they do things they know to be not of benefit to the patients, merely to cover their backs in court.

Mrs Robinson said there is evidence from the USA that litigation improves clinical practice. She gave us the example of doctors keeping better notes. Is that the best she can do? I am interested in the care of the patient. It might help the legal system to have better notes but I am only interested if it helps the patient.

I accept that studies have shown that by better monitoring mortality, and especially anaesthetic deaths, can be reduced. Legal cases are not needed to prove that. Our own associations and professional bodies have been in the forefront of such monitoring—and the perinatal mortality and the anaesthetic studies are examples of this. Such work requires additional resources. If health authorities are as interested in maintaining quality, as Mrs Robinson implies, I suggest they give the resources for the doctors to have better monitoring equipment and adequate staff.

Mr D. R. Smith *(Rehabilitation Studies Unit, Edinburgh University):* Mr Bolt referred earlier to the financial problems of health authorities when a very large claim sweeps up all the budget for the year. There is no bar to government bodies insuring—if that is what they want to do. The Ministry of Defence indulged in insurance for its employers' liability risks some time ago. Insurance consortiums have protected the UK Atomic Energy Authority's (UKAEA) works because of the sheer size of the problem.

If there is a feeling that the health authorities do not want individually to go down that particular road, they might like to explore pooling their problems by paying jointly, between all the health authorities, claims over, say, £100,000.

If I interpreted Dr Ham's remarks correctly, he said that a no fault scheme for medical accident victims would take the place of the tort system. It seems to me that in the present climate that is asking a great deal. The most to be hoped for is to have a no fault system in front of the tort system, so that the tort system is there as a final incentive (if that is the correct word to use). Above all, any change should be associated with freedom of information because, time and again, the complaint is heard about delay and lack of information. In many of those cases a settlement, or an understanding, could be reached with the patient and/or relatives without any question of litigation. That is a road which needs to be explored a very great long way.

Mr M. C. T. Morrison *(Orthopaedic Surgeon, Swindon):* My first points are primarily direct to Dr Ham about revisions of the present system. Mrs Brahams has already talked about the judiciary wishing to make payments on an annual basis. I am sure this would go a long way to helping the legal problems; it might also help the problems of medical defence subscription, for it would be much easier to work out the annual overall need if the annual amounts separately being paid out in compensation were known.

The implication is that there are a lot of patients who ought to be suing doctors and ought to be getting compensation for what has happened to them during the course of treatment. I would suggest that this may be so to some degree, but that quite a lot of the claims now are, if not frivolous, at least without foundation in law. One of the problems is with the present legal aid system. At present, as Mrs Brahams has rightly said, quite a large proportion of the population is denied legal aid, and yet is not wealthy enough to pursue a legal action through the courts because of the time it takes and the cost it incurs.

I would suggest that some of the cases that are lost by the litigant have no cause in law, and if the legal aid system were changed in two directions the situation would be improved. We need

1. To make legal aid available to those who are slightly better off.
2. To ensure that if a legally aided litigant lost his case, the legal aid fund would pay the cost of the defence.

One of the problems with our present medical defence subscriptions is that they are high because of the legal costs involved in defending cases. As Mrs Brahams mentioned, we do not have a chance of getting the costs against a legally aided litigant.

With regard to no fault compensation, I think we want to be clear what our aims and objectives are. No fault compensation goes far wider than just the medical field. I suggest that it is quite wrong to restrict it to the medical field because, if this happens, and if it becomes a legal process, there will be a publicity campaign against the doctors suggesting that they are the baddies who are going around injuring patients.

By far the majority of accidents occur at work, in the home and on the road. With the present tort system, as Mrs Brahams has suggested, it is largely a lottery whether or not someone wins his case for cause, and thereby gets damages. If, as a caring society, we really want to support people, who have suffered—and continued to suffer—a disability, then we need either no fault (or no blame) compensation or a better social security system to support them in their need, regardless of the cause of their disability.

If that is what is wanted, we do not want exclusion clauses relating to known complications of medical treatment.

Mr Bolt: I think we must face the fact that we have a problem, which is with us now. The scheme now being suggested is a fantasy and if it happens, it will be in 25 years' time. Something needs to be done *soon* because, if it is not, we are heading for disaster.

I sympathise with the views about not differentiating medical mishap from accidents on the road and so on, but I have to say that only a narrow scheme has any remote prospect of getting off the ground in the foreseeable future.

Dr Ham: I agree with Mr Bolt. Ideally, we would have a very broad scheme as suggested by Mr Morrison but, realistically, a special scheme for medical accidents is the only one remotely possible at the moment.

Mr Smith mentioned the pooling of risks. That already happens in most health regions where district health authorities are expected to bear the first part of the damages that are awarded, but the rest are pooled across the region.

Tort could operate alongside a no fault scheme, or we could have the New Zealand alternative. I am not clear in my own mind which of those two is the better arrangement. That is one of the issues that needs to be discussed further.

With regard to Mr Ross's sensitivity about negligent action, if I put it in terms of promoting high standards of medical practice that is trying to convey the same point—but more acceptably to Mr Ross and his colleagues. I accept entirely that doctors are motivated to do the best they can for their patients. I did not intend to imply anything other than that.

The Confidential Enquiry into Peri-Operative Deaths (CEPOD) clearly demonstrates that, while standards are generally very high, there are nevertheless some causes for concern in that particular area. CEPOD has identified weaknesses in clinical practice on the part of surgeons and anaesthetists, and these weaknesses now need to be put right. CEPOD shows that about half of the surgeons and anaesthetists in the study are not doing regular audit and that seems to me unacceptable. Indeed that is one of the issues which the White Paper will consider.

Dr B. E. Banks (*University College Hospital, London*)*:* Dr Ham more closely represented the feelings of victims of medical accidents than anyone else when he stressed the request for a full and frank explanation of what had happened, what had gone wrong, and for reassurance that practices will change in the future in order to prevent a repetition of whatever caused the accident under discussion.

I must ask Mrs Brahams, in view of her earlier comments, whether the Medical Defence Union (MDU) is as lenient in the matter of pressing for costs with privately funded litigants as it claims to be in not pressing for costs for legally aided unsuccessful litigants?

Mrs Brahams: I have tried to make it clear that one of the advantages of the Finnish and Swedish schemes is that the patients receive an explanation *immediately* and they also receive their notes. If they receive compensation, they get an explanation and compensation; if they do not get compensation, the law provides that they must be given a clear explanation—and they can come back and ask more about it. I think fears on this issue are unfounded.

I was impressed that the Swedish and Finnish schemes were so ''user-friendly'' compared with the mounds of paper work required in Britain just to get a hearing.

I do feel that I represent victims as well as the doctors.

So far as pressing for costs is concerned, Dr Wall is far better placed to give the view of the MDU.

Dr J. A. Wall (*Secretary, Medical Defence Union*): The MDU regularly waives costs in cases brought against doctors by non-legally-aided plaintiffs who fail. [**Dr Banks:** I lost my home] I am not in a position to comment on individual cases but am grateful to Dr Banks for declaring her interest. I do not feel free to comment on her case. She has been kind enough to say that she is a plaintiff, I gather unsuccessful, in a case in which the MDU was involved but I do not think this is the forum to pursue a personal matter any further.

By ''regularly'', I do not, of course, mean invariably, but the MDU frequently refrains from enforcing the payment of costs by unsuccessful plaintiffs. It depends upon the circumstances of the case.

In 1988, 1.3% of practising doctors in Britain had claims paid on their behalf— assuming, for the sake of argument, that the MDU figures are typical. Ten years ago it was 1 in 1,000. It has increased to 13 per 1,000 in 10 years, which is a rapid rate of increase. This applies to claims made, not to complaints made, writs issued or letters before action.

The figures published by the defence societies in their current annual reports give figures at 31 December 1987. The damages paid by the MDU in the year to that date (13 months ago) are declared as a worldwide total of £17 million. Our American friends ask how many members do we have. When we reply that there are 150,000 worldwide, half in Britain and half abroad, they say that £17 million cannot be the total damages—it must surely be the average, or perhaps the biggest, claim! When we repeat that is the total, the Americans say that we are talking very small money.

Looking at the American approach, because we are sometimes asked if we are tending in that direction, I would like to give an example from a new no fault compensation scheme which started in the State of Florida in October 1988.

In the explanatory literature sent to all doctors in the State, the question is put:

''What is the Florida birth-related neurological injury compensation plan and why was it established?''

The answer is that—

''The Florida birth-related neurological injury plan was created by the 1988 Florida legislature to provide no fault compensation for birth-related neurological injury claims occurring on or after January 1989.''

This applies to *claims made* after 1 January 1989, even if the baby was delivered in 1979 and is a crucial point which would have to be answered in the introduction of any scheme here. If the scheme only related to injury *occurring*, let us say, after 1 January 1990, that would be unacceptable to the existing defence societies. If such a new scheme covered claims brought, regardless of when the injury occurred that would be feasible. The Americans have faced that problem, and are dealing with claims brought after 1 January 1989. In other words, the right of action has been wiped of plaintiffs whose rights of action have already accrued.

The plan limits payment to the infant's actual health care expenses, both past and future, and reasonable expenses incurred in filling the claim. The plan also provides for a maximum:

"$100,000 award to the parents for intangible damages, such as pain and suffering."

What type of infant injuries are covered under the plan?
The answer in the Florida scheme is:

"The plan covers birth-related neurological injuries which have been defined as an injury to the spinal cord or brain of a live-born infant weighing at least 2500 g at birth."

which ignores the many premature babies who now sue for failure to get them through to the normal state at the date when they should have been born.

"The injury must have been caused by oxygen deprivation"

—that begs the question about the premature brain.

"or mechanical injury, and must have occurred in the course of labour, delivery or resuscitation in the immediate post-delivery period in the hospital. The injury must have rendered the infant permanently and substantially . . ."

—those words also beg questions—

"mentally and physically"

We wondered whether they meant and/or, but the wording is "mentally *and* physically—

"impaired. The legislation does not apply to genetic or congenital abnormalities."

Professor Illingworth's article in the *British Medical Journal*, entitled, "Why blame the obstetrician?", makes the same point as Mr Simmons has made, that because *post hoc* it is said to be *propter hoc*. If just after the delivery something is found to be wrong with the baby, is that birth-related? According to our experts recognising injury or defect at birth does not mean it occurred at or around the time of birth.

The following sentence is from the covering letter that went to all the doctors:

"We are optimistic that this new legislation will help relieve the pressures of escalating malpractice awards and provide a positive first step in retaining the qualified obstetricians Florida desperately needs."

In other words, the collapse of the service, as Mr Simmons has warned, has produced the need for rapid institution of a no fault scheme for brain-damaged babies, damaged at birth, with all the questions begged in the haste to introduce the scheme.

I do not know if we are so near to needing a scheme in this country, and whether it is feasible, affordable, or fundable. The funding mix in Florida (and there is a very similar scheme in the State of Virginia) is $20 million of state funds, $5000 from every doctor who wants to deliver babies, $250 from *all* other doctors, some money from the funds of privately run hospitals, and some from the insurance companies—a mix of public and private funding. I mention it as a possible combination of a government-funded scheme or the alternative, privately-funded one, to which Dr Ham alluded.

Dr Banks: To what extent did the BMA consult either victims of medical accidents or organisations that represent victims of medical accidents, as opposed to patients, to ask them what they would see as a reasonable scheme to replace the totally unsatisfactory system that we have under tort? In other words, what consultations did the BMA undertake before arriving at the proposals that have been put forward and which, as I recall, are concerned exclusively with money?

Mr Bolt: I have been Chairman of the Working Party only since the end of November 1988, so I do not know. There were exchanges with the Action for the Victims of Medical Accidents previously, but I do not know to what extent, or what ground was covered.

Mr Ross: The Action for the Victims of Medical Accidents was invited to meet the BMA Working Party, and we met Mr Simanowitz and Dr Banks. I cannot remember the exact details but we spent about half-an-hour to an hour talking with them.

Mr P.F. Carpenter *(Alza Corporation, CA, USA):* I agree with Mr Bolt about the urgency of the issue. Much of what I have heard is reminiscent of discussions in the USA about a decade ago. It is, therefore, important to encourage you to focus on the fundamental issues, the first of which often gets overlooked, and that is the difference between expectations and reality on the part of the patient. Our modern society creates tremendous expectations of the great things that will happen, particularly in medicine and these are not always reasonable, or, indeed, possible.

The second fundamental issue is risk versus perceived benefits. Several people have spoken about the difficulties of obstetricians. It has certainly been the experience in the USA, in specialties like obstetrics, anaesthesia and orthopaedics (which are perceived by the recipient as having relatively low benefits, particularly in the case of otherwise healthy people, and significantly higher risks) that those are the areas that become the ''cutting edge'', and are harbingers of things to come in other specialties.

People do not perceive that the benefits they receive from these specialties, in the case of injury, equate with the risks to which they are exposed; whereas someone who is seriously ill, for example a heart transplant patient, tends to disregard what are perceived by other people as significant risks.

Lastly, there is the question of professional self-discipline versus the use of the tort system. I spent a number of years as Executive Director of the Medical Centre at Stanford University and in my experience when meetings are called on these issues the physicians who attend are far from being a representative sample of physicians.

I would be loath to suggest that any physician in this audience was lacking in either competence or compassion. Yet studies throughout the USA indicate that the degree of negligence far exceeds the degree of discipline provided by the profession. Unfortunately, any attempt to discuss the issue results in discussion with the best, most competent, and the most compassionate doctors and who quite rightly say that they are being inappropriately accused. It is their colleagues who do not bother to come to the meetings or to participate in those discussions who are sowing the seeds for the disaster that may have to be faced by us all.

Mr J. E. Woodyard *(Stafford):* Dr Carpenter's comments lead on to what I wish to say, and that is that we are sometimes a little disingenuous about our views on negligence. Wounded pride leads us sometimes to overlook the patient's problems. Too often we see the whole issue of negligence as something that is hurting *us* rather than the injured, or unnecessarily-injured, patient.

I am not sure how to overcome this. Perhaps it should start with medical students who should not be frightened but instead told "first, do no harm".

I am sceptical about audit too, because it is often difficult in terms of practical organisation, to initiate a proper audit system in an area where there are perhaps only two consultants.

Mr Bolt implied that the BMA view of no fault compensation is that the medical profession will be largely responsible for funding it. As an employee, however, I feel that insurance is my employer's business.

Finally, the extra costs of no fault compensation have been discussed but there is a bigger issue here than money. If we want less negligence, then the Government must be persuaded to provide more doctors and nurses, so that individually they handle fewer cases. Many of the problems with negligence arise because people are too busy and too tired, largely caused by doing too much work, for too long, too early in life.

Mr Bolt: I did not suggest that the medical profession should fund a no fault scheme but that they would have a major responsibility, as they do in the present arrangement. I then went on to suggest that it was highly desirable, and to be sought, that the health authorities should join in funding the scheme.

At the moment there is a relationship with the defence societies by which the costs of those matters in which the health authority has the responsibility are split between them. That is one approach to the problem, but it would be better from our point of view if they made appropriate contributions to financing the scheme if it comes into existence.

Dr Mann: One of the most dramatic statements that has been made in this session is that if something is not done about it the obstetric service will fail. I would like to ask Mr Simanowitz to speak, but I would also like to invite other obstetricians present, and those connected with the obstetric services, to comment on whether they too feel that the threat is of these massive proportions. If it is, something must be done about it.

Mr A. Simanowitz (*Action for Victims of Medical Accidents*): I was pleased to hear Mr Woodyard support the victims' point of view, because that has been singularly lacking. Exception seems to have been taken to Dr Ham's comments although, in my view, they were put in a mild-mannered way. It is sad that as soon as the patient's point of view is put, some doctors see that as "doctor bashing". The last thing that my organisation wants to do is to attack doctors, but we do try to put forward the view of the patients.

Mr Woodyard asked how to overcome the doctors' wounded pride, when they are attacked over an accident. One way is for the medical profession to establish an organisation to help doctors when an accident has taken place. The present medico-legal organisations are involved not in medico-moral matters but only in medico-legal matters. They are legal bodies and although they give some counselling, they are not involved in the ethical problem. It is surprising that no body has been established to which a doctor can go in a crisis. I believe that doctors suffer when medical accidents occur in exactly the same way as patients and they need somewhere to go where they can get help.

There would then be less likelihood of defensive medicine. If the practice of defensive medicine is taking place on the scale suggested by Mr Simmons, though this is debatable, then it arises out of a failure of the medical profession to counsel doctors in this difficult problem of medical accidents.

As a representative of victims of medical accidents, I felt what was said sounded like a threat: "if you do not get off our backs, we will not treat you". Perhaps this was not intended. I can understand why doctors feel embattled—the insurance premiums are going up, and for the first time they are being called to account. It is a difficult situation, one which I hope to see resolved in the best way for both doctors and patients. But doctors must understand that such a reaction will create a difficulty for dialogue. I hope that difficulty will not increase, and that meetings like this will help to reduce that difficulty, not exacerbate it.

Dr Mann: We all hope that meetings like this will be helpful. Perhaps the specific problem is the assumption that a brain-damaged baby is necessarily the product of negligence. That is biologically wrong.

Mr Simmons: In my view, what I said was in the interests of patients. It was not a reaction to something that happened on this occasion. We are deeply concerned about recruitment to the discipline of obstetrics and I took the opportunity to make a point which is very germane to our discussions. It is not an academic point, but a genuine anxiety about the future of the discipline. We do not want to see in the UK the problems that exist in the USA.

To emphasise the point, our problems arise because we are victims of our own success. Babies are now saved who, a few years ago, would have had no chance of survival and expectations are now so high that there seems to be no room for error. It is often not the senior people who are in the "front line" but the trainees.

If I seemed to be reacting, and trying to safeguard the interests of my colleagues, it is unintentional. I am genuinely anxious for our future.

Prof. V. R. Tindall (Manchester): In Manchester we have one of the largest medical schools in England. At one time, obstetrics and gynaecology was an attractive discipline. It deals with fit, healthy women in the majority of cases, the students enjoy delivering babies, and in many of the gynaecological problems we are also dealing with fit patients.

The MDU and MPS regularly speak to our final-year students, and we have had one of the highest intakes into the specialty from our university. Over the past 10 years, however, the intake has gradually fallen. Mr Simmons is correct in saying that the profession of obstetrics as a whole is losing its attraction. We are becoming a shortage specialty and Mr Simmons and I, who have been involved with this for some years, are worried about the quality of people who are coming in, and who are motivated to look after patients.

Professor Martin, in Western Australia, has just retired and when I met him recently he mentioned that since he started practising about 25 years ago obstetric successes had brought the perinatal mortality rate down but, due to the success of his colleagues in the *in vitro* fertilisation field in introducing multiple births, the perinatal mortality rate when he retired was twice that to which he and the other obstetricians had reduced it.

It is a sad fact we are being penalised by our own success—but our successes become the problems of our paediatric colleagues. The decision that often has to be made is whether a baby is safer in the mother's uterus or in the care of the paediatrician.

Mrs L. Lamont (The Patients' Association): Many of those who come to us with health problems—problems which sometimes lead to litigation but sometimes cause people to give up in despair—could be resolved if there was more opportunity to talk about what went wrong and to discuss the difficulties openly and frankly at an early stage. This discussion of no fault compensation will not have been wasted if it leads to a more open dialogue between doctors, patients and their representatives. Patients would then feel that they would get an explanation of what went wrong. Often, people say that they do not want money, they just want someone to admit that a mistake was made, and to understand what went wrong.

Two points raised on this occasion have encouraged me on behalf of patients. Mrs Brahams spoke about the aspect of the Swedish system which involves lay people in discussing negligence and where things have gone wrong, and Dr Ham said there was a great need to improve the complaints procedure.

I hope that in future discussions on these subjects the medical professionals will involve other professionals, that is, the patients, who do actually know something about their own bodies.

9

The view of the plaintiff's lawyer

Mark Mildred

My starting point is that of the plaintiff's solicitor. I must therefore be extremely self-critical when making public my reservations about a system which, on the face of it, would weigh the scales in the plaintiff's favour.

I remember when I decided to become a lawyer being told by a lecturer that the no fault system proposed in a limited form by the Pearson Commission in 1968, which then seemed to me the most fair and obvious thing in the world, was opposed as much by lawyers with a large plaintiff practice in the personal injury field as by the insurance interests. So I must guard against my then naiveté being replaced by a similar self-interest. I am unsure, being invited to contribute to this symposium, what is the ambit for a no fault system under consideration. If it is solely to the field which is now known as medical negligence, the pros and cons are relatively simple. Even so, it is necessary to examine the problem from first principles and I shall begin, before proceeding to practical considerations, by asking what is the philosophical basis for no fault compensation.

Compensation is presumably meant to compensate those who have suffered damage or injury. Traditionally we have allowed individuals to insure themselves against such damage or injury and to rely upon that insurance when the damage or injury could not be shown to be or to have been, the responsibility of a third party.

For a third party to be liable to pay compensation, concepts of fault, for example, negligence, recklessness, breach of contract, defective products, have been prerequisites.

Obviously, in most cases the person injured by another is not morally superior to a person injured without such intervention. If he is, it can only be on the basis that the latter has been guilty of negligence or some other fault on his own account, for example by slipping over his own banana skin. If it is thought right that fault should no longer be a relevant criterion in the former case, why should it preclude recovery in the latter?

It seems to me, therefore, that if there is to be a no fault based system, it is illogical in principle to discriminate between the provision of adequate financial recompense to those who have and those who have not, been injured at the hands of another. The extension of this is clearly the provision of a welfare system adequate to give a decent standard of living to anyone injured or chronically sick or deprived, by reason of a medical condition, of reasonable financial security.

Even more clearly, such a Utopia is inconceivable in general and, particularly, in the current and foreseeable political climate. Even a change of Government would surely not lead to the establishment of such a system.

To sum up, if there is a *moral* case for no fault compensation, it must apply to everyone and not be dependent on the intervention of a third party. This is too remote a prospect to be discussed in the real world and, therefore, the desirability of the introduction of such a system must be judged by practical considerations.

The background against which the debate takes place is that a remedy is only available to about 20% of those who suffer accidental injury (the rest sustaining accidents for which no one is liable) and of that 20% only a quarter pursue the remedy which is in theory open to them. Anything which increases availability and improves the rate of take-up is to be welcomed.

What stands in the way of the 75% of those who have, but do not pursue, a remedy? Experience suggests strong subjective factors without objective validity such as fear of publicity, fear of upsetting people and simple ignorance.

Problems of the legal system

There are also the problems which are hurdles introduced by the legal system itself. The most important of these are five in number: delay, cost, definition of damage, proof of causation and the regulation of standards.

1. Delay

If a no fault system could reduce the sometimes unacceptable delays in the present judicial system, that would be a powerful argument in its favour. This delay has many sources including the reluctance of plaintiffs to assert their rights, delay in formulating a claim by their advisers, delay in obtaining Legal Aid and expert evidence, delay in making proper discovery, delay by the defendants' advisers or insurers dealing with the claim and delay (when all parties are ready) in obtaining a trial date. The remedy for all of these may exist without the introduction of a no fault system and in some cases steps have been taken towards this. I shall examine these causes of delay in turn.

The way to prevent a delay in the assertion of rights is to insist on prompt prosecution of the claim once proceedings have been issued. Three years to issue and one year to serve will very soon be a thing of the past.

Delays in Legal Aid are more of a problem, particularly given the Government's wish to control Legal Aid expenditure. There is marked variation between different area Legal Aid Authorities in the speed with which they deal with applications for certificates or amendments to certificates and the latitude which they are prepared to give to plaintiffs' advisers who prosecute the claim, once certificates are granted.

Again, the Civil Justice Review has recommended that solicitors should have more power and responsibility in the future and that the regular march to and from Counsel's Chambers, costly in terms of time and money, each time a question needs to be resolved, should cease. The new Legal Aid Act gives the Lord Chancellor power to make regulations to permit the Legal Aid Board to contract for the services of specialist lawyers in appropriate cases. An obvious use for this would be in multi-plaintiff litigation where time and costs could be saved by the uniformity so given to the plaintiffs' case.

All these points provide hope that delays caused by the plaintiffs' side may be minimized in future. Of course they will still exist but the increasing trend towards specialisation (again likely to prosper after the Civil Justice Review) should greatly diminish the effect.

We must now turn to delay on the part of the defendants. Justly or not, insurance companies are reputed to do their best to keep their money as long as possible. The 2% rate of interest on general damages does nothing to discourage them. Unfortunately, the Health Authorities and Defence Organisations appear to adopt the same attitude. Until recently they have been notoriously difficult about the disclosure of medical records where requests for disclosure impose an administrative burden, that burden is discharged by the undertaking for costs given by the plaintiffs' advisers. It frequently appears to be no more than a gambit intended to discourage the litigant and deter an adviser who may not be confident of his ground. In medical negligence cases in which I have been involved, it has been perfectly obvious what were the facts and what were the risks to the defendants from the date of disclosure of the medical records onwards.

Whilst the approach of the trial date concentrates the minds of both sides, it appears to have an inordinate effect on the minds of some of those who represent defendants in these cases. If the medical world is now in favour of cutting down delays, it could begin by instructing its advisers to give more realistic advice earlier on and to indicate promptly when only quantum was likely to be in dispute. The fact that Health Authorities and doctors from different defence organisations are separately represented is often a major cause of delay and is something which a no fault system would not change. In a case to which I shall refer later, the alleged negligent act took place on 8th April 1983, the Statement of Claim was served on 18th July 1986 and the trial began in the week commencing 1st January 1989. At the beginning of December 1988 (about twenty working days or so from the beginning of the trial) I was told that an illustrious firm of solicitors (who shall remain nameless) were about to serve a Notice to say that they were now acting for the Defendants in place of another illustrious firm. The defendants had not changed. The act of alleged negligence had not changed; it was and always had been an act by a member of the Defence Organisation represented by the new solicitors. A week later it emerged that this change would not now take place: the "new" firm would simply continue behind the scenes to pull the strings operating the "old" firm. Until the defendants can act in a more straightforward manner, a no fault system may be premature.

Next, the delay in obtaining expert evidence is a very real problem from the plaintiff's point of view. It is much easier than it used to be to obtain appropriate expert assistance but any such expert will fit his or her role as expert into an already crowded timetable.

This problem would not be cured totally (although it might be eased) by the introduction of a no fault system, simply because expert reports on causation and damage will still be required in every case. The "simple" question of negligence rarely takes up much of the experts' time.

Delays in obtaining proper discovery and other procedural matters are symptoms of the extraordinarily laissez-faire attitude which both sides and the Court have hitherto been inclined to take towards the timetables imposed by the Rules of Court. The remedy lies in the hands of the plaintiffs (who are getting better at cracking the whip) and the Court which is likely to be given more "hands-on" powers following the recommendations of the Civil Justice Review.

No fault will not have a great effect on delays owing to waiting lists and the Court timetable. There are very few trials in personal injury cases already (2% according to the Civil Justice Review). If under a no fault system, there will be disputes on causation, damage and quantum and if the parties in general and the defendants in particular will not come to terms earlier, the problem will remain and may even increase and can only be answered by increased provision of judicial time and other Court facilities.

2. Costs

Turning to the subject of costs, I must be more self-critical than ever. When I first heard that some solicitors create work by writing unnecessary letters etc, I was aghast. The US experience (and it is only the comparatively small number of outlandishly large awards which make the news) is ceaselessly paraded in front of the Courts and the public with considerable deterrent effect.

I accept that there are a number of exceedingly rich American trial lawyers. That owes almost everything to the existence of the jury and the contingency fee system in the US. To me, the case against the first is equivocal and that against the second unconvincing. *The major injustice in the British system is that the combination of the financial limits on eligibility for the Legal Aid Scheme exclude probably half the population of this country from the judicial process.* That cannot be right or fair. However, in very few cases will the absence of the fault criterion give the non-legally aided plaintiff the confidence to embark upon litigation with all its attendant worries as to costs. The case for extending the financial eligibility for the Legal Aid Scheme in claims involving product liability or medical negligence, where the complexities of science and medicine, let alone those of law, are matched only by the imbalance of resources between the parties seems to be unanswerable.

Delay and the deterrence of the costs discipline are in one sense peripheral issues. If a no fault system radically simplified litigation in practice, means could be devised to surmount those obstacles.

I will now discuss the two major conceptual (as opposed to procedural) matters, namely the identification of damage and the proof of causation.

3. Definition of damage

For reasons discussed earlier, damages for all is unlikely and the intervention of a third party and the act or omission of that third party (whether negligent or otherwise) is likely to be essential to found a claim. Is a defendant or its insurers prepared to pay for the outcome of all such acts and omissions?

In the medical field there seem to be the following categories:

1. Those whom treatment fails to make well.
2. Those whose health is adversely affected by their treatment.
3. Those whose health is improved by a treatment which itself causes undesired side effects.

There is little reason in principle and no chance in practice of establishing a scheme to compensate those in the first category. An insurance-based scheme (since any extension of the National Insurance Scheme appears to be out of the question at present) could as a matter of practice be made to work for the second category. If the cases in the third category are not to be paid, the justification must be an extension of the concept of the informed consent. Whether patients would gamble with the risk described or be put off treatment completely, to their detriment, is impossible to say.

At present the doctor or hospital administering a potentially life-saving drug with potentially serious and occasionally lethal side effects would be absolved from liability by the risk–benefit ratio doctrine. Under a no fault system, the damage would be attributable to the act or omission of the doctor and there would be liability. If the answer is to obtain a better (that is more informed or more encyclopaedic) form of consent from the patient, one would simply be using the law of contract to take away rights which the existing system protects and which the no fault system is advertised as enhancing.

In the case I mentioned earlier, whose trial began this week, my client sustained a perforation of the uterus in the course of a surgical termination of pregnancy. The defendant's experts tell us that this is a recognised complication and occurs in one in a thousand cases. "Quite right", says our expert "But that does not tell you why it occurs". In this case we say it occurred because of a very specific act of incompetence by a doctor. Indeed, the consultant who undertook the laparotomy and corrective procedure demonstrated and recorded in the notes why it had happened. Under the present system my client has a chance of obtaining damages. Under a system which precludes recovery for an acknowledged risk she would have none, even if she had in fact been injured by the fault of her doctor. This is a direct example of a no fault system diminishing rather than increasing the rights of the patient.

Again, it would be necessary to think very carefully how the defence of *volenti non fit iniuria* and the means of diminishing the damages payable in the event of fault on the part of the claimant (contributory negligence) should be fitted into a no fault system. In logic, they have no place at all since, if the conduct of the defendant is left out of account, that of the plaintiff can surely not be brought into account. Would it, however, not be wholly inimical to society if damages in full were awarded to the entirely negligent drunken pedestrian who lurched into the path of the wholly blameless driver? Certainly, the pedestrian will need equal medical care and may have suffered equal financial loss to that of the wholly blameless claimant but firstly, as I have argued above, the requirement of intervention of a third party robs the no fault system of most of its moral force and secondly, as a matter of practical politics, is it likely that such a result would find favour in the current social and political climate?

4. Proof of causation

Proof of causation is always (except in the simplest case) the most difficult hurdle for the claimant. For pedestrians run down on pedestrian crossings, passengers in ferries with open bow doors and workers on exploding oil rigs causation is no problem and it is easy to settle those claims. The defendant is insured and the insurers pay up. I consider the initiative recently launched for no fault insurance available for example to football clubs and restaurants to be an excellent idea which could genuinely, if administered as advertised, make life very simple for those suffering at the hands, or rather on the premises, of those insured. But they are not the difficult cases.

The classic problem is in the pharmaceutical claim. Here there are two major areas of difficulty. The first is that cause and effect can never, for ethical reasons, be demonstrated experimentally in the human. What survives by way of evidence is of four types. The least useful is animal evidence whose significance can never really be more than exclusionary. The second is biochemical where a theory may be plausible but is inherently hypothetical. The third is epidemiological. This is useful and perhaps necessary. However, the plaintiff never has the choice of studies which he would like to be done at his disposal. Almost all studies are either vulnerable on methodological grounds or, if sound, too small for their results to be more than ambivalent. It is easy for the defendants (upon whom no burden of proof rests) to pick holes in them. The last type of evidence is clinical evidence which may often be effective but is vulnerable to the existence of non-specific side effects.

The second difficult area is caused by the fact that no pharmaceutical product causes a unique side effect. The lower the background rate, the easier the cause and effect of the relationship is to detect and prove. But how is the Court to cope with the common side effect or with the difficulty of showing that the side effect in a particular individual case was one caused by the product rather than one of the background?

I know of no answer to the first question and the answer which was thought to exist in the second has recently been dealt a mortal blow.

That putative answer was provided by the case of **McGhee v National Coal Board [1973] 1 WLR HL**. A worker in a brick works contracted dermatitis. It was accepted that the failure to provide showers to wash off the brick dust was negligent and it was proved that the incidence of dermatitis was lower after a shower than without it. The House of Lords decided (or until recently we thought they did) that, where the negligence of the defendant caused a material increase in the risk of a condition and that condition then appeared in fact, the burden of proof then passed to the defendant who, in order to avoid liability, had to show that his negligence did not cause the injury, rather than that the plaintiff should be obliged to prove that it did. They acknowledged that it was impossible to say for certain whether a particular injury was one caused by a product or process or was one of the pre-existing background number.

In a complex case this was the major weapon in the claimants' arsenal. It did not diminish the difficulties of epidemiology but, if some respectable statistics could be found, it saddled the defendants with the necessity of showing that the plaintiff was a background case rather than a case caused by their product.

That weapon has, since the decision of the House of Lords in **Wilsher v Essex Health Authority [1988] 1 AU ER 871** on the 10th March 1988, been torn from the Plaintiff's grasp. Wilsher was a medical negligence case. The facts were that a premature baby suffered, amongst other things, from oxygen deficiency. Whilst in a special baby unit a catheter was twice inserted into a vein rather than an artery. On both occasions he was given excess oxygen and later discovered to be suffering from an incurable condition of the retina resulting in near blindness. This could have been caused by excess oxygen but it also occurs in premature babies suffering from five other common conditions, all of which the plaintiff had. The medical evidence was inconclusive as to whether the excess oxygen or one of the other conditions caused or materially contributed to the plaintiff's retinal condition. The decision of the House of Lords was that where a plaintiff's injury was attributable to a number of possible causes, one of which was the defendant's negligence, the combination of the defendant's negligence and the plaintiff's injury did *not* give rise to the presumption that the defendant had caused the injury. Instead the burden remained on the plaintiff to prove the causative link between defendant's negligence and his injury although that link could legitimately be inferred from the evidence.

Since there were six potential causes, the plaintiff failed because he could not say that it was more likely than not that it was the negligent acts of the hospital which were the cause of his condition. In other words, it is now necessary to show a specific cause before the defendant is offered the escape hatch of showing that this is one of the background cases. This is likely in practice to diminish the chances of plaintiffs obtaining judgments in complex cases where there are a number of different possible factors at work. For this reason I do not believe that the question of fault is determinative or even crucial in most complex litigation.

Further evidence for this proposition can be found in the outcome of product liability cases, particularly in the pharmaceutical field. Where causation is clear (for example, thalidomide, Eraldin and, to some extent, Opren) the defendants or their insurers prefer to gain in public relations terms and avoid a costly fight on the question of negligence by settling. Where there is genuine doubt as to causation (e.g. Primodos and Debendox) the cases are defended even where the plaintiff's case on negligence may appear strong. Where the benzodiazepines will fit into this picture remains to be seen.

The ultimate irony in this area is comprised in the closing remarks of the judgment in Wilsher by Lord Bridge who said "Many may feel that such a result serves only to highlight the shortcomings of the system in which the victim of some grevious misfortune will recover substantial compensation or none at all according to the unpredictable hazards of the forensic process. But, whether we like it or not, the law, which only Parliament can change, requires proof of fault causing damage as the basis of liability in tort. We should do society nothing but disservice if we made the forensic process still more unpredictable and hazardous by distorting the law to accommodate the exigencies of what may seem hard cases".

The expression of this sympathy (which we must all share) for the plaintiff must have led Lord Bridge to forget that the reason for which he had just decided the case in the Health Authority's favour had absolutely nothing to do with the fault principle (and therefore the no fault system would not have helped the plaintiff at all) but was that the plaintiff could not prove causation to a satisfactory standard.

5. Regulation of standards

There is no doubt that Westminster and Brussels between them publish an ever-increasing amount of regulations at the same time as the Government is attempting to roll back the frontiers of the State and diminish the proportion of the National Income devoted to Government expenditure. It seems therefore that the effective policing of regulatory standards must be difficult to achieve. It may follow from this (and I put this forward tentatively as a suggestion rather than a concluded view) that the private sector in the shape of litigants may have a role to play in the upkeep of standards which would be threatened by the introduction of a no fault system.

The professions probably believe that they can regulate themselves: my experience is that their confidence is not always shared by the consumers of their services. I therefore remain to be convinced that the disadvantages of a no fault system would outweigh its advantages.

To bring about a net advantage, I would need to see persuasive evidence that no fewer categories of injury than before would be compensated, that costs to the consumer would fall, that the Court and the parties (and especially the defendants) would improve upon past records on delay and that standards could be maintained without fault criterion. I believe that a no fault insurance system for straightforward cases of the occupiers' liability type would be acceptable and desirable and indeed would fit in with existing insurance arrangements, such as those in the transport field. If an insurance system or a system of law could be devised which met the particular difficulties of the plaintiff in the pharmaceutical field, it should be introduced, provided it dealt adequately with the problem of causation and did not diminish the categories or definition of damage for which a manufacturer is presently liable. This is one field where the savings in terms of legal costs might justify the change of standard of proof from "more likely than not" to "a reasonable medical possibility".

I am conscious of having made several remarks which may be interpreted as rather negative. Change is certainly needed but I believe that much necessary change could be and will be effected through the procedural changes which are presently being or about to be implemented.

To end on a positive note and to prove my caution against self-interest, I recommend the following panacea: expedite the procedural changes, freeze lawyers' fees and double damages.

References

1. McGhee *v*. National Coal Board (1973). 1 WLR HL.
2. Wilsher *v*. Essex Health Authority (1988). 1 AU ER 871.

10

A prescription for medical negligence

D. A. McIntosh

Unlike most of the contributors to this Symposium my reputation is founded upon defending personal injury litigation, usually on behalf of major corporations, including pharmaceutical companies and their insurers. Although I am influenced by this role I hope to demonstrate that I cannot be included within the category of British lawyers described by Diana Brahams as having a vested interest in maintaining the status quo by jeopardising the implementation of a Swedish-style no fault scheme for medical injury because of "selfish, short-term interests". Indeed, I wonder if such a group of legal charlatans exist, other than in the imagination of a few.

I make these points because those who do not welcome in every respect the urgings of an ever-growing band of consumer activists, run the risk of being vilified, even where their criticisms are objective and, in the context of no fault compensation scheme proposals, sensibly linked with the difficulty of financing an acceptable alternative to the present adversarial tort system.

Although the previous speaker, Mark Mildred, and I are regularly in oppostion, most notably in the Opren litigation, we share the view that if a practical no fault compensation scheme can be devised and implemented for the victims of medical accidents, we, and the vast majority of lawyers who now benefit from the tort system, would welcome it and redeploy their talents on other work. I hope, therefore, these proceedings will lead to the setting up of a working party which will be effective in introducing a pilot scheme which, if not to replace, will run in tandem with the tort system and reduce the incidence of adversarial litigation in the medical negligence and drug-related fields.

As I am not a physician, I cannot offer a full prescription for the malady which professional negligence constitutes. I do, however, urge all those involved to take cognisance of the fact that for fiscal reasons a complete cure may not yet be available, and it would be a pity to shoot the pianist when the piano is out of tune. It is, I believe, necessary to examine the extent to which the short-comings of the present tort system can be overcome, before assuming that the only way forward is the introduction of an affordable no fault scheme which would be attractive enough to all of the vested interests to make it a practical proposition.

The present tort system

We are all entitled to expect that others will conduct themselves with reasonable care in their dealings with us, and that if they do not, and as a result cause us injury, they will have to make good our loss by way of monetary compensation. If, on the other hand, any one of us suffers the misfortunes that the vicissitudes of everyday life deal out, such as the contraction of a major illness, we have no right to demand that our fellows compensate us for it.

The main criticisms of the tort system, as it stands, are that:

(1) only a proportion of the persons injured in accidents recover compensation;
(2) the evidence necessary to establish fault is often difficult to gather and present;
(3) it is impossible to assess compensation accurately or to establish uniformity of awards;
(4) the legal process is adversarial and very much in contrast with the caring relationship which it tends to replace after a medical accident has occurred;
(5) by no means every plaintiff is able to obtain the services of a solicitor with all of the relevant expertise to pursue complicated litigation;
(6) the procedures involved in pursuing a claim for damages are lengthy and expensive for both plaintiffs and defendants and only available to the wealthy and those who qualify for Legal Aid;
(7) the deterrent effect of penalising those who have perpetrated the "fault" giving rise to the claim for compensation is undermined by the widespread availability of insurance coverage.

These criticisms are heightened when these shortcomings are exposed in an exaggerated way by litigation of a type which the rules of procedure cannot properly accommodate or which cannot be easily financed; for example, the Opren litigation; where defendants refuse to admit liability or accede to the now regular plea for a voluntary compensation scheme immediately after a mass disaster has occurred or a drug-related case arisen; for example, the Bradford City Football Club Fire, the Abbeystead Waterworks Explosion, the Zeebrugge disaster, the Piper Alpha Rig collapse and the pertussis vaccine and Opren cases; where fault and/or causation are in dispute, as in the pertussis vaccine and the Wilsher case, or where cases, irrespective of their outcome, reach trial or are settled far too slowly, as in the Keith Blackburn and Malinka Head cases, which I will be discussing later.

When any of this occurs, the media not only criticise defendants for choosing to do no more than to defend themselves, but also complain about the system of compensation itself. The press, radio and television are not, however, as quick to focus on the fact that in many of the above cases justice has been speedy and effective because of the skills of plaintiffs' lawyers and the co-operation of defendants and their insurers, and that in other cases the real fault lies with the inefficient way in which the claims have been pursued.

The pressures for change

It is not a coincidence that as the debate on the merits of replacing the present tort system of compensation with no-fault schemes is gathering pace, United Kingdom consumer action groups, who are vociferous in harnessing the media, astute on lobbying Governments, and skilled in targeting their campaigns, are proliferating. These groups always have easy access to plaintiffs' lawyers who, although not, as yet, rewarded by way of US-style "contingency fee" payments, nevertheless have, understandably, vested interests in easing the path towards recovering compensation for personal injury, however and wherever an accident occurs.

Whether we welcome it or not, we all now live in a consumer-led society and the trend to which we are reacting today is likely to be a continuing one, only impeded by what society as a whole can afford to do by way of compensating the injured. On this, the United States' "tort crisis" experience stands as an example.

Escalating jury awards, sometimes with a punitive element, applied within a "strict liability" system of law, advanced year-by-year without, until recently, causing any second thoughts on the part of society as a whole. It was only comparatively recently, when the medical profession, municipalities and others providing essential services, began to find it impossible to obtain insurance coverage at an affordable price that, belatedly, steps have been taken, albeit inadequately, to redress the balance.

Europe is not yet facing a "tort crisis" of the type which has been experienced within the United States but it is clear that the basis for recovery of damages and the size of awards has a very long way to run in Europe before the momentum of European consumerism backfires upon itself.

There is a perception that it is far too difficult for injured claimants to prosecute their claims successfully in the courts of the United Kingdom. As a result, we have recently been subjected to a major review of civil litigation in the United Kingdom conducted by the Lord Chancellor's office, which has recommended substantial procedural change and calls for a better way of financing personal injury litigation, especially mass tort cases, than is currently the case under the present Legal Aid rules. The ensuing debate has provided the perfect forum for consumer groups who clamour for even greater change. Prominent amongst these is the UK's Citizen Action Group (CITCOM) who have put forward a number of proposals aimed at improving the present system and in increasing the levels of damages recoverable.

Lord Scarman, as well as being associated with CITCOM's proposals, is a prominent supporter of the introduction of a no fault scheme of compensation with, in his case, an emphasis upon introducing it for injuries caused by motor vehicles and into certain fields of strict liability. This he urged in an article in The Times on the 21st June 1988 in which he concluded that, "In a high technological society, accidents will happen: and the casualties must be properly and promptly compensated at reasonable cost". Those words can easily be applied to medical and drug-related accidents.

It is not, therefore, surprising that because of its caring nature the medical profession is in the vanguard of seeking a no fault solution so far as medical injuries are concerned. Indeed, it is impossible to disagree with the opening paragraph of the Report of the British Medical Association's No Fault Compensation Working Party which was published in 1987 and which read as follows:

"As a caring profession, we wish to see adequate arrangements to provide compensation and support to those who suffer personal injury, given according to need and not according to cause. It is clear that patients with similar disabilities may receive different benefits under current provisions. A child may remain brain damaged following (a) encephalitis, (b) vaccine innoculation, (c) traumatic birth delivery. The needs of all three children may be similar. There will be great sympathy for all three sets of parents. However, the available compensation will range from no compensation at all, through £20,000 to some hundreds of thousands of pounds. This cannot be logical, fair or sensible."

The Report's recommendations, which were accepted by the Council of the BMA, were in favour of:

(a) supporting the principle of a non-statutory scheme within defined limits which will provide compensation for medical accidents without apportionment of blame;
(b) seeking to interest Government and other concerned parties in a pioneer pilot scheme to provide adequate compensation and support for those in need.

These objectives understandably represent the pre-disposition of this meeting and are something which I suspect most speakers and panelists will support. I do, albeit with some qualification.

The medical profession's concerns

By its nature, the medical profession and the pharmaceutical industry should always demonstrate a caring approach and should not be discouraged from openly participating in procedures designed to establish accountability. The present adversarial system of resolving disputes over entitlement to compensation not only discourages openness but encourages a closing of ranks and an "arm's length" approach through solicitors. Although I have no doubt that those from the medical and pharmaceutical ranks personally involved would like to see individual injured claimants compensated, those sentiments become subsumed to other interests such as:

(a) behind the scenes apportionment of blame between a number of individuals and organisations who might be implicated. Problems of this type most commonly occur when the medical accident occurs in hospital where, for example, there is scope for blaming nursing staff as well as the doctors or surgeons in charge. More than one doctor or surgeon can find themselves "in the frame". The multiple involvements do not, however, stop there, for the interests of the nursing staff are looked after by their employers, the Regional Health Authorities, and the doctors by one or more of the three Medical Defence societies. Even where it is plain that a claimant should be compensated on a "fault" basis, if these competing interests cannot reach agreement long drawn-out litigation can ensue.
(b) the requirements of Circular 54(32), which came into effect in 1954, and which set out the procedures to be adopted when more than one doctor may have been negligent in the treatment of a patient. This Circular was designed to limit defendant doctors joining others of their fraternity as third or fourth parties to litigation and, instead, requires apportionment of blame disputes to be resolved privately. It continues to be followed but provides little guidance when deadlocks occur between Health Authorities and Defence societies. Its effect contributes to the widely-held impression that doctors close ranks when professional negligence is alleged.
(c) cash restraints which appear to impinge very substantially on the willingness of Health Authorities to contribute to financial settlements in substantial personal injury cases.
(d) the fear of personal stigmatisation which can dissuade medical practitioners and nurses from accepting blame, particularly where they feel that others are equally or to some extent blameworthy.

The above factors contribute in no uncertain way towards the delay for which the medical profession and other defendants are regularly blamed. Nevertheless, some of the delays which have occurred are indefensible.

Perhaps the best, or should I say worst, example of this is the Keith Blackburn case where he and his family had to wait 12 years for civil justice. That delay brings into question the approach of the three firms of solicitors who first represented Mr Blackburn. Luckily, he finished up in the hands of the fourth firm, namely, Mark Mildred's, and a £490,000–plus award was obtained where previously Mr Blackburn had been told he had no case.

Not surprisingly, this outcome received a great deal of media attention and the Medical Defence Union's advisers found it necessary to write to The Times newspaper in, *inter alia*, the following terms:

"The doctors were acquitted of negligence. The Judge, Sir Frederick Lawton, found that the cause of Mr Blackburn's brain damage was the failure of a nurse to clean out the tracheotomy tube sufficiently frequently.

This allegation was added to the pleadings in 1986, ten years after the event. By this time, the nurse who was caring for Mr Blackburn at the time could not be traced.

The significant clinical notes were disclosed in 1982. It is true that the secretary of the hospital declined to disclose them initially because he was not told what was being alleged. The Judge declared his decision reasonable but complained that the secretary failed to alert others who would have taken steps to protect the intensive-care unit's detailed records, which might have enabled the Health Authority to vindicate the actions of the nurse."

Surely the Medical Defence Union and the Health Authority's advisers knew from very early on where the fault, if any, lay, and yet, no doubt for some of the reasons I have identified, the doctors were advised not to blame the nurse and, rightly or wrongly, Mr Blackburn's then lawyers failed to hone their allegations properly. Bad publicity was inevitable had Mr Blackburn given up or had he, at the end of the day, lost instead of won.

The case of Malinka Head who, in October 1988, recovered £800,000 seven years after suffering brain damage as a result of hospital staff giving her too much fluid intravenously following the removal of her ruptured appendix when she was eight years old, is another bad example. Liability was kept in issue until December 1986 and, thereafter, the dispute was limited to the amount of the damages recoverable. The Regional Legal Adviser for the Health Authority involved is reported to have admitted after the hearing that it was a matter of regret that it had taken so long to admit liability. This expression of regret occurred, notwithstanding, as I understand it, that the civil litigation was underscored by references to the Medical Services Committee and to the General Medical Council, from which I believe there was an unsuccessful appeal on behalf of one of the doctors involved.

Twelve and eight years delay respectively in single-plaintiff cases, however complex, strikes me as unforgivable and, in view of their outcome and attendant publicity, something which ought to have been avoided by all of the parties' legal advisers.

Although the primary responsibility for efficiently prosecuting personal injury litigation lies heavily upon plaintiffs' solicitors, it is not only plaintiffs, the courts and, eventually, the media who should be concerned over unnecessary delay: in my experience the vast majority of defendants and insurers dislike personal injury cases dragging their heels.

Awards of damages have, over recent years, risen markedly, and the longer a case runs the more it costs in legal expense on both sides. It is in the interests of defendants and defendants' practitioners not to allow undue delay, particularly as in most cases it is only too easy to blame defendants for it, even where the fault lies elsewhere.

The possibility of out-of-court settlements which reflect the merits and likely values of claims should always be explored but, if settlements cannot be achieved amicably, there are steps open to defendants' lawyers to ensure that cases are as quickly as possible pursued towards hearings. In some cases, defendants who feel confident as to the merits of their defence ought to be anxious to have their names cleared by way of judicial decision.

I make these observations as the way in which the medical profession often appears to respond to professional negligence claims is damaging to its overall image and, as a result, undermining of one of the objectives of defending, namely, to avoid the stigmatising of individual professional reputations. Furthermore, it cannot be attractive to any medical practitioner to have a legal case pending for many years.

The practice of nearly always defending to the hilt (for that is the public perception of Regional Health Authorities and of the medical profession as a whole when involved in personal injury litigation) does, of course, have a deterrent effect, and I do not know to what extent this may have saved Health Authorities, the medical profession and the Medical Defence societies a great deal of money by way of discouraging claims, either from the onset or by wearing down opponents. I do, however, wonder whether the sort of publicity generated by cases of the type I have mentioned makes those savings worthwhile.

Because of its current preoccupation with the attractions of a no fault system of compensation, there is a risk that the medical profession will not make every possible effort to improve the way in which the present tort system operates and, in particular, the way in which it defends those cases which are brought against it.

Instead, and I know this is unwitting, the medical profession gives the public the impression that it would like to wash its hands of the present tort system. On first impression, that is something with which everyone is likely to sympathise but, on analysis, it might prove unwise to burn all of the bridges unless and until a medically–comprehensive no fault alternative can be organised, financed and put in place.

It must be remembered that the adversarial system has, with all of its defects, served society reasonably well, and that whilst it is open to a great deal of criticism, we are not suffering from a crisis in confidence so far as the practice of medicine and the prescribing of drugs is concerned, and we do have a State-funded benefits system which prevents extreme hardship.

There is also a danger if it is perceived that the medical profession in promoting a no fault system, is intent on doing so at somebody else's expense. If such a system can be devised which replaces or minimises recourse to adversarial litigation, then surely the medical profession and the Regional Health Authorities as the main beneficiaries, should, with appropriate Government support, stand a very substantial proportion of the expense involved. This outlay would, at least in part, be provided by way of savings upon the financial contributions they make under the tort system. In addition, the pharmaceutical industry ought to be willing to contribute in line with the incidence of claims in which its products are implicated.

The real savings and the ability to deflect monies into a no fault scheme, will come from reducing the amount spent on the legal costs of adversarial litigation:

not only in lawyer's fees but in the substantial sums expended on experts. Annual defence costs (including the sums paid by defendants to successful plaintiffs' lawyers) are said substantially to exceed the aggregate sum paid out by way of damages. That may amount to a testimonial to the skills of defence lawyers but, nevertheless, constitutes a waste of money if that same sum can be more usefully used as compensation for a greater number of victims of medical accidents.

The pharmaceutical industry's concerns

Cases like Opren demonstrate that the pharmaceutical industry is often at the "sharp" end of medical negligence cases. Indeed, wherever a pharmaceutical product is implicated, the drug company which supplied it becomes the "target" defendant. It is seen as a potentially liable party with bottomless pockets and as an entity more likely to contribute towards an out-of-court settlement than are doctors, Health Authorities and Government defendants, such as the DHSS in its licensing capacity. Indeed, within the Opren litigation, there was a policy decision amongst the lead firms of solicitors involved not to blame doctors, even in those cases where there might have been a case against them. It is fair to observe that one of the reasons for this was the recognition that the last thing that elderly patients would normally wish to do is to sue their own trusted General Practitioner when other targets were available.

Many of the pharamceutical companies who supply products here in the United Kingdom have also experienced the effect of the medical malpractice/tort crisis in the United States, with the result that they are unable to obtain worldwide product liability insurance cover to the same extent or at the same rates of premium as used to be available. This is hardly surprising, given the importation of US consumerist trends into Europe, as evidenced by the EEC Products Liability Directive and the legislation in all of the EEC countries to bring it into effect.

Nobody is yet able to measure the extent to which the importation of strict liability, albeit with the state of the art defence retained here in the United Kingdom, will have upon pharmaceutical companies. It is, however, recognised that the incidence of claims is bound to increase.

The pharmaceutical industry lobbied hard and long for the retention, within the EEC Directive, of the "state of the art" defence, which has been retained in most, if not all, of the member states.

Our Consumers' Association take the view, on the basis of English legal advice, that the "state of the art" defence, as contained in the Consumer Protection Act, is wider than permitted under the Directive. The Association's legal officer, David Tench, has described the "development risk" defence wording of the Act as "flabby" and has likened it to allowing the rest to remain one of "negligence" as opposed to one of "strict liability".

In contrast, the Association of the British Pharmaceutical Industry (ABPI), which campaigned to have that defence included in the Act, says that it is happy with the wording of the Act because it introduces a notion of "reasonability".

Although I have no doubt that the pharmaceutical industry would support a workable alternative to the present adversarial tort system, within which it often sees itself as a victim, it would no doubt shy away from supporting any scheme which imposed upon it the financial burdens which exceed the present cost (whether by way of insurance premiums or directly) it undertakes in defending itself, if at the same time it is not insulated against claims which are not reasonably foreseeable.

Furthermore, as an industry, it is bound to be sceptical with regard to any suggestions which appear designed to pass onto it financial obligations which are out of line with the incidence of claims which the industry faces under the present tort system.

Cognisance must also be taken of the fact that even if a satisfactory no fault solution can be devised for the United Kingdom, it will not insulate many members of the pharmaceutical industry against the risk of adversarial litigation being pursued against them in the United States where the necessary predicates for the exercise of US jurisdiction over particular companies exist. Nor would such a scheme, unless it supplanted the right to sue in the English courts, negate high profile litigation where plaintiffs, or more likely groups of them, decide to pursue, with media backing, claims for compensation where the issue in dispute is causation and/or the adequacy of warnings. Had a no fault scheme been in place working in tandem with the tort system, I wonder whether it would have answered the needs of the Opren and pertussis vaccine claimants and whether their litigation in the courts would still have been necessary.

The concern of the government

Whilst the Government and the individuals who comprise it are no doubt sympathetic towards the plight of the victims of accidents, they are looking at a much wider context in considering where to invest the wealth of the United Kingdom insofar as they consider that to be a matter for Government. If there was an overwhelming case for a no fault substitute for the present tort system which would cover all accidents, not just medical cases, then, subject to affordability, the Government ought to be involved in promoting the idea. Even then, however, one would expect governmental responsibilities to take into account the distinction which would still exist between those disabled by accidents and those disabled by nature. Why should one category of "victims" be favoured by way of access to compensation and not the other?

Albeit with reluctance in many quarters, this gathering appears to have accepted that there is no short-term prospect of our present Government underwriting a comprehensive no fault scheme and, if that is so, it is perhaps naive to expect it substantially to underwrite a pilot scheme tailor-made by and for the medical profession. I suspect the most that can sensibly be anticipated is a willingness on the part of Government to re-direct the money which it already provides through its responsibilities to the public health sector, in responding to medical negligence claims.

Indeed, recent indications suggest that the Government is hoping that private insurance-backed solutions will be found. The Prime Minister was said to be more than passingly interested in the limited Personal Accident Insurance Scheme devised by my firm as a partial solution, so far as injuries to visitors to premises are concerned. Mrs Thatcher so indicated when she was being questioned in the House regarding the Piper Alpha disaster in the context of opposition demands that the no fault provisions of the Pearson Report should be implemented.

Any Government wishing to side-step the issue of no fault compensation has ample opportunity to do so by expressing an intent to wait and see how implementation of the Civil Justice Review recommendation improves the operation of the present tort system in 1991 and beyond, and can also point to the "importance" of waiting until the late 1990s when the EEC Products Liability Directive provides for a review after 10 years of its implementation within the member States.

Other interested viewpoints

The legal profession

The legal profession in general appears unwilling to support the replacement of the present adversarial system (which has no financial limitation on the amounts recoverable) by any scheme which has financial capping of compensation built into it. Plaintiffs' practitioners, in particular, appear firmly set against financial capping. It does, however, seem to me, if you accept my view, that the vast majority of tort practitioners are not solely interested in their continued ability to make their living from the adversarial system, that it would be extremely difficult for the legal profession to resist a partial solution by way of a compensation scheme that ran in tandem with the tort system, with the claimant able to sue, as at present, for damages at large if the compensation scheme does not satisfy him.

Nobody argues against the entitlement of the victims of criminal injury to sue for damages at large in the civil courts if the compensation recoverable from the Criminal Compensation Board is not sufficient. The recent £25,000 award to the victim of a rape who decided to take her case into the courts of this land demonstrates the usefulness of the tort system in overcoming, where fault can be established, the deficiencies, as to amount, of other systems of compensation.

Trade unions

Although trade unions do not have an involvement in most cases of medical negligence, they fulfil a very important role in underwriting claims on behalf of their members in respect of accidents which occur at work. To this end, they have cushioned the Legal Aid system by making it unnecessary for their members to apply for public aid and they have also been able to underwrite claimants who could not have met the means test. The unions, quite rightly, will not lightly give up this role. They influence the main opposition party and even if a Labour Government came into power and appointed Jack Ashley as the Minister responsible in this field, I doubt whether he would be given sufficient financial resources to be able to introduce the ideal comprehensive, no fault scheme, to replace or run in tandem with the present across-the-board tort system.

Partial solutions

Improving the present tort system and the way it is operated

It is important to consider to what extent the current adversarial regime can be improved. Possible improvements include:

(i) implementation of the Civil Justice Review recommendations. Those most likely to impact favourably are:
(a) the introduction of court control of cases once proceedings are commenced. This ought to make impossible the sort of delays I have mentioned.
(b) provision for the exchange of witness statements which ought to encourage settlements in advance of hearings.
(c) widening the extent of pre-trial review hearings.
(d) extension of representative and class actions or the introduction of other procedures and methods of funding large numbers of personal injuries litigants where claims have a common basis.

(e) arrangements to expedite the release of medical records and police accident reports.

(f) court power to order split trials (that is so that liability and quantum can, where appropriate, be decided separately with savings in time and expense) without the need for a party application as this can often speed the course of justice.

(ii) Specialisation amongst solicitors should be encouraged and recognised. Although relaxation in the Solicitors' Rules on advertising has enabled prominent plaintiffs' lawyers to market their undoubted skills to the benefit of their newly-found clients, there is a risk of less competent solicitors packaging themselves in such a way as to attract the unknowing. Special skills should be recognised and the benefits of specialist panels of solicitors made available to the public.

(iii) The CITCOM proposals, insofar as they go beyond those recommended by the Civil Justice Review, should be very carefully considered and in some cases implemented without delay. I am particularly attracted by the following suggestions:

(a) the creation of a Compensation Advisory Board. This should include representatives from industry and its insurers and should not be lawyer dominated. Most damages awards are financed by insurers from premiums funded by commerce and consumers. It would be helped if increases in levels of damages were to be phased so that insurance premiums could be raised in anticipation and, by such means, the price spread fairly throughout society.

(b) the introduction of contingency fees. The criticisms which are levelled at the United States system of reward by result are dominated by the amounts involved which in many cases have vastly over-rewarded lawyers and encouraged "ambulance chasing". With proper controls there may be a place for contingency fees in this country, if only to fill the gap between the abundantly rich and those whose limited means entitle them to Legal Aid.

(c) reform of the way in which Legal Aid Funding is administered and upwards revision of the means test threshold. This, of course, flies in the face of the Government's efforts to contain the funding of civil litigation within the present budget.

(iv) Rationalisation of the way in which the medical professions respond to the admixture of professional conduct criticisms and civil litigation when medical accidents occur.

The litany of criticisms, which I hope I made in a constructive way earlier, relate to circumstances which ought to have been avoided.

Recourse to first party insurance

The tort system operates on the basis that the blameworthy pay the financial bill. Unless claimants are injured in a way which makes establishing blame a simple matter; for example, by being injured as a passenger in a motor car, the tort system is recognised as a lottery where the odds are often stacked against individual plaintiffs. Accidents are nevertheless, like bad health, a risk which confronts all of us. Most of us have the good sense to insure against damage to our property, and life and health insurances are also commonplace precautionary measures taken by a large proportion of our population.

If we were all wise enough to take out personal insurance against disabling or fatal accidents, then, at a stroke, the problems which immediately confront the victims of accidents, namely immediate impecuniosity and delay in obtaining redress, even where it is available, would be mitigated.

If first party insurance against accidents became "the norm", it would take out of the equation personal hardship. Litigation could then be conducted in an orderly way with less emotional pressure and prejudice and compassionate media attention.

Surely this could be encouraged by the Government allowing tax relief on the premiums to be paid. In the context of my firm's Visitors' Personal Accident Insurance initiative, Mr Norman Lamont, as First Secretary of the Treasury, has written to Elaine Kellett-Bowman, the MP for Lancaster who was concerned with the search for justice on the part of the victims of the Abbeystead Waterworks Explosion, in the following terms:

> "You wrote to me on 8 August on behalf of Alan Fisher of Davies, Arnold & Cooper, Solicitors of 12 Bridewell Place, London about the tax treatment of premiums paid under a "no fault" insurance scheme, enclosing details of the scheme. I am sorry for the delay in replying.
>
> I asked the Inland Revenue to look at the material you provided and they have confirmed that traders who invite customers on to their premises for ordinary trading purposes are, indeed, likely to be able to claim a deduction for premiums paid under the type of policy described."

Surely tax relief could also be provided on premiums paid for individual accident protection which would reduce the burdens of the tort system.

I urge those who campaign for a better personal injury compensation system to give serious thought to the solution which personal insurance can provide. Consumerists should note that such a route would not only benefit insurers. Because victims of accidents are a small minority of the population at large, premiums should not be prohibitive and, if widely taken up, the insurance answer is an excellent way of spreading the cost of compensation across society as a whole. It would not take away an individual's entitlement to sue a tortfeasor in the civil courts. Indeed, the prompt receipt of insurance monies could, in some cases, make it possible for a victim to pursue a claim for greater damages which he might not otherwise have been able to finance. I do, however, believe that in the main it would reduce the incidence of adversarial litigation of the speculative nature which occurs now because victims cannot otherwise recover damages beyond the state benefits level.

Unfortunately, first party insurance is unlikely to provide a complete solution for there is little prospect of everybody availing themselves of it. Prudence does, however, demand that this type of personal protection should be taken up by a far greater proportion of the population than is the present case.

A possible prescription

(a) A pilot no fault scheme tailor-made for medical and drug-related accidents—if it can be financed;

(b) to run in tandem with tort system with sensible financial caps;

(c) incorporating a clawback provision—to discourage recourse to litigation in minor cases or where the scheme's levels of damage are adequate or nearly adequate;

(d) with its cost of administration and the compensation it pays out funded as between the Government, the medical profession and by the pharmaceutical industry in a manner which bears a relationship to their current exposures to expense and the payment of damages under the tort system.

Inherent problems

There are, however a number of problems which must be recognised and debated. The United Kingdom is arguably only second to the United States as a litigious society and because of this it is likely that any no fault scheme introduced here would attract a massive incidence of claims, many of the "me too" type. On this, the example which the Opren case provides should be heeded. The extending of the normal limitation period not once but twice has not deterred a substantial number of claimants who, despite widespread publicity, missed those dates from attempting to pursue late claims because of the court supervised settlement scheme organised for much earlier claimants. It would be most unwise to discount the "me too" effect. The costs could therefore be massive in damages and very high in administration and might (even with financial capping built in) compare unfavourably with the expense of paying damages and lawyers' costs within the present adversarial tort system. This is bound to affect the viewpoint of the Government. Furthermore, the pharmaceutical industry is unlikely to be interested in contributing a great deal of money in excess of that which it expends on its present liability insurance and non-insured claims.

Even if a well thought out no fault scheme can be brought into effect, there will still be residual problems of considerable compass; for example:

(i)   continued unfavourable and misleading comparisons with the United States system where there will always be exhorbitant damages awards handed down by juries.

(ii) proof of causation will still be essential and thus cases like pertussis vaccine, Debendox and many of the individual Opren claims would probably not qualify for compensation, unless the benefit of very considerable doubt were to be exercised in favour of claimants. If those types of cases were not compensated, I suspect that the likes of Jack Ashley MP and Des Wilson would not remain quiescent.

(iii) adequacy of warnings regarding the inevitable risks of medical procedures and products and the question of "informed consent" will remain a fertile area for disputes and criticism whatever form of compensation scheme is devised.

(iv) I have the impression that some of the regular consumer campaigners have an insatiable appetite for change and are really looking for unlimited "instant and rubber-stamped" justice, as if by way of social welfare benefit entitlement. If that be the case, the real argument ought to be for increased welfare benefits across the board to all people who are disabled whether caused by accidents or not with a right to sue for damages at large very much curtailed.

The dangers of allowing the debate to be dominated by consumerist campaigners and activists, however well motivated, needs to be considered. Their attractive ideas sometimes need to be tempered by fiscal realities. Society will only provide what it can afford and is willing to pay to its accident victims and this is so wherever the monies directly come from. Further CITCOM proposals are to be offered during this symposium. Not all of CITCOM's arguments or ideas are good, although nearly all of them make good media copy. One does not need to be a consumerist spokesman to be compassionate about the injured. I hope that neither this meeting nor the media reporting upon it will be hi-jacked by CITCOM which should, in my view, only play a part, albeit an important one, in these proceedings and beyond.

Despite having focused on many of the problems which confront the introduction of even a pilot no fault scheme in the UK, I believe they should be looked at as if an obstacle course which must somehow be navigated. That is certainly an aim to which I am prepared to contribute my efforts and I am therefore grateful for the opportunity of participating in this meeting.

11

No fault compensation—short-term panacea or long-term goal?

Arnold Simanowitz

We are well into the second day of this Symposium in which speakers have been addressing what they, at least, believe is the same subject, namely "no fault compensation". Those who have already spoken include some very prestigious names. Yet I wish to try and convince you—and indeed them—that you are under a misapprehension about what we are discussing. I approach this not in a spirit of arrogance but rather in a spirit of complete humility.

Not only will I try to demonstrate that the subject is not what we *should* be discussing, my even more daunting task is to try and persuade you that what we are discussing is something that is entirely different from what we all say or think we are discussing.

The subject chosen for discussion at this Symposium is no fault compensation. What is this concept of no fault compensation? The words are, in my view, totally misleading and as the representative of victims of medical accidents, I must and do reject them emphatically.

Other contributors will, I suspect, be able to show that even in its technical meaning, and in the way the words have been portrayed to and understood by the public "no fault" does not mean no fault.

I want to point out at the outset that when people, and in particular the media, use the term, "no fault compensation", they intend to convey something entirely different from what they do, in fact, convey. I must, however, stress that I am talking only in the context of medical accidents. It is unfortunate that in a meeting hosted by the Royal Society of Medicine, it has not been made absolutely clear that we are, in fact, talking only about medical accidents. I hope that all speakers will make it clear that that is what we are debating, because it is not immediately apparent when one looks both at the title of other papers and at the names of the authors.

It is precisely because the problem relating to medical accidents insofar as victims are concerned, is so different from that of "ordinary" accidents, that it is of fundamental importance to me that I emphasise that I am talking about medical accidents only.

Let us be quite clear that in the case of ordinary accidents, the issue of causation and of definition do not present the same problems as they do in medical accidents. If someone walks across the road and is knocked down by a car, there can be no doubt that an accident has taken place and if that person has been injured, there will similarly be no doubt what the cause of that injury was.

Likewise, if a person's finger is chopped off in an industrial accident, there will be no argument as to whether an "accident" has taken place, nor will there be any difficulty in establishing that there was a connection between the machine and that accident.

To talk of no fault compensation in that context might be appropriate although there would, I submit, be some argument even about that.

Why then, in the context of medical accidents do I say that we are talking about the wrong subject?

The reason is that what is understood by the term no fault compensation looks only at the question of compensation, and fault is of no importance. Far be it from me to suggest that the medical profession, or at least the leaders of that profession in the British Medical Association, the Royal Colleges, and others have some hidden agenda behind the words "no fault compensation" whereby, in concentrating on a scheme that excludes fault, fault will not be considered. Nevertheless, the *effect* of using the term, insofar as the medical profession is concerned, is that the issue of fault disappears. Because of the way the profession presents its case, and goes about its propaganda for no fault, victims cannot help feeling that there *is* a hidden agenda, that the medical profession is only concerned about compensation and wants the issue of blame swept under the carpet, forgotten about, or simply conjured away.

Why else does the profession insist on using a term which is entirely inappropriate? Of course the majority, if not all, of the people attending this meeting are not talking about a scheme which excludes finding fault, if fault there was on the part of a doctor—or indeed drug company. Nobody here, I hope, would dream of simply allowing medical accidents to go on happening without identifying the cause of the accident, whether that be a person, a process, or an instrument. What people mean, I hope, when they talk about no fault compensation, is compensation which is paid automatically, which does not involve our cumbersome, tortuous, costly, and patently unfair legal system. They certainly do not wish to exclude an investigation into fault!

Then why not say so? The British, and the media in particular, are supposed to be proud about calling a spade, a spade. So why continue to use a term which, at best, is ambiguous and, at worst, is misleading, simply because it trips easily off the tongue?

It may seem strange to those who come new to the subject, and even to some who have been wrestling with it for a while, that the only organisation that deals exclusively with medical accidents, is, at best, lukewarm to a concept which appears to offer a better deal for victims. Should you not stop to think why we have that attitude? Should the British Medical Association, when it blunders on "negotiating" with the Department of Health for the introduction of a pilot scheme for no fault compensation, stop to ask itself why Action for Victims of Medical Accidents (AVMA) is not happy with it? Or did they stop, and do they realise why we, on behalf of victims, are unhappy about it, and are they pressing on regardless?

Not only do they persist in calling the scheme a no fault compensation scheme which downgrades, if not eliminates, the issue of accountability but, knowing that AVMA considers that accountability is more important than compensation to the vast majority of victims, they, nevertheless, press on with this propaganda and their discussions with the Department continue to relate only to the issue of money compensation and ignore the issue of accountability.

You must forgive me if this meeting only wishes to talk about money. I can only speak from the victims' point of view. And if this meeting, under the influence of eminent doctors, lawyers, and academics wants to confine itself to the issue of money, then you will find my paper an embarrassing irrelevance. If, however, you want to know what it is that victims' want, then perhaps I will be able to persuade you to listen to what I have to say on their behalf.

I regret to say that I believe that the medical profession has forfeited any moral authority it may have had to put forward proposals for the compensation of victims of medical accidents. The British Medical Association (BMA), it must never be forgotten, is a trade union and has a primary responsibility to look after its members' interests. Its whole involvement in the issue of compensation is absolutely consistent with that role and discloses little concern for the real needs of victims.

Take, for example, its relations with AVMA, the only victims' organisation, on the question of compensation. AVMA, on behalf of victims, has said from the time the BMA started investigating the issue, that unless there is included in any change, an improved system for ensuring the accountability of doctors, there is no point in even looking at the BMA's ideas on compensation. That was the evidence we gave to the Working Party, that is what we have repeatedly said since then, and that is what we are saying now. Yet when the BMA talks about its so-called no fault scheme, it never mentions accountability.

It is in favour of the Swedish scheme, but neatly omits to mention that in Sweden there is a Medical Responsibility Board which, whilst by no means perfect, makes our FPC Service Committees, hospital complaints procedure, and General Medical Council (GMC) Disciplinary Committee look like a cosy arrangement specifically designed to avoid accountability for doctors.

I said earlier that the medical profession has no moral authority for acting to improve the position for victims.

What efforts have they made to try and find out what victims actually want? We do not claim at AVMA to be the sole arbiters of the needs of victims, but surely the profession must recognise that we do know more than they what those needs are. I would not pretend to know more about the needs of surgeons than the Royal College of Surgeons and if I were setting up a scheme for the benefit of doctors, I would do my best to involve those organisations which speak on behalf of doctors at every stage of my deliberations.

But the medical profession is different. Apart from their one request to us to give evidence they have never approached us for help on the issue. On the contrary, they have put a proposal to the Department of Health for a pilot scheme without our knowledge. When we tried to involve the BMA in discussions, we found it extremely difficult. We approached the BMA about a conference on this subject and it took so long to materialise that the Royal Society of Medicine set up its own conference in the meantime and we were graciously allowed one speaker. I was however allowed only 10 minutes on a programme lasting two days—ten minutes for the views of the people most affected by the issue. I now have 20 minutes, which is still hopelessly inadequate properly to put forward the victims' case; but even that had to be squeezed out of the reluctant organisers. That is certainly not what we had in mind. Does that smack of a profession that wants to do something for victims or is it the protective "knee jerk" reaction to the hysteria which has developed as a result of the "huge" increase in insurance premiums?

The mention of premiums brings me to the position of the defence organisations which are, after all, also part of the medical profession. They, too, must be seen for what they are when they put forward proposals which are supposed to be for the benefit of victims. They are, or course, medico–legal organisations and proud to be so. They have no concern with the moral issues surrounding the question of compensation for patients—I have been told this in so many words by a responsible member of at least one of the societies and, in any event, it must be obvious from their role. They are there to protect and to defend doctors and can only agree to anything which may be of benefit to victims provided that neither in the short term nor in the long term does it adversely affect their protective or defensive role.

It is that perspective which allows, and indeed encourages, the Medical Protection Society (MPS), for example, to come up with the extraordinary idea of asking the Government to introduce a limited no fault scheme to cover babies brain damaged at birth. Dr Palmer, Deputy Secretary of that society, talks today under the heading "The Faults in No Fault Compensation Schemes". I have heard him on the subject before and insofar as he deals with the practical rather than the philosophical objections to these schemes, this is an area where AVMA and the MPS have perhaps the most in common. He is very persuasive on the faults in no fault schemes. Yet notwithstanding those objections, in the absence of any published research into the particular issue raised or of any discussions with victims' representatives or other organisations, the MPS suddenly comes out with a proposal of this nature. Its only attraction it seems to me, is that it will indeed protect doctors—it will stop their insurance premiums rising, or even reduce them, whilst at the same time avoiding what the medical profession perceive as the major evil, the assumption of the insurance risk by the Government altogether with what the profession always sees as the concomitant loss to their clinical freedom.

But what about the objections to no fault compensation? Why do these objections fall away insofar as brain damage at birth is concerned? Why is it that this is such a special category apart from the fact that it happens to carry with it the major awards of damages? In my view, it is in that very category that the major defects in the system of no fault lie. Strange that it is in that very area that the MPS suggests that it is actually a good idea.

In discussing the role of the defence organisations, I must add something which might appear to be irrelevant to our subject but I think it throws a light on the attitude of the profession towards the whole problem of accidents. It cannot be right that when a doctor suffers a medical accident—and I use the word "suffers" deliberately because a doctor suffers as much as a patient in many ways— the body to which he or she immediately turns for help is a legal organisation, concerned about the law and insurance. How can the attitude of doctors ever change towards victims, how can they ever view the problem as an ethical one, if after such a traumatic incident they must write or speak to a lawyer or to someone whose prime concern is a legal or insurance one but certainly not an ethical one? Surely the time has long since passed when the medical profession should have an organisation specifically to help doctors in the difficult problem of medical accidents—much in the same way as AVMA tries to help victims? It is to such a body that the doctor should be able to turn for advice and counselling after an accident; it is such a body that should be looking at ways to educate doctors from the time they begin their studies as to how to handle themselves and patients after an accident, and it is such a body which would have a major role in discussing what compensation scheme would best replace our present one.

I have spent some time trying to show how the attitude of the medical profession towards the problem of medical accidents makes the consideration of no fault compensation inappropriate. The role of the medical profession is, however, crucial to any system of compensation and from the victims' point of view there is no sense in setting up a new system which is just as susceptible, if not more so, to the control of the medical profession, particularly if the profession continues to demonstrate its current attitude to such problems.

In order to demonstrate the scope for such control, I would like to mention one of our more specific objections to so called no fault compensation to which I alluded earlier.

It is one of the misconceptions of almost all who debate this subject that no fault means what it says. Bring in no fault compensation and with the wave of a magic wand, the issue of whether someone, a doctor perhaps, is to blame, disappears. That, certainly, is what the rank and file doctors believe—that is the main reason why they are so keen on the scheme, is it not—others at this meeting will demonstrate perhaps more adequately than I why that is not the case.

I would just like to use a very simple example. Take the case of the man who is rushed into hospital with a heart attack. His family are extremely distressed and think he is going to die. He does, in fact, die. Clearly, in that situation, no no fault scheme is going to compensate the family even though they may have been dependent on him and he may have been earning £100,000 per annum or more. If, however, he died, not because of the heart attack but because when they got him to hospital they misdiagnosed him, or gave him the wrong drug, or an overdose or underdose, or the consultant wasn't contactable and a junior house officer was unable to cope, then it was a medical accident and the family might be entitled to hundreds or thousands of pounds.

Two facts emerge with crystal clarity from this example: firstly, that in order to decide whether there has been an accident it will be necessary to establish that someone has been at fault. Secondly, whether that fault is established will, under the bureaucratic administrative system of a no fault scheme, depend even more on the medical profession than it does now when the forensic skills of the much maligned lawyers are available to establish the facts.

I do not believe that the general public, and even some doctors, understand the way in which the medical profession has always failed, and continues to fail, to help victims of medical accidents because of its attitudes towards those victims. I would like to give you an illustration which I hope will help them to understand.

The AVMA was consulted by the wife of a man (I shall call him Mr Smith) who in March 1982 had undergone an operation for the replacement of the mitral valve in his heart. This of course is a serious operation. Immediately after the operation he appeared to be recovering but some 12 hours later, while in intensive care, there was a grave setback and he suffered severe damage to his eyesight.

Mrs Smith consulted us in November 1983. She wrote to us *inter alia* that "I feel my solicitor is doing his best, but it takes five months to get a reply from anyone in the medical profession. It took five months for my husband's records to be made available and it took five months for the consultant to send my husband's solicitor a report . . . . The hospital have admitted that there was a lack of oxygen but they say they do not know how the deficit arose".

At the time we were consulted the solicitors had obtained a report from an independent consultant neurosurgeon who had been through all the records and had reported that no negligence was involved but, "the most likely cause of this is a blockage of a main artery in the brain due to a small blood clot being carried from the heart into the arterial system of the brain. This would be a recognised risk of the condition from which Mr Smith suffered and also a risk of the operative procedure".

In addition to this report, the solicitors had a letter from the Health Authority's Legal Officer to Mrs Smith dated August 1982 giving a detailed description of what had happened and stating that "in summary, your husband suffered a serious complication of heart surgery namely a temporary stroke . . . . This type of complication happens in differing degrees of severity to approximately 10% of patients undergoing open heart operations". The letter goes on "The possible causes are clot or air in the cerebral circulation, cerebral haemorrhage or a low cardiac output, all of which produce hypoxia of brain cells. This particular case was presented and reviewed at the Weekly Cardiothoracic Unit meeting which all surgical medical and nursing staff of the unit attend and full discussion of the possible causes failed to clarify why he suffered this complication".

We gave Mrs Smith certain advice and her solicitors obtained a further independent expert's opinion—which took until July 1984. This was from a consultant neurologist. His view on negligence was that "I cannot see that this sequence of events could have been prevented and would assume that the removal of the intra-tracheal tube at 3.45 am was standard practice in view of his condition. I have explained to Mrs Smith that this view would almost certainly be taken by a cardiac surgeon".

Mrs Smith again turned to us. It seemed like the end of the road. She wrote "I feel in my heart that there must be an explanation but I doubt very much whether we will ever get to the bottom of this matter". I too was unhappy. I turned to a consultant anaesthetist known for his honesty and forthrightness in matters of this kind. I asked him simply to look at the reports so far obtained and give an opinion as to whether the matter had been properly reported. Mrs Smith was at that stage naturally unable to obtain legal aid for a third full report.

The anaesthetist, experienced in intensive care immediately noticed, simply from the correspondence in front of him (including from the legal officer which he described as an "amalgam of what he was told by the doctors concerned"), obvious discrepancies and inconsistencies which demanded investigation. He suggested (kindly in my view) that the two previous experts had not noticed these discrepancies because "neither of these doctors worked full time in intensive care units".

The anaesthetist reported in full in due course after having considered the medical records. He had found that the hypoxia had been caused by the premature termination of ventilation and the removal of the endotracheal tube and that the decision to do this was grossly negligent. The detailed report showed obvious and gross mismanagement. That was in October 1985. The anaesthetist suggested that an additional report be obtained from a cardiac surgeon.

In July 1986, such a report was obtained. After detailing the gross post-operative mismanagement the report concludes "It is my opinion that this patient suffered avoidable cerebral damage due to post-operative mismanagement".

Notwithstanding this clear and unequivocal opinion the Health Authority continued to defend the case. It was due to go to trial on the 8th November 1988. On the 4th November an offer of £35,000 was made. Shortly before the hearing this was increased to £45,000. In order to avoid the further trauma of a trial following six and a half years of torment Mr & Mrs Smith decided to accept.

Let us look at what this story tells us. I do not wish to dwell on the details of the legal process involved save to say that had both sides been competent and properly monitored, and had the experts on both sides behaved with a sense of urgency the time could at least been halved for the matter to come to trial.

I am more concerned at looking at what this tells us in the so called no fault debate. Make no mistake, under neither the Swedish system nor the New Zealand system, nor under any other system now proposed, without the goodwill of the doctors, would Mr Smith have received a penny. Worse still, the behaviour of the entire hospital staff would never have been subject to criticism. How many of the 10% of these accidents even now will continue to be seen as "known risk" accidents?

There is no answer in this case for the protagonists of no fault. Some will say that as there was no trial and the claim was settled out of court, there is no proof that there was in fact negligence. In that situation, however, Mr Smith would have got nothing under a no fault system because it would have been accepted that his damage was caused by a known risk complication which is excluded.

If on the other hand it is said that under no fault Mr Smith would have got his damages automatically then it pre-supposes that the Health Authority was defending an indefensible claim from the beginning, or their experts, like the first experts of Mr Smith, were being less than forthcoming.

The lesson to be learnt from this case is the one I am trying to convey to you today—that until the attitude of the medical profession changes, no fault will be a retrograde step, to the benefit of that profession only. There will never be the kind of analysis of a claim such as Mr Smith finally got, under any no fault system. It will be far more like the analysis given by the Health Authority or the two experts who were first consulted by the plaintiff.

Until there is a change of attitude, until it is known that doctors will voluntarily seek the truth we cannot hand over the question of compensation, let alone accountability, in its entirety to the medical profession which has to date let victims down so badly. Unfortunately until that time comes it is necessary to have good lawyers doing their forensic detective work to ascertain the truth.

Because of the control that the medical profession has exercised over the issue of medical accidents the legal system has provided a window on a world which the rest of us would otherwise not see. I urge you to understand that no fault compensation as it is put forward in conferences of this kind would, whilst of course helping some people, be a curtain drawn neatly across that window. Even a conference like this would have been unthinkable if that window had not been available. Do not let us cover it over.

I hope I have managed to go a little way towards showing you that the primary issue from the victims' point of view, is accountability, and the attitude of the profession towards victims. Before I close let me illustrate how the medical profession itself regards this issue.

One of the fundamental problems is that the profession does not, and will not, see such accidents as an ethical problem in any way. This can be clearly seen in the three booklets which deal with ethics and standards in the medical profession, the GMC's blue book, the BMA's handbook of medical ethics and the recently published BMA's Rights and Responsibilities of Doctors. Where in those booklets is there mention of what doctors' responsibilities are towards victims? It was the later book, The Rights and Responsibilities of Doctors, which concentrated my mind on this issue. It is a book about the responsibilities of doctors but I searched its pages vainly for any mention of the responsibility towards victims. And this in a booklet published as recently as July 1988!

The fact is that the profession is concerned about compensation, as conferences of this kind demonstrate, and as long as the public, supported by the media, continue to pander to this obsession by ignoring the issue of accountability and concentrating on so-called no fault compensation, we will not get the changes that victims want.

Before we consider changing the system of compensation or discussing the merits or otherwise of so-called no fault compensation, there must be a change in the attitudes of the medical profession towards victims of medical accidents, and a firm commitment from that profession to the interests of victims. Then we can introduce not a system of no fault compensation but a system of "accountable compensation".

12

The case against no fault compensation

Andrew W. Morrison

Background

When this proposed two day meeting was being discussed at the Council of the Royal Society of Medicine (RSM) it appeared to me that no one was intending to present a case against no fault compensation for medical accidents, a situation which would result in considerable bias, hence my involvement, somewhat reluctantly, in this discussion.

As a Vice-President and Council member of the Medical Defence Union (MDU) for the past two decades, advising mainly on matters pertaining to otolaryngology and head and neck surgery, I have accumulated and kept records of a very large number of instances of negligence, or alleged negligence, by my colleagues. You will appreciate that one cannot divulge specific information gained in confidence, but patterns and trends have become only too obvious. These trends, though extracted from otolaryngology mishaps, could be applied equally to any branch of medicine or surgery.

Before proceeding I should like to make it quite clear that the views and opinions which I am about to propound do not, in any way, reflect MDU thinking or conclusions. They are purely personal.

Trends in medical negligence

1. The number of claims has risen year by year and the relative size of awards or settlements has risen by several orders of magnitude compared with twenty years ago. These two factors together, well recognised by all, largely explain the present "crisis" and the desire for so many to become involved. The virtually compulsory demands for doctors to pay ever increasing membership fees, has stimulated benevolent thoughts of no fault compensation, and the sudden proposed introduction of differential subscription rates by the Medical Protection Society (MPS) has precipitated panic activity.

To digress for a moment, the recently published report from the Centre for Socio-Legal Studies in Oxford[1] summarised its attitude in the following quotation: "In so far as there is a malpractice crisis, it concerns the difficulty facing patients and their relatives in bringing a claim against doctors." Amongst its recommendations were proposals to help potential claimants identify medical negligence solicitors, to have them advertise their services, to encourage solicitors to pass cases to such legal specialists by fee-splitting arrangements, and to improve access to Legal

Aid. In my view these remarkable attitudes, perhaps designed to endear themselves to the legal profession, would spell further disaster for the medical profession.

2. I suspect it is not so well recognised that the same mistakes occur over and over again, and that the majority of these mishaps (over 50%) are indefensible. This repetition of medical accidents is not confined to otolaryngology. In every branch, danger areas could be identified. The various publications of the MDU, MPS and MDDUS (Medical and Dental Defence Union of Scotland) sometimes highlight these but they are probably not widely read. It is sad to relate that negligence has to be admitted in so many instances. But out-of-court settlements minimise costs under the law of tort.

In most of the other cases the alleged negligence can be defended, though there is likely to be some disagreement amongst experts. The pre-trial exchange of reports has helped to clarify the situation and conserve funds.

3. A minority of cases are spurious, that is to say there has been absolutely no negligence or mismanagement by any of the medical or nursing staff involved. To some extent the profession is to blame for this since in lay radio, television or press coverage, we tend to give the impression that everything is possible, all ills can be cured and death is avoidable.

To a greater extent, however, and this is equally sad to relate, there is a scattering of doctors who appear to make a profession, and even a livelihood, out of acting as expert witnesses for plaintiffs, often when there is no real case to answer. Malevolence may be the motivation for their actions. Sometimes their misguided action is due to failure to examine the facts in sufficient detail. I am concerned that if the recommendations of the Oxford group[1] were adopted these spurious cases would escalate with further wastage of Legal Aid and public funds.

4. My final group of observations concern the difference between the National Health Service (NHS) and private medicine. Litigation is relatively rare in private practice despite its expansion in recent years, even into many areas of high technology. Presumably this is because the doctors in private practice are more senior and can spend some time explaining things to their patients, thereby developing a rapport. There is also the fundamental truth that people are more appreciative of services for which they pay.

By contrast, much NHS practice with indifferent bureaucratic efficiency, long delays, busy clinics and changing junior staff (who perform a high proportion of the work) offer little opportunity for the development of good patient relationships, and must leave many patients frustrated when their treatment result does not match their expectations. Complaints follow, even when there has been no negligence.

In recent years there has been much publicity about reduction of NHS Services, while the topical subject is the long hours worked by junior staff. Whereas limited resources must to some extent prejudice standards, this aspect is seldom advanced in mitigation or defence of a doctor, unless the consultants in charge have previously warned the Health Authority of impending disaster[2].

For the purposes of this paper I propose to consider Consultants, Professors, Senior Lecturers and Senior Registrars as "senior staff", all others constituting "junior staff". An analysis of MDU otolaryngology members reveals some two-thirds to be senior and one-third junior; two-thirds of our otolaryngology negligence actions involve senior staff. The inference is that NHS consultants in otolaryngology make as many mistakes as junior staff, or at least attract as many complaints.

The balance between senior and junior ear, nose and throat staff in England and Wales is approximately 50/50 with no growth of the former[3]. Roughly similar ratios exist in general surgery, orthopaedic surgery and general medicine where the consultant growth will soon reach equality. The average annual growth of consultant anaesthetists (Table 1) means that they now outnumber their juniors; an attempt no doubt to put their house in order, for anaesthetic mishaps account for many of the largest negligence claims. Compare this with the situation in radiology, histopathology and dermatology (Table 2) where senior staff far outnumber junior colleagues; in all these specialties negligence actions are unusual.

Now examine the data for obstetrics, for paediatrics, especially for the neonatal variety and for accident and emergency departments where claims are so common and in the case of the first two potentially so expensive; for example, brain damaged infants. Juniors outnumber seniors very significantly (Table 3), nor is there any indication from the rates of growth of consultants that any drive from within these disciplines to rectify things has been effective. At least the Royal College of Surgeons of England has examined the accident and emergency problem and the Working Party has made appropriate recommendations to improve the deficiencies and raise standards[4].

It is interesting that cardiology has a similar high ratio of junior medical staff, yet no particular litigation propensity. Concealed in the figures for general medicine must be many consultants with a special interest in cardiology to balance this ratio. Furthermore, there is lay acceptance of the high morbidity and mortality from cardiac disease.

Table 1 *Ratio of senior to junior staff in selected specialties*

Specialty	Senior	Junior	Consultant Growth
Otolaryngology	449	421	1
General surgery	1135	1238	4
Orthopaedic surgery	836	966	10
General medicine	1560	1862	37
Anaesthetics	2393	1705	58

Table 2 *Staffing ratios in selected specialties*

Specialty	Senior	Junior	Consultant Growth
Radiology	1300	231	36
Histopathology	771	154	6
Dermatology	288	93	5

Table 3 *Staffing ratios (cont)*

Specialty	Senior	Junior	Consultant Growth
Accident and Emergency	241	1304	10
Obstetrics	928	1754	13
Paediatrics	828	1336	26
Cardiology	172	788	2

Objections to Crown indemnity or no fault compensation

It could be argued that a no fault compensation scheme for medical accidents is essentially a socialist or left-wing concept, the State deciding upon quantum and eligibility and legislating, as in New Zealand, so that the employer or self-employed largely fund the administration and payments. The greater the element of State control, the greater the fear of bureaucratic interference in medical affairs and the greater the risk of ultimate loss of clinical judgement by government directive. This is a real fear with the profession.

The awards for damages to patients in both New Zealand and Sweden are small compared with those in the United Kingdom (or in the United States), yet the New Zealand costs have escalated since the scheme was introduced in 1975. British experience with criminal injury claims, which reached record proportions of £52 million in the year 1987–88 (a single payment was almost £0.5 million) suggest that the costs of Crown indemnity for medical negligence or non-negligent accident would soon become prohibitive.

Although in theory the Swedish schemes still allow a dissatisfied patient to resort to the law of tort, the legislation is designed to prevent this, thereby striking at the very root of the law of tort in a free society. This is a matter for the legal profession, as is the threatened interference with judicial discretion in assessing quantum, or making case law.

The introduction of a no fault compensation scheme for medical accidents in Britain would remove the deterrent effect of possible litigation on doctors, thereby tending to lower rather than raise health care standards. Two decades of medico-legal work have left me in no doubt about the power of this factor. In this respect the recommendations of the Oxford group[1] have some merit.

To my mind the principal objection to Crown indemnity is the failure to rectify the causes of medical negligence. The questions to be addressed are "Why are there so many mistakes?" and "how should standards be raised?" The inescapable answers to the first question are that there are too many unsupervised junior staff, too many inexperienced senior staff and insufficient specialisation.

Medical negligence—the remedy

The remedy, naive though it may be, must be to raise standards to acceptable levels. This is a complex problem which requires actions of a medical and of a political nature, sometimes with difficulty in differentiating the one from the other. An old adage says that "The best medicine should taste nasty". This certainly applies to some of the suggested therapies.

1. The introduction of differential subscriptions would help to stimulate curative action in the high risk specialties. The majority of MDU members favoured selective rates in the 1986 survey[5]. Since 1988 full-time hospital staff subscriptions have been partially reimbursed to ease the financial burden on junior staff and to introduce some parity with general practitioners and HM Service medical personnel whose payments are refunded. In view of the altered circumstances a new survey is planned.

I am not privy to the MPS data on which they base their proposed subscriptions. I was privileged to be a guest of the Sou Medical in Paris last Autumn. They have ten years' experience of computer-based information on some fifteen different specialties and as detailed and accurate a method as they can devise of assessing different premiums. Their system is very impressive and is constantly being modified by circumstances. Obstetricians are the most costly; anaesthetists, plastic surgeons, general and orthopaedic surgeons are also expensive; junior doctors form a separate category below the middle of the scale; while general practitioners cost least.

I consider we require similar accurate information before asking the British medical profession to accept differential subscriptions which would be equitable.

2. Consultants in the high risk specialties should exert as much pressure as possible locally and nationally for a higher proportion of senior staff. In England and Wales it would be a good start to increase all medical staffing levels to those which apply in Scotland, where there is so much less negligence activity.

Differential basic salaries would not be acceptable to the profession, but the awards system could be modified to assist with the high premiums.

3. Undergraduate medical students should have a greater exposure to medico-legal problems. The danger areas of each specialty and the mistakes which are a recurrent theme should be emphasised. The MDU prize essays have stimulated interest but the subject should form part of the curriculum.

4. The profession should teach and practice more defensive medicine. Many raise their hands in horror at this suggestion. I consider it to be good practice to explain things in detail including the risks of treatment. Patient anxiety should not influence this approach. Written as well as verbal information may be necessary. The lack of informed consent has become a major factor, sometimes the only one, in negligence actions; the consultant is usually blamed. Patients should be given every opportunity to decline elective surgery, or risk associated medication.

Increasing numbers of negligence actions are based on "failure to diagnose" or "delay in diagnosis" of some condition often with disastrous results. These mostly stem from an unwillingness of general practitioners or hospital doctors to seek special opinions or initiate adequate investigation. This is inforgivable. As the barrister, Michael Powers, puts it so succinctly "One doctor's defensive medicine, it should be remembered, is another doctor's prudent medical practice."[6]

5. The defence organisations might make greater use of their "powers of veto". Doctors who have been "struck off" the General Medical Council (GMC) register automatically cease to be members of the MDU. Rarely will a surgeon be told that he can no longer look to the MDU to cover him for a particular operation.

6. Specialist standards must be maintained at a very high level, especially for the surgical subjects. The new Intercollegiate Specialist Fellowship examinations, which will eventually be established in most of the branches of surgery, including general surgery, will be a step in the correct direction. At present, one suspects, there may be a difference of standard between say the English FRCS and that of Edinburgh, Glasgow or Dublin, at least in otolaryngology.

7. Compulsory post-graduate courses and assessment both for general practitioners and senior hospital staff may well come in the future. The Royal Colleges and post-graduate tutors and deans would have an important role to play. There is a need to improve methods of assessing clinical competence[7] but it should not be an impossible task.

The logical extension of continuing assessment is that consultant contracts should be renewable after an agreed interval and dependent upon progress. The other logical action would be the termination of the recently introduced sub-consultant grades.

8. My final suggestions are more of a political nature. It seems likely that the GMC disciplinary powers may be extended but presumably in the field of ethical and criminal misdemeanour rather than clinical negligence.

In a recent letter to *The Times* Sir Douglas Black and my old colleague from The London Hospital, Sir John Ellis[8], point to the very high standard of training of medical students in this country, and rightly so. But a large percentage of junior doctors—many of whom subsequently achieve National Health Scheme consultant status—are overseas graduates from many different countries. One wonders if the GMC should not consider the introduction of an examination or assessment comparable with the British medical qualifying tests before granting registration. Other countries do so. European laws might present a problem but surely the EEC could not interfere with a post-graduate assessment which applies to all, and upon which depended continuing registration or employment.

Finally, I should like to repeat that these views are purely personal.

References

1. Ham, C., Dingwall, R., Fenn, P. and Harris, D. (1988). *Medical negligence, compensation and accountability*. Centre for Socio-Legal Studies, Oxford. King's Fund Institute, London.
2. Hill, G. (1988). The MDU and NHS cuts. *J. Med. Defence Union*, **4**: 1.
3. Department of Health and Social Security. Medical Manpower and Education Division (1988). Medical and dental staffing prospects in the NHS in England and Wales 1987. *Health Trends*, **20**: 101–109.
4. Commission on the Provision of Surgical Services. Report of the Working Party on the Management of Patients with Major Injuries. Royal College of Surgeons of England. November 1988.
5. Anon. (1988). Differential subscriptions survey and results. *J. Med. Defence Union*, **4**: 52–54.
6. Powers, M. J. (1988). Editorial. Litigation. *Brit. J. Hosp. Med.*, **39**: 365.
7. Maguire, P. (1988). Assessing clinical competence. Need for improvement. Editorial. *Brit. Med. J.*, **298**: 4–5.
8. Black, D. and Ellis, J. (1988). "Doctors' insurance". Letter to *The Times* dated November 25, 1988.

13

Faults in no fault compensation schemes

R. N. Palmer

Widespread concern about escalating costs and damages in personal injury claims in the United Kingdom coupled with the many anomalies of the tort-based system has led to the search for a better alternative. In the context of personal injury claims arising from medical negligence, added impetus has been given by the steep rise in the subscriptions required by the medical defence societies.

The tort-based system is widely acknowledged to be far from ideal. Among the many criticisms are the requirement for proof of fault or negligence, dissatisfaction with the lump sum system of awards, dismay at legal delays and at the cost of litigation. Many would-be litigants may go uncompensated because they are too "rich" to qualify for Legal Aid but not "rich enough" to fund their own litigation. There is a groundswell of support for change at every level, from grass roots to leaders in the *British Medical Journal*[1]. What, however, is to replace the current common law, tort-based system? Many have suggested a scheme of no fault compensation such as those which exist in New Zealand, Sweden and now Finland. This conference is to look at no fault compensation and it is hoped that the scrutiny will indeed be thorough, critical and searching. Many issues must be faced in arranging any replacement for the current tort-based system, evolved by the common law over many centuries. Before the enthusiasm for change born of dissatisfaction with the current model leads to a vote for some system of no fault compensation, it is as well to remember, *caveat emptor*!

It is suggested that there is a very special problem in the United Kingdom at present—that of the "brain-damaged" baby. If that problem could be solved then the wider aspects of medical negligence could resume more manageable proportions once more. There is a special problem for "brain-damaged" neonates because our civil law requires proof on the balance of probabilities only and this leads to fundamental problems over causation. Coupled to this is the fact that, through the advancement of medical science, the survival of the "brain-damaged" baby is now likely to be of many years' duration, but in a form demanding round-the-clock care and attention from dedicated individuals—a resource which requires great expense.

In the consumer-oriented society in which we live there is an expectation that every pregnancy carried to term will result in a happy, healthy child. Where those very human expectations are dashed, and a "brain-damaged" infant eventuates, the birth attendants, medical and nursing, may be held responsible. Notwithstanding that causation may be seriously in issue (as between the alleged negligent acts and the state of the nervous system of the child), it must be recognised that the civil common law requires proof only on the balance of probabilities. This dilemma was encapsulated in a lecture to students of the faculty of law of the University of Manitoba, Winnipeg, delivered by Krever J (1986)[2] in which it was said that a tendency is sometimes discerned among judges to grant awards of damages from what are erroneously seen as insurance company funds on something less than the full burden and standard of proof strictly required in law. Krever J is quoted as saying that in order for totally innocent plaintiffs who suffer catastrophic injuries to be compensated by wealthy insurers of equally blameless defendants, judges will tend to find fault where none exists. Krever J is reported as saying that judges sometimes tell themselves:

> "This is a case in which everybody agrees damages should be paid to the plaintiff. I know that nothing can be paid to the plaintiff unless I can find fault so I am going to find fault. I know perfectly well that if I find fault, even though the evidence, intellectually applied, does not enable me to find fault, the Court of Appeal will not interfere with my finding of fault because it is a finding of fact made by a trier of fact who saw the witnesses. So I can get away with it. I am therefore able to (make a finding of negligence)."

Whilst no one of humanity can deny the sad plight of the child or wish to block adequate provision for its care, it equally should not be overlooked that doctors are not the insurers of their patients' misfortunes. To deny the child compensation may be considered to be an injustice. To award the compensation against the doctor in circumstances where causation is not clearly established may simply replace one injustice with another.

That said, however, it must not be overlooked that, as Mrs Diana Brahams' papers in the *Lancet* show very clearly, the "brain-damaged" infant may not recover compensation under the schemes of no fault compensation in Sweden, New Zealand and Finland. It is my understanding that no compensation has been paid to a brain-damaged infant under at least one of those schemes to date, not least because of the very issues of causation which I have just touched upon. I will return to this later.

Aims and objectives—recompense or retribution?

Before the United Kingdom embarks upon any change to the current system, it is as well for society, through its Parliament, to stand back and to decide what it seeks to achieve in its systems of compensation and, secondarily, whether its wishes can be achieved at affordable cost. Until the underlying aims and objectives and costings have been decided upon, it is impossible to plan sensibly and constructively.

Whom do we wish to compensate and upon what basis? Are we aiming at recompense or retribution?

Punishment and prevention are intertwined with compensation in the UK tort-based system. However, recompense without retribution appears to be the underlying philosophy of the no fault schemes. So be it, but then this must be appreciated and plans must be made accordingly, ensuring, for example, that the means are provided to maintain professional standards—indeed every effort should surely be made to strive always to raise standards. It may be necessary also to provide means whereby patients can discover what happended to them, obtaining adequate explanations and not merely purses of money.

In raising numbers of issues in this paper the author wishes to do no more than to contribute constructively to a critical and informed debate in the hope that "the grass is greener on the other side of the fence" syndrome will not lead to a replacement of one flawed system with another in the enthusiasm for change borne of dissatisfaction.

Population and precedent

The UK population is of the order of 56 millions. The UK is made up of two nation states (England and Scotland), one principality (Wales) and one province (Northern Ireland) with different laws and legal systems. We may have a Union, but we are not all that united! Our friends in Sweden, Finland and New Zealand live in countries whose populations are far smaller—ranging from about 3½ million to 8½ million.

It remains possible for those with small populations to operate, effectively and sensibly, a central bureaucracy for their compensation system and to maintain effective control over precedents and policies. It is very difficult, I would say impossible, to exercise central control of case precedent for a population the size of ours in the UK. Our own legal system is not without examples of conflicting decisions of the High Court and indeed conflicting decisions of the Court of Appeal—as every law student knows. In our criminal law we have examples of the different motoring fines imposed by different benches of magistrates round the country for similar offences. Nearer to our own subject matter we have the example of the wide divergences of decisions of the local panels appointed to assess claims under the Vaccine Damage Payments Act—some panels being far more ready than others to admit claims and to award the statutory sum to those who can establish a causal connection between the vaccine and the neurological damage subsequently sustained. This was shown neatly in a paper presented to the VIIth World Congress on Medical Law in Ghent in 1985 by R. G. Lee[3] of the University of Lancaster.

Incidentally, one wonders what are to become of payments under the statutory scheme in the light of the decision in the High Court by Stuart-Smith J in the recent case in which he ruled that there was no causal link between pertussis vaccine and brain damage, at least in the case which he was called upon to try.

If we are to replace one set of anomalies with another we must address and solve the issues of precedent and population size in any alternative to replace our tort-based system.

Policy and politics

In this section there is no intention to discuss nakedly political matters but rather a wish to state what some might regard as the obvious. That which works satisfactorily in one country might not suit the society of another country. The basis of the provision of housing, medical benefits, social welfare and other such matters is fundamentally different in, say, Sweden from that applicable in this country. A simplistic attempt to import into the United Kingdom the best features of a Scandinavian no fault system may fail dismally in the absence of a more thorough and far-reaching reform of our own taxation and social welfare infrastructure.

In decisions about funding any possible alternatives, society through its Parliament must address fundamental issues such as taxation. For example, there are financial limits in the New Zealand no fault scheme. In August 1986 the New Zealand official review of the Accident Compensation Corporation (ACC) reported that there was "acute financial pressure on the current scheme" and continued "the trends to increasing numbers of claims and to increasing real costs of health care and compensation have led us to the view that the balance in the choice between objectives needs to be shifted . . . decisions on trade-offs are necessary as to the extent to which there should be differentials in funding arrangements and the extent to which victims themselves bear the costs of the losses they face".

Important matters such as these must be addressed by society as a precondition to proposals for change.

Access to courts—"to sue or not to sue, that is the question"

Our friends and colleagues in New Zealand, in implementing their own scheme of no fault compensation, addressed the question as to whether or not citizens should be allowed to bring tort-based actions in the courts. The New Zealanders decided that the right to sue in the courts should, for all practical purposes, be abolished.

In contrast, the Scandinavian schemes allow citizens to sue in the courts as well as to apply for compensation under the no fault schemes. Diana Brahams in her article in the *Lancet* of January 1988[4], reports the case of **Mpanda *v.* Uppsala County Council (1987)** in which a claimant refused to apply for compensation under the no fault scheme but, instead, brought an action in the courts and received an award, capitalised, equivalent to £4 million.

If we are to contemplate change to our system in the UK consideration will need to be given as to whether or not the right to sue in the courts is to be statutorily excluded. It may not be regarded as entirely acceptable if citizens are entitled to two forms of redress, one through the courts and one based upon some no fault scheme of compensation.

Definitional problems

In a personal communication from Messrs MacAlister Mazengarb, solicitors to the Medical Protection Society in New Zealand, it is understood that there is a blossoming case law in New Zealand arising from contested decisions of the Accident Compensation Corporation/Commission (ACC) over matters of interpretation of the statutory scheme and its rules. It is pointed out that not all cases of medical negligence come within the scope of medical misadventure. While acts of operational negligence will obviously be included, an act of omission (for example, a failure in responding to a call for treatment) may not be included. The whole rationale of the scheme in New Zealand was to remove damages claims for personal injury from the lottery of the courts and to replace them with a code which would compensate victims of personal injury by accident. Although the scheme works well in the area of motor vehicle accidents, sports injuries, etc, it is stated authoritatively by Messrs MacAlister Mazengarb that in medical misadventure cases the act has simply replaced one lottery by another. Many claimants will have to go through the whole legal panoply with no certainty of ultimately receiving compensation. Notwithstanding these difficulties, there is a consensus that the no fault scheme is preferable to the common law system which it replaced and that no one seriously suggests a reversion to tort-based compensation.

Size of awards

Generally speaking, more people receive a smaller award under a no fault scheme and fewer people receive a larger award under a tort-based scheme. That is of course a generalisation but it is hoped that it is not inaccurate or unfair. It must of course be a political matter as to whether society wishes to share the same cake amongst more persons or whether to make some alternative provision— ideally a very much larger cake.

In Sweden[4] the average award under the patient insurance scheme was £3,500 in 1986. Large lump sums are seldom paid but awards are made to meet nursing bills or loss of earnings and are payable only as annual sums. Tariffs for loss of amenity, pain and suffering are comparatively low, the Swedish current maximum being rather less than half the UK maximum.

In New Zealand MacAlister Mazengarb tell us that the corporation has had difficulties in assessing the levels of compensation applicable for ''brain-damaged'' babies. The lump sum award for severe loss of amenities is NZ$10,000. Lump sum awards appear infrequently to be awarded, however. Expenses such as medical and transport expenses will be met by the ACC which may in some cases provide the parents with a motor vehicle and provide the child with other special equipment. Because the child is under the age of 16 years it will qualify for the loss of potential earning capacity and currently will receive NZ$338 per week. MacAlister Mazengarb say that as an example of the unfairness of the system this is double the unemployment and sickness benefits currently paid in New Zealand.

Rejection rates

Amongst the more alarming features of the Scandinavian no fault schemes are the high rejection rates. In the introduction to his paper, Dr Carl Oldertz tells us that the Swedish patient insurance scheme has been in force since January 1975. In the first 13½ years some 60,000 cases had been notified of which 35,000 have received or will receive compensation. This represents a rejection rate of nearly 42% and, in passing, one wonders how many of those whose claims are rejected go on to sue in the courts as they are entitled to do. One further wonders how many would sue in the courts of the United Kingdom were that an option in circumstances where we had a no fault scheme but the claim under it had been rejected.

The figures for Finland are even more alarming—but the Finnish scheme has been in force only since 1987. Miss Paula Kokkonen, Director of the Department of Administration, National Board of Health, responsible for patient insurance in Finland, states that of 1,381 claims for compensation decided between 1st May 1987 and 30th April 1988, 38% were awarded compensation and 62% were denied compensation.

In the UK Vaccine Damage Payments Act scheme, Lee[3] tells us that only 13% of initial determinations led to an award and that, of those claims rejected, about half went to appeal and that 72% of appeals upheld the decision to make no award.

It is hoped that these figures speak for themselves and require no further comment except that in designing any alternative tort-based system in the United Kingdom, provision must be made, and made clearly, to deal with rejected applications for compensation.

Professional standards and accountability

Albeit that the stated aim of the common law, tort-based system of compensation is to do no more than to compensate (the system is not designed for retribution or punishment), there is no doubt that many medical practitioners fear being a victim of litigation and believe that this fear is at least in part responsible for the maintenance of high standards of clinical practice.

Be that as it may, what is plain is that in any system of delivery of health care steps must be taken to ensure the maintenance of the highest standards of professional practice and conduct. Further, a machinery must exist to enable patients to seek explanations and, where appropriate, to enable them to make complaints and to have them dealt with fairly and expeditiously.

One theoretical objection to a no fault system is that by paying compensation without asking questions it may lead to a lowering of professional standards unless, alongside it, is put into place some system of professional accountability. In New Zealand there exists a system of Medical Practitioners Disciplinary Committees. There is some anecdotal evidence that the numbers of complaints to these committees has risen in the decade since the introduction of the ACC no fault scheme. It would be interesting to know if statistical data are available.

It is argued by some that the existence of a no fault scheme makes it easier for the medical profession to admit errors. As against that are to be heard at least two different arguments. The first is that it may be more difficult rather than less for patients to obtain explanations about the "accident" which befell them. Secondly the argument has been heard that some medical practitioners, knowing of the strict need to prove "personal injury by accident" and being sympathetic toward the plight of their patient, may analyse matters more liberally in the formulation of their reports to the ACC. Medical men will be concerned by some of the anomalies arising from no fault schemes of compensation. For example, the drunken driver returning home after the office party who is involved in a road crash and loses a leg will be able to recover compensation. On the other hand, the diabetic arteriopath who loses his limb through a disease process will recover nothing. If, however, that diabetic arteriopath with a toe of dusky hue happens to trip over an uneven paving stone, adding an element of trauma to his misfortunes and, thereafter, loses a limb, the recovery of compensation may be somewhat easier.

Her Majesty's Government approach

The attitude of HMG towards no fault compensation has been voiced in both Houses of Parliament in recent months and in correspondence between 10 Downing Street and Members of Parliament.

The Government position was stated by Lord Skelmersdale[5] in a House of Lords' debate on Tuesday 10th November 1987:

". . . several noble Lords referred to no fault compensation so far as medicine is concerned and indeed we seem to have a pretty balanced opinion on this matter. I find it difficult, I must confess, to be persuaded of the merits of such a no fault compensation scheme . . . one major problem is that giving compensation to those who have suffered adverse results of their medical treatment—where no negligence has been proved—puts them in an unfair position compared with those whose disabilities are not the result of treatment but merely the inevitable progression of their disease. For example, the man who suffers brain damage—through no one's fault—on the operating table is compensated. The man who suffers equivalent injuries by a stroke would get none . . . I do not think that anyone has made out a convincing case for root and branch reform".

Causation (again)

In concluding this paper it is appropriate to look again at issues of causation.

It is crucially important to understand that many cases deserving of compensation without the need to prove fault go uncompensated in no fault schemes just as they go uncompensated in tort-based schemes.

Take three girls. Marjorie is born happy and healthy but is unfortunate enough to contract viral encephalitis which leaves her profoundly disabled.

Penelope, on the other hand, is born happy and healthy and is taken by her mother for her routine childhood immunisations. After the injection she suffers brain damage and requires, like Marjorie, lifelong care and attention.

Susan is born following a long labour and a failed attempted forceps delivery. Following her birth by caesarean section she is found to be profoundly "brain-damaged" and subsequent analysis of her case attributes that brain damage to obstetric mismanagement.

All three children have similar disabilities, similar needs in terms of nursing care and attention etc, and similar life expectancies. Marjorie will receive absolutely nothing other than the benefits which the National Health Service and Social Security systems can provide. Penelope may (or may not) be able to persuade the local Vaccine Damage Payments Act tribunal that there was a causal link between her immunisation and her brain damage. If she succeeds in convincing the panel (Stuart-Smith J notwithstanding) she stands to recover Parliament's statutory award of £20,000.

Susan on the other hand will recover a lump sum award from the Court in the region of £½ million to £1 million.

It is submitted that a system which produces such divergent awards of compensation for three children with like needs is unfair, illogical and unjust. *However, it is important to recognise that similar, nay identical, results would be achieved under any of the existing no fault schemes of compensation.* The child who suffers one of nature's misfortunes or a complication of a disease process will recover no special award under a no fault scheme.

Lee concludes his 1985[3] paper by stating that the UK Vaccine Damage Payments Act was an ill-conceived piece of legislation, pointing out that, ". . . in view of the unhappy state of medical knowledge in relation to the extent of, and reason for, severe adverse reaction to vaccines, a strict liability system which had at its heart the need to prove causation was never likely to prove satisfactory. Indeed it has not satisfied even those parents who were awarded what they considered to be a paltry sum. They are once again reverting to common law actions . . .".

Needs-based compensation

It is submitted for consideration that the only fair system of compensation is one which compensates according to need and not according to fault or blame or cause. The needs of Marjorie, Penelope and Susan are well-nigh identical, as is their life expectancy. It is absurd that they should be compensated in widely divergent ways. A system of compensation based on Swedish, Finnish or New Zealand models would still leave uncompensated significant numbers of severely disabled people. If the United Kingdom is to design an improvement to its flawed tort-based system it is to be hoped that it will be upon the basis of need and not a no fault system which, though satisfactory in some respects, still remains fundamentally flawed.

The sad plight of the brain-damaged infant may provide an ideal model for the establishment of a pilot scheme of needs-based compensation. Causation in these children's brain damage is frequently complex and may never be satisfactorily established, no matter what legal test is applied. In medical, human and social terms these children require all possible assistance if they are to lead their lives to the fullest of their limited potential. Their parents, too, require support and help. Their needs are likely to be acknowledged by those from the legal world with whom they come into contact, from solicitor through counsel to judge. It has been seen that the use of video film recordings of the practical difficulties faced by these children has a profound emotional impact upon the judge. Unfair and inappropriate weight may be attached to isolated events during the labour to the extent that the judge feels able, on the feeble test of the civil law, to make a large award of compensation knowing that this is the only hope to provide for the child the level of care required. Such awards may do less than justice, however, to the health authority and to the medical and midwifery staff who have worked hard and to high standards despite shortcomings in the relatively underfunded service.

English legal history contains many "legal fictions" which were designed to assist deserving litigants to overcome apparently formidable legal hurdles. Perhaps it is time finally to bury legal fictions (of which, it is submitted, this is but a 20th century example) and instead be open in acknowledging the problem and constructive in finding a solution to it.

Finally, it is hoped that friends and colleagues from countries with well-established no fault schemes will accept these critical comments in the constructive manner in which they are intended, accept thanks from their common law cousins for being pathfinders towards a better solution and join us in searching for a better and fairer system for all those who are deserving of society's help but who are, as yet, denied it.

References

1. Smith, R. (1988). No stopping no fault. *Brit. Med. J.*, **297**: 935.
2. Krever, J. (1986). *Ontario Lawyers Weekly*, **5** (39): 24.
3. Lee, R. G. (1985). Liability for vaccine damage in Great Britain. *Proceedings VIIth World Congress on Medical Law*, Ghent, 1985, **3**, 162–8.
4. Brahams, D. (1988). *Lancet*, **i**, 45.
5. Skelmersdale, Lord (1987). Official Record *Hansard* (Lords) 10 November 1987, **489** (32), Col: 1359.

14

Discussion

Chairman: Dr John Havard

Dr Havard: I was interested to hear Mr Mildred refer to the risk–benefit ratio and say that doctors were at very little risk of negligence in life-saving procedures. If they make a mistake during an acute appendix, does that mean they are unlikely to be sued in negligence?

Secondly, we have, of course, noted advertisements in local papers from solicitors inviting patients who think they have not been properly treated in hospital to get in touch with them. Mr McIntosh reassured us that the Law Society would see that this sort of thing does not happen. In fact, we have written to the Law Society and asked whether this is in the public interest, and we have been told that it is. I wonder whether these are solicitors who are capable and competent to deal with these cases.

Mr McIntosh: With regard to local firms trawling for cases, the Law Society, in considering the response to the Civil Justice Review, has taken the position that the profession is there to serve society as a whole, and that it is quite wrong that individual victims of accidents should not be made aware of their ability to take legal advice and perhaps seek damages. One would be hard pressed to suggest that is wrong.

The reason I feel that the Law Society needs to move towards specialised panels is to make sure that the wrong firms do not attract the wrong work for them. If there was a panel, and it became commonly known, it would take a fairly unintelligent claimant not to want to be represented by a specialist person or injury firm. We are not allowed to call ourselves "specialists". We can say we are "experienced", but are forbidden to say that we are specialists. That seems to me to be somewhat outdated.

Dr Havard: Dr Wall, Mr Mildred expressed astonishment at the statement made yesterday that the Medical Defence Union (MDU) had paid out claims on behalf of 1.3% of its members in the last year; he said that he found it difficult to believe as a result of his own extensive experience. Would you wish to confirm that?

Dr J. A. Wall (*Secretary, Medical Defence Union*): I said yesterday that the claims paid frequency (the term used by the actuaries, Baker and Woodrow, who have advised the MDU for nearly two decades) of the MDU was 13 per thousand— which most of us at the MDU immediately translate to 1.3%, (the figure I gave). Claims paid are facts. Claims made, initiated or threatened, proceedings brought, complaints made, are not.

Actuaries draw a graph of claims paid for each year. They have to wait an average of four years before being able to say with certainty what is the rate of claims paid, say, for 1980. Their graphs prove extremely reliable. It is a projection of their graph which says that for the year 1987 it would prove that we had paid claims, in the time it takes to do it, for claims which arose in 1988 at 1.3% of all practising doctors in 1988. That is not astonishing, except that that rate, as I pointed out, is to be compared with 1 per thousand (0.1%) 10 years ago and 7 per thousand (0.7%) only 4 years ago. We have announced publicly that the frequency of claims paid for British doctors has doubled in the last 3 years. Since the severity (as the actuaries call it)—in other words, the amount paid per claim—has also doubled, that is the reason why subscriptions to defence and protection societies have quadrupled in the last 3 years. It simply reflects outside facts.

It may be deplorable but subscriptions have to reflect what is paid out.

There are two points linked with that. First, Mr Bolt is reported in *The Times* today (13 January 1989) as saying that tens of millions of pounds are paid by way of subscriptions to the defence societies, of which only half reaches the patients. In a sense that is true, in that the subscriptions received in 1988 produced what appears as a working surplus in the accounts when they are duly published. The most recently published accounts for the MDU, 31 December 1987, show a working surplus of £25 million, and it is true that the damages paid that year were less than half the income of the MDU.

I must point out, however, that the damages paid in 1987—and the same is true for 1988—reflect facts going back an average of 4½ years, and in many of the more expensive cases 8, 10, 12 or even 15 years. The income received in any one year is not meant to be used on a pay-as-you-go basis, simply paying out what we need that year and having a small working surplus rather than an overdraft. We have to take in in 1988 and 1989 what the actuaries tell us will be required to pay claims in 1992 and 1993 arising out of treatment given this year.

The Times has oversimplified by isolating the suggestion that the MDU paid patients only half the money it took in. The other half is for paying patients in the future for facts which have occurred where the claims have not yet arisen, and indeed where many of the patients do not know they have a cause for action—the symptoms and signs may not become apparent for some years. The long tail of the business is the reason for that aspect.

Secondly, it was said in Mrs Brahams' paper that it can cost nearly £1 of costs to deliver £1 to the patient. I again refer to the most recently published accounts of the MDU in our current annual report, showing that £17 million damages were paid for the whole of our membership of 150,000. I gave that figure yesterday, and said that the Americans thought that must perhaps be our maximum single claim. It is not; it is the total.

Our legal costs (also given in the annual report) are £5.3 million. Even on the most simplistic approach, it cannot be said that we spend £1 on costs for every £1 paid to the patient. I would point out that that £5.3 million also needs to be subdivided (which is not feasible in the annual report). In 1988 the MDU opened 13,000 files, but my 1.3% claims paid figure is for only between 1,000 and 2,000 claims paid. The reason, which applies to all three traditional defence societies, is that over the decades we have had a very large medico-legal advisory service. We pay our lawyers to go to inquests, to the General Medical Council (GMC) disciplinary inquiries, and to appeals in the health service machinery. Of the £5.3 million we pay to lawyers including, but by no means exclusively, the leading firm to which Mr Mildred alluded, only a minority proportion is expended on costs involved in delivering £17 million to patients.

Dr Havard: As I understand it, the British Medical Association (BMA) scheme does claim to reduce delays. Mr Mildred said that it would not have much effect on delays because there would continue to be competing solicitors and so on.

Could Mr Bolt give us some indication whether he expects that the scheme will have all these adversarial disadvantages?

Mr D. Bolt *(Chairman, BMA No Fault Compensation Committee):* With regard to the delay criticism, I confess that I do not see it. It is not clear to me what major legal involvement there would be in the generality of no fault cases. We have obviously to look to the legal profession to achieve the maximum delay. The machinery, as in Scandinavia, would surely be that the patient makes a claim and appropriate medical comment is received—or medical comment is sought—by the organisation administering the scheme. I do not understand at all the idea of where delay comes from.

Equally, in the context of what Mr Mildred said, he spoke as if it is part of the no fault concept, as presented by the Association, to restrict the rights of patients to litigation. It was, in fact, specifically stated that the right of patients to litigate should be unaltered. I wish to correct that point.

I also wish to correct two points made by Mr McIntosh. First, he said—I think unfairly—that the profession is looking for somebody else to pay their bills. I stated clearly that the bulk of the expense of a no fault scheme must inevitably fall upon the profession.

Secondly, although Mr McIntosh is keen on the idea that our field should extend to, as it were, intrinsic defect in drugs, in the scheme put forward by the BMA neither Opren nor the problems that have arisen with the pertussis vaccine would be within it.

I have said that it would probably be a sound idea if, as in Scandinavia, there was a separate scheme, financed by the major drug producers, to cover that problem. I do not see it as coming into our scheme because it would take the finances of the exercise out of this world.

Mr McIntosh: I did not say that I believed the medical profession is looking for others to pay their bills. I noted carefully that Mr Bolt underscored that it was not. It seemed to me that there was such a perception before he clarified the situation. Unfortunately, my paper was prepared before I heard his, and I was not sufficiently quick to amend that point in delivering it.

With regard to the drug companies, of course it would be excellent if they had a scheme and the BMA had a scheme. If those two schemes were properly organised so that they could dovetail with each other when both were in the frame in the case, it would make sense. If, however, the medical profession has a scheme and the drug companies do not, and problems occur in their cases—as they would with the Opren and vaccine cases anyway—the entire medical profession would be to some degree embarrassed because the general public look on these cases as medical cases, when doctors, nurses, health authorities and drug companies are all involved.

Of course, we are all searching for a sort of Utopia, but I accept the good sense of having two schemes. It is no good saying that those massive cases would not have stayed outside; such cases are food and drink for the consumer campaigners. There are many other cases involving the medical profession and drug companies which are far easier to accommodate, where there is a liability, but they are settled; and they are handled with a high degree of co-operation between those involved. Those would fit into the scheme, but the big cases make it quite difficult to dovetail two schemes.

Mrs D. Brahams *(Legal Correspondent, the* Lancet*):* I took my figures from the Civil Justice Review, which said that it could cost £1 or more in legal costs for every £1 paid out to plaintiffs. Of course, the total cost must be included, not just the cost for one side.

So far as small claims are concerned, claims of under £5,000—which presently have to be fought in the county court—are even less economic to fight.

If I may turn an old legal adage on its head, we have a saying in the law that "hard cases make bad law"—which is what was said about the Wilsher case—and say that bad law makes for hard cases. I think there are too many hard cases, and therefore we have bad law. I would like to see it changed.

Causation keeps being referred to—causation is easier to establish in a no fault scheme simply because people are more willing to accept it. It does not have the adversarial process, and there is a basic willingness to accept that causation may exist. In practice, in the various countries in which no fault schemes are run, causation is not found to cause enormous practical problems. They may compensate perhaps a few too many cases, but I would rather err on the side of generosity than meanness.

Eventually, of course, there will be a dispute because somebody will fall outside the line. The fact that a no fault scheme has some defects but has great advantages is not necessarily a reason to exclude it.

With regard to Mr McIntosh's remarks that our adversarial tort system has served us relatively well over the years, I do not think it has served us particularly well in this area. It has never served private litigants very well. It has never been economic to fight relatively small claims—these end in costs greater than the damages taken out. I think adversarial litigation is a poor way of settling disputes, although of course it is the best we have at the moment.

As far as Wilsher is concerned, the whole point is that it took 10 years to get this case to the House of Lords, at an *enormous* cost. In a no fault system, that decision would probably have been taken after six months, at no cost to the plaintiff and very little cost to the public. I understand that the costs in Wilsher are about £100,000. Any system that produces cases like that is unsatisfactory.

Mr McIntosh: In Utopia, I agree with Mrs Brahams. I do not claim that the tort system is the best, but it is what we have. If I may say, at the risk of being slightly impolite, some of her ideas are unrealistic. We can all say that we would like to err on the side of being generous. I am not just a defendants' lawyer, I am a consumer, and a potential victim of a tort or of tort fees, as we all are. We would all like to see unlimited damages easily given out, but society will not provide the money. A no fault system across-the-board would be excellent.

The inquisitorial system of resolving disputes in mainland Europe is far less expensive and far less open to the criticism of our tort system. If the view is taken that everybody with a grievance should be able to run their case and get damages, the inquisitorial system does not seem to serve that.

Looking at the tort system over the years it is not as bad as is currently being suggested, and much of what is wrong with it can be rectified. That is the compromise—and it is a compromise, if it is compared with Utopia—that we had better address now because a no fault scheme will not come in quickly, even as a pilot scheme. Let us get the tort system right. Let us make sure that the yardstick which is being criticised is made into something better than it is, so that the comparison is also Utopian.

Mr Mildred: I was not in any way trying to criticise Dr Wall's figures. I am surprised that as many claims are paid as he said, but of course I accept it.

If I may take it slightly further, within this system (within which everybody has been saying that it is extremely difficult for a patient to succeed) the MDU is nevertheless paying for 13 per 1,000 doctors practising in Britain. Why? Who are these doctors? What have they done wrong? There is no jury to feel sympathetic to the patient. I do not understand the reason.

Dr Wall: Let me give two figures. The American College of Physicians recognising differences between city and country, between eastern and western seaboards and the centre of the USA, and between the specialties, gave an average across the USA for 1986 of 15 per 100 (15%) of American doctors having damages paid on their behalf.

In France, the Soù Medical, in Paris, the equivalent of the protection and the defence societies, pays damages for four doctors for every 100 in practice. I do not know why Dover and Calais should be so different. Perhaps it matches Mr Mildred's point that very few claims are paid here compared with other developed countries—and perhaps he argues that more should be.

Rabbi J. Neuberger *(The Patients' Association):* I chair the Patients' Association and most of my relations are doctors and lawyers. However, I am neither, since I am a member of the clergy (and we have our restrictive practices too).

I was rather appalled by Mr McIntosh's view that quite a lot of consumer campaigns are ''not all good''—I think those were the words he actually used. They may not all be good, and they may not all be correct, but I think they are helpful and that in many cases they direct the attention to improvements which could be made.

In the Patients' Association we cautiously welcome the idea of no fault compensation. That is not to say that we agree entirely with any of the current proposals, and certainly feel that there is a need for a pilot scheme before we can go very much further.

I would like to take up Mr Mildred's view. We too are disturbed about the definition of eligibility. He asked for the best medical minds and the second- and third-rate legal minds. We propose some fourth-rate patient minds as well to take some part in deciding who should be eligible.

We also take the point that even if a no fault compensation scheme were introduced in a pilot scheme it could only go along with considerable improvements in the personal injuries system that there is in Britain. I take Mrs Brahams' point fully, because I was involved in responding to the Civil Justice Review at the beginning. It has not worked well for the interests of individual patient plaintiffs, and there are considerable improvements that could be made. One of them, mentioned by Mr McIntosh, is the possibility of class actions, which could, of course, make a major difference.

Therefore, we welcome the proposals, but please do involve the consumers and do not always criticise them.

Mr McIntosh: Rabbi Neuberger misconstrues me. I said that not all of the consumer groups' ideas are good. I elaborated that by suggesting that some were not practical and some of them did not take fiscal reality into account. I certainly welcome consumer groups. Without them, tort law would not have moved forward at all. There have been questions at this meeting from people who represent those groups, and they seem to me to have been just as important a contribution as those from the speakers.

Mr J. E. Woodyard (Stafford): I would like to take up the point that has been made—for the first time—about the responsibility of the Health Authorities in this matter. As a practising surgeon, I can say that their interest in standards of practice is virtually nil. There is a failure of management that is reflected in many ways in how doctors do their work. Reluctantly I have to say that in the changing pattern of medical practice, if we are to see improved standards (which have been hinted at), the Health Authorities will have to organise themselves in some way to encourage higher standards of practice. We get no support, and little interest, in cases taken against us. There is no interest in why an individual case has been brought, whether it is because a doctor is unsatisfactorily trained, not properly supervised, tired, or simply past his best. There is considerable room here for improvement in medical standards when the Health Authorities take up what the general public believes to be their true responsibilities.

Dr Havard: In nearly every case it is the Health Authority which is sued.

Mr A. J. P. Ross *(General Surgeon, Member of the BMA No Fault Compensation Committee):* I get the impression that there is general agreement that the lump sum system in medical negligence is not an appropriate system. Does Mr Mildred agree that it is not appropriate and, if so, what does society have to do to change it?

Mr Mildred: For continuing care, a structured settlement—a system in which there is payment according to need each year for actual expense to be incurred—would be much better. The present system can only guess at requirements. It was said yesterday it is intended that at the end of his or her life the patient has a lump sum to leave to the family. That is not how it is meant to work. The intention is that by a mixture of spending income and capital for the presumed life expectancy of the invalid all the money will be exhausted at the date of that invalid's death. Because it is not known when that invalid will in fact die, there may be too much or indeed too little. I suspect that in many cases, particularly in periods of inflation, there is too little.

One of the few things on which I can agree with Mrs Brahams is that there is an almost unanswerable case, in cases of nursing care, etc. for money to be paid out in the future on a regular basis of structured settlements or annual payments. For damages for pain and suffering, there is a philosophical problem as to whether it is appropriate. Is there any correct figure for how many thousands of pounds for a broken limb, and so on?

If it is decided to have a system which compensates people for physical or psychological injury with money, I think there have to be arbitrary figures. There is no right or wrong figure. Defendants want the figures as low as possible; plaintiffs seem to want them fairly high. I think that should carry on in a lump sum form.

Prof. J. A. Dudgeon *(Great Ormond Street Hospital, retired):* I heartily agree with Dr Palmer's reference to brain-damaged children. One of the problems is that the causes are multifactorial from events in conception, during pregnancy, at birth, or untreated meningitis, for example, after birth.

There was reference yesterday to Lord Justice Pearson's Commission on Civil Injury. The Vaccine Damage Act was passed during the time the Commission was sitting. In his comments on antenatal and medical injuries Lord Justice Pearson and his colleagues, without dissent, clearly said that it seemed to be invidious to compensate a handicapped child for one cause and not take into account all the causes. It seems to me that that very good and careful analysis wants to be looked at again.

Taking the case of handicapped children, from whatever cause, I personally feel that it is a mistake—it is wrong—to compensate for one cause and not for the others. I would agree with Dr Palmer and try to introduce a scheme whereby those children, from whatever cause, come into a compensation scheme.

Mrs D. Brahams *(Legal Correspondent, the* Lancet*):* May I correct an inaccuracy in Dr Palmer's talk. He referred to the Mpanda case in Sweden, which was capitalised up at £4 million. In fact, the local Health Authority admitted liability for the claim, and he would have been perfectly entitled to claim under the scheme. The scheme, however, had a cap on it of £300,000 (or the equivalent in kroner), and he chose not to do so because the scheme does not like to recognise private nursing. As a result, he brought an action in the courts which were able to award unlimited damages. That is how it arose and I wanted to make it clear that he was not refused under the scheme. It is the only case that has succeeded in Sweden.

Dr Palmer: Thank you for the correction, but I do not think it destroys the point I was making. If there are two systems side-by-side in this country, and one has a cap on it but the other does not, guess who will go for the better one.

Dr C. R. Blakeley *(Cambridge):* I was rather puzzled by Mr Simanowitz's presentation. He complained bitterly of the short time he was given to present his case and the defensive attitude of the medical profession as a whole to his organisation. He made out a strong case for increased accountability, linking this with increasing standards within the profession. Yet he made no attempt to make constructive suggestions as to how this might be achieved, or how his organisation thinks it could be achieved. In fact, these suggestions came in Mr Morrison's talk.

I might suggest to Mr Simanowitz that he would get a more sympathetic response from the medical profession if he spent time making constructive suggestions rather than simply seeming to be interested in retribution.

Mr Simanowitz: I am sorry that I seem—at any rate to Dr Blakeley—to be interested in retribution. I do not think that was the thrust of my talk.

Insofar as suggestions were concerned, I would have thought that they were inherent in what I said. In the very limited time available to me, it is possible to make only one strong point and the point I make is that accountability must come to the fore. There were a number of suggestions made: that we should have something like the Medical Responsibility Board in Sweden; that there must be education for doctors so that they understand that victims are patients, as they were before the accident; and that there is an improved sense of responsibility towards them. How the medical profession actually approaches dealing with that is not for me to say. That is very much the responsibility of the medical profession. It is not up to me to put forward specific suggestions as to how the medical profession should come to terms with its responsibility to victims.

Dr R. A. Williams *(Bloomsbury Health Authority):* If a no fault compensation scheme was fully implemented, would it then be possible for all doctors to stop paying all subscriptions to medical defence societies? If that happened, what would happen to the finances of the defence societies?

Dr Palmer: No, indeed. The defence societies clearly provide a great many services to their members other than settling claims for compensation. If there was a willingness to introduce a scheme of no fault compensation—a pilot scheme, if you like, for the brain-damaged neonate (because of these problems of causation I have touched upon) then, at a stroke, that would remove the majority of the extremely high value claims. There were three in one afternoon in the high court this week which will cost, between us all, well over £1 million.

That would mean that a number of things can be done. There could be a very much lower mutual subscription, but even if all claims for compensation are removed there will still be a need, I suggest, to maintain the many other services now provided—but they could be made available at a modest subscription level. It is the huge awards for brain-damaged plaintiffs, notably the neonate, who may survive 30 or 40 years and attract awards of £500,000 to £1 million, that produce the major problem for us in funding. And, of course, there may be very many more in the pipeline about which we do not yet know.

Dr Havard: Can you remind us what happens to the lump sum payment if the injured neonate perishes?

Dr Palmer: One of the major problems of the current common law system is that the estate then comes in for what I have heard described as a "windfall".

Dr R. D. Mann *(Royal Society of Medicine):* I noticed some of the features of Mr Simanowitz's paper, and was slightly puzzled by his position that no fault is a misnomer. As this meeting is essentially about no fault compensation, I would like to comment on that.

I have previously referred to the fact that there are unavoidable drug accidents amongst the causes of medical accident. There are situations in which a drug can be effective and its benefit to risk ratio perfectly acceptable in serious disease, and yet perhaps 1 in 30,000 patients suffers catastrophic harm from it. This is a known risk. In that situation, one patient suffers all the harm and 29,999 enjoy the efficacy of the drug. No one can possibly tell who will be the unlucky patient. The suggestion amongst those who believe in this concept is that that is an example of a no fault situation.

It is not a misnomer; it is a reasonably accurate description of the fact that there are medical accidents which are literally nobody's fault.

Secondly, in my paper I defined no fault compensation as being a scheme which abandons the rule that an injured person has to show that someone was negligent in order to obtain redress. This is a further meaning, that we are talking about the fact that fault does not have to be demonstrated by the injured patient. That does not stop others investigating in the cause of prevention. No fault is not always a misnomer. I think that generalisation is supremely inaccurate.

It is true, of course, that negligence is a severe problem. I mentioned the strengthening of professional accountability in opening this meeting and noted that the Society is likely next year to hold a symposium, parallel to this one, on accountability and audit. For Mr Simanowitz to suggest that he believes it would be in the interests of his people to have a system of "accountable compensation" seems to me something that should be challenged. If we are going to compensate only when someone has been held to account then we will be back into the position of the poor fellow who suffers the 1 in 30,000 risk, and who either never gets compensated or who gets compensation only after a long period of years. We need a number of improvements moving forward in tandem.

Mr Simanowitz: I think we are arguing about semantics. Dr Mann used the term himself, that it is not always "no fault". Then he suggests that we want to compensate only where it is proven that someone is accountable. Dr Mann talks about my people. Let me remind him that they are not "my people"; we are talking about the public, the victims of medical accidents.

I am not suggesting that we should not look for a system that compensates everyone who has suffered an accident. Possibly we can even go further and look at the broader sweep discussed by Dr Palmer. What I am saying is that terms like "no fault" must not be used because they imply different things to different people. We are actually talking about some sort of automatic compensation.

The accountability comes first. We have seen about 6,000 people over the last 6 years, and the vast majority of them talk about accountability. They do not come into my office looking for money; they want to know what happened, why it happened, and what will change so that it does not happen again.

Our fear is that by concentrating on something that calls itself "no fault compensation", that deals only with compensation, the issue of what happens will be swept under the carpet. Dr Palmer has said (and I agree with him) that if there was some sort of system which deals with automatic payment, alongside that there must be an adequate scheme for accountability. If that is brought forward first, the problems of compensation will be much smaller.

Mr R. K. Greenwood *(Leicester):* Mr Morrison has raised a new and fundamental issue. He talked about the way forward, and mentioned unsupervised junior staff. As we know, the whole profession is trying to reduce the numbers of junior staff in order to correct the career structure. The corollary of this·is that we want to expand the consultant grade in the acute specialties. Unfortunately, that is not occurring. There is neither governmental nor departmental will to expand the consultant grade. This means, of course, that we are left with the existing cadre of consultants who will be put under ever increasing pressure, losing their junior staff. May I press the point that the importance of expanding the consultant grade in the acute specialties must be brought to everybody's attention.

I must endorse the remarks concerning defensive medicine. I have practised them for years now. After listening to Mr Simanowitz, I shall practise them even harder. I think it is a terribly retrograde step.

Dr P. Green *(Private General Practitioner):* There has been a lot of talk today about prevention, and those remedies that lie in that direction. As a clinical forensic specialist, I am acutely aware of the fact that very little forensic medicine is now taught at undergraduate level. Have any of the speakers or the Chairman any comments about that?

Dr Havard: The British Medical Association (BMA), giving evidence to the Royal Commission on Medical Education, said that it was vitally important that forensic medicine, and indeed the basic principles of medical practice and ethics, should be taught to medical students. It is not mentioned in the Report, although at Lord Todd's press conference he emphasised it—so the omission must have been pointed out.

Mr Morrison: When I qualified in Glasgow 41 years ago medical jurisprudence was part of the final examination. As far as I know, it still forms a large part of the curriculum.

I did not have time to complete my recommendations. Some of those I did not present would probably not have been so popular with the profession, including general practitioners such as the suggestion that continuing assessment is needed, not only of practitioners but of specialist staff. I also think that consultant appointments should not be made permanent, but should be renewable dependent upon progress. The Royal Colleges have an enormous part to play here.

I would also like to have had the opportunity of saying that I think the General Medical Council (GMC) should consider introducing examinations comparable to our final examinations for overseas doctors who come to practise in this country. I know that is very controversial—but, of course, it should not be forgotten that the health service could not function without the overseas doctors.

Dr C. Oldertz *(Skandia Insurance Co. Ltd., Sweden):* As I am the only representative of the Nordic no fault schemes, I think it is necessary for me to make some comments and clarifications.

First, the amount of compensation is an important question. In the western countries' systems it is not possible to give compensation for the full need in every case. That is out of the question.

It may be asked why certain patients who are injured while seeking health care should receive better compensation than other people. It is because there is a negligence liability system, which means that if a fault occurs in seeking health care then the patient will be compensated. There are many criticisms of such a system, and these give rise to ideas on how to avoid those criticisms.

Another question is that of prevention. It is very important to avoid injuries—because if injuries are avoided, there will be no need for compensation. As we have seen, a negligence system will not gain anything real with regard to prevention. But if there is the possibility of identifying the cause of injuries—even if those causes are not considered to be negligent—then the data provide a good starting point for studies on the prevention of injuries.

Mrs M. Vennell (*Accident Compensation Corporation, New Zealand*): In view of Dr Palmer's invitation to be of assistance, perhaps I could expand on some aspects of the New Zealand scheme.

First, it is true that there are some difficulties in New Zealand in relation to the definition of personal injury by accident. The number of cases that actually go on appeal on that point has, however, been remarkably few. Rather like the iceberg, one-eighth is above sea level, and seven-eighths are below sea level. It is only the one-eighth that causes difficulties (it may even be less than one-eighth), and on which we focus.

The difficulty of bringing people into the scheme or excluding them is, of course, overcome by having a much wider based scheme—which I think Dr Palmer would favour—which covers sickness, disability arising out of sickness, as well as disability arising out of accident. That is the logical extension of our scheme. Indeed, it is the one that Sir Owen Woodhouse, the architect of our scheme, would favour. That is very costly, even in a country with a population of 3½ million. Our Government has not been prepared to take on the costs of such a scheme.

Our threshold of personal injury by accident is not necessarily the ideal threshold—or perhaps it is the interpretation that has been put on it which is not ideal. I would hope that here you would learn from our mistakes.

In my formal paper I have tried to analyse some of the medical cases that have come before the courts in this country to try to decide whether or not they would come within our scheme, in the hope that would be of assistance.

In relation to the brain-damaged babies, I should explain that the first child, who was injured as the result of contracting viral encephalitis, would not be compensated in New Zealand. Both the vaccine-damaged child and the child who was damaged during delivery would be compensated by our scheme: they would both have suffered personal injury by accident, and would both recover exactly the same compensation. They would not have money in their hands as such because clearly they were both non-earners. They would be cared for by the Corporation from the cradle to the grave. We would provide all the aids they needed, all the medical care and attention, all the home assistance—absolutely everything the child needed until the day it died—but its parents would not have a lot of money in lump sums. Probably the child would not qualify for either of the lump sums, because to qualify for the lump sum of about £3,500 for pain and suffering the individual has to be aware that he has had some pain.

A few days before I left New Zealand a case was reported in the papers which the media picked up and highlighted. A little boy had acquired immune deficiency syndrome and became AIDS-positive as a result of a blood transfusion. The Corporation had not paid the lump sum for pain and suffering on the grounds that the parents had not yet told the child that he was AIDS-positive. The little boy, who was 8-years-old, had not had any mental suffering, so the Corporation had said it was not prepared to pay him compensation until he becomes aware of the situation. The media said what a terrible body the Accident Compensation Corporation is—but I assure you that once the child becomes aware of the situation, he will qualify for the lump sum.

In relation to the legal profession, interestingly the legal profession is very little involved with the scheme. It does get involved in a few of the difficult cases, but in the main the legal profession is outside it—and I think glad to be outside it.

Mr D. Bolt (*Chairman, BMA No Fault Compensation Committee*): I think we were all seized with the emotional appeal of Dr Palmer's suggestion about a no fault compensation system to cover the brain-damaged infant. Nevertheless, while it has emotional appeal, the main impact—as Dr Palmer pointed out—is upon the pockets of the profession. That is not primarily what we have been concerned about in preparing the Report of the No Fault Compensation Working Party. We have been interested in being fair to patients and eliminating some, at least, of the lottery that is involved in the compensation field.

May I say that I regard Dr Palmer's suggestions, in practical terms, as unrealistic but the problem of the massive award for brain-damaged children would be solved by the scheme put forward by the BMA.

Dr Palmer: I accept that I have spoken about an ideal and I think it is still something for which we should try to strive. I do not accept Mr Bolt's last point.

15

Informed choice as a way to reduce risks and prevent injury

Peter F. Carpenter

I wish to thank the Royal Society of Medicine and the British Medical Association for inviting me to participate in this meeting; I also want to share with you my experiences from the United States and from the pharmaceutical industry. I am not a doctor, nor a lawyer, nor British. I am a philosopher businessman, if the two are compatible, from a virtually unique US pharmaceutical firm.

I wish to focus my attention on the nature of risks and the ways of eliminating or reducing risks. I shall also discuss remedies to injury, and the corporation's role—and here my remarks will also apply to institutions such as the Royal Society of Medicine and the British Medical Association. I will then present a brief history of informed consent and the philosophical basis for informed choice, and finally, I will offer a specific proposal regarding pharmaceutical informed choice.

I want to begin, however, with two cautionary statements. First, the situation in the United States with respect to medically related injury and compensation is not a path that I would encourage anyone to follow, particularly those of you in the United Kingdom. Second, it is important that our concern with no fault compensation does not allow us to overlook the vital importance of trying to avoid injury when at all possible. That is an essential element to keep in mind.

A critical issue is how we deal, individually and collectively, with change. Most of us spend our lives in ruts. Ruts happen to be deep and long—easy to fall into and hard to climb out of. We do not have a very good perspective when we are in a rut. The situation in the United Kingdom, regarding the consequences of unfortunate medical outcomes, is in many ways akin to being in a rut. Under these circumstances innovation (effecting a change in the established order) is extremely important. It is important to recognise that many people are committed to an established order; that is, in fact, what an established order is—something on which a lot of people agree. Innovation, on the other hand, is concerned with changing the established order. One thing I wish to consider is how Alza has been innovative in the area of informed choice.

The aim of informed choice is to minimise the occurrence of avoidable injury. Once that is done, no fault compensation becomes a desirable and appropriate safety net. But if avoidable injury keeps occurring, it could both overwhelm and discredit even the best no fault compensation scheme.

Relating the nature of risks to risk prevention

To distinguish between categories of risks, we can look at some risk dyads, for example: unavoidable versus avoidable risks; unknown versus known; non-disclosed versus disclosed. Having distinguished them, we can examine them with a view toward moving risk situations to the right side of the dyad, for example:

Unavoidable v. *Avoidable*. Through research we can create new chemical compounds which are potentially safer. Some risks will be avoided through the provision of fuller information at appropriate decision points in the drug development process.

Undisclosed v. *Disclosed*. There are many levels of disclosure, including disclosure by manufacturers to physicians who use our products and disclosure by physicians to patients. To be on the right side of this risk dyad requires that corporations and all other providers of health care (physicians, hospitals, etc.) do a much more thorough job of disclosing risks.

Involuntary v. *Voluntary*. This dyad takes us into an area of great social controversy. It also provides a marvellous opportunity for innovation. Examples are pre-surgical informed consent—much more common today than in the past. Another example is an innovative patient package information leaflet that Alza issued for the Progestasert—our intrauterine contraceptive product (IUD). Interestingly, we were not allowed to introduce this labelling into the United Kingdom; the authorities considered it inappropriate to provide such detailed patient information.

Unknown v. *Known*. Supplementing sound clinical trials with vigilant post-marketing surveillance is essential, as Dr Mann has pointed out, in order to detect unusual or rare side effects. These often emerge in postmarketing populations that are many orders of magnitude larger than even the largest clinical trial populations can be. I think it is important to acknowledge the leading efforts of Professor Inman and Dr Mann in this area, as these efforts deserve much broader recognition and support worldwide.

Remedies to injury as a function of type of risk

Let us now consider examples of some remedies to injury as a function of type of risk. A situation involving a side effect that was known but not disclosed creates a strong case for payment of damages to an injured patient. Similarly, if a product involved a known and avoidable risk that was disclosed by the pharmaceutical manufacturer to the physician—and perhaps even to the patient—but the product was administered so that a mentally competent patient did not voluntarily accept the intervention, then from a philosophical standpoint, there is a strong basis for payment of damages. I stress "from a philosophical standpoint" because I am not a lawyer—but it is my philosophical belief that under these circumstances some form of damages would be more appropriate than no fault compensation. However, had the patient been physically and/or mentally incompetent to comprehend the risks presented to him—for example, a victim of Alzheimer's disease or someone heavily sedated—then it would have been appropriate for another person to have acted on his behalf. The question here is who that person should be.

An even more difficult situation could involve a known but unavoidable, disclosed, and voluntarily accepted risk. Here one could argue that a no fault compensation scheme would be most appropriate. One example involves vaccine-related injuries. In widespread vaccination programmes, we ask individuals to take risks not only to protect themselves from a particular disease but also to protect society at large from it. In that case, there is a strong case for no fault compensation in the event of severe adverse effects. A similar case—but with one essential difference—would involve a cancer patient undergoing chemotherapy who suffers hair loss. That hair loss was also a known, unavoidable, disclosed, and voluntarily accepted side effect. Yet one could easily argue that under those circumstances neither damages nor no fault compensation would be appropriate because the treatment was solely for the patient's benefit, not society's, and because the known and disclosed risk was minor compared to the benefits received or hoped for.

As Dr Mann and others have suggested, in the practice of medicine there are unknown risks. Until these emerge as adverse events in reasonable numbers and in a form observable by practictioners, little can be done to prevent them. In some cases, little can be done even once they become known. In such cases, to continue to have all the societal benefits from medical innovation it is essential to find a way to compensate for injuries. Or if something is unknown—not because of negligence, but unknown even though everyone did the right thing and the risk still did not become apparent—then some form of no fault compensation is highly appropriate.

It is important to point out that an unknown risk cannot be avoided, disclosed, or voluntarily accepted. This is why it is very important that unknown risks be minimised by proper testing and, more importantly, by proper post-marketing surveillance. In the case of medical practice risks, some type of audit should exist to identify otherwise unknown risks.

More importantly, undisclosed risks cannot be either avoided or voluntarily accepted. That, I think, places a heavy responsibility on those of us who are aware of risks to make sure that those risks are properly disclosed.

Finally, I would like to make one more comment: never underestimate the value of an explanation and an apology in the event of injury. I find it profoundly disturbing that good bedside manners seem to disappear in the case of an unwanted medical outcome—perhaps in response to the intrusion of the tort system. When I served as Executive Director at the Medical Center at Stanford, I encountered some distressing situations when the physician had exhausted all of his or her capabilities and the patient was near death. Frequently the physician found it impossible to deal with this situation. Thus, just when the family and patient most needed the services, help, and support of the physician, the physician had mentally and physically withdrawn. In an analogous situation—a patient's serious adverse reaction to a pharmaceutical product—I hope we will not forget the value of acknowledging the event and expressing our concern.

Roles of corporations and other societal groups

Let us consider the role and the responsibility of a corporation—and by implication the role and responsibility of both the British Medical Association and the Royal Society of Medicine—because there are significant parallels. First, it is important to realise that the "marketplace" in which we exist is changing. It is changing for the pharmaceutical industry, and it is also changing for the medical profession. The most significant change involves the expectations of patients. This is particularly true in the United States, but I doubt that patients in the United Kingdom will be far behind. We have succeeded in creating a society that expects that medical miracles will be commonplace, and that the medical profession and the pharmaceutical industry will solve all of society's problems at a reasonable price without risk.

The media and consumer advocacy groups are major agents in changing expectations. It is crucial to listen closely to one's critics; to ignore them is a fatal arrogance. Certainly, the best advice we received while going through the difficult process of deciding whether our company should keep the Progestasert system (a controversial and potentially expensive product from the product liability viewpoint) in the marketplace in the United States came from the harshest critics we could find. Acting on their advice, we made fundamental changes in the way we presented our product; every other company then in the IUD field abandoned the marketplace and turned away from customers who wanted and needed their products. We made our harshest critics part of our review process and made their suggestions part of the solution.

With respect to product liability issues, it is important to recognise that the tort system is failure-oriented. We would do much better if we focused more attention on increasing the successes in the health care system rather than putting so much time and attention on coping with the failures. That view speaks to the comments made by Mr Morrison and others in the course of this symposium. For all of its successes, the tort system is in fact dedicated to dealing with failure. A good portion of our energy and resources should go into increasing the ratio of success to failure in providing health care, as opposed to trying to decide what to do in case of failure.

Corporations, certainly in the United States, have no constitutionally granted right to exist. In the United Kingdom also there seems to be no inherent right of a corporation to exist. All corporations, associations, and other institutions exist because society feels that they are going to do something beneficial. Some people say corporations exist solely to make a profit. Actually they exist, particularly in the United States, because they are chartered by the individual States to do things not achievable by individuals acting alone or in an unlimited liability partnership with other individuals. Society empowers corporations to do these things in order to meet society's needs. To the degree that society and the state grant specific privileges to corporations, those corporations have a corresponding responsibility not only to fulfil their own objectives, but to fulfil the public trust placed in them. Once public trust is lost, it is difficult if not impossible to regain. In the United States, the one-to-one patient–doctor relationship is alive and well, in the sense that individuals effectively served by their physician retain great respect for that person's capabilities. Yet many people have lost the public trust that they once had in the medical profession, broadly defined. I hope the United Kingdom will not follow us down this particular path. Both the medical and pharmaceutical industries in the United Kingdom, however, are in grave danger in this respect. But these are observations by a visitor.

The history of informed consent

Let us look now at the history of informed consent, because understanding that history is important to understanding the proposal that I shall make at the close of my contribution. Informed consent first emerged as a legal concept and remained a legal concept for years before being examined as an ethical concept; finally it developed as a medical concept. Many of my legal and other citations are from United States sources because that was the environment in which Alza developed its philosophy regarding informed consent. But I think that this analysis is applicable to most Western European countries.

The first case I would cite is, however, a case from the United Kingdom in 1767 **Slater** v. **Baker and Stapelton:** ". . . and indeed it is reasonable that a patient should be told what is about to be done to him, that he may take courage and put himself in such a situation as to enable him to undergo the operation."[1] It is interesting that this case occurred over 200 years ago. It is equally interesting that a tremendous hiatus followed: the legal literature both in the United States and the United Kingdom shows that after **Slater** it was a long time before the courts again addressed this issue directly.

In fact, the next really pertinent citation was **Schloendorff** v. **Society of New York Hospitals**, 1914: "Every human being of adult years and sound mind has a right to determine what shall be done with his own body; and a surgeon who performs an operation without his patient's consent commits an assault, for which he is liable in damages."[2] In both of these cases the essence of what the courts are saying is that you cannot do things to a human being without providing a certain amount of information and without obtaining his consent.

Following the tragedies of World War II, the Nuremberg Code was adopted in 1948. In part, it states: "This means that the person involved should have legal capacity to give consent; should be so situated as to be able to exercise free power of choice . . . and should have sufficient knowledge and comprehension of the elements of the subject matter involved as to enable him to make an understanding and enlightened decision".[3] This code was not the creation of the medical profession but of the international legal and political system. Once again, this code specifies not only the process of consent but also the provision of enough information to allow people to consent knowledgeably.

Within medicine the process of patient consent began primarily with surgical procedures, was extended to medical procedures, and has over the last 20 years become standard in clinical trials of pharmaceutical products. I hope, on the basis of some innovations Alza introduced, that obtaining consent will become far more commonplace for marketed pharmaceutical products.

The medical profession first addressed this issue of consent in clinical trials in The Declaration of Helsinki (1964): "In any research on human beings, each potential subject must be adequately informed of the aims, methods, anticipated benefits and potential hazards of the study and the discomfort it may entail [and] that he is at liberty to abstain . . . . The doctor should then obtain the subject's freely given informed consent"[4]. For those of you who feel concerned or even threatened by this, I would like to quote from Ruth Faden's description of the United States' medical community's response in the early 1970s to the concept of informed consent: "Predictably, much medical commentary in the 1970s was negative: Physicians saw the demands of informed consent as impossible to fulfil and—at least in some cases—inconsistent with good patient care. . . . Dire predictions were voiced that fearful patients would refuse needed surgery after disclosure"[5].

The predictions of the United States' medical community turned out to be largely incorrect. Eventually the American Hospital Association's position was stated as follows: ". . . The patient has the right to receive from his physician information necessary to give informed consent prior to the start of any procedure and/or treatment . . . The patient has the right to refuse treatment to the extent permitted by law and to be informed of the medical consequences of his action"[6].

In 1984 the American Medical Association came out very strongly in support of informed consent: "The patient's right of self-decision can be effectively exercised only if the patient possesses enough information to enable an intelligent choice. The patient should make his own determination on treatment. Informed consent is a basic social policy . . . . Social policy does not accept the paternalistic view that the physician may remain silent because divulgence might prompt the patient to forego needed therapy. Rational, informed patients should not be expected to act uniformly, even under similar circumstances, in agreeing to or refusing treatment"[7]. This important statement should be read carefully, noting its extension of informed consent to the status of a social policy, as well as its advocacy of patients' rights to know and to respond differently to the same information.

Two British authors, Dukes and Swartz, writing in 1988, bring us up to date: "Although the general principle of proper patient information was formulated long ago, the process is commonly inadequate"[8]. I think that is a fair assessment of the process of informed consent as we face it today.

Informed choice

Let us look at the philosophical basis for what I am calling informed *choice*. I have made the transition from informed consent to informed choice for the following reason: Informed consent is viewed by many people as a legalistic term because it derives in many respects from the practice of law. Our objective in informing patients is not to protect *ourselves* legally, but to protect *them*. By using the words "informed choice" I mean to state that objective: to place the patient in a position to make a free choice about the treatment offered.

Three elements are involved: first, non-maleficence—the non-infliction of harm; second, beneficence—the provision of benefit; and third, autonomy—the right of individuals to make their own choices. With respect to non-maleficence, the medical profession has a long history of performing well. As to beneficence, our intentions have always been grand, but only in relatively recent years has a patient interacting with the medical system had better than 50–50 odds of emerging from the encounter with improved health as a result of the treatment received. In recent years—as a result of better medical education, the progress of science, and the benefits of technology—the interactions of most patients with the medical system provide much better than 50–50 odds of improvement. Finally, the most controversial of the three philosophical bases—autonomy, the right of individuals to make choices—is recognised to greatly varying degrees from culture to culture and even from generation to generation. Public and individual demands for autonomy, however, will surely grow.

On the basis of these principles, and my experience in the marketplace of the United States, I have developed the following proposal for further consideration. Once again, it rests on certain assumptions: that each individual is master of his or her own body and has the right to decide to use or refuse a pharmaceutical product (or any other medical intervention); and that in order to make such a choice, the individual must have adequate information (the concept of being informed). My specific proposition reads as follows: "The patient's right of self-decision can be effectively exercised only if the patient possesses enough information to permit an intelligent choice. Therefore, the physician and the pharmacist should be provided with adequate information regarding a pharmaceutical product and its alternatives in order to assist in the presentation to—and understanding by—the prospective user. Whenever pharmaceutical product information is directed to patients, the objective should be to inform them regarding benefits and risks rather than to promote the use of the product."

Dukes and Swartz[9] have also pointed out that, "The fact that the correct information is given is not enough. It should also be presented in such a way that it serves its purpose". In this respect, Alza has made the distinction in our own company between pharmaceutical hardware and pharmaceutical software. The pharmaceutical hardware is the physical product for example, the drug or device. The pharmaceutical software is the entire context in which that hardware is provided to the physician, the pharmacist, and ultimately to the patient.

If there is an under-invested area in the pharmaceutical industry where we need to do more, it is in the research and development of pharmaceutical software. The analogy to the medical profession is quite clear: the hardware is in pretty good shape, but this profession's software leaves a lot of room for improvement.

Some issues deserve further consideration. What is the appropriate balance between too much and too little information? How do we resolve the conflict between standardised worldwide labelling versus conformity to local regulations and customs? We find that, country by country, regulatory agencies will not accept labelling that other countries' agencies have either approved or even demanded. This refusal creates an interesting conflict for multinational corporations such as mine. There are other questions. How can we encourage consistent utilisation of patient information by physicians? What should the specific role of the pharmacist be in acting as a learned intermediary?

Conclusions

In conclusion, the patient has the right to make an informed choice. Its exercise requires that we provide patients with adequate information on the benefits and risks of the products and services we offer. The physician and the pharmacist are essential intermediaries in this process, and the industry has the capability of assisting them to act effectively. Finally, despite its difficulties, the long-term benefits of pharmaceutical informed choice outweigh the risks.

A move towards pharmaceutical informed choice, however—as with any change or innovation, such as those discussed in this meeting—will, and should, involve controversy, debate, and dissension. Challenges and criticisms are inevitable. It is often tempting to shun controversy, and if you live in a glass house, you may not want to throw stones—but that does not mean that you shouldn't keep your windows clean. In all of this we should never forget that our first priority must be the welfare of the patient. In this respect, I need to emphasise that openness and honesty are essential if we are to deserve and maintain the trust of the public.

References

1. Faden, R. F. and Beauchamp, T. L. *A history and theory of informed consent*. New York: Oxford University Press, 1986: 117.
2. *Ibid.*, p. 123.
3. *Ibid.*, p. 282.
4. *Ibid.*, p. 156.
5. *Ibid.*, p. 91.
6. *Ibid.*, p. 94.
7. *Ibid.*, p. 96.
8. Dukes, M. N. G. and Swartz, B. *Responsibility for drug-induced injury*. Amsterdam: Elsevier, 1988.
9. *Ibid.*, p. 176.

16

The CITCOM initiative

Des Wilson

A feature of British democracy, or what remains of it, and of the British political system, is the substantial contribution to policy-making of non-party political organisations, known as voluntary organisations, pressure groups, citizen groups etc. Some historic social changes, from the abolition of slavery and votes for women onwards, have come about as a result of political activity beyond, or in addition to, that of the conventional political parties. Citizen Action comes from that tradition. It is a non-profit-making organisation set up to coordinate a number of campaigning activities. In 1987 it was approached by some of the victims of the drug Opren for help and the campaign known as CITCOM—the Citizen Action Compensation Campaign—is part of our response to their problems.

I differ from most other contributors in that I am neither a lawyer, nor a medical man. My only qualifications are that I am a concerned citizen, and that I represent others who have been able to put together a campaign with a set of objectives that have won the support of a remarkable consensus—from consumer organisations to practising lawyers, and over 200 MPs of all parties.

I want to make two other brief points by way of introduction.

First, I want to emphasise that our campaign is not anti-lawyer (as I have said, it involves many lawyers), not anti the medical profession, and not anti-business or industry. We do not wish to weigh the scales of justice to bear more heavily on any of those professions—we merely wish to ensure that injured individuals have an equal chance before the law.

Second, we accept that there are many different issues involved in major multi-claimant cases like thalidomide and Opren as compared with individual cases. Nevertheless, I begin with one or two conclusions from the Opren case, for it did more to draw attention to the inadequacies of the British system of compensation than any since the thalidomide cases of the 1960s and 1970s and the Pearson Royal Commission which reported just over 10 years ago.

From the Opren case came what one can only describe as a judicial request for our involvement, for when announcing the settlement offer, the Judge paid particular tribute to two or three of those now involved in CITCOM, and said "once the Opren litigation is finally disposed of, those who have worked so hard on it will have, I feel sure, a great contribution to make in the future in finding solutions to the problems which have come to light in the handling and financing of litigation of this kind".

Likewise Mr Justice Hirst, commenting on the low levels of settlement said "there is nothing wrong with people questioning or condemning these levels

. . . . so long as they recognise that only parliament can change them. While they remain in force, the courts have no alternative but to apply them''.

CITCOM is effectively a response to that challenge.

Our experience, but much more critically, the experience of all those other organisations and individuals involved in CITCOM, is that there are six problems which have to be overcome:

First, there is the ability of the ordinary citizen to achieve access to justice. Their ability to afford it.

Second, if they are able to afford to pursue their case, there is the difficulty in finding a lawyer who is suitably qualified in either the personal injury or medical negligence field.

Third, there is the lengthy time it takes. The delays.

Fourth, in some cases it is arguable that the burden of proof is unfairly loaded in favour of the defendant—there is the difficulty of proving one's case.

Fifth, if all these problems are overcome, the levels of compensation in the UK are often deplorably low.

Finally, the handling and financing of multi-claimant cases present particular problems.

CITCOM exists to press for appropriate solutions to these problems.

It seeks to be open-minded. That is to say, it is not wedded to any particular proposal at this point, but it is promoting ideas in the hope that it can develop a consensus around the most appropriate to emerge. There is perhaps one exception to this—the Bill it is currently introducing in the House of Commons, with the assistance of Lawrence Cunliffe MP, which I refer to below.

Clearly, however, a form of no fault compensation, if it proved acceptable to all interested parties, has the potential to solve many of these problems. The Campaign has been criticised for not making no fault its priority. Instead, we have begun by seeking reforms in the tort system.

There are two reasons why we chose to do this:

First, the only no fault schemes that have been proposed to date are for minor road traffic accidents—a recommendation of the Civil Justice Review—and for medical negligence cases. Our campaign is aimed at the whole range of personal injury litigation and there is still need for reform to enable victims of many other kinds of accidents or negligence to pursue compensation in the courts.

Second, it is clear that the medical negligence no fault schemes which are operating in New Zealand and Sweden raise many questions, and that before either system is transplanted to the United Kingdom, much work needs to be done and much controversy will take place.

For these reasons, our view is that we should fully participate as a campaign in the debate about no fault, with the hope that an acceptable approach may emerge, but in the meantime proceed to some improvements in the tort system so that at least some people can achieve more appropriate levels of compensation.

However, without committing our campaign in any way, I should say that we would be most enthusiastic about a form of no fault compensation which did encompass a procedure for medical accountability which was both independent and involved a significant lay input.

As has probably emerged from earlier papers, the New Zealand system is distinguished from the Swedish system in a number of respects, but most fundamentally by its failure to make proper provision for monitoring, improving and controlling the performance of the medical profession.

The Swedish system on the other hand, is much more geared to encourage higher standards of care and to minimise the incidents of medical accident. The

Medical Responsibility Board, an autonomous body which governs medical accountability, is by all accounts truly effective in maintaining the highest standards of practice.

Effective accountability is a form of discipline without which a system of compensation is incomplete.

I make no apology for leaving the issue of no fault, and devoting the rest of my remarks to our other proposals.

I do so, because it is useful to take into account that whatever discussions take place will not happen in the short term. Apart from all the problems and difficulties in thoroughly working out the detail of any proposed scheme, political commitment to it has to be won. The late-lamented Edwina Currie in a letter last September to a Labour MP concerning the introduction of a no fault scheme, stated that "the government considers that the basis for seeking compensation for injuries suffered should continue to be through litigation in the courts". While government minds can be changed, as Mrs Currie has herself discovered, it does appear that the government is resistant to the idea of no fault, mainly for financial reasons. It is with this in mind that we seek not only to influence events in the long term, but also to eradicate in the short term the injustices in the existing system.

We have begun with the question of low levels of compensation for personal injury. Remember what Mr Justice Hirst said about the Opren settlement: "there is nothing wrong with people questioning or condemning these levels . . . . so long as they recognise that only parliament can change them. While they remain in force, the courts have no alternative but to apply them".

While in spectacular cases, such as the Piper Alpha disaster, and to some extent the King's Cross and Clapham disasters, higher settlements tend to be reached under the full glare of publicity, the fact remains that in many everyday cases, the levels are still based on Kemp and Kemp; Kemp and Kemp is about precedent, and the precedents have been too low.

The question is how to break the vicious circle?

We have made a practical proposal, encompassed in Lawrence Cunliffe's private members' bill, due to come before the House of Commons shortly. It would establish a Compensation Advisory Board to recommend the levels of compensation that should be awarded to injured persons; it would place a duty on the courts to have regard to such recommendations and also to actuarial evidence in awarding compensation; and it would increase the amount of damages paid in the event of bereavement and extend the categories of persons entitled to receive such damages.

The Board would be advisory, but we believe that many judges would welcome it as a more sensitive and up-to-date guide. Its chairman would be a high court judge appointed by the Lord Chancellor. It would consist of no fewer than eight and no more than eleven members, appointed after consultation with relevant organisations and would include one medically-qualified person specialising in, and with current experience of, the treatment of injured persons; one medically-qualified person specialising in the rehabilitation of injured persons; one clinical psychologist specialising in the counselling of injured persons; two persons having experience of personal injury litigation, a practising solicitor and a practising barrister; and three persons appointed after consultation with voluntary organisations providing advice or service to injured or disabled persons.

Within a year it would be expected to recommend compensation levels appropriate to injuries in a number of classes listed in the schedule to the Act. It would from time to time review its recommendations. It would place a duty on the court, in awarding damages to an injured person for pain, suffering, loss of quality of life, resulting from his or her injuries, to have regard to its recommendations.

We do not pretend this is a world-shattering innovation or that it alone solves the problems to do with personal injury compensation, but it is a practical, reasonable, step in the right direction and we will hope it will have the full support of everybody.

The Bill would also increase bereavement damages. As you know, bereavement damages are governed by the *Fatal Accident Act 1976* and the limit on the amount of damages recoverable is £3,500. We believe that this amount is unacceptably low. A belief which is borne out by the recent settlements in both the Zeebrugge and Clapham disasters in which the defendants paid out almost three times the legal minimum. We therefore propose an increase to a basic £10,000 per claimant with a ceiling of £50,000.

It really is unacceptable that individuals can win sums of £1 million (in the case of Elton John) or £500 thousand (in the case of Jeffrey Archer) in the courts for damage to reputation and yet can obtain a relative pittance for physical damage that can wreck a life, or the loss of a loved one.

This Bill has wide support. No doubt everybody will have their detailed suggestions that can be dealt with in committee but we are encouraged by the fact that the Law Society supports its second reading, and more than 200 MPs have indicated their broad support, many of the members of the government party.

Let me deal very briefly with some of our other objectives.

First, funding of litigation. We will campaign for increases in Legal Aid, but, we intend to provoke debate about other ways of funding actions. It is clear that the number of individuals who are eligible for Legal Aid has fallen during the last few years. An increasing number of people are deemed to be too affluent to qualify for Legal Aid and yet are not wealthy enough to contemplate financing an action on their own.

We cannot tolerate a situation where an individual, Mr Godfrey Bradman, had to put £5 million of his own money at risk to enable pensioners to stay in the Opren case because they were judged to be too affluent for Legal Aid on the basis of their life savings. In that case, a huge multinational company with comparatively unlimited resources had the dice hopelessly loaded in its favour.

We are therefore putting forward a set of proposals which will call upon the government and the Legal Aid Board to remedy a number of problems in the present system. These include:

The establishment of an enquiry into the decrease in the numbers of people eligible for Legal Aid. We find it unacceptable that there have been no detailed government studies over the last 10 years into the coverage of Legal Aid. The government has consistently attempted to make out that the numbers eligible for Legal Aid have remained the same, despite substantial evidence to the contrary and despite the fact that in 1986 it actually reduced the numbers eligible in money terms.

A drastic cut in the time taken to process Legal Aid applications. The Civil Justice Review found that the average time taken was 130 days—well over four months. This is before an individual will even know whether a claim can be started or not, let alone all of the other formidable delays in the system. The delays in the administration of Legal Aid have been described by one judge as ''a deplorable state of affairs''.

I have already mentioned the particular difficulties faced by the Opren claimants. I cannot emphasise too much the unfair effect of penalising elderly people for having life savings which are often used to supplement low incomes. We are therefore calling on the Legal Aid Board to adopt a more flexible approach to varying the limits when required.

One possibility, in addition to an increase in the levels of Legal Aid, is wider adoption of the Scottish system of allowing lawyers to take a case "on spec". We are not proposing American-style contingency fees; but in Scotland for years a lawyer has been able to charge nothing if a case fails and charge the ordinary fee if a case succeeds. And unless a better answer is put forward, and quickly, there is no defence for not allowing this to operate in England.

Second, we propose that there should be greater specialisation in this area. The recent Blackburn case of a man who suffered brain injury in a medical accident and whose parents had to fight for 12 years with three different sets of solicitors before finding a solicitor who could competently handle the claim, has once again highlighted the need for specialisation. A study published last year by the Centre for Socio-Legal Studies at Wolfson College, Oxford, heavily criticised the lack of expertise in the legal advice available. It established that specialisation is necessary not only in the highly complex field of medical negligence, but also across the whole field of personal injury law.

We will support the recommendations of committees, review bodies and Royal Commissions for the last 20 years that there should be greater specialisation in this area. We would like to see an acceleration in the process of establishing specialist panels of lawyers and in the drafting of written standards of professional conduct. We will also seek to ensure that such panels provide the public with truly specialised lawyers.

Third, we will be campaigning to support proposals by the Civil Justice Review and from other sources to cut the delays and the exorbitant costs inherent in the present system. We will also support the measures which will increase the amount of disclosure in the process.

There is however one important exception to this. The Review proposed that the small claims court should handle personal injury claims of £1,000 or less. This would mean that claimants, who would for the most part be unrepresented, would be pitched against insurance claims inspectors who are immensely experienced at litigating. We feel that such a move would gravely undermine a claimant's position. I have already referred to the need for the increased availability of specialised legal advice in this area and I can only say that it would be absurd if a large number of people were not able to avail themselves of it because they found themselves in the small claims court.

We will be pressing for a reform of the payments-in procedure. This was intended to promote fair out-of-court settlements. And we believe it has failed to achieve this aim. One individual who was badly injured in a road traffic accident has described it as "a shameful game of brinkmanship". We believe that its use by defendants to tempt needy and desperate claimants to accept less than their due must be stopped. We will be proposing that a system should be adopted which will encourage both sides to negotiate as fully and openly as possible so that speedy and fair settlements are reached and the costs of going to trial are avoided.

We will be advocating that the courts should have the power to award periodic payments as opposed to the traditional lump sum award. Recent developments in the insurance world have enabled schemes to be set up after out-of-court settlements which enable victims to receive periodic payments of damages. This means that victims do not run the risk of their compensation award being eroded by inflation.

We feel that the law in this area is lagging behind.

We will therefore be supporting the Pearson Royal Commission recommendation that courts should be obliged to award damages in cases of death or serious and lasting injury in the form of periodic payments, unless it is satisfied that a lump sum award would be more appropriate.

Finally, the Opren case demonstrated the need for reform to deal with multiple claimant cases. With the Ativan tranquilliser, British nuclear test veterans and haemophiliac HIV positive cases looming on the horizon we believe that urgent action is required in this area.

The Campaign, in conjunction with the National Consumer Council, has put forward proposals to reform the existing inadequate procedures. This approach would mean that the informal process which took place in the Opren litigation would be replaced by a system which would be governed by the court and which would not allow the defendant to buy off the lead actions.

Secondly, we will be campaigning for a reform of the financing of such actions. If ordinary people who are injured by defective products are to be allowed to challenge the government and corporate manufacturers, the Legal Aid means test will need to be relaxed. The cost of such actions is so immense that those who do not qualify under the present Legal Aid limits just cannot contemplate taking proceedings. We propose therefore that in multi-party claims all the plaintiffs should be entitled to Legal Aid and that there should be a limit of £1,000 on the amount an individual has to contribute towards their case.

No system of justice is perfect, but it is imperative in a society that likes to consider itself fair and democratic that people believe that they have a good chance of justice.

When, as a result of what they believe to be the negligence of others, they are injured, or a member of their family is injured or even killed, they are entitled to believe that the negligent should be held to account, and that they should be compensated.

It is an undeniable fact that apart from major disasters, where there is so much public attention, every day people are deciding they simply cannot pursue compensation because they cannot afford to. Or they wait years, and, after a lengthy struggle, they are awarded derisory sums. This does not encourage those who have the capacity to injure, by negligence, or deliberate cost-cutting, to be more careful.

Thus, the system is inadequate and this has been known for years. And yet, as an issue, it simply does not have the political priority that leads to real change and improvement.

That is why our campaign has been launched: to add political priority to the many good ideas—not just our own, but those of other people—that are around and to force debate and action. Our private members' bill, if it is passed, as I believe it will be, is but a small first step, but it is a first step—a beginning.

My colleagues and I approach it with some humility because we recognise the complexities. On the other hand, there is no field of activity, no matter how complex, from which public opinion should be denied expression, and on which the concerned layman should not have the chance of making a contribution.

We look forward to working with you over the next two or three crucial years, not only on the subject of no fault compensation, but on the whole area of personal injury law.

17

No fault compensation—a perspective from the view of the UK insurance industry

Barry R. West

Insurers are faced regularly with actual or proposed measures for law reform. They tend to be neutral on the principles on which proposals are based. They feel it is for society generally to decide such matters and see their role as commenting on the effect on the insurance mechanism in terms of practicality and cost. They do have a particular vested interest in seeking clarity in law reform and related issues since it is insurers who usually have the commercial need to estimate in advance the financial effect of change.

If the law was changed to introduce a no fault concept in respect of compensation for medically related injury, then insurers would expect to fulfil their obligations to their policyholders by continuing to offer insurance in respect of the enhanced legal liabilities that would arise.

Whilst the financial effect would depend on the nature and extent of the change, claims costs, and therefore premiums could be expected to increase significantly in the areas affected.

However, in this case discussion is related to the development of a no fault scheme on a voluntary basis. This presents something of a problem in terms of the appropriate response. It is not possible to deliver a view on behalf of insurers overall. In fact it may be appropriate to say something about the UK insurance industry as its nature and structure is pertinent to how it may look at an issue such as this.

It is an important industry. It collected non-life premiums in 1987 totalling some £25bn, nearly half of which is in respect of overseas risks. It is the biggest contributor to the invisible exports of the UK. London is still the biggest and most influential insurance market in the world with a deserved reputation for innovation and flexibility.

However, it is also a very competitive industry—not only domestically but also internationally. In comparative international terms it is lightly regulated (apart perhaps from the life sector) in that, whilst government is rightly concerned to see that insurers are financially viable, unlike many other countries, there is virtually no regulation in detail on policy wordings, rate levels, etc. Market forces prevail.

Insurers are commercial undertakings. In the non-life sector the mutual element is not significant. Shareholders have to be satisfied and performance is under constant scrutiny by the stock market and others. It also contains the unique element of Lloyds which has at least an equal commitment to commerical considerations.

The nature of insurance, particularly in the area of personal insurance, added to the instincts of the industry, produce a high level of social responsibility. However, insurers would not normally see themselves as social engineers. Any proposition would have to make sense in commercial as well as technical insurance terms to succeed.

At this stage, therefore, the input from insurers can only be to set out some of the considerations that would arise from the perspective of an insurance underwriter related to the broad concept of a voluntary no fault scheme. The natural starting point would be to look at the forms of cover written currently that may be pertinent to the subject.

As it happens, the premium income that UK insurers receive from the UK medical sector, even in its widest sense, is not substantial. The National Health Service does not insure. Drug manufacturers are large and international and few in number with a significant element of self insured retention and/or non-traditional insurance arrangements particularly for product liability. Professional indemnity cover is largely the preserve of the defence societies (perhaps insurers, but not in the sense of being part of the general insurance industry). The largest element of medically related premium received in London is, in fact, probably American medical malpractice cover.

In looking at relevant cover currently provided it may be convenient to use two groupings, "first party" insurance and "third party" insurance.

First party insurance is effected to provide specified compensation to the policyholder in the event of injury or illness or death. Cover may be effected by the individual or on a group basis; for example, by or through an employer.

There is a large range including life insurance, medical expense insurance, personal accident insurance, long-term disability insurance etc. These are covers designed to provide specified compensation for specific events. To the extent that any insured event may be caused or exacerbated by medically related action then compensation is paid usually at the level specified in the same way as any other cause.

Another form of insurance that could be pertinent is legal expenses insurance. This provides cover in respect of legal expenses incurred in pursuing an action for damages in defined circumstances. This group of insurances does give some means whereby the prudent individual can mitigate the financial effect of injury, including medically related injury.

However, the area more pertinent to the subject is third party insurance which is effected to provide an indemnity to meet damages awarded in the event of a legal liability to pay compensation; in addition, claims are defended. The policy will usually provide an indemnity up to a specified limit for one event and/or one year.

In this latter grouping we can identify two broad categories of cover.

Firstly, cover provided to commercial concerns. They would normally carry general third party cover to respond to any legal liability arising from the enterprise including liability from any defective product sold or supplied. This category would include drug and medical equipment manufacturers. (The recent *Consumer Protection Act* has, from March 1988, imposed a general regime of strict liability in respect of defective products put into circulation after that date. However, certain defences are allowed, notably the "state of the art" defence.)

Also in this category would fall private hospitals and nursing homes and similar facilities run by charitable organisations and the like where insurance may be effected to protect the enterprise on similar lines.

The second category is medical malpractice or professional indemnity insurance. This defends and indemnifies the policyholder against claims arising from allegations of professional negligence. As mentioned previously, for the United Kingdom medical profession this is almost entirely the province of the defence societies. This area of third party insurance is more pertinent since it is these covers that would be extended to respond to additional liabilities emerging from the development of a no fault concept.

There is no United Kingdom precedent for providing cover to indemnify for liability arising under such a concept. However, as mentioned earlier, if the law was changed to introduce such a concept then insurers would respond. In fact policies would respond automatically. Inevitably, however, premium levels would have to be adjusted.

Third party cover is, therefore, concerned with providing an indemnity in respect of the policyholder's legal liability. There is an ultimate objective standard that can be applied to any claim made by a third party, in that the issue of liability and the level of damages can if necessary go to litigation. In practice litigation is unusual but it is, of course, established precedents and decisions which determine the resolution of claims in this area.

Turning now to the concept of a voluntary scheme. This aspect of the necessity for an independent arbiter of liability would cause problems for insurers as a matter of philosophy.

Whilst the essence of a no fault system is that the issue of legal liability for the injury does not arise it will, nevertheless, still be necessary to establish a causal link between the medical activity and the injury and the level of damages still has to be determined.

In theory these matters could continue to be dealt with within the current legal framework with recourse to litigation if necessary. However, presumably this will be seen as maintaining too much similarity with the current tort system that is the subject of criticism.

So far as the level of damages is concerned, a level of compensation could be provided based on fixed scales. These scales would need to be complex if the objective is to match compensation to the victim's circumstances with reasonable accuracy.

Another possibility is determination of the causal link and/or compensation by use of a tribunal or similar independent body. This would, of course, have to be acceptable to both parties including claimants' advisers. Rules of operation would have to be established. Presumably there would have to be an appeal system. Some care would be needed to ensure that this was a cost effective alternative.

As mentioned already, the bedrock of third party insurance is an indemnity for legal liability as established by the legal system and interpreted by the courts. Clearly an insurer could not provide cover where the determination of the policyholder's liability to a third party and/or the level of damages was a decision for the insurers. Similarly, any tribunal would have to be seen to be totally independent of insurers. It has to be said also that even if independent, cost effective, and generally acceptable to claimants and their advisers, the use of a tribunal or similar body to determine issues of liability and/or compensation on an artificial system of liability for payment by an insurance policy is unlikely to attract insurers.

There are some additional points from the insurance perspective that may be pertinent.

Whilst a voluntary scheme could reduce the incidence of tort-based claims as an additional or alternative means of securing compensation, depending on the nature of the scheme and the degree of support secured, such claims will still occur. It would still be necessary to maintain insurance or other protection to deal with these.

Also some large commercial concerns—for example, major international drug manufacturers—may have problems in responding. Modern practice is for very large companies to manage actively their risk exposures, often resulting in substantial risk retention and use of captive insurance companies. They may not find it easy to slot in a voluntary scheme for part of their exposures. Also if additional cost were involved they would no doubt need to consider the effect on their competitive position in their industry.

Widespread, preferably near-universal, support from the medical sector for a voluntary scheme would seem to be highly desirable to reduce situations where claimants had different standards of compensation available depending on whether the defendant supported the scheme. This would need careful explanation to the public. A similar consideration would arise in respect of the date of introduction. Unless the scheme were to apply retrospectively—which would certainly result in inundation—two standards will apply depending on the date of injury. This is of course a consideration that would arise equally with change through law reform. These considerations would seem to make the development of a pilot particularly difficult.

Finally, to touch on the financial implications, whatever form a voluntary scheme takes it will be difficult to assess the compensation costs that will develop. In particular, the impact of a scheme in attracting claims for compensation which are not presented currently. A considerable technical research commitment would be required. Also the need to establish resources to administer the scheme could require a significant investment. So far as insurers are concerned these aspects would have to be justified by the expectation of a worthwhile return.

In making these comments I am very conscious that they are negative in tone. This is a subject of significant social importance and could involve substantial sums of money. It would not be helpful if insurers did not list the problems that they perceived from their perspective, and which had to be taken into account if the proposition of a voluntary scheme is to be progressed with insurers' involvement.

I said in my introduction that there was no settled insurance industry view. Having given this input, insurers will be happy to look at the conclusions reached at this meeting and engage in further discussion.

Perhaps I can conclude by summarising, simply, the salient points made. Firstly, insurers' participation in a voluntary scheme would require justification on commercial as well as technical viability. The subject is too significant for it to be dealt with as a matter of goodwill. Secondly, insurers would find difficulty with the philosophy of a scheme designed to provide third party compensation on a system that was not based, in whole or in part, on actual law. Thirdly, they can see a number of practical problems, particularly if the scheme is not supported widely.

From this I think the conclusion has to be that if the concept of no fault is seen as socially desirable for medically related injury, then perhaps the way forward is through law reform. Insurers would be involved automatically through continuing the current basic system related to new rules. In the long run, if shortcomings in the legal system are perceived it must be preferable to seek to change the system rather than to seek alternatives by voluntary arrangements.

18

Discussion

Chairman: Sir David Innes Williams

Dame Rosalinde Hurley (*Queen Charlotte's Maternity Hospital*): When Mr Carpenter spoke about informing patients on alternatives, did he mean the consequences of alternative therapy or the consequences that might arise for them if they did not accept the advice given to them?

Mr Carpenter: We have an obligation to do both, to inform patients with respect to alternative products to any product that we offer in the market–place as well as alternative therapies. This is precisely what was done in the patient leaflet presented on the particular product that we have in the US market–place.

The brochure begins by saying:

"Do not use this product unless you have read this information."

It then proceeds to make sure that patients are aware of the alternatives to the use of that product.

Sir David Innes Williams: It seemed to me that Mr Wilson put forward a series of proposals in regard to changes in the law, some of which would achieve considerable support. May we hear from the legal members of the audience which of the Citizen Action Compensation Campaign (CITCOM) proposals would be acceptable?*

Mrs D. Brahams (*Legal Correspondent, the* Lancet): As far as the Review Board suggested by CITCOM is concerned, I think it is a good idea in principle and indeed Finland tried this. They had a "halfway" procedure, with a committee which looked into trying to improve their fault system as well as developing a no fault compensation arrangement.

A review panel was set up to help patients bring their claims. If patients thought they might have a claim, they took their case there—or were entitled to do so— and this panel investigated the case. It called for evidence, assessed that evidence to see whether it was worth pursuing, and issued a report on it. That seemed to me quite a good system; it did not cost patients anything and their whole claim was investigated. The Panel would also advise patients on compensation.

However, few extra patients were compensated and the system was perceived to be very little improved. The theory was excellent, but the practice was inadequate. The real problems were, firstly, that the board quickly became overwhelmed and was rather bureaucratic and slow; secondly, the problem of proving negligence seemed to be insuperable.

Mr Wilson was unable to stay for the discussion. Mr H. Witcomb answered questions on his behalf.

Whilst I applaud CITCOM's initiative I doubt very much that it will do a great deal for the process. It will perhaps improve computation of personal damages, but while we still have lump sums, the law will be inadequate. I would prefer to see in their Bill something to get rid of lump sum damages and something on annual awards.

Mr H. Witcomb: We will be campaigning for the courts to be able to award people periodic payments. It is 10 years since Pearson recommended that system, and we cannot see any reason why that should not be taken up. It is also worth noting as Mr Wilson said, that the insurance industry can arrange for out-of-court settlements to be made as "structured settlements" for people who are injured—which is a form of periodic payment. That the courts cannot give these periodic payments but, out-of-court, they can be given seems an absurd situation. We will therefore be campaigning for periodic payments.

With regard to the Review Board, it will not handle individual cases. It will act for one year or eighteen months, laying down guidelines, very similar to those produced by the American Medical Association. The concept is of *A Guide to Permanent Impairment,* and is a thorough look at all forms of injury, laying down guidelines for the judiciary then to use.

That is the idea behind the Board. It will not deal with individual claimants except in very unusual circumstances. For instance, if after drawing up those guidelines a particular unusual injury arose, such as the photosensitivity in the Opren case, which had not been dealt with previously, then the case would go to the Board.

Sir David Innes Williams: CITCOM is proposing considerable enlargement of the Legal Aid function. Would it also propose that the Legal Aid authority ought to pay the costs of the defendant in failed plaintiff cases—if not, why not? At the moment, if a doctor is sued by a legally aided patient and he—the defence—wins, he gets no costs. This is perceived by the medical profession as a very serious injustice.

Mr Witcomb: It is our view that Legal Aid eligibility has fallen substantially over the last 10 years, despite the Government's persistent but, in our view, mistaken views about the level.

We will be making two proposals on Legal Aid: first, to cover the general case, we propose that (as happened in 1979) the Government should set up a study to see how many people are covered by Legal Aid now. We find it absurd that there should be no detailed investigation as to this principle of our judicial system—which is access to the courts.

Secondly, in terms of product liability, the major multi-claimant cases, we will argue that in such cases there should be an exception to the general Legal Aid rule because the costs are immense. In Opren there were literally millions of documents and costs of millions of pounds. No claimant who falls outside the present Legal Aid rules could possibly even contemplate taking up that sort of action. Therefore, we want to see an exception made in those cases.

In general, we want more Legal Aid, but primarily we want the Government to investigate how far the Legal Aid eligibility levels cover the population.

With regard to Legal Aid providing defence costs in a failed case, I cannot speak for the Government or the Legal Aid board. It is for them to make up their minds and decide whether reform is necessary.

Sir David Innes Williams: But CITCOM is proposing a reform of Legal Aid, and putting it all one way.

Mr D. A. McIntosh *(Davies, Arnold & Cooper, Solicitors):* First, it is refreshing to listen to such a well balanced and carefully considered presentation by Mr Wilson. He referred to differences between he and I. Those differences basically stem from the way in which some of the press campaign was conducted in the Opren case. People with comparatively little—and sometimes cosmetic—knowledge about the case spoke on it when those of us who, with our colleagues, had looked at some 1200 medical reports and 700 sets of records actually knew about the cases. That is in contrast with what we have heard today. I am today in agreement with most of the CITCOM proposals. There are only two that worry me, one of which has not been mentioned today—the urging of preliminary inquiries following disasters being the forum for deciding civil liability. I feel this runs the risk of being too hasty and emotional a process.

Secondly, the cry for levels of damages to be increased. We are talking about a pilot scheme which would have to have limitations. We are studying other countries' schemes which do have financial caps and we are concerned about financing the scheme. If we are to consider any scheme which involves levels of damages higher than the English ones—which Mr Wilson described as derisory—I think the exercise is stillborn. I do not know where the comparisons come from. They were not stated, but I imagine that when English damages are described as "miserly" they are being compared with the USA. Damages in this country happen to be higher than in most of Europe, and most other countries. We hear about exorbitant awards in the USA from time to time, and some very bizarre ones.

It is interesting that as recently as 5 January 1989, a joint study by the Socio-Legal Society, Oxford, and the Bar Foundation, presented a report on English asbestos litigation. In that report they compared the way in which that litigation was handled in England and in the USA and reached a few important conclusions. First, that the English tort system worked exceedingly well in those cases, but they stressed that was because he conduct of the cases was in the hands of a very small group of plaintiffs' solicitors who were union experienced and extremely competent. The defendants' case was in the hands of an even smaller group of lawyers. They were able to work the tort system knowing the likely outcome, and to achieve speedy settlements on the basis so that total costs bill in the case sampled was found to be less than 25% of the damages paid (not a deduction from that, just less than 25% of what was paid). That was one-fifth of the expense in the USA.

With regard to the English damages, when they are increased by applying a dollar rate, when contingency deductions are taken into account, as well as the fact that a large element of American awards involves medical care (which is nearly always provided free in this country), the awards themselves are comparable.

The report concluded that the handling of that litigation in this country was more equitable, efficient, speedy and cost-effective. There was one main criticism, that in England not enough potential claimants were trawled. There was a higher incidence of take-up of claims in the USA. I think that is fairly important.

The Opren case is emphatically *sub judice* because parts of it are going on. I make no comment, other than to say that my firm has looked at the number of medical reports and records I mentioned (no other plaintiff's firm has done so because there were groups of firms, and not every one of them is in every case). It is very frustrating that *sub judice* and confidentiality rules prevent my clients and myself, whatever public utterances they or I may have been able to make, from actually referring to individual medical records. If that had been possible, we would have been able to redress some of the misinformation in the public domain. Unhappily, we cannot—rightly, incidentally, because the records are confidential to patients.

Finally, if there is going to be a debate, I for one would like to sit down with Mr Wilson and CITCOM—and other action groups of equal importance, one of which is represented here—and clear up our misunderstandings, and see whether the debate can be carried in the very moderate and intelligent way that he put it today.

Mrs Jean Robinson: I would not like this occasion to pass without saying on behalf of lay people how important was Mr Carpenter's contribution, and how I beg medical, legal and pharmaceutical people here to listen to it. I have never before had the urge to embrace heartily a member of the pharmaceutical industry!

This question, not of informed consent but of informed choice, is extremely important to get over to medical students and to members of the medical profession. I remember sitting on an ethics committee where we approved a study and the written information which the doctor was to give to the patients. A couple of months later the doctor said that he wanted to alter what the committee told him to tell patients because some of them were refusing to take part in the study. He had not realised, as many doctors do not realise, that informed consent also means informed refusal. It would be better to talk about choice.

When I say "choice" and "information", I do not mean what the obstetricians mean. They have not been giving basic information and permitting informed choice.

When it comes to doctors giving the kind of information about which Mr Carpenter is talking, the problem is that many of them are woefully ill-informed. General practitioners (GPs) are often not in a position to help patients make informed choices.

Secondly, the paternalistic attitude still prevails. Mr Carpenter's particular example concerned contraception. As an increasing number of epidemiological studies reveal previously unsuspected risks, for example, the possibility of breast cancer risk or of cervical cancer risk, the kind of response found in what one would expect to be the most informed journal, the *Journal of Family Planning*, was that it was possibly worrying, but there is no need to change prescribing practice. What should be changed, of course, is information practice to patients, to help them make better choices.

As a result of Mr Carpenter's work American women choosing an intrauterine device (IUD) are apparently told that if they have a sexually promiscuous partner, that increases the risk. It helps them to make a better choice. The Department of Health and Social Security (DHSS) is not allowing British women to know that—and why not?

Mr Carpenter: Dialogue is the key issue here. As I mentioned earlier, we struggled with a very difficult issue. I think everybody is familiar with the US scene with respect to the Dalkon Shield and the bankruptcy of A. H. Robins. The product that we have on the market–place is a trivial product in terms of turnover, an intrauterine contraceptive system called Progestasert. My Board of Directors gave me the responsibility of making the decision whether we should stay in that market–place after every other IUD manufacturer had left it. In making that decision, I chose to consult the harshest critics I could find, saying to them that we were the last people in this market–place and should we stay or leave? The answer universally was, please do not leave because women need this alternative. I asked how we could responsibly stay. Out of that discussion evolved the concept of informed choice with this particular product.

A seven page long patient package begins by saying something like: "Do not use this product until you have read this leaflet, and be aware that it can cause you serious injury".

We make every effort to ensure that the woman understands the risks, as well as the benefits, of the product.

We told our marketing people that their objective was not to sell the product, but to make sure that the people who use the product are well informed. We also altered our rules on compensation and fundamentally re-addressed the values that we hold as a Company.

I particularly enjoyed Mr West's presentation from the insurance perspective because anybody who ever wants to get close to the truth should talk to insurance people. They are actuaries; they deal with facts. I think that Mr West is being factually correct when he says what the public opinion is on many of these issues, and the degree to which people are willing to vote, with their dollars, on these propositions.

Although I am supportive of no fault compensation, I do not think there will be either public or political support for it until both the pharmaceutical industry and the medical profession do everything possible to prevent avoidable injury. When that has been done, I think society will join with us and help solve the problem of unavoidable injury.

Dr P. G. T. Bye *(Schering Health Care):* I think it is ironical that Mrs Robinson, speaking as a lay person, should have chosen the oral contraceptive as an example. There is no product in the history of medicine that has suffered more from ill-considered criticisms by lay people (in this I include most of the press) than oral contraceptives. There is no product on the market, I believe, with such a lengthy package leaflet as the standard combined oral contraceptive. This leaflet contains the most minute details about contraindications, warnings and precautions.

One of the problems is, of course, that however much a pharmaceutical company tries to make sure that the users of its products give informed consent, there is no way of ensuring that the information gets across to the patient. We provide almost exactly the same information in data sheets as is provided in patient leaflets—as, in fact, we are required to do. All the essential information in the one, must be in the other. It is put in the leaflet in language as plain as we can make it.

It is inconceivable that a doctor prescribing the Pill for a patient the first time will go over everything that is germane in making a decision about using the Pill and accepting the risks that are known or suspected to go with it. In my family planning clinic I certainly do not have time to go over the whole gamut every time with a new patient. What I invariably do, however, is to extract a promise from the patient that she will read the leaflet from end to end before starting to take the Pill; and if she fails to understand any of it, or is unhappy with anything she reads, that she will come back and talk to me again before starting the Pill.

I do not see what else we can say.

Again, it is ironic that Mrs Robinson should have talked about failure to inform women about the consequences of promiscuity. I was present at a meeting at which the subject of cervical cancer and the Pill was being discussed. Very properly, the question of the sexual habits of women, and the influence that might have on the incidence of cervical cancer, was raised. Mrs Robinson chose to take the attitude that any suggestion that the sexual habits of women had any bearing on the incidence of cervical cancer was a slur on British womanhood.

Mrs Robinson: In reply to what I am alleged to have said about cervical cancer, I have published perfectly respectable epidemiology on cervical cancer (published by the Royal College of Obstetricians and Gynaecologists).

This is, in fact, a very good example of the selectivity of information which is provided to people. The public were informed that female promiscuity was a risk factor, and that husbands' occupations in dirty industries like mining, oil, chemicals and so on, also had a possibility of risk—that it is, in fact, a multifactorial disease.

I wanted balanced information presented to the effect that oral contraceptives have been known to be a risk since 1981, following the work of a very good Oxford team.

All I am asking is that people are given balanced information, and that it is not "filtered" through—in this case—largely male medical minds to female consumers of the Pill, so that they receive only some information and not other information which women themselves consider very relevant.

The conclusion of the report of the Royal College of General Practitioners study from 1974 was that the study had shown that it was a risk that women, well-informed, would happily take. I took that study up and down the country to women —not a single woman who read the study wanted to continue taking the Pill.

With information, we may take different choices for ourselves from the ones that the doctors take for us. That is precisely what Mr Carpenter said and what I, as a consumer representative, am saying.

Sir David Innes Williams: I am interested to continue the matter of the big pharmaceutical firms. In the British Medical Association (BMA) scheme Mr Bolt excluded the big drug actions. We hear from Sweden that there are two separate systems. I think it is important that we should look into this further. Dr Oldertz, how much do the two systems interact? Are there many drug actions which involve both the doctors and the drug firms?

Dr C. Oldertz (Skandia Insurance Co. Ltd., Sweden): It should be remembered that in Sweden there are about 200 drug-caused injuries each year, which means that the number of drug injuries which could be referred to the medical sector will be comparatively few. I cannot give an exact figure, but a probable figure is 10, 15 or perhaps 20%.

Sir David Innes Williams: Mr Bolt, the BMA system seems to have two arms to it. Do you think that one can be put on without the other, or do they necessarily come together?

Mr D. Bolt (Chairman, BMA No Fault Compensation Committee): At the start, when we were working on the paper and when we wrote it, it was our clear conviction that developmental defects in drugs should be excluded. For the purpose with which we were dealing it was thought that they were too unpredictable. When they occurred they might involve very large numbers of people and very large sums of money. For these reasons, they were not comfortable bedfellows for the sort of scheme being designed.

There has been discussion here, and I accept the principle that something similar would be appropriate for the drug firms. However, I continue to feel that the scheme should be set up, financed and run by the major drug companies.

Mr Carpenter: Both in the USA and in the UK there is a class of medicines which are available by prescription only, which means that those drugs can be used only under the supervision of a physician. For that reason, however, we deal with compensation on drug-related injuries, I think it is important to have some co-ordination with respect to whatever compensation arrangements are made for physician-related injuries. The two can, in fact, overlap substantially. I do not wish to suggest that all drug-related injuries are the responsibility of misguidance or misuse by physicians, but I also feel that the pharmaceutical companies, the physicians and the chemists have a close partnership in ensuring that these products are used properly.

There must be some co-ordination between those systems if we are going to deal with drug-related injury which does not occur in a vacuum, but in the context of a medical system. On occasion, there are totally unknown factors which show up after the drug has been reviewed and approved, and which are outside anybody's knowledge. As I indicated in my presentation, this may well be the basis for some no fault compensation. However, in my opinion, many other drug-related injuries are eminently avoidable by well informed companies, physicians and patients.

Mr Bolt: I think that I have been slightly misunderstood. Those things are covered in our scheme. What is being turned out are those unpredictable events which are, let us say, inherent defects in a drug—we think those should be unacceptable.

Dr Oldertz: I think the scheme put forward by Mr Bolt is very reasonable. It is a practical solution.

Sir David Innes Williams: Can the representatives of the drug firms present tell us—without any commitment—whether they feel that the British pharmaceutical industry would be in any way agreeable to discuss the setting of a no fault organisation for them?

Dr D. M. Burley (*Centre for Pharmaceutical Medicine*): I do not work in the pharmaceutical industry any longer, although I have worked in it for 30 years, and anything I say is not said on the industry's behalf. I have for a long time advocated that the pharmaceutical industry should give serious consideration to this. At this meeting we have heard talk about pilot schemes of one sort or another. I feel that in the UK at the moment it is likely that such a scheme would only be set up by the pharmaceutical industry. It is up to them to take a lead, and they would do themsevles a great deal of good in the eyes of the public if they were seen to be taking a lead in this matter. That could provide a lot of data of extreme value to the medical profession and others who are looking at similar types of schemes.

I urge (and did in December 1988) the industry to consider this. It is a pity, perhaps, that representatives of the Association of the British Pharmaceutical Industry (ABPI) are not here to give their opinion. At the moment, as far as I am aware, they have not formed a view on it.

Dr R. D. Mann (*Royal Society of Medicine*): I should make it clear that the ABPI were invited and have an observer present.

Mr Carpenter: One of the points I stressed was the concept of innovation. It is an unfortunate dilemma of society that very seldom are trade associations' leaders in the area of innovation. A trade association is an association of a number of companies and, to a large extent, the policies of that association will invariably reflect what I would like to describe—or *not* to describe—as the lowest common denominator amongst the members.

This is a marvellous opportunity for what I described as competitive advantage. I would hope that individual companies who perceive themselves as being leaders in this field will take up the challenge and begin to innovate. But, with the trade associations in the USA, and from what I know about pharmaceutical industry associations elsewhere, I think it is unrealistic to look to associations for leadership. We will have to look for leading innovative companies to come in with mechanisms which provide basically a challenge to their partners in the market–place to be responsive.

Dr G. D. Parr (*Ciba-Geigy Pharmaceuticals*): I would like to support substantially what Mr Carpenter has just said. I would also ask the audience to remember how he listed in his presentation the various circumstances in which damages should be awarded, and those in which perhaps a no fault scheme would be helpful to patients and indeed defendants.

It seems to us at Ciba-Geigy that this kind of discussion is very much to be welcomed. It should be going on at the moment. It is obviously appropriate. Something that we have worried about considerably is the concept of accountability. We are concerned to see that there is accountability.

Mr West: I would not for one moment suggest that I can talk on behalf of the drug industry. However, I have some connection with them in involvement with the product liability insurance of, I think, four of the biggest six companies. When this subject is raised, with one exception, they say that they would be resolutely opposed to a no fault concept.

That is not quite as it sounds. In recent years there has been a considerable problem facing the big drug companies, in that they have not been able to buy as much insurance cover as they feel they should carry—it just has not been available. Therefore, they have reverted to alternative mechanisms which involve insurance and forms of off-shore banking to build up funds in order to discharge these liabilities if they arise.

They also say that they can, if they wish, be innovative, but rather than design a scheme they would prefer to wait for the event—they may be legally liable anyway. If they are not, and there is a case whereby it would be appropriate for them to make some gesture, they could make it—but they want to make that decision case by case, situation by situation, not be committed either individually or collectively to a no fault concept (as I say, with one exception).

I would stress that is what the drug companies tell me at a particular level. I am not so naive as to believe that our policyholders always tell their insurers the full truth.

On the subject of the literature, the software to the product, with product liability claims on every form of product in the UK (not related to the medical and pharmaceutical industry only) the statistics indicate that the biggest single cause of product-related injury is not following instructions.

Sir David Innes Williams: Dr Mann, you were one of the proponents of the no fault scheme. It is clear that you will not get it in one go. I think it is very important to identify the common ground we have here: what can be done, whether there are pilot schemes which are viable in any way? Would you like to give us a lead on that?

Dr R. D. Mann (*Royal Society of Medicine*): I think the meeting has been enormously instructive. No fault has been discussed very carefully in the context of personal injury.

I thought that Rabbi Neuberger's comments were extremely apposite in that it was suggested that there might be a cautious welcome for no fault compensation, provided serious consideration was given to a pilot scheme and any scheme was introduced in tandem with considerable improvements in the other aspects of the personal injuries system in Britain. There has, in fact, been a great deal of emphasis on accountability in this meeting and near unanimity that negligence and tort need to be looked at carefully.

With regard to the pharmaceutical question, as an ex-pharmaceutical industry man, I would say that there is reason to think that three things can be done. Firstly, in respect of the BMA type of proposal, there is an extant Working Party which might, in view of all the helpful material raised at this meeting, be encouraged and broadened a little. The help of the Department of Health is clearly needed. Secondly, I would hope that the major pharmaceutical companies might consider establishing their own Working Party to review the pharmaceutical issues. Thirdly, I was much attracted to the comment of Professor Laurence that there is actually a medical job to be done in looking at these issues of accountability, causation and severity—and I hope that the Royal Society of Medicine might give thought to that very practical proposal.

Clearly, all this will not happen overnight, and none of us expected that it would. I would, however, differ from friends and colleagues in the BMA regarding drug-related damage because I think this is one of the first things to look at.

My reasons include the fact that something about the size of the problem is already known. In 1987 there were 16,000 adverse reactions reported to the Committee on Safety of Medicines in this country. Those 16,000 represent perhaps 10% of the actual number of reactions, so we are talking about a presumed total of 160,000 suspected reactions. Not more than one-third are serious and only a proportion of these are prolonged—and this provides an estimate of what one might want to provide compensation for. There are perhaps 70,000 active prescribing doctors in the hospitals and practices of this country. Adverse drug reactions are, therefore, uncommon. On average, clinicians will see two or three *a year*—and only a minor proportion of those seen will be of the serious prolonged kind for which compensation might be thought appropriate.

Some of these reactions may be avoidable. In fact, many may be. But some are not; they arise by the operation of malign chance—and those patients should be helped in a charitable and kindly way, without having to sue for negligence when, in fact, no negligence has been involved. It is also unfortunate that pharmaceutical companies should be subjected to the kind of comments that do crop up when these non-negligent difficulties arise. Thus, I hope that the pharmaceutical industry will be as innovative in this matter as it has been in the process of drug discovery. I hope that innovative progress can move forward on the three fronts I've mentioned in parallel with progress on many of the CITCOM initiatives.

Sir David Innes Williams: It appears the complete scheme, as proposed by the BMA, will not be obtained at once. Mr Bolt has told us about the disadvantages of pilot schemes. Is there a specific instance in which something will have to be done fairly soon? Is the question of brain damage in the newborn such that it imperils the service? Is there any chance of setting up a no fault compensation for that subject alone (as, I think, has been suggested), or would that require some specific action by the Government, some Crown indemnity for that alone? Is there a crisis?

Mr Bolt: I do not feel wholly equipped to answer that question. Mr Simmons, who unfortunately cannot be here in this session, would be much more able to answer. I had the impression that while there were visible adverse events, if you like, taking place in the obstetric world, we are not rapidly approaching an actual crisis— although it is obviously a field in which the sooner something is done the better.

I am open to conviction, but do not think that getting a no fault scheme for brain-damaged infants is a realistic proposition. Such a scheme would have to be funded by Government. Any process which involves getting significant sums of money out of Government is not likely to be viable.

As far as the scheme as a whole is concerned, I have never deluded myself that it would happen in the very near future. All that I hope is that there will be enough publicity to persuade Ministers to start talking to us about it so that the possible ways of assessing the cost could be studied. That is critical. I do not think we can find out that ourselves, but need assistance from the Department of Health to tackle that sort of problem.

I have always been rather dubious about pilot schemes. A pilot study is fine if we then go on to the full scheme. If, however, we embark on a pilot study, say, for 12 months, and then find it has to be stopped because it does not work or cannot be afforded, we are left with extremely difficult problems. I would hate to start a pilot study unless I was very sure we could go on.

19

Closing remarks

Sir David Innes Williams (President, British Medical Association)

We have had a most informative two days. I am certainly very much better informed, and hopefully a little wiser.

I think we all agree that it is vital to improve the standards of care. We have talked peripherally about accountability. That was not really the subject under discussion, but I do not believe that anybody in the profession would doubt the need for these improvements in audit and in evident accountability in proper postgraduate and continuing education.

It seems to me that everybody on the legal side is agreed on the need for some reforms of the tort system. I am encouraged to think that the legal people here have a very considerable community view on this matter. I hope that they can do something about it.

I wonder whether the medical profession itself should do something. We find it unedifying that experts oppose one another in the courts, that the adversarial system fuels their mutual antagonism. There is the possibility of pre-trial conferences, but they are not made much use of at the moment. Can we not, in the profession, identify experts who are available, and who really believe in a pre-trial conference, so that the refusal of either side to partake in it would count against them? There is something here with which the profession can concern itself, as well as the legal side.

With regard to the possible costs of a no fault scheme there is no doubt that more information is needed. It is very disappointing that the health authorities and the health departments have not yet been able to give us the information. Dr Oldertz told us how important it is not simply to know the number of claims but, for instance, the age of the claimant and many other factors.

These data ought to be available, and I am disappointed that nobody from the Department of Health appears to have taken part in this discussion. This is a matter of very great importance, not simply to the profession but also to the Department of Health and the public as a whole.

I think, therefore, that there are certain matters about which we are agreed. Clearly, there are some on which we are not in any way agreed. I believe, though, that what has emerged from this meeting will be a most important stimulus to further progress along these lines.

I would like to close by thanking Sir Christopher Booth, Dr Mann and the Royal Society of Medicine for providing this opportunity for discussion.

Sir Christopher Booth (President, The Royal Society of Medicine)

I hesitate to follow the words of wisdom just given by the President of the British Medical Association (BMA), who has summarised so very clearly some of the discussions of this meeting.

Unfortunately, I have been unable to attend as much of this meeting as I would have wished, but I can say that those parts I have attended have been extraordinarily fascinating and extremely rewarding.

I will not sum up the meeting in any ordinary sense. I cannot do that because the subject is far too wide, and I have not attended enough of the meeting.

I would like, though, to make a few personal remarks and comments.

On a personal note, I was first involved in the question of no fault compensation when I was Chairman of the Department of Medicine at the Royal Postgraduate Medical School, Hammersmith, about 15 years ago. It was a department of some 300 people of which I was then head, doing a lot of clinical research and publishing about 200 or 300 papers a year. A young man in the department spent a year in Sweden working on the technique of muscle biopsy. When he came back he asked why did we not have some insurance or no fault compensation for individuals who had submitted themselves to experimental studies within our institution, since we were doing clinical research in this big department.

I stress that because I do not think that research investigation has, in fact, formed part of the discussion at this meeting.

It is intriguing also that in the 11 years that I was Chairman of this very distinguished Department of Medicine, working in the field of clinical investigation, there was no case of litigation based on an investigational study.

I then went to Northwick Park, where I was Head of the Medical Research Council's (MRC) Clinical Research Centre, with a yearly budget of £11 million, and publishing between 700 and 800 papers a year in the general field of clinical research. Again, in the 10 years I was Director there was not a single case of litigation based on a research procedure, and I can recollect only one on the health service side of an individual patient complaining about the research being carried out. There were complaints about waiting in outpatients, about kindness and all sorts of aspects, but never about research.

I think that is extraordinarily interesting because it illustrates that, at least within the field of medical research, the introduction of the ethical committee structures that we now have has made it almost impossible for litigation problems to arise—it has not entirely, but to a large extent, relieved us of that sort of problem.

If we then move to the question of drugs, obviously there is a problem—and there is a problem with no fault compensation. If we consider the vexed question currently being addressed by the BMA on benzodiazepines in the treatment of anxiety, and the question of dependence and so on, these are unforeseen problems which relate to drugs brought in with the best of intentions by the pharmaceutical industry, and seized upon by the medical profession and public brought up to the idea that "for every ill there is a pill".

I would like to say a word in defence of the pharmaceutical industry, some of whose representatives are present. I heard it said at a meeting recently that one of the great bogeys of the 1930s was the armaments industry. We were all told about those wretched armaments factories and so on. As the years have gone by, however, there is now a situation in which that is called the "defence industry". That is splendid: all the weaponry we spend our money on, like torpedoes that run ashore, for example—this huge expenditure on defence is now respectable. For that reason, the pharmaceutical industry is the bogey man of the system, as a result of being attacked by all sorts of people who now attack it for the relatively minor amount of problems that it produces although, for the individual, as in the thalidomide tragedy, these can be major issues.

At the end of the day, however, the pharmaceutical industry is our health defence industry. Without it, I, as a physician, would be totally ineffective. I may be ineffective anyway, but I certainly would be if it were not for the pharmaceutical industry. I think we should pay tribute to what they do, and also to the research laboratories that they run. After all, vitamin B12 was discovered in a pharmaceutical laboratory (Glaxo Laboratories) by Lester Smith, who was awarded an FRS for that. We may consider the Wellcome Laboratories which have done so much. Both here and in the USA they have 27 Fellows of the Royal Society to their credit—and not many universities can claim that. We should also remember that the Nobel Prize for Medicine in 1988 was awarded to James Black, George Hitchins and his colleague at Research Triangle in America for specific developments in the drug industry. Those are all major achievements to which everybody should pay tribute.

Two other points about the pharmaceutical industry are worth making. The two areas of life which have been dramatically transformed by science, technology and the industry are, first, the control of pain, and secondly, birth control. We have only to look at any of the descriptions of illness in the 18th century and the early 19th century, or at the problems of surgery which were exposed by the Editor of the *Lancet* in the early 19th century, to recognise what has happened to humanity as a result of scientific, technological and medical developments through the years. We no longer have to suffer acute untreatable pain. That has been a major achievement.

My mother was a friend of a very remarkable lady, Marie Stopes. She will be remembered in this country as the great pioneer of birth control. Her papers are preserved in the Wellcome Institute for the History of Medicine. Anybody reading the extraordinary letters she received—at a time when the medical profession and many other people were accusing her of the most disreputable behaviour by making recommendations on birth control in the 1920s—would be quite shattered and shocked by them, and by the absence of education in sex matters, particularly in birth control. There are letters there from Irish farmers' wives, for example, who had no idea that there was any way of performing sex other than in the way done by a bull and a cow. It is quite extraordinary, and very moving, to read those letters.

Progress has been made. This is the point I want to make. What we have been discussing here is trying to make more progress. I think that the points made here about the need for audit, for care and attention, and the need for improved communication, are tremendously important and heartening for all of us present.

May I thank all the speakers who have come from far and wide to join with us. We have had a remarkable multidisciplinary discussion. As Sir David has said, it has been extremely interesting for all of us, and very rewarding in terms of informing us about the whole problem of no fault compensation which has been the subject of the meeting.

I think certain people in particular should be thanked. Mr Bolt, in putting the BMA view so clearly, has been very important. As he said, the publicity the meeting has achieved, with widespread reports in today's press, has been of great importance.

We should thank Dr Mann, who has done a superb job in bringing together everybody here, all the speakers from around the world as well as the BMA.

I very much hope that this first meeting we have had with the BMA at the Royal Society of Medicine will be the beginning of a trend. I worked for the BMA for a year as President. I am now Chairman of their Board of Science, so I go to Council and other meetings at Tavistock Square. Of course, there we are in a more formal position, in the sense that in Council we state our position. The debates at Council are, as stated by Scrutator in the current issue of the *British Medical Journal*, extremely effective and good. The recent one on junior doctors' hours was probably one of the best structured debates ever held by the BMA, and it came to very effective and helpful conclusions.

I hope that the BMA members here who have joined with us and so fruitfully contributed to the discussions have felt it possible perhaps to let their hair down a trifle more than they would be able to do in the confines of Tavistock Square. That is what was intended, and I very much hope it is something that will continue for the future.

May I thank Sir David and the BMA warmly for their co-operation. It is something that we have keenly appreciated.

20

APPENDIX 1

Undertaking to disburse indemnity for drug-related injuries.
Indemnity provisions as of 1 January 1988

§ 1 Indemnity will be provided in accordance with this undertaking for an injury caused by a drug which a manufacturer or importer, who has endorsed this undertaking, has in the normal course of his business distributed in Sweden for consumption.

§ 2 According to this undertaking the term drug is understood to mean

—products intended for human consumption to which the Drug Ordinance (1962:701) applies,
—radioactive drugs even if the Ordinance does not apply to such drugs, and
—products that are used in tests on humans as part of the testing of a medicine (clinical drug trials and pharmacological tests on humans).

§ 3 A drug-related injury is understood to mean an illness or other bodily injury which with preponderant probability has been caused through the use of a drug.
A drug-related injury is not considered to include an illness or other injury which

—is due to lack or absence of effect, on the part of a drug, or
—has occurred in the course of an activity which is unsuitable with respect to the intended or predicted effect of the drug in question.

A series injury is understood to mean injuries which during one or more calendar years are suffered by several persons and are due to the same sort of property of, or substance contained in, one or more drugs which, due to their side-effects, have either been deregistered or, if they have not been deregistered, have been distributed for consumption before the appropriate public authority or manufacturer has issued information regarding the extent of their side-effects.

§ 4 A drug-related injury will only be indemnified if, as a consequence of the injury, the injured person

—has been on the sick list with at least 50% incapacity for work for a period exceeding 14 days, or
—has sustained permanent disability of some significance, or
—has died.

Regardless of what is stated in the first paragraph reasonable compensation will be provided for the costs and loss of income related to treatment of a drug-related injury if the costs and loss of income combined exceed SEK 1,000 after the deductions have been made in accordance with §8.7.

§5   Indemnity shall not be payable for a drug-related injury if in view of

—the nature and severity of the disease for which the treatment was given
—the general health status of the injured person
—the severity of the injury
—the reason for the medical professional to expect the side-effects of a drug and the possibility for him to foresee the consequences of them

it would have been reasonable to accept the injury as a consequence of using the drug.

§6   Nor will indemnity be paid if the drug, with the injured person's knowledge, has been provided contrary to whatever

—is prescribed with respect to trade with drugs, or
—has constituted a prescribed condition for possession of the drug.

§7   Indemnity for a drug-related injury shall not be provided if the injured person or—should the injury result in death—the deceased has wilfully or through obvious misuse of the drug caused the injury himself.
Indemnity for a drug-related injury may be reduced in the event that the injured person or—should the injury result in death—the deceased has contributed to the injury through gross negligence in cases other than those that are described in the first paragraph.

§8   Indemnity for a drug-related injury shall be determined in accordance with Chapter 5, §§1–5, of the Tort Damages Act (1972:207) to the extent that nothing else is prescribed below.

8.1   Indemnity for pain and suffering during acute illness shall be provided in the form of a lump sum and shall be calculated in accordance with the norms established each calendar year by the Drug Injury Committee.

8.2   If the injury results in permanent disability indemnity for permanent pain and suffering and loss of amenities shall be determined when it can be established that no changes will occur in the future. The indemnity shall be provided either in the form of a lump sum or an annuity and shall be calculated in accordance with the norms established each calendar year by the Drug Injury Committee.

8.3   Indemnity for other permanent inconveniences, as described in Chapter 5, §1, Paragraph 1 (3) of the Tort Damages Act (1972:207), is to be paid if the injured person, in spite of being disabled because of the injury, returns to work.
Indemnity according to the preceding paragraph shall be provided in the form of increased compensation for permanent pain and suffering and loss of amenities in accordance with the following norms.

Degree of medical disability	Increase of indemnity for permanent pain and suffering and loss of amenities
— At most 10%	At most a half compensation sum at the appropriate degree of medical disability
— At most 20%	At most one compensation sum at the appropriate degree of medical disability
— At most 30%	At most one and a half compensation sums at the appropriate degree of medical disability
— More than 30%	At most one and a half compensation sums at the 30% degree of medical disability

8.4   Compensation for future costs is included in the indemnity for permanent pain and suffering and loss of amenities pursuant to §8.2 and in the indemnity for other permanent inconveniences pursuant to §8.3. However, if future costs of a more substantial size can be expected to arise, a special indemnity in the form of an annuity will be provided.

8.5   Compensation for future loss of income will be paid if the injured person has been disabled by the injury and his capacity to obtain income through work has thereby been decreased by at least one-fifteenth and the annual loss is more than one-fourth of the base amount, according to the Social Insurance Act, which is applicable at the time when the right to such compensation is determined.
Compensation for future loss of income is determined in the form of

—an annuity if the compensation is of substantial importance regarding the injured person's support, and no special reasons indicate otherwise,
—a lump sum if the yearly loss of income can be assumed to be less than 10%,
—an annuity or a lump sum in other cases in accordance with the request of the injured person.

8.6   The annuities are value-guaranteed in accordance with the Act on Modification of Damages Annuities (1973:213).

8.7   In determining the amount of the indemnity, the benefits mentioned in Chapter 5, §3, of the Tort Damages Act (1972:207) shall be deducted as well as

—such compensation which the injured person obviously has a right to from the security insurance, the patient insurance or traffic insurance or
—compensation from other insurances (for example a sickness, pension, accident or business interruption insurance) in regard to compensation for costs and loss of income.

8.8   Compensation shall not be provided for extra costs for the State, a county council district or a municipality benefit or service that relate to a higher billing rate because of the fact that the injured person has a right to indemnity for costs from the pharmaceutical insurance.

8.9   Indemnity shall not be paid for any loss that can arise if the examination of the claim or the payment of indemnity is delayed due to war, warlike occurrences, civil war, revolution or riot, or because of an action by a public authority, a strike, a lockout, a blockade or other similar events.

§ 9   Liability for drug-related injuries in accordance with this undertaking is limited to

—SEK 3 million for each injured person, including the value of annuities capitalised in accordance with commercial insurance principles,
—SEK 100 million for each series injury and to a total maximum of SEK 150 million for several series injuries which are to be attributed to the same calendar year.

Injuries which are part of a series injury shall be attributed to the calendar year during which it first became apparent that a series injury had occurred and the Drug Injury Committee was notified about this by the policyholder or the insurer.

§ 10   If the amounts specified in § 9 are insufficient to fully indemnify all of the injured persons who are entitled to indemnity from those amounts, their indemnity shall be reduced by the same proportion in each case. If there is reason to expect that such a reduction will be necessary after an injury has occurred, the Drug Injury Committee may determine that until further notice only a certain proportion of the indemnity shall be paid.

§ 11   Liability in accordance with this undertaking shall be covered by a collective insurance. Indemnities for drug-related injuries shall be disbursed by the insurer.

§ 12   A person who wants to claim indemnity for a drug-related injury in accordance with this undertaking shall report the injury in writing within three years of the time when he became aware of the injury to the insurer or the manufacturer or importer of the drug. If this is not done, he will lose his right to indemnity in accordance with this undertaking.

§ 13   Questions of principle or disputes in indemnification cases, at the request of the injured person, the insurer or the policyholder, shall be referred to a specially appointed committee—the Drug Injury Committee—for an opinion. The injured person may not request an opinion from the Drug Injury Committee later than six months after he received the insurer's decision regarding his indemnity claim as well as information about what he should do if he does not accept the insurer's decision.

§ 14   The Drug Injury Committee consists of eight members. The chairman and three members are appointed by the government. Of the latter three members, one represents medical science and one represents the interests of patients. The county councils and the insurer each appoint one member. The policyholder appoints two members. The chairman has the casting vote. The rules of procedure for the Drug Injury Committee are laid down by the government in accordance with the proposals submitted by the policyholder in consultation with the insurer.

§ 15   Disputes between the insurer and the injured party are to be settled by arbitrators in accordance with the Arbitrators Act (1929:145). If one of the arbitrators appointed by the parties so requests, a third arbitrator shall be appointed by the government.

The arbitration proceedings shall be based on written medical documentation. The parties shall present their pleadings in writing. The arbitrators also decide whether an oral hearing is necessary to elucidate the disputed question. If an arbitrator so requests, the arbitrators shall call upon a person who is an expert regarding the issue in dispute and provide him with the opportunity to present his opinion.

If the injured person had reasonable grounds for having the dispute determined by arbitration, the insurer will be liable for the compensation of the arbitrators and the experts called in in accordance with the second paragraph.

§ 16 Arbitration in accordance with § 15 may be requested only if the Drug Injury Committee previously issued an opinion on the indemnity matter pursuant to § 13. If either party wants to refer to new circumstances or a new investigation which has not been examined by the insurer or the Drug Injury Committee, the matter shall be remitted back to the Drug Injury Committee for a new opinion.

The injured person may not request a decision by arbitration later than six months from the time he received the insurer's final decision, on the basis of the opinion of the Drug Injury Committee, regarding the indemnity matter as well as information about what he should do if he does not accept the insurer's decision.

§ 17 An injured person who accepts an award of indemnity that is offered pursuant to this undertaking must assign to the insurer his right to tort damages from anyone who could be held liable therefore.

However, this duty does not apply to compensation from the security insurance, the patient insurance or traffic insurance which has been deducted in accordance with § 8.7.

If the injured person does not accept the indemnity offered by the insurer within six months of the date he was notified regarding his duty according to the first paragraph, he loses his right to indemnity in accordance with this undertaking. He also loses his right to indemnity if he does not assign his right to tort damages.

§ 18 This undertaking comes into force on 1 January 1988. However, it does not cover series injuries which include indemnifiable injuries that according to the last paragraph of § 9 of the previous undertaking shall be considered to have occurred prior to 1 January 1988.

APPENDIX 2

Patient insurance

Indemnity provisions as of 1 April 1988

§ 1   Indemnity for a treatment injury shall be paid to a patient who is injured in direct connection with health and medical care, or to the survivors of such a patient, in accordance with the following conditions.

Healthy persons who voluntarily participate in medical research activities, which are approved by an ethics committee and do not pertain to testing of drugs, will be considered to be equal to patients.

§ 2   A treatment injury shall be understood to be an injury or disease of a physical nature which

2.1   has occurred as a direct consequence of an examination, treatment or any other similar procedure, on the condition that it does not constitute an unavoidable complication of a measure which was justified from a medical viewpoint.

2.2   has occurred as a direct consequence of a diagnostic measure, unless the complication reasonably must be accepted as a consequence of such a risk-taking because it was motivated by the nature and severity of the injury or disease to be treated and the general health status of the patient.

2.3   has occurred or has been impossible to prevent as a consequence of the fact that examination results obtained by means of technical equipment were incorrect or symptoms of illness actually observed in connection with the diagnosis were not interpreted in a manner which corresponds with generally accepted medical practice.

2.4   has been caused by an infection due to an infectious matter that was probably transmitted to the patient by means of health and medical care measures, but not if the infection is a consequence of

—an operation or other measure in the intestines, oral cavity, respiratory system or other area which, from a bacteriological viewpoint, is deemed unclean

—an operation in tissue which had considerably reduced vitality or other similar characteristics

—a treatment which causes an increased risk of infection such as prolonged catheterisation, drainage, external fixation, traction, transplantation surgery, etc.

216

2.5   has been caused by an accident

—as a consequence of a sudden external event which has a connection with an examination, treatment or any other measure that has been undertaken by the medical personnel
—that occurred during the conveyance of the patient
—that occurred in connection with a fire or other kind of damage to the health care facilities or equipment, or as a result of a defect in the medical equipment.

§ 3   However, a treatment injury shall not be understood to mean an injury or disease which

3.1   is a consequence of a necessary risk-taking, from a medical point of view, for diagnosis or treatment of an injury or disease, which if untreated, is life threatening or entails a risk of severe disability.

3.2   to a preponderant extent, other than those cases mentioned in 2.3, has its origin in or is caused by a disease or comparable condition in the patient.

3.3   has been caused by a drug to which the drug regulations apply and which in view of the directions for use of the drug could not be avoided.

§ 4   A treatment injury will be indemnified only if, as a consequence of the injury, the injured person

—has been put on the sick list with at least 50% incapacity for work for more than 30 days or
—has been required to stay in a hospital for more than 10 days or
—has been inflicted with a permanent disability that is not without importance or
—has died.

Regardless of what is stated in the preceding paragraph reasonable compensation will be paid for treatment costs and loss of income in connection with treatment of a treatment injury if the total amount of the costs and the loss of income exceed SEK 700 after reduction according to § 5:7.

§ 5   Indemnity for a treatment injury is to be determined in accordance with Chap. 5, §§ 1–5 of the Tort Damages Act unless otherwise prescribed below.

5.1   Indemnity for pain and suffering during acute illness is to be paid in the form of a lump sum and is calculated in accordance with norms established by the advisory committee appointed by the Federation of Swedish County Councils and the insurer.

5.2   Indemnity for other permanent pain and suffering or loss of amenities is to be paid when it can be established that the situation will not change in the future. The indemnity is to be paid either in the form of a lump sum or an annuity determined according to the norms established by the advisory committee appointed by the Federation of Swedish County Councils and the insurer.

5.3   Indemnity for other permanent inconveniences, as described in Chap. 5, § 1, Paragraph 1 (3) of the Tort Damages Act, is to be paid if the injured person, in spite of being disabled because of the injury, returns to work.
Indemnity for other permanent inconveniences is to be paid in the form of increased compensation for permanent pain and sufferings and loss of amenities in accordance with the following norms.

Degree of medical disability	Increase of indemnity for permanent pain and suffering and loss of amenities
— At most 10%	At most a half compensation sum at the appropriate degree of medical disability
— At most 20%	At most one compensation sum at the appropriate degree of medical disability
— At most 30%	At most one and a half compensation sums at the appropriate degree of medical disability
— More than 30%	At most one and a half compensation sums at the 30% degree of medical disability

5.4   Compensation for future costs is included in the indemnity for permanent pain and suffering and loss of amenities pursuant to 5.2 and in the indemnity for other permanent inconveniences pursuant to 5.3. However, if larger future costs may be expected to arise, a special indemnity in the form of an annuity will be paid.

5.5   Compensation for future loss of income will be paid if the injured person has been disabled by the injury and his capacity to obtain income through work has thereby been decreased by at least one-fifteenth and the annual loss is more than one-fourth of the base amount,
according to the Social Insurance Act, which is applicable at the time when the right to such compensation is determined.
Compensation for future loss of income is determined in the form of

—an annuity if the compensation is of substantial importance regarding the injured person's support, and no special reasons indicate otherwise,
—a lump sum if the yearly loss of income can be assumed to be less than 10%,
—an annuity or a lump sum in other cases, in accordance with the request of the injured person.

5.6   The annuities are value-guaranteed in accordance with the Act on Modification of Damages Annuities (1973:213).

5.7   In determining the amount of the indemnity, the amount shall be reduced by such benefits as are mentioned in Chap. 5, § 3, of the Tort Damages Act, and a reduction shall be made for compensation which the injured person has a right to from insurances which are meant to provide compensation according to torts principles, e.g., security insurance for work-related injuries, traffic insurance or pharmaceutical insurance as well as from health and accident insurance but only with regard to indemnity for pain and suffering, disfigurement, disability, costs, rehabilitation and loss of income.

5.8   Compensation is not provided to the extent that the loss or cost is provided for by government benefits or services and the injured person thereby has a right to compensation from those sources.

5.9   Indemnity for treatment costs is to be paid only if these costs were incurred in Sweden.

5.6   For indemnity in accordance with this undertaking, the rules regarding contributory negligence in Chap. 1, § 6, of the Tort Damages Act are correspondingly applicable. However, indemnity is not to be paid if the injured person or, in those cases where the injury has led to death, the deceased intentionally caused the injury.

§ 7   Indemnity is not to be paid if the claim regarding pain and suffering, disfigurement, permanent disability or other injury is based on an assignment.

§ 8   A person wishing to make a claim for indemnity for a treatment injury during a period of time when the insurance policy was in effect shall present his claim within three years of the time when the injury became apparent, however, no later than 10 years after the time at which the measure which caused the injury was undertaken.
In case of special reasons a claim can be examined even if the time stipulated in the first paragraph has been run over.

§ 9   Indemnity is not to be paid in connection with nuclear damage according to the definition in § 1 of the Nuclear Liability Act, or for an injury whose origin or extent is directly or indirectly caused by or connected with an earthquake, volcanic eruption, invasion, war or other enemy action, revolution, rebellion or action by a power that has illegally taken over the government.

§ 10   Indemnity for a treatment injury is paid by the insurer.
If the insurer has paid indemnity for a treatment injury he will take over the injured person's right to damages.
The insurer is not responsible for any loss which arises if the claim investigation or payment of indemnity is delayed because of war, warlike events, civil war, revolution or rebellion or because of a government action, a strike, a lockout, a blockade or similar situation.

§ 11   This undertaking is limited for each loss event to a maximum sum of SEK 20 million, and to a maximum of SEK 3 million for each injured person. For injuries that occur during one calendar year the total liability of the health care authorities, according to this undertaking or on other grounds, is limited to an aggregate of at most SEK 125 million.

§ 12   Questions of principle or disputes in indemnification cases shall, upon the request of an injured person, a health care authority or an insurer, be referred to a specially appointed committee—The Patient Claims Panel—for review. The Patient Claims Panel consists of six members. The Government appoints the chairman and two other members, one to represent the interests of patients and the other to represent medical expertise. The health care authorities appoint two members and the insurer one. The rules of procedure of the Patient Claims Panel are laid down by the Federation of Swedish County Councils after consultation with the insurer.

§ 13   Disputes between the insurer and the injured person are to be settled by arbitrators in accordance with the Arbitrators Act (1929:145). If any of the arbitrators appointed by the parties so requests, the third arbitrator shall be appointed by the Government.
If an arbitrator so requests, the arbitrators shall call upon a medical expert and provide him with the opportunity to present his opinion.
The arbitration proceedings shall be based on written documentation unless special grounds exist.
If the injured person had reasonable grounds for having the dispute determined by arbitration, the insurer will be liable to the compensation of the arbitrators.

§ 14 Arbitration in accordance with § 13 may be requested only if the Patient Claims Panel has previously issued an opinion on the indemnity matter pursuant to § 12. If either party wants to refer to new circumstances or a new investigation which has not been examined by the insurer or the Patient Claims Panel, the matter shall be remitted back to the Patient Claims Panel for a new opinion.

The injured person may not request an opinion from the Patient Claims Panel later than one year after he received the insurer's decision regarding his claim for indemnity.

The injured person may not request a decision by arbitration later than six months from the time he received the insurer's final decision, on the basis of the opinion of the Patient Claims Panel, regarding the indemnity matter.

APPENDIX 3

Indemnity for pain and suffering (1987)
(=personal suffering during a period of acute illness)

By pain and suffering is understood such pain and inconvenience that the injury has caused during the duration of the acute illness and its treatment. The size of the indemnity depends on the nature of the injury, its treatment, the time for healing, etc.

Every injury must be assessed individually. This means that a higher indemnity than normal can be assessed, e.g., for severe cerebral damage, treatment with traction or extensive plastering.

On the other hand the indemnity will be lower if the inconvenience is slight or if the injured regardless of the treatment injury would have been on the sick list or been treated in a hospital.

	Indemnity per month in SEK		
	For 3 months from date of injury	Thereafter for at most 3 months	Thereafter
1 *Hospitalisation*			
1.1 Severe injury (Note 1)	2,800	2,000	1,400 (Note 2)
1.2 Other injury	2,000	2,000	1,400 (Note 2)
2 Other care during *period of illness* (Note 3)	1,200	1,200	600

· 1 Severe crush or burn injuries, severe lacerations, severe skull or face injuries, substantial lesions on different parts of the body, fractures which are difficult to heal and the like.

2 For 6 months at the most. Eligibility for longer periods is subject to special assessment.

3 If there has been an initial period of hospitalisation, this estimate will start out instead from the date of discharge from the hospital. The amounts will be reduced if a patient is not on the sick list to 100%. If the patient is on the sick list exclusively pending the commencement of occupational therapy or a disability pension, the extended period will not be regarded as a period of acute illness. Periods of acute illness of more than three years are to be assessed individually.

The basic amount may be increased by 10–50% due to special circumstances. The increase is calculated on the basis of the applicable basic amounts according to "other care during period of illness". Such circumstances could be the following,

50%   During intensive care

40%   Skull traction, a body cast, or at least 2 extensive casts

30%   External fixation of a fracture of the pelvis, traction of the tibia or femur, fixation of the jaw or a thoracobrachial cast (stronger arm)

20%   A thoracobrachial cast (weaker arm), high arm cast (stronger arm), colocecostomy

10%   High arm cast (weaker arm), whole leg cast or external fixation of the lower leg.

Less than 10% will not result in an increase. Thus there will be no increase regarding the plastering of a lower leg or arm, the plastering of fingers, the necessity to use one or two crutches for walking or trestles or simple draining even if draining is used for a long time.

Severe pain during treatment outside of a hospital motivates—for six months at most—an increase of 20% normally. In exceptional cases the increase may be up to 40%, but including all additions the total increase may not exceed 50% in total.

4   If the basic disease as well as the treatment injury would have resulted in hospital treatment, the indemnity will be 50% of the amounts under 1.2. If the treatment injury results in hospitalisation, but the basic disease would only have resulted in care in the home the indemnity will be 75% of the amounts under 1.

5   If the basic disease as well as the treatment injury would have resulted in care in the home the indemnity will be 50% of the amounts under 2.

If the basic disease results in hospitalisation but the treatment injury would only have resulted in care in the home the indemnity will be 25% of the amounts under 2.

For painful *denial treatment*, painful *physiotherapy*, or other *painful treatment* that is administered during a period when a certified illness is not at hand, and which accordingly is not covered by the above definitions, an indemnity will be provided at a rate of SEK 115 per treatment occasion.

APPENDIX 4

Indemnity for permanent pain and suffering and loss of amenities 1988

The indemnity belongs to the injured person himself and refers to compensation for losses caused to him by the treatment injury. The indemnity is calculated with respect to the losses which the injury should have caused a person who, when the injury occurred, was healthy and fit for work and refers to permanent:-

—physical and mental suffering e.g. pain and suffering, reduced morale or feeling of humiliation because of disfigurement
—reduced possibilities to enjoy leisure time and practise spare-time activities.

The size of the compensation is related to probable remaining life time and is calculated according to the following Table.

Degree of disability %	Indemnity SEK Lump sums
100	230,000
90	200,000
80	175,000
70	150,000
60	130,000
50	106,000
40	82,000
35	70,000
30	58,000
25	50,700
20	43,400
15	35,700
10	27,900
9	25,100
8	22,300
7	19,500
6	16,700
5	14,000
4	11,200
3	8,400
2	5,600
1	2,800

The Table pertains to cases in which the injured person is not older than 25 years of age. With increasing age the amounts of indemnity shown above will be reduced proportionately so that, at the age of 50, the amount awarded will be 75% of that stated in the Table and, at the age of 65, the award will come to 50% of the amount stated in the Table.

The Table regards indemnity to a person who was normally healthy and able to work immediately before the injury.

The injured person, regardless of the treatment injury, has sustained disfigurement and permanent disadvantage in any of the respects mentioned above or if there has been risk for such disfigurement or disadvantage regardless of the treatment that led to the injury, reasonable consideration shall be taken of this when establishing the indemnity.

APPENDIX 5

Statistics: Patient and drug no fault insurance

A **Patient Insurance**

Premium areas (type of care)

01 County Council and State
02 Private dentists
03 Private physicians
04 Private nursing homes
05 Private hospitals
06 Municipalities
07 Company health care
08 Private physical therapists
09 State otherwise
10 Private dental technicians
11 Opticians

Type of institutions

21 University or region hospitals
22 County hospitals
23 Partial county hospitals
24 Other hospitals
25 District hospitals
26 Medical specialist practice
30 District dental and out-patient department
31 Specialist dental out-patient department
99 Other care

Locale of injury incurred (for premium areas 1 and 9)

3 Injury which occurred within care premises (in-patient)
4 Injury which occurred within care premises (out-patient)
5 Injury which occurred on other care premises
6 Injury which occurred in connection with transport with motor vehicle
7 Injury which occurred in connection with other transport outside hospital premises
8 Injury which occurred at another location

Type of reserve

1   Transient injury with estimated sick leave of less than 3 months
2   Transient injury with estimated sick leave of more than 3 months
3   Disablement cases   0–15%
4   Disablement cases   16–30%
5   Disablement cases   over 30%
6   Death

Basic illness (the illness whose treatment led to the injury)

Is coded according to ICD (International Classification of Diseases)
Hospital–clinic
    according to the classification of the Swedish National Board of Health
Kind of treatment
    according to the classification of the Swedish National Board of Health

Cause of injury

A   Diagnostics
A1   Radiology
A2   Laboratory test
A3   Clinical assessments
A9   Other reason

B   **Operation or Treatment**

DIAGNOSTIC METHOD

B1   Puncture
B2   Open biopsy
B3   Examination
B4   Angiography
B9   Other diagnostic operation

SURGICAL OPERATION WHICH INVOLVES OR CONCERNS

E1   Brain, spinal marrow, nerves
E2   Endocrinal organs
E3   Eye
E4   Ear, nose, throat
E5   Mouth, oesophagus (not dental treatment)
E6   Heart and mayor arteries
E7   Bronchi, lungs, thorax
E8   Mammary gland
E9   Liver, gall ducts

F1   Pancreas
F2   Spleen
F3   Ventricle, duodenum
F4   Small intestine
F5   Colon, rectum
F6   Urinary ducts

F7   Male genitals
F8   Female genitals
F9   Childbirth

G1   Abortion, legal and spontaneous
G2   Placement of interuterine contraceptives (spiral, etc.)
G3   Caesarian section and other obstetric operations
G4   Skeleton in injuries (not remaining condition)
G5   Joints, muscles and other soft parts in case of illness (even discs)
G8   Hands
G9   Amputation and exarticulation

H1   Peripheral arterial surgery
H2   Skin and subcutaneous tissue (plastic surgery, etc.)

K9   Other surgical operations

ANAESTHESIA

9C   With intubation
9F   Without intubation
9X   Information about

LOCAL ANAESTHESIA

L1   Spinal anaesthesia
L2   Epidural anaesthesia
L3   Sacral anaesthesia
L4   Nerve blockade
L5   Infiltration anaesthesia
L6   Anaesthesia of the surface
L9   Miscellaneous

OTHER TREATMENT

N1   Physical therapy
N2   Radiation treatment
N3   Infusion
N4   Blood donation
N5   Injection, puncture (even vaccination)
N6   Catheter, drainage
N7   Casts, bandaging, etc. (not surgical measure)
N8   Bandaging of wounds
N9   Prothesis treatment (private dental care)

P1   Tooth and bite treatment
P2   Physical therapy
P9   Other treatment

ACCIDENTAL INJURY

R1   Fall from stretcher, bed operating table
R2   Fall from previous level (such as sliding)
R3   Fall on stairs

R4   Injury in connection with work therapy, rehabilitation
R9   Other causes

Other causes of injury

T1   Drugs not used according to the instructions
T2   Health care equipment, defective material
T3   Defects in treatment material
T4   Defects in diagnostic material
T5   Other defects in material
T6   Contamination (without connection with A–C)

X9   Other cause

Injury effects

01   Sore infection, *staph. aureus*
09   Sore infection, other bacteria
10   Salmonella or other intestinal infection
11   TB
12   Hepatitis
13   HIV—AIDS
19   Other contagion
20   Sepsis
21   Haemorrhage
22   Thrombosis—embolism
30   Breathing effect
31   Circulation effect
32   Heart failure
33   Physic injury
34   Allergic reaction
35   Toxic reactions
36   Condition of pain
50   Injury to nerves and central nervous system
51   Injury to ducts
52   Injury to liver
53   Injury to kidney
59   Injury to other internal organs
60   Injury to skeleton
61   Injury to teeth
69   Injury to other tissue, for example skin
70   Reoperation
80   Unchanged or extended state of illness
99   Other injury effects

x) Does not have to be stated in connection with cause of injury =
accidental injury and only in connection with certain reasons for refusal.

Reasons for refusal

01   Not a patient
02   Injury occurred before the insurance came into effect

03 7.2 Injury reported after period of limitation
04   The injured party has not kept to his claim
05   Accident without connection with treatment
06 2.2 Not a diagnosis injury
07 2.1 Probable consequence of a measure motivated from a medical point of view
08 3.3 Drug with side effects
09   Diagnostic surgery—injury not more severe than basic illness
10 3.3 Health care material used according to instructions
11 3.4 Contamination, not transferred
12 3.4 Infection, unclean operation
13 4   Cost or loss of income less than the deductible
14 4   Injured person not on sick list for more than 14 days
15 2.1 Injury not caused by treatment
16   Not insured patient
17 3.4 Infection, clean operation but patient had reduced resistance or impaired tissue vitality
18 3.4 Infection, clean operation but infection due to method used (major resections or remaining catheters)
19 3.1 Intentionally risk taking
20 3.2 Injury/illness would have continued, arisen or developed regardless of care
21 5.3 Another insurance shall pay for the injury
22 2.3 Not caused by an accident
23 2.4 Accidental injury outside the hospital area
24   Injury compensated by pharma-insurance
25   Injury caused by the injured himself
26   Not bodily injury
27   Accident caused by the basic illness
50   Other reasons
70   Surgery in unclean part of the body
71   Surgery in tissue with reduced vitality
72   Catherisation over a long period
73   Increased risk of infection as a result of transplantation, etc.
75   Reduced immunity resistance
80   Injury caused by faulty material

B   **Data—jointly for patient—and pharma insurance**

Sickness period of less than 3 months
Sickness period more than 3 months
Permanent disability 1–15%
Permanent disability 30–15%
Permanent disability 16–30%
Permanent disability of more than 30%
Death
BASIC DISEASE = 3 numbers and one letter
              According to 1987 International Classification of Diseases
Number of compensated days during acute illness must be registered when compensation is paid for
—Pain and suffering
—Loss of income

—Date for report of injury
—Date of occurrence

	Code
Acute illness	01 = cost for hospitalisation, etc.
	02 = pain and suffering
	09 = loss of income
Rehabilitation	16 = cost of rehabilitation
	19 = loss of income during rehabilitation
Disability	10 = loss of income—annuities
	11 = cost for capitalisation of annuities
	12 = compensation for costs as annuities
	14 = loss of amenities and permanent pain and suffering
	15 = other permanent inconveniences
	22 = lump sums for loss of income
	41 = lump sums for loss of income
Death	20 = cost for funeral
	21 = annuities for loss of breadwinner
	42 = lump sums for loss of breadwinner

C Drug insurance

Premium area	50 for a serial injury
	40 for other injuries
Prescription	1 bought without prescription
	2 bought with prescription
	5 used within a hospital
	6 used in tests on voluntary human beings
	7 used in clinical trials
	8 prescribed with licence
Drug number 1	The name of the drug which has caused the injury
	Code according to FASS
Name of the drug	Name en clair according to FASS
Side effect 1	The most serious side-effect coded according to list published by the National Board of Health and Welfare
Unknown adverse reaction	If side-effect, was not known when the drug, was prescribed
Side-effect 2	The next serious side-effect
Drug number 2	Other drug which may have contributed to the injury

The main reason for injuries not being compensated

02 —Occurred before 1 July 1978
03 —Barred by the statute of limitations
04 —The injured has not maintained his claims
14 —Incapacity for less than 14 days
31 —The manufacturer not insured
34 —Not caused by the drug
39 —Severe basic disease
40 —Not on sick list of more than 3 months
44 —Referred to Patient Insurance

APPENDIX 6

TABLES

Patient insurance

1. Premium for 1987
2. Number of reported injuries and amounts of compensation
3. Number of reported injuries and amounts of compensation divided in proportion to seriousness
4. Number of yearly reported injuries
5. How serious were the injuries?
6. Number of reported injuries in proportion to age and sex
7. Number of reported injuries according to the cause of injury
8. Examples of number and costs for some kinds of injury
9. Examples of number of injuries and amounts of compensation referred to different kinds of treatment
10. Cases decided in the patient claims panel

Pharma insurance

11. Number of reported injuries and amounts of compensation
12. Number of reported injuries and amounts of compensation divided in proportion to the degree of seriousness
13. Number of injuries caused by known side effects
14. Examples of injuries and amounts of compensation divided in proportion to treated basic diseases
15. Cases decided in the claims panel
16. Disputed cases decided in the claims panel referred to the reason for the refusal

Patient and Pharma Insurance

17. Average cost for reported injuries
18. Paid out compensation divided in different kinds of economic or non-economic losses
19. The main reasons for injuries not being compensated

Table 1 *Patient insurance: Premium for 1987—outcome per December 1987 in SEK (1000) (not including the premium for the administration)*

Insurance year	Paid preliminary premium	Paid out compensation	Difference
1979	900	948	−49
1980	1,700	4,005	−2,305
1981	2,700	3,315	−615
1982	3,900	3,377	523
1983	6,300	4,182	2,118
1984	7,500	7,313	187
1985	9,400	9,764	−364
1986	8,100	6,256	1,844
1987	2,700	2,121	586
	43,200	41,281	1,919*

*If deficit this had been paid from special claims reserve fund

Table 2 *Patient insurance: County councils—number of reported injuries and estimated compensation with regard to the year when the injury was reported, January 1975 through August 1988 (in SEK million)*

Year reported	Total number	Compensatable	Under investigation	Total estimated compensation	Paid out compensation	Not compensatable
1975	682	349	—	6.1	5.4	333
1976	2,255	1,165	1	17.9	14.7	1,089
1977	2,076	1,110	1	16.4	15.4	965
1978	2,273	1,153	—	20.9	15.9	1,120
1979	2,662	1,389	2	26.7	20.4	1,271
1980	2,694	1,443	1	34.3	24.8	1,250
1981	3,111	1,652	6	38.7	30.2	1,453
1982	3,710	1,901	12	41.1	31.2	1,797
1983	4,359	1,936	54	38.7	30.2	2,369
1984	4,592	2,068	74	41.9	30.7	2,450
1985	4,796	1,869	206	58.6	30.3	2,721
1986	4,575	1,563	495	67.7	27.8	2,517
1987	4,630	1,257	1,385	94.6	13.8	1,988
1988	3,071	276	2,221	46.9	1.9	574
	45,486	19,131	4,458	550.5	292.7	21,897

Table 3 *Patient Insurance: County councils—estimated cost for not refused claims reported January*
1975 through June 1988 (in SEK 1,000)

Not refused claims	Number	Total estimated cost including reserves	Finalised claims	Compensatable but not yet finalised	Still under investigation
Degree of seriousness					
1. Sickness period less than 3 months	5,814	10,508,856	4,795	274	745
2. Sickness period more than 3 months	8,190	49,275,748	6,218	389	1,583
3. Permanent disablement 1–15%	7,305	237,746,661	3,952	1,369	1,984
4. Permanent disablement 16–30%	1,297	94,571,877	970	223	104
5. Permanent disablement more than 30%	660	147,659,203	427	182	51
6. Death	483	11,744,482	388	38	57
	23,749	551,506,827	16,750	2,475	4,524

Table 4 *Patient insurance: County councils. Number of yearly reported injuries*

Reported year	
1983	4,359
1984	4,591
1985	4,796
1986	4,572
1987	4,630

Table 5   *Patient insurance: County councils—accepted claims—1 January 1975 through 31 June 1988 (in SEK 1,000)*

How serious were the injuries?	Number	%	Total cost SEK milion	%
Sickness period of less than 3 months	5,814	24	10.5	2
Sickness period more than 3 months	8,190	35	49.3	10
Permanent disability 1–15%	7,305	30	237.7	43
Permanent disability 16–30%	1,297	6	94.6	16
Permanent disability of more than 30%	660	3	147.6	27
Death	483	2	11.7	2
	23,749	100	584.4	100

Table 6 *Patient insurance: Reported claims (all) according to age and sex from January 1975 through December 1987 (in SEK 1,000)*

	Total reported claims			Permanent disability 1–15%			Permanent disability more than 15%		
	Number	M%	F%	Number	M%	F%	Number	M%	F%
00–19	2,911	50	50	444	50	50	149	51	49
20–29	5,407	42	58	860	40	60	90	34	66
30–39	8,725	37	63	1,262	40	60	203	40	60
40–49	9,043	37	63	1,186	38	62	198	40	60
50–59	10,558	40	60	1,277	37	63	315	52	48
60–69	9,584	43	57	1,218	41	59	400	48	52
70–99	9,106	35	65	1,243	30	70	583	31	69
	55,334			7,490			1,938		

Table 7   *Patient insurance: County councils—number of compensated injuries according to the cause of injury reported from January 1975 through December 1987*

	Number of injuries
Caused by diagnostics	
Radiology	185
Laboratory test	42
Clinical assessment	919
Other reason	198
	1,344
Caused by operation or other treatment	
Diagnostic operation	1,052
Surgical operation	7,560
Anaesthetics	1,842
Physical therapy	50
Radiation treatment	28
Infusion	224
Blood donation	89
Injection, puncture	573
Catheterisation	112
Casts, bandaging, etc.	247
Bandaging of wounds	34
Prosthetic treatment	49
Tooth and bite treatment	952
Physiotherapy	46
Transfusion	65
Other treatment	340
	13,263
Accidental injuries	
Fall from stretcher, bed, operating table, etc.	891
Slipping on a floor, etc.	1,701
Falling down stairs	63
Injury in connection with work therapy, rehabilitation	123
Other accidental causes	642
	3,420
Other causes	
Drugs not used according to instructions	122
Health care equipment, defective material	62
Defects in treatment materials	35
Defects in diagnostic materials	7
Other defects in materials	10
Contamination	26
Other causes	193
	455
In all—compensatable injuries	18,482

Table 8 *Patient insurance: What kind of injuries occur most frequently—some examples 1975—August 1988*

	Number	Total cost in SEK (1,000)	Average cost
Injuries caused to			
— Teeth	2,472	5.2	2,086
— Skeleton	2,484	35.5	14,311
— Nerves and central nervous system	2,833	130.5	46,061
— Liver	27	0.3	11,267
— Blood vessels	263	8.2	31,486
Injuries caused by			
— Staphylococcus	2,139	36.4	17,030
— Hepatitis	195	3.6	18,764

Table 9 *Patient insurance:—Examples. Reported and accepted claims 1974—August 1988*

Group	Reason for treatment	Number	Estimated total cost 1,000 SEK	Average cost SEK
650–662	Partus	252	11,675	46,328
655	Partus complicatus e disproportione fetopelvina	9	96	10,659
656	Partus complicatus e presentatione fetus	15	1,145	76,301
755	Congenital hip joint dislocation	64	1,745	27,402
772	Laesiones intra partum	7	638	91,178
776	Anoxia (lack of oxygen)	15	3,564	237,601

Table 10 *Patient insurance: Cases (1369) decided in the patients' claims panel 1 January 1975– 31 December 1987*

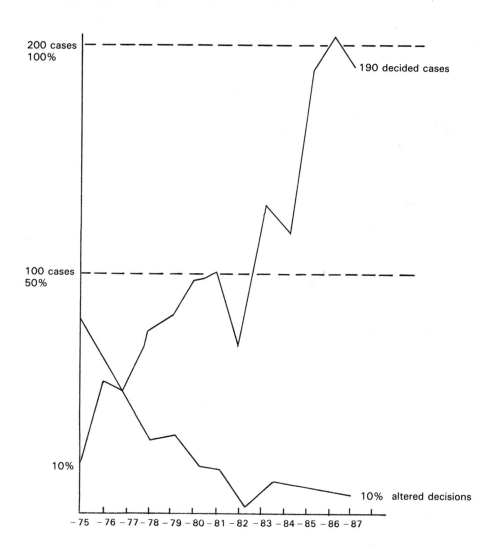

Table 11 *Pharma insurance: Injuries reported 1 July 1978—1 July 1988 paid out compensation and reserves in SEK (1,000)*

Degree of seriousness	Number	Paid out compensation	Total cost including reserved	Number of finalised claims	Not finalised claims
Insurance year 1978					
1. Sickness period less than 3 months	9	17	24	6	3
2. Sickness period more than 3 months	11	84	˙92	10	1
3. Permanent disablement 1–15%	24	217	1,015	6	18
4. Permanent disablement 16–30%	2	277	277	2	—
5. Permanent disablement more than 30%	3	545	545	3	—
6. Death	2	10	10	2	—
Not compensatable	274	14	14	274	—
	325	1,167	1,978	303	22
Insurance year 1979					
1. Sickness period less than 3 months	7	22	24	6	1
2. Sickness period more than 3 months	21	137	141	20	1
3. Permanent disablement 1–15%	9	177	266	7	2
4. Permanent disablement 16–30%	4	178	178	4	—
5. Permanent disablement more than 30%	12	2,335	3,082	9	3
6. Death	10	270	321	9	1
Not compensatable	120	16	16	120	—
	325	3,135	4,028	175	8
Insurance year 1980					
1. Sickness period less than 3 months	9	21	21	9	—
2. Sickness period more than 3 months	16	217	217	16	—
3. Permanent disablement 1–15%	9	185	460	3	6
4. Permanent disablement 16–30%	4	413	473	2	2
5. Permanent disablement more than 30%	7	944	4,768	2	5
6. Death	2	24	33	1	1
Not compensatable	91	11	11	91	—
	138	1,815	5,983	124	14

continued

Degree of seriousness	Number	Paid out compensation	Total cost including reserved	Number of finalised claims	Not finalised claims
Insurance year 1986					
1. Sickness period less than 3 months	13	24	45	5	8
2. Sickness period more than 3 months	33	194	265	15	18
3. Permanent disablement 1–15%	64	507	2,894	3	61
4. Permanent disablement 16–30%	3	4	385	—	3
5. Permanent disablement more than 30%	2	238	608	1	1
6. Death	1	—	23	—	1
Not compensatable	71	23	23	71	—
	187	990	4,243	95	92
Insurance year 1987					
1. Sickness period less than 3 months	12	4	30	2	10
2. Sickness period more than 3 months	27	94	245	3	24
3. Permanent disablement 1–15%	72	119	3,239	—	72
4. Permanent disablement 16–30%	3	16	288	1	2
5. Permanent disablement more than 30%	1	34	370	—	1
6. Death	2	41	59	1	1
Not compensatable	21	2	2	21	1
	138	310	4,352	28	110
Insurance years 1978—July 1988					
1. Sickness period less than 3 months	93	416	483	63	30
2. Sickness period more than 3 months	294	1,946	2,498	229	65
3. Permanent disablement 1–15%	481	11,814	28,199	103	378
4. Permanent disablement 16–30%	61	3,473	8,474	31	30
5. Permanent disablement more than 30%	75	9,830	27,875	44	31
6. Death	62	1,478	2,273	49	13
Not compensatable	1,242	163	163	1,242	—
	2,308	29,121	69,965	1,761	547[a]

[a]in 259 cases liability has been accepted

Table 12 *Pharma insurance: Specification of paid out compensation and reserves 1 July 1978–31 December 1987 paid out compensation and reserves in SEK (1,000)*

Degree of seriousness	Number	Paid out compensation	Reserves
Insurance year 1978			
1. Sick leave of less than 3 months	9	19	6
2. Sick leave of more than 3 months	10	84	0
3. Permanent disability 1–15%	18	219	541
4. Permanent disability 16–30%	2	277	0
5. Permanent disability of more than 30%	3	545	0
6. Death	3	174	69
Not accepted		14	
	45	1,333	616
Insurance year 1979			
1. Sick leave of less than 3 months	7	22	2
2. Sick leave of more than 3 months	21	137	4
3. Permanent disability 1–15%	9	177	89
4. Permanent disability 16–30%	5	386	157
5. Permanent disability of more than 30%	11	1,942	472
6. Death	9	88	0
Not accepted		16	
	62	2,768	724
Insurance year 1980			
1. Sick leave of less than 3 months	9	11	2
2. Sick leave of more than 3 months	15	152	0
3. Permanent disability 1–15%	10	244	391
4. Permanent disability 16–30%	3	317	13
5. Permanent disability of more than 30%	7	929	3,593
6. Death	2	24	8
Not accepted		7	
	46	1,684	4,007
Insurance year 1981			
1. Sick leave of less than 3 months	7	56	0
2. Sick leave of more than 3 months	33	226	194
3. Permanent disability 1–15%	20	560	161
4. Permanent disability 16–30%	10	696	682
5. Permanent disability of more than 30%	3	414	627
6. Death	5	84	0
Not accepted		23	
	78	2,059	1,664
Insurance year 1982			
1. Sick leave of less than 3 months	12	17	10
2. Sick leave of more than 3 months	45	324	23
3. Permanent disability 1–15%	24	425	265
4. Permanent disability 16–30%	8	482	203
5. Permanent disability of more than 30%	14	2,176	5,538
6. Death	6	79	0
Not accepted		15	
–	109	3,518	6,039

continued

Degree of seriousness	Number	Paid out compensation	Reserves
Insurance year 1983			
1. Sick leave of less than 3 months	10	36	2
2. Sick leave of more than 3 months	39	183	54
3. Permanent disability 1–15%	49	672	987
4. Permanent disability 16–30%	10	663	925
5. Permanent disability of more than 30%	15	1,658	730
6. Death	11	341	508
Not accepted		13	
	134	3,566	3,206
Insurance year 1984			
1. Sick leave of less than 3 months	10	176	7
2. Sick leave of more than 3 months	32	251	30
3. Permanent disability 1–15%	47	998	1,298
4. Permanent disability 16–30%	11	454	2,033
5. Permanent disability of more than 30%	17	505	4,447
6. Death	10	191	143
Not accepted		12	
	117	2,587	7,958
Insurance year 1985			
1. Sick leave of less than 3 months	9	31	9
2. Sick leave of more than 3 months	34	205	29
3. Permanent disability 1–15%	63	587	2,234
4. Permanent disability 16–30%	5	206	831
5. Permanent disability of more than 30%	9	535	517
6. Death	11	190	61
Not accepted		19	
	131	1,773	3,681
Insurance year 1986			
1. Sick leave of less than 3 months	12	20	17
2. Sick leave of more than 3 months	32	158	84
3. Permanent disability 1–15%	57	222	2,289
4. Permanent disability 16–30%	2	4	274
5. Permanent disability of more than 30%	1	238	0
6. Death	2	0	53
Not accepted		7	
	106	649	2,717
Insurance year 1987			
1. Sick leave of less than 3 months	13	4	25
2. Sick leave of more than 3 months	13	4	74
3. Permanent disability 1–15%	39	40	1,747
4. Permanent disability 16–30%	3	4	303
5. Permanent disability of more than 30%	0	0	0
6. Death	1	15	0
Not accepted		2	
	69	69	2,149

Table 12 *continued*

Degree of seriousness	Number	Paid out compensation	Reserves
All years			
1. Sick leave of less than 3 months	98	392	81
2. Sick leave of more than 3 months	274	1,724	492
3. Permanent disability 1–15%	336	4,144	10,003
4. Permanent disability 16–30%	59	3,489	5,421
5. Permanent disability of more than 30%	70	8,942	15,923
6. Death	60	1,186	843
Not accepted		128	
	897	20,005	32,763

Table 13 *Pharma Insurance: Injuries caused by known side effects—not including reports of non-compensated injuries*

Year reported	Total number	Compensatable	Under investigation	Compensation and reserves	Average cost SEK (1,000)
1978	7	7	—	59	8
1979	44	43	1	2,414	55
1980	26	26	—	1,296	50
1981	62	62	—	5,103	82
1983	109	108	1	7,179	65
1984	116	103	7	8,350	76
1985	105	98	7	9,073	86
1986	133	106	27	7,483	56
1987	130	61	69	5,841	45
1988	109	13	96	4,791	44
	910	702	208	54,703[a]	

[a]of this amount SEK 22.1 million has been paid out

Table 14 *Pharma insurance: Example of types of injuries reported and accepted claims 1 July 1978–31 August 1988*

Group no	Indications for treatment	Number	Estimated total cost 1,000 SEK	Average cost 1,000 SEK
1	Digestive organs and metabolic system	20	2,084	104
2	Blood and haemapoietic organs	120	16,605	138
3	Heart and cardiac system	59	1,775	29
4	Dermatoloses	2	10	5
5	Urine and sex organ	117	9,624	82
6	Infectious diseases	126	3,588	28
7	Central nervous system	185	13,189	71
8	Respiratory system	5	72	14

Table 15 *Pharma insurance: Cases (83) decided in the pharma claims panel 1 July 1978–*
31 December 1987

77%

Disputes

(64 cases)

23%

Decisions in principle

(19 cases)

72%

Not compensatable

(60 cases)

28%

Altered decisions

(23 cases)

Table 16   *Pharma insurance: Disputed cases (64) decided by the pharma claims panel and referred to the reason for refusal 1 July 1978–31 December 1987*

86%

No alteration

(55 cases)

14%

alteration

(9 cases)

According to

§ 3   30 cases

§ 5   17 cases

§ 3 + 5   6 cases

Table 17 *Patient and pharma insurance: Average estimated cost for injuries which were reported in 1987 and which has caused*

1.	Sick leave of less than 3 months	2,500
2.	Sick leave of more than 3 months	6,700
3.	Permanent disability 1–15%	46,300
4.	Permanent disability 16–30%	138,800
5.	Permanent disability of more than 30%	354,200
6.	Death	29,200

Patient insurance

Average actual cost for injuries which have been accepted between January 1975 and August 1988

1.	Sick leave of less than 3 months	1,835
2.	Sick leave of more than 3 months	6,192
3.	Permanent disability 1–15%	32,102
4.	Permanent disability 16–30%	73,095
5.	Permanent disability of more than 30%	222,540
6.	Death	25,178

Pharma insurance

Average actual cost for injuries which has been accepted between January 1975 and August 1988

1.	Sick leave of less than 3 months	5,552
2.	Sick leave of more than 3 months	7,814
3.	Permanent disability 1–15%	60,217
4.	Permanent disability 16–30%	124,380
5.	Permanent disability of more than 30%	366,315
6.	Death	39,214

Table 18 *Patient insurance (31 December 1987)*

Paid out compensation (SEK 279 million	M SEK	%
— Pain and suffering during acute illness	59.0	20.0
— Permanent pain and suffering or loss of amenities	96.0	36.0
— Other permanent inconveniences	30.0	10.0
— Loss of income	25.0	8.0
— Costs for medical treatment	24.0	8.0
— Future loss of income	17.0	6.0
— Funeral costs	4.0	1.5

Pharma insurance (31 December 1987)

Paid out compensation (SEK 26 million)		
— Pain and suffering during acute illness	3.7	14.0
— Permanent pain and suffering or loss of amenities	12.3	50.0
— Other permanent inconveniences	1.3	5.0
— Loss of income	2.5	10.0
— Costs for medical treatment	2.0	8.0
— Future loss of income	0.5	2.0
— Future costs	1.6	7.5
— Funeral costs	0.7	2.5

Table 19 *Patient insurance: The main reason for injuries (25,349) not being compensated 1 January–31 August 1988*

	Number
— Not caused by treatment	4,420
— Not possible to avoid	3,376
— Barred by the statue of limitations	2,364
— The cost for the injury should be paid by another insurance	2,115
— The injured has not maintained his claim	1,490
— A consequence of the basic disease	1,293
— Not caused by incorrect diagnoses	986
— Not on the sick list during at least the stipulated minimum time	897
— Occurred before 1 January 1975	846
— Accidents caused by the medical care	714
— Consequence of an intentional risk taking	571
— Caused by pharmaceuticals	301
— Loss less than the deductible amount	129
— Claimant was not a patient	63

Pharma insurance: The main reason for injuries not being compensated 1978–1986

	Number
— Severe basic disease	397
— Not caused by the drug	333
— Not on the sick list of more than 3 months	214
— Occurred before 1 July 1978	151
— Referred to Patient Insurance	69
— The injured has not maintained his claim	45
— Incapacity for less than 14 days	21
— Barred by the statute of limitations	33
— The manufacturer not insured	0

APPENDIX 7

Patient Injury Act issued at Naantali, 25 July 1986

In accordance with the Decision of Parliament, it is enacted that:

Section 1

Scope of application of the Act

Compensation is payable under this Act for personal injury caused to patient in connection with health and medical care (patient injury).

Persons voluntarily undergoing medical research shall also be regarded as being patients.

Section 2

Patient injury

Compensation for patient injury is payable for any injury which:

1) probably has arisen as a consequence of examination, treatment or any similar action, or neglect of the same;

2) has been caused by an infection or inflammation which probably has originated in the circumstances connected with examination, treatment or any similar action or;

3) has been caused by an accident:

a) connected with examination, treatment or any similar action; or

b) occurring during ambulance transportation or in connection with fire or other damage to treatment premises or treatment equipment; or

c) resulting from a defect in medical care equipment or in a medical care device.

Consequences of medically justifiable treatment that could not have been avoided by other procedure equally effective in the care of patient shall not be regarded as being patient injury in the sense of Points 1 and 2 of Subsection 1 above. An injury resulting from diagnostic incision shall, nevertheless, be compensated as patient injury if the consequence is unreasonable considering the quality and severity of the illness or injury to be diagnosed and the state of health of the patient as a whole.

Section 3

Assessment of compensation

The compensation for patient injury shall be assessed in compliance with the provisions of the Tort Damages Act (412/74), Chapter 5, Sections 2–4, and

Chapter 7, Section 3. Compensation shall not be payable, however, for minor injury.

If the patient suffering the injury has intentionally or through gross negligence contributed to the occurrence of the injury, compensation thereof shall only be paid to the extent to which the other circumstances have contributed to the occurrence of the injury.

Section 4

Liability to insure

Those engaged in the practising of health care or of medical care shall be covered by insurance against liability under this Act.

Any party that has neglected to take out insurance shall be liable to pay an insurance premium that is at most tenfold for the period of neglect.

The insurance premium including interest for delay is enforceable without judgement or decision.

Section 5

Insurer

A policy under this Act may be granted by a domestic insurance company that has a licence to engage in liability insurance business.

All insurance companies engaging in patient insurance business shall belong to the Patient Insurance Association. The Association may issue policies and attend to the claims settlement procedure for its member companies. The Association shall be liable for damages when the taking out of an insurance policy has been neglected, and shall assess and collect the increased insurance premium referred to under Section 4, Subsection 2. It is for the Ministry of Social Affairs and Health to confirm the Articles of the Association.

Section 6

Confirmation of the terms and the premium basis of patient insurance

It is for the Ministry of Social Affairs and Health to confirm the insurance terms and premium basis that are to be complied with in patient insurance policies, upon application by the Patient Insurance Association and upon hearing the respective leading parties liable to carry insurance and their organisations.

The bases for the insurance premium shall be so confirmed that, in combination with the interest proceeds of the claims liability, they shall suffice for the expenditure arising out of the patient insurance activities intended herein and for the maintenance of the liability-bearing capacity of the company engaged in this business.

Section 7

Liability to issue insurance

The Patient Insurance Association shall not refuse to issue or maintain a policy under this Act if an insurance company referred to under Section 5, Subsection 1, shall have refused to do so.

Section 8

Primacy of claims reserve

The party suffering the injury shall be entitled to receive compensation for patient injury from the insurance company mentioned under Section 5, Subsection 2, irrespective of whether the party suffering the injury is entitled to compensation on any grounds other than those laid down in this Act.

If compensation has already been paid to the party suffering the injury on the basis of any other Act, the amount paid shall be deducted from the compensation under this Act.

Section 9

Transfer of right to compensation and of right of recourse

If the party suffering injury is entitled to receive compensation for patient injury under any other Act, such right shall be transferred under this Act to the party paying the compensation, up to the amount which it has paid as compensation.

If the party suffering the injury is entitled to receive damages from the party causing the patient injury or from that party's employer, such right shall be transferred under this Act to the party that has paid the compensation, solely in the case, however, that the injury has been caused intentionally or through gross negligence.

Any contract under which the insurer reserves to himself greater rights against the party liable for recovery than those provided under Subsection 2 shall be without effect.

Section 10

Presentation of claim

When a claim for compensation for patient injury is made under this Act, the claim shall be made to the insurer within three years from the date when the party entitled to compensation has learned of the injury. When particular reasons exist, claims made later shall also be taken up for examination. Any claim shall be made, however, not later than within 20 years from the event leading to the injury.

Section 11

Patient Injury Board

At the Ministry for Social Affairs and Health there shall be a Patient Injury Board, appointed by the government for three years at a time, whose responsibility shall be to issue recommendations for decisions on compensation for patient injury to anyone claiming, or against whom is claimed, compensation for patient injury, and to anyone who carries insurance against liability under this Act. It shall moreover be the responsibility of the Boards to issue statements to courts dealing with cases of indemnity for patient injury. In discharging its duties, the Board shall strive towards uniformity in the compensation practice of patient injury.

The composition of the Patient Injury Board shall be regulated by decree.

Section 12

Right of the Patient Injury Board to obtain information

In order to examine a case with which it is dealing, the Patient Injury Board is entitled to obtain the necessary information from the authorities and from those engaged in the practice of health care or medical care, notwithstanding the provisions on the obligation of confidentiality of authorities or physicians or nursing staff.

Section 13

Obligation to observe secrecy

Anyone who has taken part in the processing of a case covered by this Act, or has ex officio or otherwise in his work learned thereof, shall not without permission divulge to an outsider a matter that by law or statute shall be kept a secret.

Anyone violating the confidentiality prescribed in Subsection 1 shall be convicted of violation of confidentiality prescribed in the Patient Injury Act and fined or imprisoned for at most six months.

The public prosecutor shall not raise a charge of violation of confidentiality unless the complainant shall have reported the case for prosecution.

Section 14

Legal venue

An action for damages based on the provisions of this Act may be pursued under the process for civil action also in the court of first instance with jurisdiction in the locality in which the plaintiff has his domicile under the Population Records Act (141/69).

Section 15

Statutory power

Detailed provisions on the implementation of this Act may be issued by decree.

Section 16

Enter into force

This Act shall enter into force on 1 May 1987.

The Act shall apply to patient injuries occurring after its entering into force.

Steps necessary for the enforcement of this Act may be taken prior to the entering into force of this Act.

Naantali. 25 July 1986
President of the Republic
MAUNO KOIVISTO

Minister of
Social Affairs and Health   Eeva Kuuskoski-Vikatmaa

APPENDIX 8

Articles of the Finnish Patient Insurance Association

CHAPTER I

General provisions

Article 1

The Finnish Patient Insurance Association consists of the domestic insurance companies indicated in the Injuries to Patients Act (585/96), Section 5, Subsection 1 that grant patient insurance policies.
The domicile of the Association is Helsinki.

Article 2

The purpose of the Association is:

1) to run the indemnity operations indicated in the Injuries to Patients Act
2) to grant patient insurance policies on behalf of its member companies
3) to accept liability for injuries to patients when the taking out of insurance policies has been neglected
4) to compile statistics and to make studies and estimates for the confirmation of patient insurance premiums, and to promote work to prevent injuries
5) to draw up the insurance terms
6) to fix and collect the increased insurance premium prescribed in the Injuries to Patients Act, Section 4, Subsection 2
7) to provide for the enforcement of agreements covering the running of patient insurance and the practical steps that it requires
8) to issue to its member companies instructions for the standardisation of operations under the Injuries to Patients Act, and to oblige them to avoid competition among themselves tending to increase the administrative costs of the insurance or to lead to procedure contrary to good insurance custom
9) to attend to information and communication and to issue pertaining instructions to its members and otherwise act to promote the patient insurance business.

Article 3

If the Patient Insurance Association is summoned to answer a suit involving compensation for injury to a patient, the Association shall forthwith give notification of the summons to the company on whose policy the claim is based.

Article 4

The Association shall notify the Ministry for Social Affairs and Health in writing of the agreements indicated in Article 2, Point 7, of these Articles of Association, and of any changes made therein, not later than one month prior to their coming into effect.

CHAPTER II

Assembly, Board of Directors and President

Article 5

The organs of the Association are the Assembly, the Board of Directors and the President.

Article 6

The Assembly, in which every member company has the right to vote, is held in Helsinki. The Assembly is convoked by the Board of Directors of the Association or by its President.

The call convoking the Assembly shall be delivered to each member company, verifiably, at least five days prior to the Assembly. The Assembly forms a quorum when at least half the member companies are represented at the Assembly. The Assembly, is legitimate, however, irrespective of any call convoking it, if all the member companies are represented therein and prior notice of the Assembly shall have been given to the Board of Directors.

If not all member companies are present at the Assembly, decisions shall be made solely on business stated in the call to convene and on the date of a further Assembly to deal with specific business. The absent member companies shall be notified of the further Assembly.

Article 7

The delegate of a member company shall not vote at the Assembly on a matter dealing exclusively with relations between his member company and the Association or otherwise dealing with the private interests of his member company.

A delegate who is also a member of the Board of Directors of the Association shall not take part in the making of a decision on the adoption of the financial statement or the granting of freedom from liability or the election of auditors with the task of auditing the administration and the accounts during his term.

At the convention, each member company shall have one vote. In the event of a tied vote, the opinion supported by the chairman shall prevail, except at elections, when the decision shall then be by the drawing of lots. Elections shall be conducted by secret ballot if any of the member companies represented so demands. Other votes shall be made by secret ballot solely if the Assembly so decides.

A delegate of a member company at the Assembly shall not be the proxy of another member company.

Article 8

An Extraordinary Assembly shall be held should the Ministry for Social Affairs and Health or a member company so demand in writing in order to deal with a specified matter. It shall also be held if the auditors so demand in consequence of their audit.

The Extraordinary Assembly shall be held within 14 days of the time at which the written demand shall have been made to the Board of Directors or the President of the Association.

Article 9

The handling of matters at the Assembly shall be directed by a chairman elected at the Assembly.

Article 10

It is the responsibility of the Assembly:

1) to adopt the general insurance terms for patient insurance policies for presentation to the Ministry for Social Affairs and Health for confirmation
2) to direct what the member companies shall do to comply with the instructions and principles indicated in Article 2 or to conduct studies
3) to decide and deal with other matters that have been brought before the Assembly for decision.

Article 11

The Ordinary Assembly of the Association are the Spring Assembly and the Autumn Assembly, the former being held not later than in June and the latter not later than in December.

At the Spring Assembly:

1) the financial statement and annual report of the Board of Directors and the Auditors' Report shall be presented
2) the question of adoption of the financial statement for the previous year shall be dealt with, and
3) the steps to which the administration and accounts of the previous year give rise shall be decided on.

At the Autumn Assembly:

1) the fees of the members and chairman of the Board of Directors as well as those of the auditors shall be decided on
2) the number of members of the Board of Directors shall be decided on, and elections shall be held of the members of the Board of Directors and the auditors, and
3) the budget for the following year shall be adopted.

Article 12

The Board of Directors of the Association shall have at least five and at most seven members, elected for a calendar year at a time. The Board of Directors shall elect a chairman and a vice-chairman from among its members.

The Board of Directors constitutes a quorum when the chairman or the vice-chairman and at least half of the rest of the members are present. Matters shall be decided by a simple majority of votes. In the event of a tied vote, the opinion supported by the chairman shall prevail, except in elections, in which the decision shall be by the drawing of lots. Each member shall have one vote.

The Board of Directors shall be convened by its chairman or by the President, and notice thereof shall be given to the members not later than two days prior to the meeting.

Regarding disqualification of a member of the Board of Directors, the provisions enacted in the Procedural Code on the disqualification of judges shall apply.

Article 13

It is the responsibility of the Board of Directors to answer for the administration of the Association and the appropriate organisation of operations, and to run the affairs of the Association that have not been assigned in the Injuries to Patients Act or in these Articles of Association to the Assembly or to the President.

The responsibilities of the Board of Directors include:

1) to prepare business to be put before the Assembly
2) to adopt the principles for the premiums of patient insurance policies for presentation to the Ministry for Social Affairs and Health for confirmation
3) to collect from the member companies the funds necessary to cover the expenditure of the Association
4) to prepare the financial statement and other reports to be made annually about the operations of the Association
5) to settle matters in which the Association is primarily liable for claims
6) to elect a president for the Association and to discharge him and to decide on the general terms of employment of the president and the officials of the Association, and to decide on the fees to be paid to experts employed in the Association's assignments.

If the revenue in the Association's budget is insufficient to cover the expenditure, the Board of Directors shall have the right, if the performance of the responsibilities of the Association under these Articles so requires, to collect the lacking amount from the member companies.

Article 14

The President of the Association shall be a jurist.

The President shall not be in the employ of any of the member companies, shall not belong to the administrative organs of any such company, shall not act as an insurance agent of a member company nor otherwise be in a relationship with a member company that would disqualify him as a judge in a case involving that company.

Article 15

The responsibility of the President:

1) is to manage the running administration and accounting of the Association
2) to keep minutes at the conventions of the Association and the meetings of the Board of Directors
3) to introduce the matters to be dealt with by the Board of Directors
4) to execute the decisions of the Assembly and the Board of Directors

When the President is prevented from managing his duties, the Board of Directors shall decide on the temporary management of those duties. The Board of Directors shall have the right to assign the duties indicated under Points 2 and 3 of Paragraph 1 of this Article, or part thereof, to an official of the company who meets the requirements for president stated in Article 14.

Article 16

A member company that has not endorsed a decision of the Assembly regarding patient insurance has the right to seek remedy by written appeal to the Ministry for Social Affairs and Health within 30 days of the issuing of the decision, before the closing of office hours. Irrespective of any appeal, the decision of the Assembly may be executed if the execution does not make the appeal futile or unless the authority dealing with the case on account of the appeal forbids the execution.

Article 17

Any decision of the Board of Directors dealing with patient insurance other than claims, or dealing with the relationship between a member company and the Association, shall be submitted for decision to the Assembly if a member company so demands within 14 days of the issuing of the decision.

CHAPTER III

Patient Insurance Commission

Article 18

The Patient Insurance Association has a Commission with the responsibility of maintaining co-operation between the member companies and the various interest groups in patient insurance.

The Commission issues statements on matters of policy and far-ranging matters concerning patient insurance, and makes propositions on the development of patient insurance.

The Commission has 13 members. The members are appointed by the Board of Directors of the Patient Insurance Association for three years at a time. The Ministry for Social Affairs and Health proposes two members for appointment, the Finnish Medical Association, the Finnish Dental Association and the Association of Group Practices together propose two members, the Trade Union of the Nursing Profession, Tehy, together with the Finnish Union of Practical Nurses one member, the Nursing and Central Hospital Districts three members, and the Consumer Guidance Association together with the association called Kuluttajat-Konsumenterna one member who is to represent the interests of the consumers of the services of health and medical care. Four members are elected by the Board of Directors of the Patient Insurance Association.
A deputy member shall be appointed for each member in the respective order.

The Commission organises itself.

The Commission draws up directives for its activities, to be confirmed by the Board of Directors of the Patient Insurance Association.

CHAPTER IV

Rights and duties of member companies

Article 19

The mutual rights and duties of member companies that have endorsed the agreements mentioned under Article 2, Paragraph 7, of the Articles of Association regarding the rights and duties arising from the management of patient insurance operations shall be determined in accordance with the said agreements.

Article 20

If the charter of a member company for the operating of liability insurance is revoked, or if the company otherwise ceases to engage in the patient insurance business, the Association shall be notified thereof and the company shall be held to have withdrawn from the Association.

Article 21

Any disagreements arising between member companies regarding compliance with the Articles of the Association shall be submitted to the Ministry for Social Affairs and Health for settlement.
Disputes associated with the agreements indicated in Article 2, Paragraph 7 of the Articles of Association shall be submitted to a court of arbitration for settlement. Each party shall appoint one member to the court of arbitration and the members thus appointed shall select an umpire. If the arbitrators are unable to agree on an umpire, an umpire shall be appointed by the Ministry for Social Affairs and Health. The parties are obliged to be content with the award.

CHAPTER V

The financial statement and the audit of administration and Accounts

Article 22

The fiscal period of the Association is the calendar year. In the accounting, the provisions of the Accounting Act (655/73) and the Accounting Statute (783/73) and instructions issued by the Ministry for Social Affairs and Health shall in applicable parts be complied with.

Article 23

For the audit of the administration and the accounts of the Association, the Association shall have at least two auditors elected for a calendar year and these shall have personal deputies. One of the auditors and his deputy shall be accountants certified by the Central Chamber of Commerce.

No person in the employ of the Association or of a member of its Board of Directors, or otherwise in a relationship with the Association or with a member of the Board of Directors that would disqualify him from acting as a judge in a case of theirs, shall be appointed to be an auditor or a deputy for an auditor.

Article 24

The Board of Directors of the Association shall for each fiscal period make a report of the activities of the Association and a financial statement, and hand them to the auditors before the end of March.

Upon receiving from the Board of Directors the report and the pertaining financial statement, the auditors shall deliver their written report to the Board of Directors before the end of April, which shall reveal whether they propose the granting of discharge from liability.

Article 25

In respect of injuries to patients for which the Patient Insurance Association is liable under the Patient Insurance Act and which it has not indemnified in full during the calendar year in which the injury occurred, the Association shall, in accordance with the Insurance Companies Act (1062/79) and with the principles confirmed for insurance companies on the strength thereof by the Ministry for Social Affairs and Health, calculate the amount equivalent to the actuarial claims liability and divide it among the member companies.

If the membership of a member company of the Association ceases during the calendar year, the Association shall determine in accordance with Paragraph 1 of this Article the share of that company in the amount equivalent to the actuarial claims liability at the time when the membership ceased.

At the cessation of the membership of a company in the Association, the company is liable to pay the Association the amount determined in accordance with Paragraph 2 of this Article unless another member company shall have accepted responsibility for its commitments. If the amount cannot be collected from the company, the other member companies shall be liable for it in proportion to the distribution of liability.

CHAPTER VI

Supervision

Article 26

The supervision of the Association rests with the Ministry for Social Affairs and Health.

The provisions of the Insurance Companies Act on the supervision of insurance companies shall, where applicable, also be complied with in the supervision of the Association. The Association shall notify the Ministry for Social Affairs and Health, as directed by the Ministry, of the convoking of any Assembly or of any meeting of the Board of Directors, and of the auditing of the accounts of the Association.

Copies of minutes kept at the meetings shall also be delivered to the Ministry for Social Affairs and Health.

Article 27

The Ministry for Social Affairs and Health shall have the right to forbid the executing of any decision by the Assembly or by the Board of Directors involving matters stated in Article 2, Paragraphs 1–3, 6 and 7.

CHAPTER VII

Sundry provisions

Article 28

The chairman of the Board of Directors and the President shall sign for the Association each singly, as shall other persons authorised thereto by the Board of Directors, any two jointly.

Article 29

The Association shall report the names and domiciles of the chairman of the Board of Directors and the President, and of the persons authorised by the Board of Directors to sign for the Association, to the Ministry for Social Affairs and Health, which shall on request issue a certificate showing the persons who are authorised to sign for the Association.

Article 30

Minutes shall be kept at the Assembly and at meetings of the Board of Directors wherein there shall be entered the decisions and the votes conducted and, in respect of the Assemblies, the member companies present and their delegates, and the members of the Board of Directors who are present.

The minutes of the Assembly shall be checked and signed by its chairman and by at least two persons entitled to vote and appointed therefor at the Convention.

The minutes of any meeting of the Board of Directors shall be checked and signed by the chairman of the Board of Directors.

Article 31

Copies of the minutes of the Assemblies and the meetings of the Board of Directors shall be sent without delay to the member companies.

Any decision by the Assembly shall be held to have come to the knowledge of a member company, for compliance, on the third day of having been sent from the Association under an address reported by the member company.

The provisions in Paragraph 2 of this Article on decisions of the Assembly shall also be applied to decisions of the Board of Directors. Whenever a decision of the Board of Directors has been submitted for settlement by the Assembly. Execution of the decision shall be deferred unless the Assembly otherwise directs.

Article 32

Any notices to the member companies in addition to those indicated above in these Articles shall be delivered in writing.

Article 33

At the dissolution of the Association, any of its funds not required to cover the commitments of the Association shall be distributed among the member companies in proportions determined by the Assembly.

APPENDIX 9

The Finnish Pharmaceutical Insurance Pool

DRUG INSURANCE

General Insurance Conditions in force from 1.7.1984

1. Indemnity is payable from drug insurance in respect of any personal damage related to medicinal use of any drug issued in the course of trade for such use in Finland by any manufacturer or importer signatory to this contract through which any person shall be entitled to indemnification in accordance with these insurance conditions.

The above statements concerning this insurance shall apply equally to any manufacturer of drugs on whose behalf any signatory to this insurance contract shall have assumed responsibility for drug-related injuries.

2. The term drug shall here be understood to mean any substance intended for human consumption to which § 1, Section 2 of the Pharmaceutical Act (374/35) applies. The term drug shall also be understood to mean any serum or vaccine and any product released for use in trials involving patients, or for contraception.

3. The term the insured shall be taken to mean those who use a drug according to paragraph 1.

4. By drug-related injury shall be understood illness or other bodily injury which with preponderant probability has been caused through the use of a drug. Drug-related injury is not considered to include illness or injury which

— is due to lack or absence of effect, on the part of the drug, or
— has occurred in the course of an activity which is unsuitable with respect to the intended or predicted effect of the drug in question.

5. Drug-related injury will be indemnified if as a consequence of the injury, the injured person

— has been incapacitated from working for a continuous period of at least 14 days or otherwise has sustained a corresponding impairment of bodily functions for a continuous period of at least 14 days,
— has sustained permanent bodily injury or
— has died.

Additions as from 1.1.86: x) or related to clinical test performed on health persons in Finland in accordance with instructions given by the National Board of Health, xx) and intrauterine contraceptives.

Notwithstanding the provision contained in the first paragraph, reasonable indemnity will be paid for costs incurred and for loss of income in connection with treatment necessitated by drug-related injury insofar as these exceed an aggregate sum of FIM 500 calculated in accordance with Section 9.

6. No indemnity will be payable for drug-related injury, if it may be considered that the injury should reasonably have been accepted as side-effect of the use of the drug, taking into account

- the nature and seriousness of the illness to which the treatment relates
- the general state of health of the injured party
- the extent of the injury
- the possibilities and the reason for experts to foresee the effects of the drug, and
- other circumstances.

7. Nor will indemnity be paid if the drug has been dispensed with the drug user's or the injured party's knowledge contrary to whatever is prescribed with respect to trade with drugs or whatever has constituted a prescribed condition for possession of the drug.

8. Indemnity for drug-related injury shall be forfeited in the event that the drug user, the injured party or, should the injury result in death, the deceased has wilfully or through obvious misuse of the drug caused the injury himself.

Payment of an indemnity in respect of a drug-related injury may be reduced or rejected

- if the drug user, the injured party or, should the injury result in death, the deceased has contributed to the injury through negligence or gross negligence in other circumstances than are stated in the first paragraph, or
- if something else than the action of the manufacturer or importer of the drug or any person acting on their behalf has been the main cause of the injury.

9. The amount of indemnity for drug-related injury shall be determined in accordance with provisions of § 2–4 of Chap 5 and § 3 of Chap 7 of the Law of Damages (412/74). Any indemnity in respect of ache and pain and in respect of permanent disability shall however be determined in accordance with the guidelines issued by the Drug Injury Board and in force at that particular time. In arriving at the amount of indemnity payable, any compensation to which the injured is obviously entitled from public funds or from statutory insurance shall be deducted from the amount of indemnity payable.

10. Liability for any drug-related injury in accordance with these insurance conditions is limited to

- FIM 2 million for each injured person
- FIM 50 million for injuries which have been inflicted on several persons and resulting from similar effects of a drug or drugs containing the same active ingredient
- FIM 100 million for injuries that have occurred during one and the same calendar year

A drug injury is considered to have occurred when the victim first sought treatment for his injury or, if the victim has died without having sought treatment, when he died.

Injuries caused by a drug or drugs containing the same active ingredient are considered one injury regardless of whether the injuries have been observed during one or more insurance periods. If such injuries are found during different insurance periods, they are considered to concern the insurance period, during which the first injury, as defined in these conditions, occurred.

In the event that the sums stated in this section do not suffice to indemnify those entitled to indemnity from such sums, their indemnity shall be reduced by the same proportion in each and every case. Should there be reason to fear after an injury occurs that such a reduction is necessary, the board referred to in Section 14 may determine that until further notice only a certain proportion of the indemnity shall be paid.

11. Indemnity for drug-related injury shall be disbursed by the insurer.

12. Whosoever may be entitled to indemnity in accordance with these conditions shall receive such indemnity only on condition that he assigns to the Insurer the right to damages which he may have in Finland or in any other country against the party instrumental in bringing about the injury or against any party otherwise liable for damages in respect of the injury.

The injured party's obligation in accordance with the first section to assign his right to damages to the insurer does not apply with respect to an indemnity to which he is entitled from public funds or from statutory insurance.

13. Any claim for an indemnity in accordance with these conditions shall be submitted to the insurer within a year of the date upon which the party entitled to indemnity became aware of the drug-related injury in question.

The claim for indemnity shall be submitted at the latest within 15 years of the date on which the injured party ceased using the drug.

14. The Pharmaceutical Injury Pool will appoint the Drug Injury Board in order to issue statements regarding indemnities in respect of drug-related injuries to the injured party, the insurer and the policyholder. If a request for statement is considered unjustified no statement need be issued.

The Drug Injury Board consists of the chairman, the vice-chairman and four members, each member having a personal deputy. The chairman and the vice-chairman shall be juristic persons with knowledge and experience in judgeship and familiar with indemnification of bodily injuries and the Law of Damages. One of the four members shall represent expert knowledge in pharmacology or clinical pharmacology and one shall be specialist for internal medicine. Two members are appointed on the basis of the representation of the manufacturers and importers of drugs. At the meeting the Chairman has the casting vote.

The rules of procedure for the Drug Injury Board are confirmed separately after the policyholder's statement on them.

The injured party must request for a statement from the Drug Injury Board no later than six months after the date on which he was informed of the Insurer's decision relating to his claim for indemnity.

15. Any dispute between the insurer and the injured party shall be settled as provided in the Arbitration Act (46/28).

If the injured party loses the case the insurer still pays the arbitrator's remuneration if the injured party had a reasonable cause for having the dispute reviewed. Arbitration proceedings may only be invoked if the drug injury board has first issued a statement with respect to indemnity.

The injured party must instigate arbitration proceedings no later than one year of the date on which he was informed of the Insurer's final decision with respect to indemnity together with instruction as to what action to take if he does not accept the Insurer's decision.

16. These insurance conditions come into force on July 1, 1984.

Drug-related injuries as specified in the Section 10 which have occurred prior to the date on which these conditions come into force, shall not be indemnified.

APPENDIX 10

Finnish Patient Insurance Association/ Jyrki Sarkamo

THE RATING FACTORS OF THE FINNISH PATIENT INSURANCE

PUBLIC HEALTH SERVICE

Policy holders are the 21 central hospital districts and the State of Finland.

Premium for total public health service = claims paid + change in claims reserve + loading for administrative expenses + safety loading.

The share of the State is 1.48% of the total premium and the rest is shared to the 21 central hospital districts in proportion of the population.

PRIVATE HEALTH SERVICE

1. Companies practising health care or medical care

	premium (o/oo of the amount of salaries)
— private hospitals practising surgical function	6.2 o/oo
— private physician centres practising surgical function	3.3 o/oo
— health services for employees	1.5 o/oo
— dental technical laboratories	
— optician companies	
— other companies practising health care or medical care	2.1 o/oo

2. Professional persons practising health care or medical care

	annual premium
— physicians and dentists practising surgical function	454 mk
— other dentists	337 mk
— other physicians	257 mk
— dental nurses	
— dental technicians	109 mk
— opticians	
— other persons practising health care or medical care	158 mk

3. Group insurance

— union of physicians
— union of dentists
— union of health personnel
— union of special dental technicians
— deaconesses of Finnish Church

FINNISH PATIENT INSURANCE ASSOCIATION

Number of patient insurance claims reported 1.5.1987–30.4.1988

Compensatable	679
Non-compensatable	1038
Not settled until	
4.7.1988	184
*TOTAL	1901

Compensatable claims reported 1.5.1987–30.4.1988 (settled until 4.7.1988)

Treatment injury	408
Infections	245
Accidents	26
TOTAL[a]	679

Number of compensatable claims classified according to the treatment function (settled 1.5.1987–5.4.1988)

	Number of claims	%
Clinical examination	22	4.6
Radiological examination	14	2.9
Other examination	4	0.8
Surgical operations	330	68.5
— Orthopaedic	82	17.0
— Urological	50	10.4
— Gynaecological	42	8.7
— Affected heart and other circulatory organs	30	6.2
— Gastroenterological	25	5.2
— Endoscopies	25	5.2
— Others or not coded	76	15.8
Anaesthesia	23	4.8
Injections, punctures, vaccinations	23	4.8
Dental care	27	5.6
Others or not coded	39	8.1
TOTAL[a]	482	100.0

Number of compensatable claims classified according to the diagnosis of patient injury (settled 1.5.1987–5.4.1988)

	Number of claims	%
Infection after surgical operation	113	23.4
Puncture or perforation	45	9.3
Accidental injury affecting nerves or spinal cord	35	7.3
Bleeding or haematoma	20	4.1
Wounds	13	2.7
Breaks of arms	12	2.5
Breaks of legs	11	2.3
Orthopaedic diseases	11	2.3
Skull fractures	10	2.1
Others or not coded	212	44.0
TOTAL[a]	482	100.0

Patient injuries reported to the Patient Insurance Association during the period of 1.5.1987–30.4.1988

Entitled to indemnity	529	38
Rejected	852	62
Claims decision made by May 1, 1988	1,381	100
Claims decision not made or statistics not yet compiled	521	
Total number of reported injuries	1,902	

Rejected (April 30, 1988)

1. The injury was not a treatment, infection or accidental injury (2.1)	178	21
2. Minor injury (3.1)	146	17
3. The injury was an accident that was not connected with examination or treatment of the patient	144	17
4. The injury has arisen as a consequence of necessary risk-taking (2.2)	124	14
5. The injury was an unavoidable complication of medically justifiable treatment (2.2)	82	10
6. The injury occurred before the law came into force (16)	70	8
7. Other grounds for rejection	108	13
	852	100

Patient injuries reported to the Patient Insurance Association within the period of 1.5.1987–30.4.1988

Claims decision made by May 1, 1988

Patient injuries that will be indemnified (section of the law in brackets)

	Number of claims	%
— Treatment injury (2.1.1)	328	62
— Infection injury (2.1.2)	178	34
— Accidental injury (2.1.3)	22	4
— Diagnostic injury with an unreasonable consequence (2.2)	1	0[a]
	529	100

[a]More since these figures were compiled